MW00533371

The Normative Animal?

FOUNDATIONS OF HUMAN INTERACTION

General Editor: N. J. Enfield, Max Planck Institute for Psycholinguistics, Radboud University, Nijmegen, and the University of Sydney

This series promotes new interdisciplinary research on the elements of human sociality, in particular as they relate to the activity and experience of communicative interaction and human relationships. Books in this series explore the foundations of human interaction from a wide range of perspectives, using multiple theoretical and methodological tools. A premise of the series is that a proper understanding of human sociality is only possible if we take a truly interdisciplinary approach.

Series Editorial Board:
Michael Tomasello, Max Planck Institute Leipzig
Dan Sperber, Jean Nicod Institute
Elizabeth Couper-Kuhlen, University of Helsinki
Paul Kockelman, University of Texas, Austin
Sotaro Kita, University of Warwick
Tanya Stivers, University of California, Los Angeles
Jack Sidnell, University of Toronto

Published in the series:

Talking About Troubles in Conversation
Gail Jefferson
Edited by Paul Drew, John Heritage, Gene Lerner, and Anita Pomerantz

The Instruction of Imagination
Daniel Dor

How Traditions Live and Die
Olivier Morin

The Origins of Fairness
Nicolas Baumard

Requesting Responsibility
Jörg Zinken

Accountability in Social Interaction
Jeffrey Robinson

Intercorporeality
Edited by Christian Meyer, Jürgen Streeck, J. Scott Jordan

Repairing the Broken Surface of Talk
Gail Jefferson
Edited by Jörg Bergmann and Paul Drew

The Normative Animal?
Edited by Neil Roughley and Kurt Bayertz

The Normative Animal?

On the Anthropological Significance of Social, Moral, and Linguistic Norms

EDITED BY
Neil Roughley and Kurt Bayertz

OXFORD
UNIVERSITY PRESS

OXFORD
UNIVERSITY PRESS

Oxford University Press is a department of the University of Oxford. It furthers
the University's objective of excellence in research, scholarship, and education
by publishing worldwide. Oxford is a registered trade mark of Oxford University
Press in the UK and certain other countries.

Published in the United States of America by Oxford University Press
198 Madison Avenue, New York, NY 10016, United States of America.

Library of Congress Cataloging-in-Publication Data
Names: Roughley, Neil, editor. | Bayertz, Kurt, editor.
Title: The normative animal? : on the anthropological significance of social, moral, and linguistic norms /
edited by Neil Roughley and Kurt Bayertz.
Description: New York, NY : Oxford University Press, [2019] |
Includes bibliographical references and index.
Identifiers: LCCN 2018038474 (print) | LCCN 2018053710 (ebook) | ISBN 9780190846473 (updf) |
ISBN 9780190846497 (online content) | ISBN 9780190846480 (epub) |
ISBN 9780190846466 (cloth : alk. paper)
Subjects: LCSH: Social norms. | Normativity (Ethics) | Standard language.
Classification: LCC GN493.3 (ebook) | LCC GN493.3 .N67 2019 (print) | DDC 303.3/7—dc23
LC record available at https://lccn.loc.gov/2018038474

9 8 7 6 5 4 3 2 1

Printed by Sheridan Books, Inc., United States of America

Contents

Part IV. Linguistic Norms?

Part V. Afterword

Foreword

This volume is not a conference proceedings. Rather, it is the product of the repeated interdisciplinary interaction of a group of scholars over several years around topics that gradually crystallised to produce the present book's focus. After an initial exploratory meeting in 2008 involving only a few of the authors of this volume, the core group met annually from 2009 to 2014, missing only 2011. Our meetings were hosted first by the Institute for Advanced Study (HWK) in Delmenhorst and later by the Centre for Advanced Studies in Bioethics at the University of Münster. We would like to express our gratitude to both institutions for their support, both financial and material. We would also like to thank Ansgar Jansohn, Stefan Mandl, Yannick Weinand, and especially Moritz Bütefür for extensive editorial assistance. Finally, the editors are also grateful to all the members of the group for their willingness to reflect on material well removed from their own home base and for the stimulating discussions that they made possible. We would like to express our particular gratitude to Louise Röska-Hardy for her long-term support of and contributions to our work.

Contributors

CHRISTOPH ANTWEILER, Professor of Southeast Asian Studies, Department of Oriental and Asian Studies, University of Bonn, Germany

KURT BAYERTZ, Professor of Philosophy, Department of Philosophy, University of Münster, Germany

JUDITH M. BURKART, Senior Lecturer, Department of Anthropology, University of Zurich, Switzerland

AUDUN DAHL, Assistant Professor of Psychology, Department of Psychology, University of California, Santa Cruz, USA

N. J. ENFIELD, Professor of Linguistics, Department of Linguistics, University of Sydney, Australia

CLAUDIA FICHTEL, Group Leader "Communication and Cognition," Department of Behavioural Ecology and Sociobiology, University of Göttingen, Germany

HANS-JOHANN GLOCK, Professor of Philosophy, Department of Philosophy, University of Zurich, Switzerland

PETER M. KAPPELER, Professor of Behavioural Ecology and Sociobiology/Anthropology, Department of Sociobiology/Anthropology, University of Göttingen, Germany

NIKOLA KOMPA, Professor of Philosophy, Department of Philosophy, Osnabrück University, Germany

KARL MERTENS, Professor of Philosophy, Department of Philosophy, Julius Maximilians University Würzburg, Germany

HANNES RAKOCZY, Professor of Cognitive Developmental Psychology, Department of Psychology, University of Göttingen, Germany

ANNE REBOUL, Senior Researcher CNRS at the Laboratory on Language, the Brain and Cognition (L2C2), Lyon, France

NEIL ROUGHLEY, Professor of Philosophical Anthropology and Ethics, Department of Philosophy, University of Duisburg-Essen, Germany

MARCO F. H. SCHMIDT, Senior Scientist, Department of Psychology, Ludwig Maximilians University Munich, Germany

JACK SIDNELL, Professor of Anthropology, Department of Anthropology, University of Toronto, Canada

HOLMER STEINFATH, Professor of Philosophy, Department of Philosophy, University of Göttingen, Germany

ELLIOT TURIEL, Jerome A. Hutto Professor of Psychology, Department of Psychology, University of California, Berkeley, USA

CAREL P. VAN SCHAIK, Professor of Zoology/Anthropology, Department of Anthropology, University of Zurich, Switzerland

PART I

Introductory

1

Might We Be Essentially Normative Animals?

Neil Roughley

Humans, it has often been claimed, are characteristically or even essentially rational, linguistic, social, or moral creatures. If these characterisations are intended to name the essence or nature of being human, however understood, then they would appear to be in conflict. This volume is built around the question of whether these characterisations may not turn out to be compatible because they all ground in a more basic feature: that of being creatures whose lives are structured at a fundamental level by their relationships to norms. The various capacities singled out by talk of rational, linguistic, social, or moral animals might then all essentially involve the orientation to obligations, permissions, and prohibitions. If this is so, then perhaps it is a basic susceptibility, or proclivity to the normative or deontic regulation of thought and behaviour that enables humans to develop the various traditionally emphasised features of their life form.

This is *the normative animal thesis*. This volume aims to investigate it by looking at the nature and workings of three types of norms, or putative norms—social, moral, and linguistic—and asking whether they might all be different expressions of one basic structural feature unique to humankind. These questions are approached here by philosophers, primatologists, behavioural biologists, psychologists, linguists, and cultural anthropologists. Their contributions are the results of extended interdisciplinary communication over a number of years around these issues. Moreover, the contributions all proceed from a commitment to the idea that understanding norms is a two-way process, involving a close interaction between conceptual clarification and empirical research.

This chapter introduces a number of distinctions relevant for the following, more specific discussions and presents an overview over the issues at stake. It begins with the sketch of an argument as to the legitimacy of talk of human nature after Darwin and some remarks situating the project within a more general trend to interdisciplinary work around features that look to be candidates to be specifically human properties. After these introductory remarks (section 1), the chapter divides into two large sections.

The first (section 2) begins by clarifying the concept of normativity that the authors are working with, in particular distinguishing it from a conceptualisation that is at the centre of intense debates in contemporary meta-ethics, theories of rationality, and practical reasoning (2.1). The second subchapter of the section then lists and discusses the primary candidates for generic features of norms (2.2). The third subchapter introduces a number of distinctions that allow fine-grained formulations of the various dimensions of the normative animal thesis (2.3).

Section 3 then presents the key issues at stake in the discussion of the nature and workings of those orientations for human behaviour that are often thought of as social (3.1), moral (3.2), and linguistic (3.3) norms. In doing so, it particularly emphasises the points of overlap, as well as the points of difference between the relevant phenomena, laying the ground for a discussion of the extent to which one should accept that all three dimensions of our behaviour are essentially dependent on generic deontic structures.

1. The Characteristic Human Life Form and Interdisciplinary Research

From the beginning of Western thought, conceptions of the specifically human have been advanced, often as accounts of "the human essence" or of "human nature." Prominent traditional candidates have been reason, language, freedom of the will, particular forms of sociality or culture, and morality.[1] Since Darwin, these ascriptions have lost any plausibility as definitive of the biological species. As species are historical

---

[1] The Aristotelian characterisation 'zoon logon echon' (Aristotle Pol. 1523a 9f.) is plausibly understood as combining the first two, proposing that humans are in some sense essentially animals who live their lives in terms of linguistically structured reason. Charles Taylor has recently advanced a trenchant defence of the second (Taylor 2016). Kant's proposal, that a human being is essentially an "animale rationabile" (Kant 1798/1800, 226) might be thought of as combining the first and the third, insisting that reason is a capacity whose realisation depends on the exercise of freedom of the will. The third characterisation is prominently advanced by Pico della Mirandola in his oration on human dignity (della Mirandola 1846, 4f.) and has seemed particularly attractive to indeterminists such as Sartre (cf. Sartre 1946). Perhaps the most publicised account to come out of the German tradition known as "Philosophical Anthropology," Plessner's characterisation of humans as living their lives in terms from "excentric positionality" (Plessner 1928, 288ff.) is arguably also best understood as a version of the third proposal (cf. Greene 1965, 104ff.). The most well-known historical variant of the fourth claim is again to be found in Aristotle ('zoon politikon') (Hist. an. 487b 33ff.; Pol. 1253a 2ff.). Varying, empirically based versions of this last suggestion are represented by the work of authors such as Bowles and Gintis (2011), Pagel (2012), Sterelny (2012), and Tomasello (2014). Both Aristotle and Kant also seem to advocate some version of the fifth proposal, the former naming "a sense of justice" alongside the two more famous characterisations in the *Politics* and the latter claiming that the human capacities of reason and freedom necessarily confer a kind of absolute moral value that he, following Pico, labels "dignity" (Kant 1785, 46ff.).

entities individuated by means of their lineage, no non-historical properties of existing individuals can be necessary or sufficient for specieshood (Hull 1978, 338ff.; 1984, 19; 1986; cf. Kronfeldner et al 2014, 643f.).

Nevertheless, the traditional descriptions of human specificity retain their plausibility as distinguishing marks of the characteristic human life form, that is, of those animals identified with a specific branch of the phylogenetic tree (Roughley 2005, 139ff.; 2011, 16ff.; Kronfeldner et al. 2014, 646f.). What is of interest here is whether any of these might be *structural properties of the characteristic human life form*. These would be properties whose instantiation by the organisms located at the relevant place on the phylogenetic tree explains the way in which many other features of the way they live their lives hang together. It would also explain the specific shape taken on by these features in the typical life of that animal. Think of the way in which the fact that humans are linguistic animals doesn't only generate a rich set of practices unavailable to non-linguistic animals. It also both pervades and reorganises the relationships between, for instance, emotion and behaviour, perception and behaviour, coordination and competition, and essentially alters the character of communicative interchanges, of self-understanding, and grounds the capacity for extended abstract thought. Similar claims might also be made for the other traditional candidates for "human nature."

Note that there is no a priori reason why a feature able to fulfil this role need be the only such property generally instantiated in one species nor why it need be unique to the species in question. It is conceivable both that one species might play host to several such structural properties, although their structural character limits the number of features that might play such roles, and that various creatures might share one or more such structural properties. What is eminently plausible is that different species might uniquely instantiate particular clusters of such structural properties. The hypothesis that this volume aims to investigate is whether what might be thought of as the specifically human cluster of social, moral, and linguistic capacities may turn out to be grounded in a generic capacity for deontic thought and behavioural orientation.

The question is approached by way of a variety of disciplinary approaches to what appear to be norms of social, moral, and linguistic kinds. In doing so, the volume's approach follows the lead of comparative psychologists, cognitive ethologists and biological anthropologists, who have developed entire research programmes on whether properties of the kinds traditionally picked out in philosophy are indeed unique to humans or whether they, or their precursors, are shared with members of other species. One strand of such research has concerned instrumental reasoning, primitive forms of which appear to be present in primates (Mulcahy and Call 2006) and in corvids, such as New Caledonian Crows (Weir et al. 2002; Weir and Kacelnik 2006) and scrub-jays (Clayton et al. 2005; Clayton et al. 2006; Raby et al. 2007). A further topic that has excited comparative empirical research over the last 30 years is primates' capacity for mind-reading (Tomasello and Call 2006; Call and Tomasello 2008).

The data provided by such research have made it possible to reframe a number of traditional theoretical issues. Moreover, conceptual work from philosophy has been taken on board by empirical research on the borderlines between human and non-human animals, where it has proven extremely fruitful. This is particularly evident in the work of Michael Tomasello and his collaborators, who have come to consider the capacities for shared intentionality as central to the specifically human life form (Tomasello et al. 2005). The interaction between empirical and conceptual work here grounds in a recognition that the investigation of key features of the human should be a two-way process: on the one hand, the application of the relevant key concepts requires their clarification, a clarificatory process that, with concepts of this nature, cannot be restricted to narrow contexts of empirical investigation. On the other hand, such clarification cannot sensibly be dissociated from the understanding of capacities only reliably detectable under observational or experimental conditions that go far beyond those directly accessible to the philosopher. There is thus a need for inter-action between philosophy and disciplines such as primatology, behavioural biology, psychology, linguistics, and cultural anthropology.

2. Normativity and the Normative Animal Thesis

One topic that has always exercised philosophers, but has been given comparatively little attention in the interdisciplinary debates, is the extent to which humans live their everyday lives in terms of what they take it that they ought to do. "Oughts" seem to be central to a number of the phenomena that have been traditionally seen as specific to the human life form. We are, so it seems, subject to a rich variety of "oughts": to take the best available means to our ends; not to describe something as a cat without being prepared to describe it as an animal; to use lexical forms ending in "-s" when we con-jugate English verbs in the third person present singular; not to park on double yellow lines or to address the Queen of England with "hey, you!"; not to steal, lie, or murder.

At first blush, it appears that there are prudential, conceptual, syntactic, legal, etiquette-related, and moral "oughts." And it seems plausible that these all apply primarily—indeed, it might be thought, uniquely—to humans, who, as we have seen, have been taken to be first and foremost reasoning, thinking, linguistic, socially organised, or moral animals. Perhaps what is common to being animals that are ac-curately classified in all these ways is the subjection and sensitivity to formal deontic structures of prohibitions, prescriptions, and permissions internal to participation in the relevant practice, deontic structures expressed in relevant "oughts." And perhaps the most pervasive structural feature of the human life form is the proclivity of human animals to live their lives in terms of "oughts" grounding in such structures: perhaps humans are primarily deontic or "normative" animals.

Perhaps. Such a thesis would presuppose two claims the truth of which is anything but clear. The *first* is that all the practices named are indeed at core deontically structured and that the relevant "oughts" ground in such structures. For this to be true in the relevant sense, the practices would need not only to involve norms in some way or another; beyond this, their identity as the kinds of practices they are would have to depend on their being built around specific sets of deontic structures. The claim is controversial. For one thing, there are disputes in both linguistics and philosophy as to whether language is in any substantial sense regulated by specific norms internal to the practice of language use, that is, by linguistic *rules* (see section 3.3). For another, philosophical ethicists do not agree as to whether there really are such things as moral norms, that is, prescriptive moral *principles* that guide, or would appropriately guide, morally required behaviour or correct moral judgements (see section 3.2). As we shall see, where "oughts" are in play, this does not guarantee that these ground in norms. For the normative animal thesis to be true, such a grounding relation would have to be in place for a significant number of key cases in each area.

Even if these doubts can be assuaged, there is still a *second* claim that would need to be true in order for the normative animal thesis to resolve the competition between the various traditional characterisations of the human life form. This is that the rules, principles, and norms shown to be central to reasoning, thinking, using language, life within institutions, and morality would have to be features of the same generic kind. It would have to be true that participation in each of these spheres of human practice and experience essentially involves being subject to, and responding to, requirements or demands, strictures that are not only appropriately described as "obligations," "prohibitions," and "permissions," but are appropriately thus described for the same reasons in each kind of case.

2.1. "Ought," Norms, and "Normativity"

The claim that we are, and take it that we are, essentially subject to normative strictures when we reason, think, speak, and otherwise act is significantly stronger than the claim that there are, and we take it that there are, things that we ought, and things that we ought not to do. In this section, I will, first, point to several such gaps between "oughts" and obligations, before emphasising and explaining a related terminological gap between the use of the term "normative" in this volume and a use that has become established in certain important philosophical discussions. It will be imperative not to conflate the two uses.

To begin with, an agent can, for instance, think that some friends of hers ought to arrive by six in the evening, where the "ought" is epistemic. Obviously, there is no entailment here that the friends are under any obligation to arrive. Indeed, the epistemic "ought" is no candidate for normative talk at all, in any sense of the term "normative." Hence, if there is a unified semantics for "ought" that includes its epistemic use—as has recently been argued (Finlay 2014, 44ff., 176ff.; Chrisman 2016, 31ff.)—the term's applicability, even to actions, in the context of the relevant practices is no guarantee that we are picking out the "normative" structures that interest us.

Moreover, it is also implausible that all non-epistemic "oughts" entail obligations, even when their contents specify actions of their addressees or owners. We ought to look before crossing the road, but that doesn't entail that we have an obligation to do so. Even in the moral sphere, it is controversial that what you ought to do is identical with what you have an obligation to do.[2] An elder brother who has been given a whole box of chocolates and sits eating them next to his younger brother arguably ought to give his younger brother some of the chocolates, although he has no duty or obligation to do so (cf. Thomson 1971, 13).

Clearly, then, the appropriateness of "ought" sentences can at most count as an indication that the "normative" features that interest us might be present. Still, even if the interpretation of the case of the chocolate-eating elder brother seems plausible, there can be little doubt that obligations constitute the core of morality and that such obligations are often and appropriately expressed in terms of "oughts." Importantly, however, there is also controversy as to what explains this linguistic appropriateness. It is worth briefly sketching this controversy, as understanding it will help us to distinguish the conception of normativity at work in this volume from a conception that has recently become predominant in analytic metaethics and theory of rationality.

What is at issue in the controversy can be clarified in terms of a distinction made by Bernard Williams between "the 'ought' that occurs in statements of moral principle" and "the 'ought' that occurs in the deliberative question 'What ought I to do?'" (Williams 1965, 184). Williams was concerned that certain substantive moral theories tend to elide the distinction between the moral "ought" and what he calls the deliberative "ought." According to Williams, the theories in question fallaciously—and absurdly—make the former appear both supreme and ubiquitous. Since Williams raised this issue, other theorists have questioned whether there really is any practical "ought" other than the deliberative or all-things-considered one. According to Judith Jarvis Thomson, the reason why we think it appropriate to say such things as "Leia ought not to lie" and "Ben ought to move his bishop" is that we frequently take it that the—moral or chess-related—considerations thus brought into play are decisive in the relevant situations (Thomson 2008, 172). Because such considerations are decisive in these cases, they can be expressed in terms of the all-things-considered "ought." Thus

---

[2] There are two further prominent uses of "ought" that have no relation to obligations. A first is in sentences such as "There ought to be no wars," which has been labelled "the 'ought' of general desirability" (Wedgwood 2007, 117) or simply characterised as "evaluative" (Chrisman 2016, 32). A second kind of case, which has been called "functional" (Finlay 2014, 48) or "teleological" (Chrisman 2016, 32), is found in sentences such as "Knives ought to be sharp."

understood, such ways of speaking provide no reason to believe that there are specific moral or chess-related "oughts."

A less rigorous version of this move is to be found in the work of John Broome, who recommends that we employ the word "ought" to single out the all-things-considered, "unqualified," or "central" usage. Unlike Thomson, he doesn't dispute the acceptability of talking in terms of qualified "oughts," as in claims to the effect that someone "morally ought" or "rationally ought" to do something. If one does so, however, it is, he insists, crucial to remember that the "oughts" thus expressed are not detachable from their adverbs (a generalised version of Williams's point noted earlier). In order to avoid the misunderstandings that are easily generated by talk of "oughts" that need qualification, Broome proposes in all such cases to talk of "requirements," where requirements can only exist if a source (law, morality, prudence, fashion, etiquette, rationality) can be identified (Broome 2013, 25ff.).

For our purposes, there are two points of importance here. The first is that the unqualified "ought," unlike the qualified "oughts" of etiquette, chess, and morality, entertains no necessary relationship to obligations, prohibitions, and permissions. It might be the case that an agent correctly believes that she ought to do something, say catch the next train to some destination, for some decisive reasons that have nothing to do with deontic categories. Perhaps she wants to see some concert and knows that the best way to ensure that she does so is to take the train.

A second point marks the juncture at which many contemporary analytic ethicists, including Broome, on the one hand, and the authors of this volume, on the other, part terminological company. For Broome, it is the all-things-considered "ought," in spite of its independence from obligations, prohibitions, and permissions, that is essentially "normative." Other considerations are "normative" insofar as they explain what an agent in this sense ought to do. Considerations that explain, or contribute to the explanation of, the central "ought" are, according to Broome's analysis, *reasons* for whatever it is that ought to be done (Broome 2013, 50, 53). According to this usage, the concepts "norm" and "normative" entertain no essential relations. Rather, the term "normative" is appropriate where reasons are in play, whatever their source.

Whereas the explanation of reasons in terms of a primitive concept of "ought" is probably a minority position (cf. Gibbard 1990, 160ff; 2012, 14f.), the understanding of "normativity" as a matter of intrinsic reason-involvement is widespread in analytic ethics and theories of practical reasoning (cf. Robertson 2009; De Caro and Macarthur 2010; Raz 2011). Many authors take the deliberative "ought" to be definable in terms of the balance of reasons, seeing reason as the primitive notion (cf. Korsgaard 1996; Scanlon 1998, 17ff.). Whichever concept is taken to be prior, "normativity" is said to be in play where some action is favoured by a reason, even if the action is not something an agent ought, all in all, to do, because the relevant reasons are outweighed by other reasons. This terminological move has the consequence that a great deal of qualified "oughts," and the norms or requirements from which they derive, may not be "normative," if they carry no intrinsic reason-providing weight.

In order to avoid terminological, and consequent conceptual confusion, it should be emphasised that the authors of this volume will not, in general, follow this terminological usage. Instead, they will stick to the rather more natural association of "normative" with "norms."[3] As we have seen, the stipulation that "normativity" is independent of norms, but essentially tied to intrinsic reasons, is well established in ethics, particularly in the distinction between normative moral theory and meta-ethics.[4] Nevertheless, the aims of this volume—to bring together debates within various parts of philosophy, and above all, between philosophy and other disciplines—strongly recommend that we work with a conceptual connection between "normativity" and norms. Social philosophers and philosophers of language frequently use "normative" in this way, as do sociologists, cultural anthropologists, behavioural biologists, psychologists, and linguists. In order to facilitate the interdisciplinary debate on our key questions, "normativity" will be used in this volume to pick out the feature or features of norms in virtue of which they are norms. Metaethicists and philosophers of rationality might want to mentally substitute the terms "deontic" and "deonticity" at the appropriate places.

2.2. Generic Features of Norms

Before turning to the normative animal thesis, it will be helpful to collate the key features that are plausibly—if not completely uncontroversially—taken to characterise norms in general.

The first is their *prescriptive* character. Norms in the sense at issue here require or demand actions, omissions, or behaviour of a certain kind under certain circumstances. This excludes "statistical norms" from the purview of our interest.

The second feature of norms can be seen as an explanation of the specific character of the prescriptions constitutive of norms. Whereas recommendations or requests are types of prescriptions in one sense,[5] these are too weak to count as the kind of

---

[3] For a speculative diagnosis as to how the meaning of "normative" moved from norm- to reason-relatedness in moral philosophy, see Finlay 2019, 205f., note 47.

[4] One might attempt to explain the subject matter of normative moral theory in terms of the "moral norms" that provide reasons for correct moral behaviour or corresponding judgements. However, this would have the consequence that certain theories' attempts to explain our moral reasons, and just about any theoretical attempts to explain certain kinds of moral reasons won't count as normative moral theory. Virtue ethicists claim that moral reasons can be explained without recourse to norms, and anyone who thinks the concept of morally supererogatory action is coherent necessarily believes that there are moral reasons not derived from norms. But virtue theory is normally classified along with utilitarianism, Kantianism, contractualism, and contractarianism as a normative moral theory and the question of whether and why there are supererogatory actions is also naturally discussed in the same theoretical context.

[5] Compare Richard Hare's initial collection of what he at first calls "commands" (Hare 1952, 4) and the class of "directives" in speech act theory (Searle 1979, 13f.).

prescriptions that norms generate. Norms *demand* or *require* behaviour, action, or omission of the agents to whom they apply. In many cases, this point may be put by saying that norms ascribe "obligations," "prohibitions," and "permissions."[6] However, perhaps the aptness of the everyday use of these terms should not be emphasised, as their apparent inappropriateness in some cases may merely result from their tight association with moral and legal contexts.

Norms in the relevant sense, thirdly, involve a dimension of *generality*. The requirements at issue need to be addressed to all agents instantiating some property: all Germans, all chess players, all members of the Humber and District Catholic River-Wideners' Club, all persons, all speakers or writers of ancient Greek. The contrast here is with individually addressed prescriptions. Someone telling another agent to perform some action does not necessarily express a norm concerning the action in question, even if that person has authority or power over the addressee. General prescriptions, we can say, *set standards* for the behaviour of certain agents within certain contexts. Descriptions of the relevant contexts will frequently appear in conditional clauses within a requirement's scope. Such conditionality is, of course, perfectly compatible with the norm's being addressed generally.

Fourth, a norm, more precisely, the applicability of a norm plausibly entails some condition on relevant *abilities of the norm's addressees*. The principle traditionally cited here in moral philosophy is *"ought implies can."* The principle raises serious questions as to how both the concepts of implication and of ability at work here are to be interpreted. The broad point of the principle is, however, easily sketched: prescriptions for agents with which the agents are generally[7] unable to comply cannot function as prescriptions, that is, as guiders of the behaviour of their addressees.

This may seem naturally to go hand in hand with a correlative negative principle according to which *"ought implies lack of inability not to."* This principle would articulate the following point: prescriptions for agents with which the agents are generally unable not to comply cannot function as prescriptions, that is, as guiders of the behaviour of their addressees.

Truths about what would be good or desirable from some point of view may be insensitive to the abilities or lack of inabilities of relevant agents. This seems implausibly to be the case with norms insofar as these involve the strong kind of prescriptions I have called demands or requirements. Norms, at least norms as addressed, hence appear to involve some presupposition of the accountability of their addressees.

---

[6] That norms ascribe permissions entails that their summary characterisation as demanding or requiring actions or omissions is insufficient. Norms can also assign the lack of a requirement, an assignation that is to be distinguished from the lack of any assignation. One way to think of such cases is in terms of prohibitions on others to apply pressure on someone not to do or omit something. For ease of exposition I will generally assume this point where I talk of norms as requirements.

[7] And not just as the result of their own previous behaviour.

How strong that presupposition needs to be in order for us to be talking about norms at all, rather than about any particular sort of norms, is likely to be controversial. Together, the two principles just named give us a version of the principle of alternate possibilities, according to which accountability for φ-ing presupposes the ability to either φ or not φ. Although this combined principle has seemed to some metaphysicians to require an indeterministic interpretation relative to moral norms, there is little plausibility to such a reading for norms of other kinds.

Finally, some authors believe that an analysis of norms necessarily involves reference to *sanctions*, i.e. negative reactions of some sort to the non-realisation of the prescribed content. If the concept of sanctions is so weak as to cover negative retrospective judgements of the form "You shouldn't have done that," this may be plausible as a general feature. Something stronger, involving either emotional reactions or even intentional punishment, has at times been thought to be the feature we need in order to explain the specificity of the kinds of prescriptions associated with obligations. What is also key to the plausibility of reference to sanctions as a generic condition is the precise relation that sanctions are taken to entertain to non-conformity. As the claim that they are necessarily activated in individual cases of non-conformity is clearly far too strong, some mediated relation that specifies their appropriateness, or the belief in their appropriateness, appears more promising.

I shall return to these features in the discussions of particular candidates for normativity in the various spheres of human activity discussed in the following.

2.3. The Normative Animal Thesis

The normative animal thesis, then, is a claim concerning the importance of norms, or of norm-related (or "normative") attitudes for animals living the characteristic human life form. The kind of importance at issue is that named by the claim that we are dealing with structural properties (see section 1). As the disjunction in the first sentence of this section suggests, there are different candidates for the "normative" feature that may have this kind of importance. In what follows, I shall, more precisely, distinguish four such candidate features. The normative animal thesis would be most importantly true if all four candidate features were extensively present in at least the three areas to be discussed in this volume. I shall also look at the relationships between the candidate features, as it is conceivable that different constellations of such features might be given in the three areas under investigation. As we shall see, one of the candidates has clear priority for the thesis.

The features that would plausibly be pertinent to the characterisation of a creature as a "normative animal" are of four kinds. We can specify them in four brief descriptions of the creatures. The third is conjunctive. As we shall see, it picks out two relations that, for our purposes, are sensibly grouped together.

(NA1) The creatures are beings to whom the norms *apply*.

(NA2) The creatures *regulate* their behaviour in line with what they take to be normatively required of them.

(NA3) The creatures are in some sense *creators* and *upholders* of the norms.

(NA4) The creatures are *enforcers* of the norms.

Although these relations may all be realised by the same creatures, the four descriptions are in principle independent of one another.

Note, first, that NA2 might be satisfied, although NA1 is not. That might be so if a creature regulates its behaviour on the basis of taking itself to be subject to certain norms, although the norms thus conceived don't actually exist. An error theory of normative beliefs is combinable with a model of self-regulation on the basis of normative beliefs or other action-guiding attitudes with deontic contents (cf. section 3.2).

The satisfaction of NA1 and NA2 is also possible without that of NA3. This might be the case if there are norms that humans are aware of being subject to, but which exist independently of them. Norms of a divine origin are obviously candidates here. Leaving views that require theological premises to one side, there is still clearly room for claims that certain norms that apply to humans are not their product. "Robust moral realists" assign moral values and norms some such "response-independent" status (Enoch 2011, 3), that is, they take them, or corresponding facts, to exist independently of whether any creature has ever thought about, or developed beliefs, desires, or emotions concerning their content. Robust realists believe further that this status grounds in the instantiation of special sui generis properties, belief in which— explicitly—spells serious conflict with naturalistic commitments and has appeared to some only conceivable as a relic of theological views (Street 2016). For NA1 and NA2 to be satisfied without NA3 in a naturalistic framework, existence of the norm applicable to the relevant agents would have to be identical with, or functionally equivalent to some natural property. This appears at most a possibility for moral principles (Brink 1989), as neither social norms nor linguistic rules seem conceivable in the absence of constitutive human practices.[8]

But even if one thinks that moral norms are implausible candidates to satisfy NA1 and NA2 without NA3, there are other highly plausible candidates for the status of a priori norms, such as the requirements of rationality, which don't look to be dependent for their existence, as opposed to their recognition or implementation, on human or other agents. Norms or requirements of rationality plausibly apply necessarily to any agents kitted out with certain sets of attitudes: believers, it seems, are necessarily subject to a requirement of non-contradiction of their beliefs; and believers-cum-intenders appear to be necessarily subject to requirements concerning

---

[8] But see section 3.3 for a use of "rule" to which this doesn't apply.

further intention formation in view of their beliefs about necessary means to ends (Roughley 2016, 184f.).

If there are norms with this status, they would be anthropologically uninteresting if they played no role in the structuring of the lives of the creatures to which they apply. In other words, the satisfaction of only NA1 would, for our purposes, be irrelevant: the mere fact that some other agent might evaluate the creatures relative to standards, independently of whether such evaluations are taken on by the creatures themselves and guide their behaviour, would not tell us anything interesting about the creatures' life form, only about the way the evaluators see them. The most basic claim of the normative animal thesis thus concerns significant guidance of the animal's behaviour as a result of the animal taking certain norms to apply to it.

NA3 and NA4 are sensibly understood in a wide sense, i.e. either of the relations they name may be thought of as being either intentionally or non-intentionally established. Both the existence and persistence of the relevant norms and the means of their enforcement may, on the one hand, be the objects of explicit decisions. On the other hand, they may alternatively, or also, be thought of as the result of processes that are less than deliberate, even intransparent to their bearers. Emotional, volitive, or perhaps unreflective behavioural processes are mechanisms that may well be at work here.

Where there are thought to be norms that exist in some robust sense independently of human agents, NA2 and NA4 might, alongside NA1, both be satisfied in spite of the non-satisfaction of NA3. In such a view, NA4 might appear particularly important. Most religions have certainly placed a premium on norm enforcement; their institutions may perhaps be thought of as predicated on the two primary aims of providing epistemic access to the relevant norms and enforcing them. Whatever the truth values of NA1 and NA3 here, the anthropological significance of the conjunction of NA2 and NA4 for religious norms is certainly enormous (cf. van Schaik and Michel 2016). However, it will play no role in this volume.

Relative to the requirements of rationality, it might seem unclear to what extent we should see NA4 as being satisfied. There is a sense in which it is in the interests of the agent herself to satisfy the relevant norms. This is related to the fact that the work done by parents and educators to help young humans to avoid believing both p and non-p counts less as enforcing the requirement than as making clear what it consists in. Indeed, it arguably counts primarily as an attempt to make clear to the young believers what believing actually is. Similar things might be said about principles of instrumental rationality and their relatives. In later life, people may be ridiculed or given well-meaning, perhaps exasperated, advice if they reveal themselves to be weak-willed, wishful thinkers, or self-deceivers. But most people presumably satisfy most of the requirements of rationality most of the time without such explicit external support. However, there is one particular agent whose role in enforcing the requirements of rationality should probably not be underestimated: the agent whose behaviour is at issue. The human capacity for self-regulation is acquired gradually and may only be upheld as a result of its regular exercise (cf. Baumeister and Tierney 2011). Perhaps, then, here we are the primary enforcers of the norms vis-à-vis ourselves.

What is fairly difficult to conceive empirically is the satisfaction of NA3 without the satisfaction of NA4. This is because, in those cases in which the animals in question are taken to be the generators and upholders of the norms, it is hard to see how the upholding and enforcing of those norms might be distinguished. The distinction is in itself easily made: if a norm n prescribes behaviour b for population P, then the second conjunct of NA3 concerns behaviour that ensures the continued existence of n, whereas NA4 concerns behaviour that ensures the behaviour prescribed by n because it is prescribed by n. Enforcement of a norm presupposes its existence, for which its upholding may be necessary. However, if n's existence is only guaranteed as a result of the relevant creatures' attitudes or behaviour, then it is highly probable that the same attitudes or behaviour will be responsible both for n's continued existence and its behavioural realisation. At least, the attitudes and behaviour that are generally cited for the two tasks tend to overlap significantly.

Many norms are enforced by patterns of behaviour that are unpleasant to, or unwanted by, those subject to the behaviour—forms of behaviour sometimes broadly labelled "sanctions" or "punishments." These are frequently mentioned in the same breath as the critical reactive attitudes they are sometimes taken to express, in particular resentment, indignation, outrage, blame, or guilt.[9] To these can be added forms of verbal criticism, admonishment, and appeals to the reason, understanding, or sense of community of the agent in question. The effect of reactions of these types, if not always the aim in individual cases, is likely to be an increase in the likelihood of behaviour that conforms to the relevant norm. The resultant strengthening of behavioural regularities can in many cases plausibly be taken also to contribute to the continued existence of the norm itself.[10]

Although forms of punishment, critical emotional reactions, and verbal criticism may all contribute to a norm's enforcement and persistence, it would be circular to take them to be—at least exclusively—constitutive of its creation. For obvious conceptual reasons, they all presuppose the existence of the norm to whose contravention they react. To be precise, they at least presuppose some independent element of the norm, to which they can be reactions. That element has frequently been taken to be attitudinal in nature, conceived by different authors in differing manners as essentially desire-like, as a matter of expectations, as involving both prescriptive and assertoric elements, as a form of acceptance, or as a sui generis kind of normative attitude. If

---

[9] The locus classicus here is Adam Smith's *Theory of Moral Sentiments* (Smith 1759/90, II, i).

[10] Where the relevant norms are taken to be in part constituted by behavioural regularities (see section 3.1), the connection is likely to be deemed necessary.

such attitudinal features turn out to be the core of the norm, their persistence is likely to entail the norm's persistence and also to contribute, either directly or indirectly, via sanctions or critical reactions, to the norm's realisation. Even a conception of (certain) norms that sees their essence as independent of any kind of critical reaction to their contravention will probably have to accept that the persistence of the relevant attitudes will need to be scaffolded at least by emotional and verbal reactions.

The normative animal thesis, as applied to humans, asserts that the relations in which humans generally stand to norms are decisive for the ways they character- istically live. The key relation is picked out by NA2. It arguably subdivides into the *epistemic* relation of believing, or subdoxastically taking it that one is subject to the relevant requirements, and the *practical* relation of guiding one's actions on the basis of such belief or subdoxastic taking. Whether the epistemic and practical attitudes are in turn explained by the existence of a corresponding norm will in many cases appear less significant. The consequences of satisfying NA2 will be intensified for creatures who are, or see themselves as, the agents of the norms' enforcement. Finally, insofar as human beings are also the norms' authors—in whatever precise way—the sense in which they are normative animals is strengthened further.

3. Three Kinds of Norms?

The strategy of this collection is to look at three—overlapping, but analytically distinguishable—areas of human activity that are candidates to be seen as normatively or deontically structured, in order to focus on the sense or senses in which norms or normative attitudes may indeed be at work in each. This then allows us to pose the overarching question as to whether there are indeed generic normative phenomena at work across all three fields, phenomena of the sorts designated by NA1–NA4, which could turn out to be structural features of the human life form. In order to prepare these moves, it is helpful first to get a sense of how normative phenomena are conceptualised by the scientists and scholars working in these areas and of the problems that the phenomena have been taken to pose.

3.1. Social Norms

The topic of social norms raises problems of a somewhat less fundamental nature than do the topics of moral or linguistic norms. Whereas in both of the latter cases there are reasons for doubting whether there are such things at all, no one doubts the existence of social norms. Moreover, no one doubts that their existence is dependent on features of relevant agents. Rather, the key questions here concerns how to circumscribe their nature and extension.

In order to know what we are picking out by means of the expression "social norms," we first need to know what the qualifier "social" picks out. It seems fairly natural to think of it as circumscribing either the norms' addressees, their bearers, or both. On one understanding of social norms, then, what is specifically social about them is the demarcation of their addressees. Social norms would be thought of as *norms only addressed, or applicable to the members of some society, subculture, or milieu, as members of that group.* Alternatively, or in conjunction, they might be thought of as norms *whose existence grounds in the attitudes or behaviour of a significant proportion of the members of some society, subculture, or milieu.*

If either form (or both forms) of distribution is (or are) semantically decisive, social norms are the norms of a specific society or sub-group of some society—where "of" picks out either or both of the relations just mentioned. Laws, even laws of an oligarch, could be social norms if only the addressees are criterially decisive. Informal norms grounding in the attitudes of all, or most, members of some community concerning the behaviour of only some of their number, for instance of members of some caste, could be social norms if only the norms' bearers are decisive. If it is the conjunction that is conceptually decisive, then the relevant attitudes or behavioural proclivities will have to be widely distributed among the society's members, as will the features of agents in virtue of which they are subject to the norms.

If the conjunction of these parameters is taken to be sufficient for the sociality of specifically social norms, then they are unlikely to include juridical norms, unless some theory is advanced according to which democratic processes entail the acceptance of laws by the society's members. Certain metaethical conceptions, in particular accounts of a contractarian structure, might subsume moral principles under the category. However, for any account that sees moral norms as necessarily universal, in the sense of applying to all persons, the classes of moral and social norms will be disjunct, unless all persons are taken to be members of a global community. This will also be true for robust realist metaethical accounts of deontic moral principles, which deny any dependence of their existence on the attitudes or behaviour of humans.

One feature that is frequently taken to be specific to the social character of social norms is their *general implementation* by their addressees. Although norms in the relevant sense are not mere statistical regularities in behaviour, social norms are often understood as necessarily involving such regularities.

There are some limit cases which might divide theoretical opinion on the sense of "regularity" at issue here. If we take "regular" here to mean "general," i.e. that the relevant behaviour takes place in the majority of cases in which specifiable conditions are satisfied, then we are not committed to the claim that a social norm must play any noticeable role in the everyday life of a society. A norm prescribing the appropriate ritual on the death of a tribal leader in the case that there are no immediate successors may not have been relevant for generations, although the details of the procedure might be passed on. As long as the prescription's antecedent is not satisfied, the society conforms to the norm whatever it does. "Regular," then, would not entail frequent observability.

Of course, if it is taken to be necessary for a norm to be social that it is psycholog-ically instantiated in the majority of members of the social group in question, then if the content of the norm is handed down among some esoteric group, perhaps the population's elders, it would for this reason not count as social. But it certainly seems sensible to understand social norms in such a way that there may be more or less cen-tral and more or less peripheral cases, where orientation relative to the central, not to the peripheral, cases is part of the everyday business of social life.

This issue is important in view of the prominent conception of social norms ac-cording to which they are at least in part distinguished from other kinds of norms by the fact that necessarily they are generally conformed to. Two classic theories of what look like closely related social phenomena make this assumption: Lewis's theory of convention and Hart's theory of social rules. In spite of important differences between the two approaches, they agree in their understanding of the precise source of this necessity. For both authors, the necessary connection between the existence of a for-mation of the relevant kind ("convention" or "social rule") and general behavioural conformity follows from the fact that the formation is identical to the generally reg-ular behaviour, insofar as the regularity is augmented by specific sets of attitudes and, in Hart's case, their further behavioural consequences.

According to David Lewis's much cited definition, a *convention* is a general behavioural regularity, known by the members of the population to be such, and of which four further attitudinal conditions hold and are known to hold. These are a doxastic condition—that general conformity is generally expected—and three conditions concerning preferences of the majority of the population's members (Lewis 1969, 78). According to H. L. A. Hart's influential analysis, a *social rule* is a general behavioural regularity of which three conditions hold. These concern the general tendency to criticism of deviation, the general acceptance of such criticism as legitimate, and the general understanding of the behaviour as setting a standard for all relevant others (Hart 1961, 55–7). It is natural to understand the role of the attitudes in both accounts as explanatory, or at least supportive of the behavioural regularity, although neither author makes such an explanatory relation a feature of his definition.[11]

One strange consequence of understanding social norms as essentially behavioural regularities accompanied or explained by attitudinal features is that there could be no social norms that are particularly ineffective in motivating behaviour. However, it seems plausible that norm revision within a social group will often result from the withering away of the motivation to adhere to norms that had formerly mustered such motivation in the group's members. One could, of course, simply say that, after a certain behavioural threshold has been crossed downwards, we should cease to talk

---

[11] Pettit, in contrast, includes such an explanatory condition (Pettit 2008, 140).

of a norm. But this move misses the fact that an essential feature of the structure that interests us may well survive such motivational debilitation on the part of the norm's addressees. We want to be able to say that prescriptions are still being addressed to the members of the social group, but that many of them no longer respond. And if this is true, then it also seems unhelpful to exclude the possibility of there being social norms of long standing in some population to which there is only a very limited level of conformity.

In his response to his critics, Hart accepted that his "practice theory of rules" doesn't cover all the legal rules for which he had originally developed the theory, as some such rules may exist "from the moment of their enactment before any occasion for their practice has arisen" (Hart 1994, 256). Even for the simple social rules that he takes as his analytic starting point, there appears to be a basic confusion in the claim that it is the empirical "pattern of behaviour" that sets the standard for conduct and for criticism (Hart 1961, 57; 1994, 255). Hart summarises his analysis as picking out a behavioural component and a distinctive normative attitude toward that behaviour which he labels "acceptance." But there seems to be no good reason why the content of such "acceptance" need be determined by a generally instantiated pattern of conduct. The case of enacted legal rules shows that the attitude may precede the behaviour; the considerations of the last paragraph show that the behaviour may follow only sluggishly or fade even when the relevant normative attitude is in place.

This insight opens the way for a conception of social norms as essentially a matter of the attitudes of a population, an approach that raises both the question as to which attitudes are decisive and the question as to what it might mean that the relevant attitudes are in place in the population. Cristina Bicchieri's influential game-theoretic approach takes the key attitudinal structure to be explicable in terms of preferences and expectations or beliefs, where these concern the conformity of others, one's own conformity conditional on that of others, and others' expectations and preferences concerning one's conformity (Bicchieri 2006, 11).[12] According to a more recent proposal by Brennan et al., the decisive attitudes are at core those that Hart saw as constitutive of "acceptance," viz. the dispositions to take on reactive attitudes such as disapproval, together with judgements to the effect that an agent or agents "must" or "should" perform some action φ, or that φ-ing is "appropriate" (Brennan et al. 2013, 29).[13]

[12] This rough sketch leaves out a crucial feature of Bicchieri's proposal: that the relevant attitudes all refer to conformity with a "rule," where the concept of a rule is itself left unanalysed. As such, its analysis could lead to an iteration of the questions concerning the concept of a social norm. For instance, is such a rule a behavioural regularity or the content of some attitude?

[13] Curiously, Brennan et al., who are highly critical of the claim that norms are practices, treat Hart as a pure attitude theorist.

This constellation of attitudes has become an important research focus in developmental and social psychology, most prominently in the work of Michael Tomasello and his co-researchers. In everyday interaction, two- to three-year-old children, according to these authors, begin taking on what they call "the normative stance," that is, a constellation of attitudes that can be summarised as the understanding that "this is how things are done" (Tomasello 2009, 35, 92f.; Rakoczy and Schmidt 2013). One important result of this research is that children at this early age do not only follow what they take to be rule or norms; they also, as the authors put it, "enforce" them. By "enforcement," Tomasello and his collaborators mean the making of assertions with deontic vocabulary, addressing imperatives, and "tattling" (Rakoczy and Tomasello 2007; Rakoczy et al. 2008; Schmidt et al. 2011). What also seems significant is the spontaneous nature of children's normative responses: young children are eager, indeed at times over-eager (Keupp et al. 2013), to interpret and respond to behaviour in deontic terms. This may be seen as support for the view that the children's behaviour not only functions to enforce, but is also in part constitutive of the relevant norms.

However, even if it seems plausible that the setting of standards necessarily grounds in the attitudes of the social group's individual members, there looks to be a gap between such distributed attitudinising and the existence of a norm, if there is nothing that binds the attitudes of the individuals together. This is perhaps one point at which the existence of a corresponding social practice may seem a necessary adjunct. For Hart, the phrase "they do it as a rule," which is applicable both to social habits and "social rules," picks out the general social phenomenon that is then distinguished attitudinally in the normative case. Most authors, however, tie the relevant attitudes together in attitudinal terms.

The standard mechanism invoked in the rational choice tradition is that of "*common knowledge*," that is, of a recursive and symmetric epistemic relation to the attitudes of the other relevant agents (Lewis 1969, 52ff.): everyone knows that the others have the attitudes, a fact that is in turn known by everyone, which may at a next level be itself known, and so on. The potentially infinite recursion is blocked in some approaches by, at some level, replacing the requirement of knowledge with the requirement that the agents be in an epistemic position to attain the relevant knowledge. However the epistemic relation between the agents is modelled (cf. Vanderschraaf and Sillari 2013), the condition is highly demanding and is likely to exclude a great deal of the phenomena we would tend to think of as social norms. The paradigm case of common knowledge is a situation in which some explicit public announcement is heard by all the agents concerned, in the presence of all the others concerned. There is unlikely to be anything comparable to this in most cases of social norms. For this reason, Brennan et al. propose a simple knowledge condition as a replacement, viz. that it be generally known that the members of the population generally have the relevant attitudes (Brennan et al. 2013, 31).

In her 1989 critique of Lewis, Margaret Gilbert proposed a quite different approach, one that has been highly influential in its own right. Gilbert argued that what is required beyond common knowledge in order to make sense of the "ought" of social norms is an understanding on the part of the relevant agents that they together constitute a collective that can, as a collective, accept the norm: "We* accept [a principle], therefore, in so far as I am one of us*, I ought to conform to [the principle]" (Gilbert 1989, 374). The basic idea is that the relevant attitudes for social norms are not those of the individual members of a population as individual members, but of the collective— or "plural subject"—of which those individuals are members. Gilbert sees the ties that bind members of some social group or society together as of exactly the same kind as the ties that bind a small group of agents when they set out to perform some, perhaps short-lived, action together. Social norms, she argues, presuppose the existence of such ties across the social entity.

Such ties have since become the object of a rich set of overlapping research paradigms that focus on what is variously labelled "*joint*," "*shared*," or "*collective intentionality*." The analyses of the phenomena thus picked out—joint attention, shared beliefs and shared emotions, joint or collective intention and action—although interesting in their own right, are only of relevance here insofar as they are taken to be the basis for social norms. Gilbert's research programme is built on the assumption that social norms and large-scale social institutions can only be made sense of on the basis of an analysis of collective intentionality. In the original version of his theory, John Searle appears to share this assumption (Searle 1995, 41, 46), although not the conception of collective intentionality. In his revised account, however, he claims that the collective recognition of social rights and obligations can be reduced to individual recognition plus mutual belief (Searle 2010, 57f.).

An account close to Gilbert's has, however, been taken on board and developed by Tomasello, for whom an explanation of why children do not only follow, but also "legislate" social norms has to draw on children's early sense of shared intentionality, that is, their sense of being part of some larger "we" (Tomasello 2009, 39f.). In an attempt to get the best of both theoretical worlds, Tomasello and his collaborators have argued empirically that such a self-understanding as part of a Gilbertian "plural subject" is a necessary precondition for the acceptance or inauguration of social rules, where these latter steps are construed in terms of the conceptual tools developed by Searle. Such rules can be either regulative or constitutive, in the first case assigning rights and obligations for participants in independently existing practices (e.g. driving), in the second assigning rights and duties that make some practice (e.g. football) possible in the first place.

If rules of these two sorts are labelled "social norms," then social norms may pervasively structure just about all of human interaction, as all social roles—from dinner party host to president—and many social entities—from money to universities—appear essentially dependent on structures of rights and obligations ("status functions") that such rules assign. Tomasello and his collaborators claim, on the basis of developmental and comparative studies, that the capacity to generate, uphold, and act according to such rules is one important feature that distinguishes humans from our nearest living primate relatives (Rakoczy and Tomasello 2007; Wyman and Rakoczy 2011). The key feature they take to be the capacity for shared or collective intentionality, which is most prominently manifested in the capacity for social rules, as well as in the ability to cooperate.

Tomasello claims, importantly, not only that shared or collective intentionality is the central structural feature of the human life form, but also that it is what makes our life form unique. The latter claim raises two questions, both of which have been articulated by primatologists. The first is the ontological question as to whether it is really true that chimpanzees, for instance, neither cooperate—as opposed to merely coordinating—nor have social norms. Counter-examples to the former claim may include hunting and patrolling (cf. Boesch and Boesch 1989; Boehm 2018); dominance hierarchies and the behaviour of the members of coalitions may appear to contradict the latter (de Waal 1998, 77ff.; van Schaik and Burkart 2018). If dominance hierarchies don't involve social norms, then talk of a chimpanzee alpha male's "status" or "ranking" is either metaphorical or involves the use of mere homonyms.

The second question raised by Tomasello's claim is epistemological or methodological: how precisely can we establish empirically whether there are social norms in some population? In the absence of linguistic behaviour that might involve deontic terms, imperatives, and expressions of criticism, other forms of behaviour need to be focused on. Depending on the concept of social norms that is taken to be germane, the relationship of that focus to the criteria for norms' existence will be more or less close. This is a point at which a social practice account is clearly going to be more productive than any account which sees the essence of social norms in attitudes of a population's members, attitudes whose contents may or may not be realised. Of course, the adoption of a different concept of social norms for non-linguistic than for linguistic populations will restrict the possibility of drawing comparative conclusions. The alternative would be to resist the idea that a social practice component is definitive of the norms, seeing it instead as an epistemically necessary tool that enables the gathering of the most relevant data possible in view of the dearth of other kinds of evidence.

Other kinds of evidence need not, however, be completely lacking. If lack of language rules out the articulation of deontic concepts, as well as explicit imperatives and criticism, it doesn't exclude the expression of negative reactions in spontaneous emotional behaviour or in action that may involve the intentional administering of preventative measures or of sanctions. The difficulty now is ascertaining whether the behaviour observed really is an expression of the relevant emotions or is appropriately described as intentional prevention or punishment. These methodological problems can, for reasons of principle, not be definitively solved. What we can hope for, however, is the collation of material that provides sufficiently strong evidence for one or the other picture.

3.2. Moral Norms?

The methodological question as to how the existence of norms can be established is given a special twist when we turn to moral norms. Whereas there are no sensible grounds for specific scepticism about social norms among humans, even for humans the existence of moral norms is controversial. Two very different kinds of scepticism should be distinguished here. One form of scepticism is local and applies to moral *norms*, in contrast to other kinds of moral facts; the other form of scepticism is global and concerns *moral* facts of any kind. Let us take the two forms of scepticism in turn.

Scepticism of the first kind doesn't concern moral facts per se. Its advocates have tended to be "robust realists" about morality: they take it that there are moral facts that are as real as other facts of human life, i.e. that are in no sense dependent on what humans think, feel, or want with respect to the relevant features of their lives. Certain robust realists, however, claim that, among the features that determine moral facts, there are none that are appropriately thought of as norms. Two reasons for such specific norm scepticism have been prominent.

The first reason for local norm scepticism is a more strident version of Judith Thomson's claim that there is no specifically moral "ought" (cf. section 2.1 in this chapter). In her influential article "Modern Moral Philosophy" (1958), Elizabeth Anscombe claimed that the concepts of a moral "ought," of moral obligation, and of moral duty are all expressions of a "law conception of ethics," a conception that can be given no sense outside of a theological framework (Anscombe 1958, 5–6). This kind of critique avoids general scepticism through the assumption that ethical judgements can only coherently be judgements of character, rather than judgements concerning specific actions. This assumption, which is central to a *virtue ethical* account of morality, is, however, itself highly controversial.

A second reason for local norm scepticism concerns not the *deonticity*, but the *generality*, of norms. According to advocates of this view, most prominently Jonathan Dancy, moral facts concerning the value or appropriateness of some form of behaviour φ in a specific situation *s* are not deducible from more general moral facts, including facts concerning the existence of prescriptive principles (Dancy 1993, 60ff.). For example, the fact that A should not lie to B in *s* is, according to such a *particularistic* view, not entailed by any norm or principle that prohibits lying. This remains so even if the principle's scope is significantly restricted by the inclusion of descriptions of *s* within the principle. The principle "Don't lie to others about things that matter to them, unless you believe that they might make dangerous use of the truth if you were to communicate it to them" would be no less invalid. And so on, independently of how much detail is built into the principle (Dancy 2004, 73ff.; cf. McKeever and Ridge 2006, 113ff.).

Particularists generally interpret the claim that any such principle is invalid in ontological terms: the claim is then that there *is* no such principle which could be the source of the moral facts of the matter in any concrete situation. Although there are moral truths about specific situations, determined by moral and non-moral properties of those situations, there are, according to this view, no moral norms that are part of the fabric of the world.

Robust realism about any kinds of moral facts, whether or not these include facts about, or deriving from, moral norms, faces a general challenge as to the compatibility of such facts with a naturalistic world view, in particular with the truth of evolutionary theory. This challenge is spelled out most vigorously by *irrealist* or anti-realist positions, which reject the very idea that moral requirements, or any other kind of moral property, could be a part of the fabric of the world. Irrealists are norm sceptics of the second sort, rejecting the existence of moral norms for the same reason they reject the existence of moral properties of any kind.

John Mackie rejected the claim that there may be elements of the world characterised by "objective prescriptivity," a claim he takes to be central to everyday folk morality, as too bizarre to have a place in a world view compatible with contemporary science (Mackie 1977, 42). More recent challenges based on evolutionary theory, so-called debunking arguments, have claimed that there is an incompatibility between the claim that our moral beliefs are true, justified representations of moral facts and the evolutionary idea that our systems of beliefs are the product of natural selection. Whereas it is plausible that our capacity to develop beliefs about the perceptual world was selected for because of its survival value—animals with true beliefs about the presence of their predators or food are more likely to survive—no such story seems plausible about the capacity to form what we take to be true moral beliefs. If moral beliefs have bequeathed a selective advantage, this will be a form of usefulness that looks to be completely independent of whether they are true or not (Joyce 2006, 179ff.; Street 2006). If arguments of this kind go through, this wouldn't make our beliefs about, for example, our moral obligations necessarily false; however, it would make them, at the very least, unjustified and would make their truth a massive coincidence.

Now, locally and globally sceptical views of the ontology of moral norms are perfectly compatible with a recognition that the members of relevant populations are anything but sceptics. In the terms of section 2.3, NA2 may be satisfied without NA1 being so. According to Dancy, individuals, or groups of individuals, may use thoughts of the form "You shouldn't tell lies" as rules of thumb in their attempts to do what is morally right (Dancy 1993, 67ff.). Such tools just shouldn't be understood as successful representations of features of reality. One of the key claims of Mackie's error theory is that everyday folk are in all their moral thinking necessarily engaged in unsuccessful attempts to represent features of reality with the scientifically inconceivable property of "objective prescriptivity." Indeed, he takes this description of everyday moral thinking to be so obviously true that he at one point considers whether it might not count as the premise for an argument for the existence of God: if there were a God who could create the supervenience relation that binds such prescriptions to natural properties, it would explain where we get the idea that requirements are part of the fabric of the world (Mackie 1982, 114ff.). Like Anscombe, Mackie rejects this explanation.

One response to a generalised scepticism about moral facts has been to argue for a *less metaphysically robust conception* of the objectivity, existence, or reality of the features that would make claims concerning moral obligations, prohibitions, and permissions true. A successful account here would, on the one hand, need to explain how the existence of such deontic features might in some way be generally dependent on the dispositions of humans to respond to certain properties of their social environment. On the other hand, it would have to make clear how these features can also be independent of responses of specific individuals, or even groups of individuals, at particular moments in time. The satisfaction of the latter condition is required to justify talk of "reality" or "objectivity," whilst the satisfaction of the former is what allows the conception to count as non-robust. Non-robustly real moral norms would satisfy NA3.

The human dispositions that have been taken to be decisive here are to emotional and desiderative reactions. Theories that work with emotional responses have generally attempted to provide an account of evaluative, rather than deontic, properties (McDowell 1985; Wiggins 1987).[14] Desires might appear better suited to explaining the prescriptive character of obligation. This may seem particularly plausible if we are dealing with a generalised reciprocal desiderative structure of the kind focussed on by the contractarian tradition: X wants Y to refrain from φ-ing relative to X more than X wants to φ relative to Y, together with a symmetrical condition concerning Y's preferences. For "X" and "Y," finally, substitute all members of some community and add some (common) knowledge condition.

Conceptions along these lines move moral norms closer to social norms. Indeed, one might think that, if one supplements a general understanding of social norms with the features that Hart took to be characteristic of obligation, it becomes clear that moral norms must be a sub-class of such social norms of obligation. According to Hart, social rules involve obligations where the critical reactions to their contravention are particularly insistent, where their upholding is taken to be necessary for the maintenance of social life, and where conformity may require sacrifice or renunciation (Hart 1961, 86ff.) Certainly, all three features appear to be prominent in our understanding of moral obligation. The contractarian takes it that commitments

---

[14] An exception is Prinz (2007, 87ff.).

to reciprocal self-restriction will concern primarily those action types that endanger social life. Hart himself thought that, where insistent critique takes the form of self-critical emotions such as guilt, shame, and remorse, we might plausibly classify the norms in question as part of "the morality" of the relevant social group.

Construing moral norms as social norms of a specific kind makes moral norms tractable objects of empirical research. In particular, it makes possible a research programme in comparative psychology or primatology that investigates the extent to which our closest relatives might also have moral norms, or something approaching them.

There has been a certain amount of research, most prominently by Frans de Waal, on the extent to which other primates may be motivated by mechanisms taken to be decisive for moral behaviour, in particular empathy (Flack and de Waal 2000; de Waal 2006). However, there has so far only been limited attention paid to the question of whether other primates might have anything approaching moral rights and duties. The extant research here naturally picks up on the three Hartian features of obligation, in particular on evidence of insistent social pressure or patterns of marked negative reactions. Such behaviour might, so it seems, point to something like general demands for the avoidance of behaviour that is damaging to the cohesion or prosperity of the population.

Candidates for relevant mechanisms are "policing," "punishment," or apparently disinterested third-party intervention (Flack et al. 2006; Clutton-Brock and Parker 1995; Vaish et al. 2011), as well as specific kinds of emotional agitation (Rudolf von Rohr et al. 2011, 14). Empirical studies of these phenomena don't aim simply to establish whether, for instance, chimpanzee communities have moral norms. The primary goal is, rather, to investigate the extent to which they may possess relevant behavioural or attitudinal precursors. As a consequence, such research promises to deliver insights ex negativo on the question as to what is required for an agent to live his or her life in a framework structured by moral obligations. The egocentric reactions of capuchins and chimpanzees to "disadvantageous inequity" documented by Sarah Brosnan (Brosnan and de Waal 2003; Brosnan 2006) may also be candidates for such a role.

Note, however, that, in talking about "the moral norms of a social group," as Hart does and as is natural for the primatological research perspective just sketched, we seem to have changed the subject relative to that which is at issue in the metaphysical discussions with which this section began. It is one thing to ask under what conditions we should think of a certain group of social norms in a society as moral. This classificatory question parallels the question of when we should think of certain social norms as rules of etiquette or as mere conventions. The answers to these question leave it open whether members of a relevant social group, or any other agents, have reasons to conform to the norms in question. It is quite another thing to ask what it might mean that there are certain things that we are morally obliged to do or omit. This latter question presupposes that an answer which provides an explanation of such obligations and prohibitions will pick out a source of reasons to behave accordingly. It is this question which, somewhat confusingly, has often been called "the normative question" (Korsgaard 1996, 10ff.), where "normative" means "provides intrinsic reasons" (cf. section 2.1 of this chapter).

Importantly, drawing this distinction does not preclude answering the second question by pointing to certain kinds of norms generated in a certain way and perhaps in some way assented to by the members of a particular population. This would provide a relativist answer to the question of reason-providing moral obligations (Harman 1977; Prinz 2007). What we do, however, need to recognise is that we are dealing with two very different questions. The latter is a particularly philosophical concern and may appear completely disconnected from empirical research. However, this is not so.

Investigating indicators of precursors to moral norms in some population does not necessarily presuppose that moral norms themselves are social entities that could be identified by empirical methods. Such empirical research might be helpful for our understanding of the morally deontic if it were true, for example, that moral normativity can only be developed or recognised by communities that have social norms. This might be the case if moral obligation, or at least the concept of moral obligation, were constructed by means of abstractions from the certain features of social norms that first need to be in place before such abstraction, and the orientation that it bequeaths, were to be possible.[15]

This possibility raises an interesting question about the status of research in developmental psychology that investigates young children's appreciation of moral norms. Tomasello and his collaborators have shown that three-year-old children react with the same forms of protest to the contravention of what look like simple moral norms—concerning, for instance, harm and ownership (Vaish et al. 2011; Rossano et al. 2011; Schmidt et al. 2013)—as they do to the infringement of the constitutive rules of games (cf. section 3.1). One way of interpreting the broad spectrum of such reactions is to see them as all indicating that children take on a generic "normative stance," being disposed to react in similar ways to a whole set of different forms of behaviour. Thus understood, "the normative stance" might be thought to involve attitudes that appear appropriate to deontic strictures of any sort, a stance that allows the addition of distinctions between social and specifically moral norms. Another view might be that three-year-olds already grasp, and indeed begin contributing to, the basic elements of social normativity (cf. Göckeritz et al. 2014), which equally cover both moral norms and game rules.

---

[15] The idea that moral reasons in general are generated through a process of abstraction from social processes—of a specifically emotional kind—is central to the naturalistic moral theories of David Hume and Adam Smith (cf. Sayre-McCord 2015).

The former view, which allows that moral and social norms may be of two different kinds, rather than the first being a variant of the second, accords with a central claim of *social domain theory* in developmental psychology. According to this theory, human agents think in terms of three distinct sets of considerations when leading their lives, groupings that allow us to distinguish the personal, the conventional, and the moral "domains" (Nucci and Turiel 1978; Turiel 1983). Elliot Turiel and his colleagues have presented a large body of evidence for the claim that, from the middle of their third year, children make a distinction between the moral and the conventional. In comparison with matters that concern convention, matters of morally right and wrong are taken to be more serious; moral norms, unlike conventional norms, are taken to be applicable beyond one's own geographical or cultural context; and moral but not conventional norms are taken to be authority-independent. Finally, Turiel claims, already young children tend to think of judgements about moral norms as justified by considerations of welfare, justice, or rights, whilst conventional judgements are taken to be justified by rules set up to facilitate social organisation (Turiel 1983, 52ff.; Smetana and Braeges 1990, 330ff.).

These claims of social domain theory have generated a great deal of discussion both in psychology and in philosophy. Discussions have concerned the precise structure and basis of the distinction, its coherence, status, and ontogeny.[16] Although these issues are all important for the topic of this volume, I shall just remark here on two points.

The first concerns the relationship between the operative notion of the conventional and that of the social. There is a widespread understanding of conventions as rules for social life that prescribe a solution to some problem, although, as is clear to the addressees, the solution could with equal justification have been another. Conventions are, in other words, arbitrary.[17] However, if this is the relevant concept of convention, the distinction between moral and conventional norms is implausibly thought of as an exhaustive disjunction, as there appear to be rules that are not in this sense arbitrary, whilst also not being moral norms. Aesthetic norms and at least some civil laws are plausible candidates. Of course, whether we may be dealing with an exhaustive disjunction here also depends on the conception of moral norms at issue. Relativists may also think that the solutions prescribed by moral norms could, in many cases, have turned out differently with equal justification.

---

[16] Doubts about the ontogenetic claims have been propounded for the most part by authors working in the tradition of cultural psychology (Shweder et al. 1987; Gabennesch 1990), who take such doubts to carry over to claims about the distinction's status. Doubts about its structure and coherence concern the relationship between the four features seen by Turiel and colleagues as in some sense definitive (Kelly et al. 2007; Shoemaker 2011, 105ff.). One suggestion as to what might really ground the distinction has honed in on issues of justification (Southwood 2011; Brennan et al. 2013, 66ff.); another has claimed that it derives above all from the type of emotions at issue (Prinz and Nichols 2010, 121).

[17] This feature is central to the phenomenon that Lewis took himself to be rationally reconstructing.

A second feature of the view propounded by social domain theory is the claim that the three domains the theory distinguishes, presumably including the relevant norms, are "constructed" by children in the course of their development (Turiel 1983, 53f.). This claim is intended to position the account on middle ground between nativist claims that morality is innate and culturalist claims that it is entirely taken on from the social environment. As the account assumes that the relevant "constructions" all develop along the same structural lines, this raises the question as to what it is that explains their regularity. Although social domain theory is less than forthcoming about the answer to this question, it does seem that it is likely to be congenial to some form of non-robust realism about moral norms.

3.3. Linguistic Norms?

Whereas there are few authors who would classify moral norms as mere *conventions*, there are many who take language to be essentially conventional (Hume 1739/40 III, iii, 2, 490; Austin 1962, 14; Lewis 1975, 7; Tomasello 2008, 102ff., 218ff.). And many authors of very different persuasions have argued that language is in some important sense *rule*-governed (Wittgenstein 1953, §§199–242; Searle 1969, 22ff.; Kripke 1982; McDowell 1984; Glock 2000). The key datum from which such claims generally proceed is that language use involves meeting *standards of correctness*.

This is uncontroversially true for various dimensions of language use. Here are some examples: first, according to what phonologists call the "assimilation rule," an "-s" added to construct plural forms in English should be voiced or voiceless, depending on whether the previous consonant is voiced. This is something that language learners can get wrong. Second, some languages provide a number of different words for "you," the correct choice among which depends on the level of formality or hierarchical character of the relation between speaker and addressee (Enfield 2010, 10; 2015, 133ff.). Third, in every language, ascribing a particular property to items of a particular kind necessitates the use of specific words, or words taken from a specific grouping. At least under normal circumstances, you won't be able to ascribe the property of being on the mat to a cat in English by saying "My hovercraft is full of eels."[18] Finally, attempts at communication are often likely to be unsuccessful if they don't attend to standards of relevance (Grice 1967, 27).

Language is, obviously, an area of activity in which human agents can make various kinds of mistakes or get it right. Where this is the case, the relevant agents may, so it seems, be guiding at least some of their behaviour in ways suited to meeting the standards in question. Indeed, humans have entire institutions dedicated to the

---

[18] Neither will you be able to request a box of matches by means of this sentence, as the Monty Python Hungarian phrasebook sketch illustrates.

upholding of linguistic standards, whether these concern the introduction of children to the niceties of their native tongue, the facilitation of second- or foreign-language acquisition, the preservation of languages threatened by linguistic imperialism, or copy editing. In all these contexts, language users are furnished with explicit linguistic prescriptions of various kinds and attempt to apply them.

It ought, however, to be clear that much of our everyday linguistic interaction is conducted in the absence of any explicit thoughts concerning standards for correct pronunciation, word-order or conjugation, address, reference or predication, and relevance. Yet, within linguistic communities, these various standards are, to a significant extent, met effortlessly. Moreover, the overwhelming majority of the speakers who meet the standards would be unable to formulate most of them. *Phonological standards* such as "the assimilation rule" are met by speakers who would need time to be taught the "rule" and would have to work hard *not* to meet it.

At this stage, we should note that, in this expression, the term "rule" evidently has a radically different meaning from that of the term as we have, following Hart, been employing it. "Rules" of the kind at work in the assimilation of consonants are not followed intentionally by speakers, but are implemented by their vocal systems in the course of the speakers' trying to say something. "Phonological rules" are thought of as algorithms in the brain for the production of "commands to the speech muscles," where these "commands" in turn specify the production of articulatory features under specific conditions. Such "rules" are essentially highly complex dispositions whose triggering generates equally complex vocal "gymnastics" (Pinker 1994, 170ff.).

The currency of these uses of the terms "rule" and "command" in cognitive science enjoinders care to keep them separate from those uses that appeal to the intentional capacities of human agents. This is, importantly, not merely a terminological issue, as there are areas in which the structures picked out by the two uses of the terms are in explanatory competition. One such area, as we will see in a moment, is that of linguistic meaning.

Before we come to "semantic rules," it is worth noting that an explanation of phonological behaviour in the terms proposed by cognitive science does not entail that no standard is in play. However, the standard—according to which an English speaker *should* voice the "-s" in constructing the plural of "bug"—is secondary, a retroactive assignment of a status to the product of a process explicable without recourse to the standard. Nevertheless, although the standard isn't what explains the process in the primary cases, it remains a remarkable fact that humans retroactively introduce such status assignations. Indeed, where such standards are not met, this can provoke all sorts of reactions, ranging from the mild—an unnoticed smirk—to the murderous—as in the biblical example of the murder of 42,000 Ephraimites by the Gileadites on the basis of the latter's deviant pronunciation of the word "shibboleth."

It is important to be clear on what these examples show. The latter use of a pronunciation standard is entirely dependent on a pre-existing murderous motive. The relevant inability of the Ephraimites had a mere epistemic status, allowing the Gileadites to identify those they wanted to kill. Any other kinds of properties could have fulfilled the same purpose; the linguistic incapacity was simply extremely handy, as it was a feature that could not easily be shed. The fact that the Ephraimites were failing to do something that, for the Gileadites, counted as following a rule is thus irrelevant here.

The case of the smirk is somewhat different. The smirk may be fairly harmless, but could also express an entrenched attitude of disdain or contempt. Moreover, it might also correspond to embarrassment or even shame on the part of the speaker. Where this is the case, dispositions to a suite of emotional reactions are in place that seem to play an analogous role to those of the reactive attitudes taken by Adam Smith, Hart, and Strawson to be at least partly constitutive of the socially or morally deontic.

A deviant pronouncer, then, might feel the embarrassment or shame as a result of not meeting a standard she accepts. And she may accept it because she believes that that is what is required by the language she speaks. It is, however, anything but clear what might be meant by the claim that *the language requires* one pronunciation rather than another. A young Yorkshirewoman studying at Oxford may feel pressure to, among other things, lengthen her pronunciation of the "a" in "grass," but such pressures derive entirely from local social norms and the desire to be accepted by meeting them. For this reason, there appears to be nothing specifically linguistic about such norms, which seem to be entirely analogous to local dress codes or table manners.

What it might mean for norms to be specifically linguistic depends on a characterisation of the point or function of language. The two most plausible candidates here are, first, that of a sound, or of a person *meaning* something, and, second, that of *communication*. In most cases, deviant pronunciation is not going to interfere with either of these goals, just as using the wrong fork at dinner party is not going to interfere with one's nourishing oneself (Davidson 1994, 9).

Let us turn, then, to the claim that there are specifically *semantic norms*. Begin with the assertion that a vocal sound's having a specific meaning depends on there being conventions, rules, or norms in place according to which the sound has that meaning. The claim is generally associated with the middle and later Wittgenstein, who explicitly argues that rules for a word's use "determine its meaning" (Wittgenstein 1930–32, 59). According to this view, the human life form has its pervasive semantic dimension because humans have developed particular sets of rule-governed customs or practices (Wittgenstein 1953, §199, §202).

Such an explanation conflicts directly with explanations of the kind pioneered by Chomsky and developed by Bickerton and Pinker, the key components of which are innate "rules" or "principles" that make up a "universal grammar" (Chomsky 1968, 69; Chomsky and Halle 1968, 4). Like "phonological rules," taken to be a subset of those of universal grammar, the "rules" taken to determine meaning in such accounts are generally inaccessible to their bearers, grounding in the algorithms of a deep syntactic structure that cannot be learned, but rather, as a complex set of innate micro-dispositions, constitutes the framework within which different languages and dialects can be acquired.[19] Even the "rules" that determine semantic features of particular languages remain, according to such accounts, largely inaccessible to the speakers, as they are constituted by the sub-personal specification of parameters opened up by the structure of universal grammar. Such "rules" are thus far removed from rules understood as purveyors of normative guidance.[20]

Anyone claiming that linguistic meaning is essentially dependent on rules that can be intentionally followed faces the challenge of providing an explanation of how such intentional guidance might be at work in spite of the fact that relevant rules are almost never explicitly consulted by agents prior to speech. Indeed, this fact needs explaining even if the decisive semantic rules are claimed to be of a form that can be articulated in everyday language and grasped by everyday agents. In the terminology of Robert Brandom, the solution will have to lie between "regulism," the implausible claim that guidance works with explicit rules, and "regularism," the misconception that mere regularity of behaviour suffices for a rule or norm to be at work (Brandom 1994, 18ff.). Wittgenstein's solution, according to Brandom and others, is that the relevant rules or norms are "implicit" in practices or institutions (McDowell 1984, 242ff.; Brandom 1994, 61).

This idea can be cashed out in terms of the reactions to deviant behaviour, particularly of those reactions that are—explicitly—thought to be appropriate. It is worth

---

[19] Although Chomsky explicitly rejects the interpretation of "rules" in terms of dispositions (Chomsky 1980, 48ff.), he seems to be primarily heading off the idea that simple forms of observable behaviour are necessary for the confirmation of their existence. As Jackendoff argues (Jackendoff 2002, 56), complex multi-track dispositions to perceive, judge, and behave seem to fit the bill.

[20] Here again, Jackendoff is helpful: "What makes elements of a language *rules* . . . is that they contain typed variables . . .– that is, they describe *patterns* of linguistic elements" (Jackendoff 2002, 57; the relevant word to emphasise for our purposes is "describe").

It has, however, been argued that there is an important sense in which the "parametrised principles" generative of our everyday speech are indeed "normative." This sense is manifest in everyday reactions to ungrammatical talk, which speakers automatically feel to be unacceptable, although they could not explain the unacceptability. According to this line of argument, developed in particular by Susan Dwyer (Dwyer 2006, 2009), not only are the "principles" that determine language use "normative"; they are normative in exactly the same sense in which parametrised moral principles are normative. In Dwyer's view, this is indicated by the phenomenon of moral dumbfounding, the inability to explain certain basic moral impermissibility judgements (Haidt 2001). Dwyer can thus be seen as advancing an idiosyncratic position on the normative animal thesis: both morality and language she takes to be "underpinned by human normative competence" (Dwyer 2006, 238), where the relevant competence is conceived as an innate "grammatical" structure, containing parameters set differently in different cultures, indeed in different individuals. It follows that the true moral principles, like the correct linguistic rules, are not followed intentionally by anyone, but simply manifest themselves in behaviour.

noting that intentional guidance or control need not be thought of as resulting from thoughts, conscious or otherwise, concerning the relevant guidelines. We can think of such guidance as being at work where behaviour is under *virtual* control: an agent may act in accordance with a set of norms out of sheer habit, but in doing so act for reasons that don't include any reference to the norms at all. We may think of her behaviour as being under virtual normative control where she nevertheless retains a sensitivity to indications that her performance is in danger of infringing against them. That sensitivity is in turn bound up with the disposition to correct her behaviour in view of the norms, should she register any such danger.

This seems a plausible description of agents' intentional relations to prescriptive social and moral norms. Whether the model is appropriate for linguistic behaviour is a further question.[21] The answer depends in part on the role in intentional action of constitutive—rather than explicitly prescriptive—rules, which specify conventional supervenience relations between a behavioural item and what it counts as in view of a specific convention (see section 3.1). As these relations, in the linguistic case, make possible an infinite number of otherwise inconceivable actions (referring to absent or abstract items, making claims and providing reasons, etc.), their understanding must play some role in the generation of the relevant behaviour. The fact that they are taken for granted in much of that behaviour again seems plausibly compatible with their habitually structuring behaviour and only needing to be explicitly consulted (a dictionary taken to hand, reading FIFA's guidelines on the new offside rule) where that habitual guidance breaks down.

The claim that linguistic meaning requires the institution of specific norms also raises the question of the natural history of the relevant practices: whether a plausible narrative can be told that explains the generation of linguistic meaning through the emergence of norms out of non-linguistic behaviour. One kind of account, inspired by Sellars, suggests that certain behavioural regularities may with time have morphed into rules in minute steps and with the help of bootstrapping mechanisms (Peregrin 2010; 2012, 91). However, such an account fails to offer any substantial explanation of the transition to the norms assumed to be the bearers of our semantics.

In contrast, Tomasello has, in explicit opposition to nativist conceptions, developed a natural history that sees linguistic meaning as grounded in a "psychological infrastructure" specific to humans (Tomasello 2008, 100ff.). It is this structure of

---

[21] Such a model might be taken to cast doubt on the claim that, in intentionally performing utterances, speakers are intentionally following relevant rules. Habitually speaking in accordance with certain rules whilst intentionally pursuing non-linguistic aims (threatening, deceiving, making someone happy) seems compatible with the relevant conformity being *non-intentional* (as opposed to unintentional: it isn't brought about by mistake). Intentional conformity might be thought to enter the scene where virtual control turns actual.

psychological features that is taken to bear the explanatory burden. The core feature, Tomasello argues, is the same one at work in the generation of social norms: the species-specific capacity to share intentions. To this is added the motivation to share information, attitudes, and emotions with conspecifics. Within this framework, humans develop shared intentions to share such states, i.e. to communicate. The step to doing this by linguistic means requires the capacity for joint attention, specifically that of role reversal. This in turn involves understanding that a sound to which one is attending together with another agent directs the attention of that other to the same item in the world to which it directs one's own attention (Tomasello 2003, 25–8). This structure then provides the basis for the introduction of linguistic conventions, which Tomasello understands as shared devices whose attention-directing use is understood, and understood to be understood, by the members of the community (Tomasello 2008, 102–4, 218–25). Finally, Tomasello claims that the internal syntactic structures of conventional linguistic constructions take on a normative dimension, that is, are taken to impose requirements that speakers have to meet in their communicative behaviour. In Tomasello's view, this normativity reduces to that of social norms: "it is," in his words, "just another case of the normativity of group behaviour" (Tomasello 2008, 292).

John Searle has also proposed a speculative genealogy of the norms that determine linguistic meaning. Like Tomasello's narrative, it begins with intentional states of individuals and sees fully developed language as a medium for communicating such intentional states. Speaker meaning, the first step on this road, involves the "imposition of conditions of satisfaction on conditions of satisfaction" (intending to make certain sounds, whilst intending these sounds to be appropriate to relevant conditions in the world). Word and sentence meaning are then generated by the introduction of socially recognised repeatable devices, linguistic conventions, which Searle understands as standing possibilities of speaker meaning. The move to public conventions, Searle believes, brings with it speech-act-specific commitments on the part of speakers, for instance, to the truth of what they assert or to the carrying out of a promise. Searle claims that such commitments impose "obligations" on speakers. Moreover, he also argues that the generation of rights and duties through the inauguration of conventional practices of asserting, ordering, promising, thanking, etc. is necessary for the generation of any other kinds of social rights and duties. According to Searle, then, the normativity of linguistic convention is the basis on which social norms, and indeed moral norms, are built (Searle 2010, 61–89). "Language," he claims, "is the basic form of public deontology" (Searle 2010, 82).

Both Tomasello's and Searle's views are clearly hospitable to the normative animal thesis, as in both views, norms are in some sense all of a piece. In Tomasello's view, all norms of the kinds at issue in this volume are essentially social, deriving from the framework of collective intentionality and the motivations to cooperate and conform.[22] In Searle's view, they all at least ground in the norms essential to linguistic practice.

Whatever the details of these particular genealogical exercises, there remains the more specifically philosophical task of specifying the content of the norms that are claimed to have come into being in such manners. A number of authors have argued that the correctness standards in play where lexical items are being used are insufficient to show that such usage is subject to genuine norms. For one thing, the standards might be merely classification criteria, involving no evaluative dimension (Hattiangadi 2006, 224; Glüer and Wikforss 2015b, 67f.). For another, if they are normative, it should be possible to specify the contents of "oughts" or requirements that follow from the standards. The challenge is substantial because it would be absurd to postulate norms according to which it is required of speakers that they apply the terms suitable for referring to items in the world to all the items to which they would be appropriately applied. Indeed, if "ought" implies "can," any such claim will also be false (Hattiangadi 2007, 180).

However, the applicability of further deontic modalities seems at least prima facie unproblematic. If a term picks out one and only one kind, then we are required, so it seems, not to apply it to other kinds. We thus appear to have a norm with the structure of a prohibition (Whiting 2013, 15; Peregrin 2014, 80). Conversely, we are semantically permitted to apply the term to items of the kind the term picks out (Glock 2010, 99). Moreover, if meaning is even minimally holistic, then it is going to be either part of, or follow from the meaning of, a term that further linguistic moves are permissible or impermissible (Brandom 1994, 89). If you have asserted that there is a fly buzzing around the room, you are entitled, without any further evidence, to the claim that there is an insect in the room. Whether such inference rules should be thought of as constitutive of an expression's meaning or as following from it depends on the details of the relevant theory of meaning.[23]

Now, although some talk of "ought" or "require" seems obviously applicable here, it may seem less plausible to talk in terms of "prohibitions" and "permissions," as these expressions may appear in some sense too strong. The reactions to non-conformity are likely to look less like the reactions to the contravention of social norms than do the reactions to locally deviant pronunciation. If someone misapplies a term, this is likely to generate confusion, amusement, concern, or even pity, depending on what appears

---

[22] Moral norms are for Tomasello also essentially social, a claim he has recently developed in detail in his *Natural History of Human Morality* (Tomasello 2016). For some worries about the model, see Roughley (2018b).

[23] An inferentialist such as Brandom will deny the distinction between "meaning-determining" and "meaning-engendered" normativity set up by Glüer and Wikforss (Glüer and Wikforss 2015a, sect. 1.1). That it is, conversely, possible to deny the claim that norms are necessary for meaning, but to accept that "'means' entails 'ought'," is argued by Allan Gibbard (Gibbard 2012, 37ff.).

to explain the misapplication. This finding admits of different interpretations. On the one hand, it may seem to be an argument for the claim that the norms at work here are sui generis, linguistic norms and not a species of social norms. On the other hand, it may appear to indicate that there are no norms in any interesting sense at work. In the words of Davidson, who advocates the latter interpretation, "[i]t is absurd to be obligated to a language; so far as the point of language is concerned, our only *obligation*, if that is the word, is to speak in such a way as to accomplish our purpose by being understood as we expect and intend" (Davidson 1994, 9).

Relatedly, it has been argued that, if norms applicable to an agent's action provide her with reasons or justification for her action (Glock 2010, 92), semantic standards cannot count as norms in any interesting sense. One argument for this claim is that the only genuine semantic standards concern truth conditions for the use of some expression (Davidson 1982, 269) and that these standards have no place in a practical syllogism explaining linguistic behaviour (Glüer and Pagin 1999, 224). Such a claim depends on specific conceptions both of the relevant kind of semantic standards and of the role of normative reasons in action explanation. If reasons are considerations that can be retrospectively cited to justify an agent's action, independently of whether they are explicitly registered antecedently, then the standard to the effect that the phonetic sequence /pɪt bʊl/ picks out a particular kind of animal can play the role of a reason. Of course, such semantic standards don't provide intrinsic reasons for intentional action. There is, however, no plausibility to the claim that the only genuine norms are those that provide intrinsic reasons:[24] if this were true there would arguably be no social norms at all.

Nevertheless, many semanticists remain convinced that, although there is a whole set of norms relevant for linguistic performance, none of these are sui generis linguistic norms (Wikforss 2001, 205ff.; Hattiangadi 2007, 181ff.). For there to be such norms, they would have to determine linguistic meaning, whereas the true determinants of meaning are, as many authors believe, very different, for instance, truth conditions or causal processes. From such perspectives, the norms associated with speech are often taken to concern further aims such as truth (Horwich 1998a, 92f.; 184ff.) or communication, rather than meaning, where the former depend on the latter, thus reversing the dependency relation argued for by authors such as Wittgenstein, Searle, and Tomasello.

The most well-known norm that has been proposed as a *norm of communication* is Grice's "cooperative principle," according to which contributions to a conversational exchange should be regulated by the common purpose of the conversation, and thus meet standards of informativeness, truth, relevance, and perspicuity (Grice 1967, 26–7).

---

[24] This claim would make the concept of "normative" in the sense of "norm-related" a subcategory of "normative" in the sense of "intrinsically reason-providing" (cf. section 2.1).

Grice himself believed that he was formulating a norm of rationality or reasonable-ness applied to the realm of "talk," a norm whose subordinate maxims have close non-linguistic analogues and the effects of whose non-observance, implicatures, do not strictly speaking belong to the linguistic ("conventional") meaning of what is said.

If, however, the category of meaning is already at work in non-linguistic human interaction and merely honed in specific ways by language, there might be grounds for scepticism as to whether the strict distinction between semantics and pragmatics can be upheld (Enfield 2009, 1ff.). This suspicion has motivated work in linguistic anthropology that proceeds on the premise that there can be no strict separation of semantic and social normativity. From such a perspective, conventional linguistic signs mark only one semiotic dimension of composite utterances, which essentially also include intonations and gestures. All these dimensions are seen as bound up with cross-modal commitments and entitlements, as illustrated, for instance, by the extent to which different languages make social structure implicit in the array of personal pronouns available. From this perspective, the standards for personal reference both pick out other agents and prescribe an encoded affirmation of a culture's structure of social relationships on the part of speakers (Enfield 2007). Thus viewed, perhaps a sufficiently stark deviation from the norms prescribing the appropriate stance to social structure might be viewed as a failure not only in communication, but also in achieving meaning.

4. Over to the Contributions

In the contributions to this volume, a group of authors from a variety of disciplinary backgrounds set out arguments and empirical evidence supporting various positions on the normative or deontic dimensions of social, moral, and linguistic behaviour. They also prominently pursue the question of the extent to which the decisive psy-chological mechanisms at work in humans in these dimensions may have substantial precursors in other social animals. The contributions refer in differing degrees of ex-plicitness to the broader normative animal thesis, but were all written with a view to enabling a more thorough examination of the likelihood of its truth.

2

On Social, Moral, and Linguistic Norms

The Contributions to This Volume

Neil Roughley and Kurt Bayertz

In the following, we present the key claims of the individual chapters. In doing so, we set the claims of the authors into relation to one another and highlight a number of issues raised by competition between some of the key claims. In this way, we prepare the ground for an assessment of the normative animal thesis in the light of the diverging accounts both of specific deontic phenomena and of normativity in general.

1. Social Norms

The first chapter in Part II, "There Ought to Be Roots: Evolutionary Precursors of Social Norms and Conventions in Non-Human Primates" (Chapter 3), is contributed by the behavioural biologists **Peter Kappeler, Claudia Fichtel, and Carel van Schaik**. The authors proceed from the assumption that the social norms and conventions characteristic of human society must have developed from precursor mechanisms, mechanisms that are plausibly at work in the social formations of our closest living biological relatives, non-human primates. The contribution sets out to identify candidates for such mechanisms.

The authors begin by outlining how the demographic development of human social formations from bands via tribes to chiefdoms leads to social hierarchies and mechanisms of social coordination unnecessary in the original small social units. They then distinguish between legal and moral rules, traditions, conventions, and social norms, before focusing on the latter two. The primary features of *conventions* they take to be their arbitrary contents and their explanation in terms of conformity to majority influences, where that explanation does not ground in the agents' insight into the utility of the relevant behaviour ("informational conformity"). The key feature the authors see as specific to *social norms* is "a sense of oughtness," which delivers a proximal explanation of behaviour distinct from the urge to copy behaviour. This feature is also taken to explain behavioural expectations on the part of bystanders in specific cases. The fact that, in both cases, it is the specific motivational profile of the agents that is decisive entails that empirical research is necessarily unable to establish with certainty whether primate societies have conventions or social norms. With this epistemological restriction in mind, the authors distinguish three kinds of data relevant for the chapter's topic: candidates for dyadic precursors of social norms, evidence for social norms themselves, and evidence for conventions (non-informational conformity).

The discussion of dyadic precursors proceeds from the assumption that social norms require certain behavioural, cognitive, and emotional features generated as exaptations by evolutionary processes, features whose functional integration then allows normativity to emerge. Key candidates for such features, it is further assumed, can be studied in the dyadic interaction between primates.

The authors focus here, first, on bonding mechanisms, which generate "expectations," the violation of which can lead to aggressive responses, responses which in turn can lead to third-party interventions. The second feature discussed is, here as in much of the literature, labelled "punishment," a label that does more to indicate the possible co-opting of the relevant mechanisms for norms than to describe the mechanism in its dyadic context. What is decisive is that an aggressive behavioural reaction functions to discourage its object from repeating a certain kind of behaviour. The authors discuss the third-party variant ("policing"), its assumed emotional accompaniment, anger, and the correlative, appeasing emotion, shame.

The third feature discussed here is that of dominance hierarchies, a feature that is not restricted to dyadic interaction, but structures entire social groups and thus appears functionally very close to social norms in human societies. Indeed, what is plausibly the key factor for its selection, intragroup competition for resources, is the same factor adduced by Hume in his genealogy of obligation.[1] The core of such hierarchies appears to lie in threat and appeasement displays, whose force may seem to derive entirely from the physical strength they express or the danger they signal. However, Kappeler et al. also point to specific examples in matriline hierarchies, where the position of each female—a position shored up by third-party intervention where necessary—is a function of their age. The explanation here seems to require reference to "social rules." This raises the striking question of the ontology of such "rules."

The kinds of social norms that have been claimed to exist in various primate species concern property, the protection of weak group members, impartial intervention

---

[1] ". . . the selfishness and confin'd generosity of men, along with the scanty provision nature has made for his wants" (Hume 1739–40 III, ii, 2, 495).

in dyadic conflicts, inequity aversion, food calls, and reactions to the infringement of dominance hierarchies. In each of these cases, Kappeler et al. see the evidence for norms as equally compatible with other kinds of explanations.

Finally, interesting cases of behavioural homogeneity that may be explained purely in terms of conformity include (i) the alternative between scrubbing or pounding fruit among capuchins in the wild, (ii) alternative food retrieval techniques made available to chimpanzees under laboratory conditions, (iii) copying retrieval-for-reward actions performed by one individual three times or three individuals once, and (iv) the induction of preferences for coloured corn among groups of wild vervet monkeys. Such forms of conformity might be thought to derive functionally from the avoidance of negative reactions from conspecifics, from the desirability of predictability among social allies, or from the tendency to minimise intragroup differences in the face of intergroup conflict. However, the authors conclude that none of these explanations is clearly superior to explanations that rely distributively on interests of the individuals involved.

In Chapter 4, "On the Human Addiction to Norms: Social Norms and Cultural Universals of Normativity," the cultural anthropologist **Christoph Antweiler** delineates conceptions of culture in his discipline as primarily constituted by social norms, describes varying ethnological approaches to studying norms, and discusses in particular the practices in child-rearing by means of which norms are successfully instilled in young members of societies.

According to Antweiler, social norms are rules specifying how people ought to behave, where those rules involve the ascription of obligations coupled with the threat of sanctions. Some cultural anthropologists conceive of such rules in terms of shared practices, whereas others, cognitive anthropologists, think of the rules as mental representations of the individual bearers of the culture. Either way, social norms provide solutions for tasks that are complex, recurrent, and important for societies and which individuals are cognitively ill-suited to solve. In cognitive anthropology, the representation of such solutions has been conceived as a subset of the mental models or "scripts" that furnish sensory and behavioural orientation.

Antweiler emphasizes that the installation of such normative models is a task faced by all societies and one which is dealt with by means of a set of universally available strategies. First, norm inculcation requires repetitive and consistent practices that deliver experiential constancy, thus providing the basis for habitual modes of reaction. Second, the relevant practices need to arouse strong and primarily negative emotions, an effect achieved through techniques such as beating, frightening, shaming, and teasing. Third, these practices tend to be accompanied by global evaluations of the children they are directed at. These three strategies function by installing in the children dispositions to act and, above all, to experience particular emotions, such as shame, in response to verbal criticism.

Antweiler also distinguishes between "mores," taken to be crucial for an acceptable way of life, and "folkways," which guide agents in all sorts of everyday tasks in ways that are hardly noticed. It seems likely that it is primarily norms of the former kind that are necessarily subject to the three inculcation strategies that aim at producing emotional dispositions with regulatory function. Someone performing a formally criminal act is nevertheless likely to be conforming to all sorts of informal and in-explicit "conventions" concerning how he dresses, perambulates, and communicates.

Finally, Antweiler places the specific constraints that he takes it give rise to social norms within a broader biological context. In agreement with Kappeler et al., he argues, first, that norms generally come into being in large social formations, many of whose members are not personally acquainted. Moreover, taking a leaf out of the book of the German school of Philosophical Anthropology, he adds that, for norms to be a relevant solution for these societies, their members have to be organisms whose behaviour is insufficiently hard-wired by genetic programmes.[2] Finally, for this latter reason and because of their general constitution, the survival of the organisms has to be dependent on behavioural coordination, requiring in particular predictability of the behaviour of others. Here, Antweiler sets the bar lower than Tomasello, for whom cooperation grounded in shared intentionality, not mere coordination, is decisive for the generation of norms (see chapter 1 of this volume, section 3.1). Consistently with his view, Antweiler claims that it is above all the capacity to anticipate the behaviour of others that appears crucial, not the more demanding abilities that feed into theory of mind or empathy.

In Chapter 5, "On the Identification and Analysis of Social Norms and the Heuristic Relevance of Deviant Behaviour," the philosopher **Karl Mertens** begins where Antweiler leaves off—with the claim central to German Philosophical Anthropology that only humans have norms and institutions, as such artefacts can only fulfil a func-tion for beings that are biologically underdetermined and environmentally deter-minable. Antweiler suggests that other social animals might also have norms, as the degree of their biological hardwiring may also be insufficient to prevent their social

---

[2] According to Arnold Gehlen, "instinct reduction" relative to that of other animals is the key to the human life form (Gehlen 1950, 26). Gehlen supports this basic claim, which has historical roots in Herder, with reference to the concept of "secondary altriciality," coined by the zoologist, Adolf Portmann. Portmann pointed out that humans are born prior to the level of neurological and physical development that characterises their nearest relatives, a fact that determines their particular need for intense and extended parental care (Portmann 1944). It also determines the susceptibility of their neurological development to cultural shaping. Stephen Jay Gould argues that, in spite of his non-Darwinian framework, Portmann recognised a key feature of human evolution, viz. the general temporal retardation of development resulting in neoteny in a whole series of dimensions that are of immense significance for the human form of life (Gould 1977, 349f., 365ff.). The evolutionary explanation for the specific phenomenon of human secondary altriciality is controversial. According to much recent research, it is not an adaptation, but an evolutionary tradeoff between pressures to bipedalism and encephalisation.

organisation suffering from coordination problems. Mertens may well agree, as he points to recent primatological research that he thinks has unseated the view that social norms are specific to humans. In his chapter, Mertens focuses on the human case, developing a substantial conception of social norms, as instantiated in human society. He accompanies the development of this account with methodological reflections that he believes show that one could be a little less sceptical than are Kappeler et al. about the possibility of detecting social norms in non-human populations.

Mertens' methodological reflections concern three points. First, he sees negative reactions as the epistemic key to the question of whether social norms are in place in a human or non-human population. This point derives from the fact that the efficacy of norms is, as the phenomenologist puts it, "non-thematic"; they are at work "in the background" and as such don't achieve their purpose mediated through explicit conscious processes of their bearers. For this reason, "deviant cases" are methodologically primary, a point that ties in with Antweiler's emphasis on the infliction of negative experiences in norm-inculcation. Second, Mertens argues that such an approach is the best way to attain a desirable theoretical equilibrium between competing considerations in two dimensions: between explanation and understanding, and between individualistic and holistic accounts. Like Margaret Gilbert, Mertens takes it that collective intentionality is a necessary condition for the existence of social norms. However, he explicitly rejects Gilbert's claim that social normativity is derived from larger-scale social interaction in the same way that "associational" rights and duties are generated in dyadic interaction between individuals. In contrast, Mertens insists on the anonymity of social normativity, an insistence that seems to locate his approach more to the holistic than the individualistic side of the divide he is concerned to overcome. Finally, Mertens sees less cause for concern about the barriers to the discovery of social norms, barriers that Kappeler et al. take to derive from the necessity of determining the motivation of agents involved. Here, Mertens sees a non-mentalistic approach to intentionality as the key.

The substantial analysis of social norms that Mertens presents aims to deliver a set of individually necessary and conjunctively sufficient conditions. According to these conditions,[3] social norms (i) generate regularities in social behaviour that are (ii) socially desirable; (iii) they provide public reasons for that behaviour; (iv) individuals' conformity to the norms is at least in part explained by the conformity of other individuals, (v) mediated by the setting of standards through behaviour; conformity to these standards is (vi) experienced as a strong obligation, which is in turn (vii) connected to the risk of sanction for non-conformity, a sanction (viii) imposed by informal, non-institutional mechanisms.

---

[3] Our numbering diverges slightly from Mertens' own.

Mertens thus proposes a conception of social norms that is significantly narrower than that presented by Antweiler. In contrast to Antweiler, Mertens excludes rules that are institutionally—above all, legally—represented and enforced. His target is what Brennan et al. label "informal" as opposed to formal social norms (Brennan et al. 2013, 40ff.). Within these, he distinguishes, as do Kappeler et al., social norms from conventions. According to Mertens, what distinguishes the two cases is an understanding on the part of the relevant agents that conventional rules could have easily had a different content, whilst such an understanding is absent in the case of genuine social rules. The difference is mirrored in the kinds of reaction to the contravention of the relevant rules. This move reconstructs the idea of arbitrariness that various authors take to be definitive of convention. The same move, when made by Turiel and other authors from social domain theory, is seen as establishing an exhaustive disjunction between social and moral norms. Mertens, however, argues that social norms form a category situated between conventions and moral norms. The latter, he takes it, are in some sense universal in their application, whereas social norms are applicable to actors in virtue of their occupation of particular social roles. Social norms, however, retain a level of importance to agents that at least rivals that of moral norms because, as agents seem to believe, such norms uphold the "core" social structures of a particular society.

The final chapter in the section on social norms is a contribution by the psychologists **Marco F. H. Schmidt and Hannes Rakoczy**. In Chapter 6, "On the Uniqueness of Human Normative Attitudes," they construe the normative animal thesis as a claim that primarily concerns mental states of the relevant organisms. Schmidt and Rakoczy identify the decisive attitudes as forms of "self-understanding": normative animals understand themselves to be bearers of rights and obligations and creators of social norms. The authors may be leaving open the question of whether "understanding" as used here is factive, thus avoiding metaphysical claims as to whether the relevant animals really have the rights and obligations, really do create norms, and perhaps have those rights and obligations as a result of their own activity of norm creation. However, the general tenor of the contribution supports a reading with metaphysical implications. "Normative animals," so it seems, understand what appear to be facts about norms, at least some of which are indeed facts: facts such as that norms set standards, thus creating the possibility of agents getting things wrong; that they apply generally in sufficiently similar situations; and that they have "normative force," i.e. their applicability entails a—presumably pro tanto—"ought." Moreover, the animals are, on the basis of this understanding, disposed to apply sanctions to enforce the norms. Finally, the acquisition of all these attitudinal features presupposes a more fundamental capacity: that of collective intentionality, which allows the formation of the standpoint of a social group that transcends that of the individuals involved.

With these clarifications in hand, Schmidt and Rakoczy turn to the data provided by developmental and comparative psychological research. Like Mertens, they specify that reactions of third parties should be seen as epistemically decisive. However, their reason differs from his, as they, like Kappeler et al., take it that the criterion, access to which is thus plausibly established, concerns the mental states of the relevant agents, that is, their own deployment of the concepts of right and wrong.

Schmidt and Rakoczy report a series of studies in which young children criticise the non-adherence to constitutive rules of games and pretend activities. Where in cases of the latter kind an object counts as something else in pretence, entitlements and proscriptions concerning actions are understood to follow. The infringement of such norms leads to third-party protests. The studies the authors report on normative learning seem to be in tension with the claim in Antweiler's article that norm inculcation requires explicit pedagogical strategies. In contrast, Schmidt and Rakoczy describe how three-year-old children spontaneously interpret apparently intentional and familiar "game-like" actions on the part of adults in normative terms. Indeed, they report findings that support the ascription of the tendency to "promiscuous normativity" to children: they tend in various contexts to assume that norms are the reasons for certain forms of behaviour, even when no such norms are in place. Older children presented with a task requiring coordination responded by creating their own norms, which they transmitted using normative language.

Interestingly for the relation of Parts II and III of this volume, the authors find similar reactive tendencies in children when confronted with the infringements of norms we think of as moral. Dispositions to protest and reprimand are triggered where certain kinds of harms are inflicted. Moreover, three-year-olds also protest where another right-holder's property entitlements are threatened. Finally, in a contribution to the debate on the relationship between moral and conventional norms, Schmidt, Rakoczy, and Tomasello have shown that protest against norm infractions depends on whether the perpetrator is an ingroup member (equal protest in the case of moral or conventional norms) or an outgroup member (protest primarily against the breaking of moral norms).

The authors conclude their survey by arguing for a more sceptical conclusion on the question of social norms among primates than that motivated by the methodological difficulties foregrounded by Kappeler et al. According to Schmidt and Rakoczy, none of the three plausible-looking candidates for social norms in primates—"policing," social learning, and resource distribution—are particularly good candidates. "Policing" in the wild is generally performed by high-ranking individuals, for whom intervention has few costs and who may have various other individual motives for the behaviour. Moreover, in an experimental study, it could be shown that dominants' "punishment" for food theft was far more pronounced in second-, than in third-party cases, which positively suggests that they are acting to achieve their individual goals, rather than to enforce group norms. Like Kappeler et al., the authors also suggest that social learning is likely to result from non-normative mechanisms—here a bias to copy dominants, rather than to imitate the behaviour of the majority. Finally, they argue that neither Brosnan and de Waal's work with the token-exchange paradigm nor behavioural versions of the ultimatum game provide evidence for the claim that primates have a preference for fairness. Unlike Kappeler et al., Schmidt and Rakoczy offer a principled reason why none of these areas will involve normative attitudinising: the lack in primates of the capacity for collective intentionality.

2. Moral Norms

Schmidt and Rakoczy diagnose strong continuities between young children's behaviour with respect to social and moral norms, suggesting that moral and conventional norms may be different species of social norms. Similarly, **Carel van Schaik and Judith Burkart** in Chapter 7, "The Evolution of Human Normativity: The Role of Prosociality and Reputation Mangagement," propose an account of moral normativity continuous with the account of social norms and conventions developed by Kappeler et al. However, the most important claim in our context advanced by van Schaik and Burkart is that moral norms are best understood not as social norms of a particular kind, but rather as the paradigm case of normativity, the existence of which allowed the development of other kinds of rules and conventions.

The argument for this claim proceeds from a functional characterisation of morality as a set of behavioural dispositions evolved to support the socioecological niche of mobile foragers that developed prior to the development of agriculture around 10,000 years ago. The foraging niche, grounding in the interdependence of the members of small foraging bands, was basically characterised by a unique form of egalitarian cooperation, the stability of which was decisive for the survival of those bands. It was the function of evolving morality to secure that cooperative stability. It did so, according to van Schaik and Burkart, as a set of dispositions to behaviour that essentially included a normative component. This component then turned out to be detachable from the function of stabilising cooperation in small-scale egalitarian interaction, becoming co-opted for the regulation of other social domains that came into being with the evolving socioecology of large-scale tribes and then even larger complex societies.

Van Schaik and Burkart see humans as "normative animals," by which they mean animals fitted out with dispositions of two sorts: first, to participate in the sanctioning of deviation from certain behavioural regularities and, second, to maintain those regularities in their own behaviour out of an experienced sense of high emotional urgency to do so. Morality, they claim, evolved through the generation of these dispositions in order to support a suite of antecedently existing further dispositions, most of which are shared by humans with other animals. Most of these latter dispositions also appear to provide motivation to cooperate in ways that both exploit and ameliorate the interdependence of the mobile foraging life style. According

to van Schaik and Burkart, they derive from independent functional contexts, including the protection of and provision for biological kin, incest avoidance, same-sex
pair bonding, raiding, and perhaps aversion to infanticide. It seems clear, however, that
the extent to which these dispositions might have helped cope with interdependence
is variable. Although, for example, the aversion to inbreeding plausibly accounts for
a component of the content of early human morality, it seems unlikely that it did so
because of any such interdependence-related role.

The two contexts emphasized by van Schaik and Burkart as decisive for the cooperative socioecological structure stabilised by moral norms are cooperative breeding and
cooperative hunting and gathering. The types of motivation generated for both kinds
of context are absent in our nearest primate ancestors, although the former is a prominent feature of the life form of callatrichid monkeys. The authors believe that cooperative breeding is the key source of what psychologists think of as prosocial motivation,
encompassing both direct and indirect reciprocity. They see cooperative hunting and
gathering as made possible by the capacity for coordination and reinforced by the
tendency to synchronised action, i.e. action aligned in behaviour and posture. Shared
intentionality, they suggest, can be understood—perhaps reductively—in terms of coordination and synchrony.

There is some unclarity about the extent to which the authors see prosociality as
exclusively grounding in the practice of cooperative breeding, as caring and sharing
are clearly at work both in the protection and support of biological kin and, certainly
in humans, in same-sex pair bonding. The empathy documented by Frans de Waal
in chimpanzees and bonobos, the workings of which he takes to be so extensive as
to constitute a "proto-morality," has its origins, he claims, in parental care (de Waal
2006, 26).

Unlike de Waal, but like Tomasello (Tomasello 2016, 45ff.), van Schaik and Burkart
see the disposition to perform joint actions as a separate source of the cooperative
life form of early humans, grounding in the context of hunting and gathering, and
presumably also equally at work in raiding. There are interesting conceptual and empirical questions here concerning the relationships between cooperative breeding and
joint action. If cooperative breeding is a type of joint action, then the mechanisms of
shared intentionality must be at work in both. This seems plausible for humans, although presumably the mechanisms controlling cooperative breeding in callatrichid
monkeys will have to be different. Were it to turn out that the specific contours of
human prosociality have their roots in cooperative breeding and were cooperative
breeding to be an instance of joint action, then the capacity for shared intentionality
would be explanatorily fundamental for, rather than on a par with, the capacity for
prosocial motivation.

Finally, a factor that plausibly plays a role in both cooperative breeding and collective
hunting, but which van Schaik and Burkart particularly emphasise in the discussion of

prosocial motivation, is reputation. As the decisive control mechanism of indirect reciprocity, its quality is likely to determine both the level of care an agent receives when in need and the likelihood of being chosen as a partner in joint action. It also retains its motivational prominence when the basic cooperative dispositions are supported by norms, which come to set the standards of goodness of reputations and to add a high level of urgency to the experienced motivation to do meet those standards.

That felt urgency is explained by van Schaik and Burkart in terms of the threat of sanctions they take to be constitutive of normativity, where such a threat may be in part represented explicitly, but is likely to also have generated intrinsic motivation through mechanisms inaccessible to the agents. One striking feature of van Schaik and Burkart's account of the transition to normativity is that, unlike that of Schmidt and Rakoczy (Chapter 6 in this volume) and pace Tomasello, it does not see norms as themselves explicable in terms of collective intentionality, but rather opts for a much thinner notion of norms or rules as behavioural regularities, deviance from which tends to be sanctioned. This allows there to be morality in other animals, in spite of them—possibly—not acting collectively. The key difference to the normativity of human morality lies in the fact that only humans appear to engage in third-party sanctioning.

A last important feature of the model is the role of language, which van Schaik and Burkart see as having two decisive effects, both of which contribute to the developing independence of norms from the behaviour of individuals. Firstly, it significantly expands the purchase of indirect reciprocity by enabling the proliferation of reputation effects. Secondly, it introduces the possibility of challenges and justifications, forms of behaviour intimately related to the establishment of an impartial perspective. This latter suggestion is given more extended consideration in the following two philosophical discussions of moral norms, both of which also argue that moral normativity is the product of the linguistic elaboration of more basic forms of interrelatedness.

In Chapter 8, "The Emergence of Moral Normativity," **Kurt Bayertz** argues that this basic form is at core volitive. The prescriptive core of the moral "ought," he argues, resides in the institutionalised collective volition of a population, a collective set of attitudes generally supported by sanctions. This core is that of social norms, some of which attain the status of moral norms when, with the advent of propositional language, abstraction from temporal or contextual features of the relevant behavioural issue comes into play. Linguistic elaboration brings with it, further, both explicit normative pedagogy and the possibility of questioning, challenging, and demanding reasons for the prescriptions that express the group's collective will. The justificatory practices thus initiated connect the "validity" of the norms to the world view of the society's members.

According to this account of moral norms as linguistically elaborated social norms, moral norms are as real as other social entities such as universities. With his tongue firmly ensconced in his cheek, Bayertz notes that the account could be classified as a variant of "moral realism." On this basis, normative moral legitimacy is necessarily relative to group-specific world views, although Bayertz leaves the question open as to how far groups may be extendable.

A key claim in Bayertz's narrative is that moral norms emerge at a fairly late stage in phylogeny, when certain social norms become subject to linguistic elaboration. He thus postulates the inverse explanatory and chronological order to that argued for by van Schaik and Burkart. A further late development, Bayertz claims, which similarly builds on the older core structure of social norms, is the practice of third-party sanctioning. This only enters the scene with the emergence of the larger social formations that are no longer built around the mechanisms of direct reciprocity characteristic of foraging bands. The account excludes the possibility that sanctions might be constitutive of normativity. On the one hand, Bayertz argues, natural counter-reactions to harm at the hands of another are as yet far removed from normative reactions. On the other hand, when such reactions become normative, that is because they presuppose the existence of the norm. Third-party sanctioning is an indication of the presence of a norm precisely because it indicates that the sanctioned behaviour is taken to negatively affect the entire community that accepts the norm.

In developing his account of the deontic core around which specifically moral norms are built, Bayertz argues that both divine command theorists and Kant had identified a key feature of the moral "ought": that it is essentially a matter of the volition of some other. Both theories must, he takes it, be wrong because of the incompatibility of their metaphysical assumptions with the facts of evolution. According to Bayertz, the evolutionary rationale for the importance of a system of orientation set up by collective volition derives from the importance of imperatival communication between conspecifics in species with decreased genetic behavioural control. He thus gives the central theorem of German Philosophical Anthropology cited by Antweiler and Mertens a new twist. He supports the claim with Tomasello's data on almost exclusively imperatival communication among chimpanzees, taking the latter to have a life form also characterised by some significant degree of reduced genetic behavioural control.

Bayertz' central claim, then, is that a—perhaps *the*—key form of non-genetic behavioural control required to ensure group functioning and thus individual fitness among humans is established through the generation of a collective will focussed on within-group cooperation. This "will" concerns action contexts that tend to occur repeatedly and has thus a certain generality. It is moreover stabilised over time, taking on the character of an "institution." For Bayertz, institutions are essentially patterns of behaviour. Where Mertens, working with a narrower, formal conception of institutions, understands social and moral norms as both non-institutional and disjunct, Bayertz opts for a conception of institutions that is essential to both social and moral norms, where the latter are a variant of the former. He sees institutions, including moral norms, as products of what he, following Leroi-Gourhan, calls an "exteriorisation" of specific mental states, i.e. volitions. As such, moral norms are biologically no more mysterious than tools, understood as the exteriorisation of bodily capacities. The exteriorised collective volitions that are moral norms can thus be handed down from one generation to the next and create a new—normative—kind of environment into which members of the species are born. Their generation, Bayertz argues, counts as a human-specific form of niche construction.

Like Bayertz, **Holmer Steinfath** believes both that moral norms are a particular kind of social norms, and that the advent of language is decisive for the generation of moral normativity. Moreover, Steinfath also concurs with Bayertz that the importance of language lies in the fact that it makes justification possible. However, unlike both Bayertz, and van Schaik and Burkhart, Steinfath doesn't take the linguistically enabled practice of justification to transform a previously existing normative structure. Rather, he argues that normativity only comes into being through the addition of justificatory practices to a prior form of non-normative connectedness of participants in a common practice.

In Chapter 9, "Joint Activities and Moral Obligation," Steinfath proposes a genealogy of dyadic moral obligations. Dyadic moral obligations are held by individuals towards specific others. They correlate with the others' corresponding rights, where these rights can only be waived by the right-holders. Their contravention warrants resentment on the part of the right-holder, who is the only agent that can exercise forgiveness in the matter. Steinfath's account of these central forms of obligation sees them as grounding in structural features of the way agents relate to each other in dyadic joint activities. Like Gilbert and Tomasello, then, he takes it that shared intentionality, as a human-specific way of forming social bonds, is the key to explaining normativity. However, in contrast to Gilbert, he takes it, firstly, that the normativity that can be thus explained is not a sui generis form of "associational" or social normativity, but the normativity of moral obligation. A second disagreement with Gilbert structures much of Steinfath's contribution: unlike her, he claims that normativity does not inhere in joint activities. Nevertheless, he claims, it is the interpersonal structure of joint activities that makes the emergence of dyadic moral obligation possible with the advent of language.

In order to stake out this position, Steinfath discusses the arguments for and against Gilbert's interpersonally normativistic conception and Bratman's rival account, according to which the only normative ties between collaborators derive from requirements of individual rationality. On the one hand, he objects to Bratman's conception that our most natural reactions to the unilateral abandonment of a joint project don't appear to involve criticism of the agent for being irrational. Moreover, unlike Gilbert's account, Bratman's provides no indication of why interpersonal normative features seem to pervade our joint activities. On the other hand, Gilbert's theory of joint commitment appears too voluntaristic, to overlook the background social context that, according to Steinfath, is implicated in the generation of rights and duties and to ignore cases where acting together implausibly generates such normative statuses.

The social bonds left unaccounted for in Bratman's account, but prematurely assigned a normative status by Gilbert's, are, Steinfath asserts, essentially emotional. Acting together, so the claim goes, involves the establishment of a primitive sense of "we" that exerts a kind of emotional pressure to uphold the common project. He sees the clearest evidence for this dimension of shared intentionality in the resentment that naturally results from reneging on such projects. In spite of frequent claims to the contrary, resentment is not, he argues, a genuinely normative reaction, but rather a natural reaction to the lack of good will of another who one sees as a partner in a common endeavour. It is, as Strawson originally put it, the expression of a "participant stance."

It is this stance and the attendant disposition to feel resentment that is converted to a normative attitude when the affect is accompanied by the belief in the justification of the reaction. And it is this idea of justified resentment that enables the move to what Strawson calls the impersonal reactive attitude of indignation, which, unlike resentment, does presuppose the acceptance of a norm. As such, Steinfath argues, it also involves the belief that the reaction is one which others in the community should also take on towards the perpetrator. The dyadic moral obligations expressed in justified resentment are thus backed by community-wide norms that make the impersonal reactive attitude of indignation appropriate.

Like Bayertz, then, Steinfath believes that moral obligations are first and foremost the products of interactions within groups. Their scope depends on the extension of the relevant common projects or endeavours. Unlike Bayertz, however, he explicitly raises the question of whether a universalist morality, which among other things assigns human rights to all humans, can be made sense of within such a framework. He briefly names two strategies that might be adopted in order to explain how such a move can be made. The first involves emphasizing the insight into the arbitrariness of exclusion from basic rights, as societies become larger and more complex. The second focuses on the ideal of relations of universal recognition among all agents. Steinfath's sceptical conclusion, however, is that both of these justificatory strategies are missing a substantial basis in anything that might be plausibly construed as a common project or community. As such, the ideals thus formulated may exert a certain attraction, but they cannot, absent the creation of a substantial worldwide community, ground obligations.

Where van Schaik and Burkart, Bayertz, and Steinfath all see moral normativity as inherent in a subset of the social norms of a population, the authors of the final two chapters in the Part III demur. The first of these is Chapter 10, "The Development of Domains of Moral and Conventional Norms, Coordination in Decision-Making, and the Implications of Social Opposition" by the psychologists **Elliot Turiel and Audun Dahl**. The authors lay out the basic assumptions of social domain theory and defend them against challenges posed by alternative psychological approaches to morality. In doing so, they argue on the basis of a large body of empirical evidence for the "constructivist" account of the differences between moral and conventional normative orientation.

Turiel and Dahl argue that there are systematic, structural differences between a number of ways of thinking about relationships, society, and culture acquired by humans in ontogeny. These structural differences in ways of thinking ("domains") depend on the clusters of properties of the objects of thought that are taken to be significant in that mode of thought. Where the mode of thinking can be classified as moral, the relevant properties are, or concern, welfare, rights, and justice; where the mode of thinking is conventional, the relevant properties concern behavioural uniformities that coordinate interaction. For Turiel and Dahl, thought oriented to these property clusters culminates in "ought" judgements that are specific to the relevant mode of thought, where such thought is essentially reasoning directed to justifying the relevant judgements. The standards against which behaviour is evaluated in thus judging are set by the active, "constructive" interpretation of the property clusters and their relation to the behaviour in question.

The authors emphasize what they see as the active relationship between developing children and the normative features of a reality they grow into. They contrast their account, first, with the claim that moral orientation is simply the product of the passive "internalisation" of the norms of the social environment, a view they associate with behaviourism and the Culture and Personality school of anthropology. They equally reject current nativist accounts, according to which morality is generated by pre-programmed modules that unfold in agents' judgements and actions. As, like Bayertz, Turiel and Dahl take the moral domain to be essentially the sphere of thought oriented to categorical deontic moral judgements, the empirical demonstration of early prosocial motivation can at most count as a precondition for the move to morality, not as evidence that it is pre-given.

Against the "social-intuitionist" account of moral judgement advanced by Jonathan Haidt and Joshua Greene, according to which moral reasoning is mere post hoc rationalisation of emotional reactions, Turiel and Dahl argue that emotions and reasoned judgements generally work in concert. In order to explain why this is so, they develop a version of motivational internalism about moral—but not conventional—judgement. According to their view, utterances or thoughts deploying terms such as "morally right" only count as moral judgements if they are backed by what Nico Frijda calls "concerns," that is, stable dispositions to prefer the realisation of the judgement's content. It is the triggering of these dispositions by judgement-incongruent behaviour that explains relevant emotional reactions.

Turiel and Dahl also argue against an influential critique of social domain theory advanced by Kelly, Stich, et al., according to which the classroom examples used in Turiel's vignettes are too simple. They claim that, once one uses examples from everyday adult life, it can be shown that Turiel's criteria of categoricity, authority-independence, universality, and justification in terms of welfare and rights don't necessarily attach to the same judgements. From this they infer that the social domain theory of moral judgements is incoherent. Turiel and Dahl respond by pointing to the discussions within the tradition of the way in which agents have to negotiate conflicting claims of different domains ("coordination"). An early example of this is Turiel's interpretation of the Milgram experiment.

One important question raised by Turiel and Dahl's contribution in the context of this volume concerns the meaning of their term "construction." Its precise interpretation has consequences for the sense in which it might be argued that humans are "normative animals." On the one hand, the term clearly picks out an epistemic concept, covering a psychological process by means of which the material provided by the social environment is actively worked with in reasoning that attempts to make sense of that environment. On the other hand, it is unclear whether the concept also has metaphysical implications.

Conventional norms, so it seems, have to be recognised as existent solutions to unavoidable problems of social organisation. Precisely because the relevant solutions might have been different and still provided points of orientation, the solutions that have been adopted in a particular society are the ones that rationally ground conventional ought judgements. So it seems that in the conventional domain the scope for metaphysical construction is extremely limited: a judgement here just is a judgement about what the given conventional norms prescribe.

However, when one turns to deontic moral judgements, the relevant property cluster—of welfare, rights, and justice—leaves considerably more scope for an account of construction that concerns not only the way developing agents conceive of the morally right, but also the morally right itself. The authors' discussions of the way in which adolescents adjudicate between considerations of honesty and welfare, and of the way in which their judgements of the acceptability of deception are modulated by considerations of equality or inequality between the relevant actors, may indicate that the correct answer in such cases is sometimes not something to be discovered, but something that emerges in the course of context-specific reasoning about particular cases.

The authors conclude with the claim that the term "moral norm" is ambiguous. On the one hand, it may pick out standards shared by many members of a community, where those standards concern matters of welfare, rights, or justice. On the other hand, it may pick out what dissenting individuals take to be morally obligatory, permissible, or impermissible in those matters in spite of the contrary orientation of other, even of most of a society's members. The fact that such dissenting judgements may, as Turiel and Dahl claim, serve to guide behaviour that brings about more just social conditions seems to presuppose that such judgements may be correct even in the absence of any social norms to which the judgements refer.

In Chapter 11, "Moral Obligation from the Outside In," the final contribution to Part III on moral norms, the philosopher **Neil Roughley** defends a slightly modified version of Turiel's moral-conventional distinction and employs it as one pillar of an empirically supported theory of moral obligation. Roughley shares a basic assumption with van Schaik and Burkart, Bayertz, and Steinfath: that the fact of moral obligation can only have resulted from the development of psychological structures specific to the human form of life. However, like Turiel and Dahl, he doesn't think this should lead us to conceptualise moral obligation as essentially the product of social norms. Rather, his method is to piece together a psychology of deontic moral judgement and to argue that moral obligation is what must be the case if such judgements are true.

It is this method that allows him to make use of two sorts of empirical material, which shed light on the psychology of agents who appear to have no access to the moral point of view, but who do seem to have some capacities that are necessary for such access. The discussion of the two kinds of case allows the development of hypotheses as to the decisive further psychological building blocks of a deontic moral psychology. Roughley first discusses Brosnan and de Waal's use of the experimental token-exchange paradigm, which has shown primates to react adversely to being given a lower-ranked reward than that given to a conspecific for the same "work." Where Brosnan takes the reactions to express inequity aversion, a primitive sense of fairness, Roughley sees a less demanding attitude at work, which he calls "resentment★," that is, an egoistic version of the everyday attitude we call "resentment," where the latter at least frequently presupposes adherence to some moral norm. According to Roughley, resentment★ is an affective reaction to an action of another that the reacting agent takes to contravene their natural dispositional demand that they not be treated with ill-will or indifference. The disposition thus to react is, he proposes, a basic building block of a deontic moral psychology, which requires supplementing before its bearer can attain the concept of moral obligation.

A second context in which resentment★ appears to be at work is, according to Roughley, that of certain reactions of psychopaths. He interprets some cases of psychopathic aggression as resulting from an affective reaction to the non-fulfilment of the demand for non-indifference, where what is counted as expressing indifference is highly idiosyncratic. Above all, psychopaths have no tendency to extend their demands for non-indifference to cover comparable behaviour towards others.

It is here that Roughley draws on work carried out in the framework of social domain theory, in particular that of James Blair. Blair has used Turiel's moral-conventional test to assess whether psychopaths make genuine moral judgements. Blair's negative answer to this question has been criticised, as has Turiel's test itself. Roughley defends both before concluding that psychopathy does indeed appear to involve an inability, or at least a significantly restricted ability, to make deontic moral judgements.

Roughley hypothesises that the inability to make moral judgements and the inability to transcend an egoistic perspective in resentment★ may both be explained by the lack of the same psychological feature that is to be found in normal human development. He characterises that feature as "Smithian empathy," after Adam Smith, for whom "sympathy" involves taking on an emotion on behalf of another. Adding this capacity bequeaths an agent the disposition to vicarious resentment★, or indignation★. Indignation★, finally, becomes a genuinely moral attitude, Roughley claims, when it is subject to the reapplication of Smithian empathy, this time from the perspective of an impartial and informed empathiser. Demands raised as from such an impartial empathic perspective are taken by Roughley to be moral demands; deontic moral judgements he takes to involve beliefs about counterfactual impartial and informed empathic indignation★ and moral obligation he conceives in terms of the facts that would make such beliefs true.

After replying to various objections to these construals, Roughley concludes with an explicit discussion of the relation of deontic moral facts, thus understood, to social norms. To this end, he reviews a proposal by Carel van Schaik and colleagues, according to which manifestly emotional reactions by chimpanzees to depictions of infanticide might be explained in three different ways. Van Schaik takes the third kind of explanation to be one which would postulate normative attitudes on the part of the chimps. According to this way of modelling the reactions, which van Schaik takes to be inapplicable to non-human primates, the reactions would be a matter of shared indignation, based on empathy. He argues that chimpanzees can have no such moral attitudes because of their inability to share attitudes—an explanation that parallels that of Tomasello.

Roughley agrees that such attitudinal constellations, plausibly part-constitutive of social norms, may have been phylogenetically necessary as precursors of deontic moral attitudes. However, he claims that only the regulation of such attitudes by representations of impartial Smithian empathising enables the step to genuine moral attitudes. Moreover, as such representations might come to be the prerogative of only a few members of a population, who may be unaware that others share their attitudes, deontic moral attitudinising doesn't require the existence of corresponding social norms. And, as the correctness of such representations doesn't depend on whether a significant number of other agents happen to share them, moral obligations are also independent of the social norms of a society. The existence of social norms is likely, Roughley concludes, to have been a phylogenetic condition of the genesis of moral obligation. Nevertheless, an agent's moral obligations are in general independent of what is socially required of her.

3. Linguistic Norms?

The book's Part IV begins with Chapter 12 from the philosopher **Nikola Kompa** on "Language Evolution and Linguistic Norms." Kompa's aim is to specify a point at which the phylogenetic development of human language requires responsiveness to norms on the part of speakers. To this end she distinguishes between natural signs, signals, and symbols, where only the latter are specific to human communication. In Dretske's terminology, natural signs indicate, rather than represent; that is, they stand in causal relationships to what they stand for, indicating only as long as they stand in that relationship, thus being incapable of mis-indicating. For such a causal connection to count as a natural sign, it must be the case that some organisms are sensitive to the causal connection in a way that can count as understanding. "Understanding," in turn, should be interpreted in an undemanding manner in terms of behaviour that contributes to the maximisation of inclusive fitness.

Unlike natural signs, signals necessarily involve both a producer and a recipient, where the effect on the recipient looks both to involve a fitness advantage for the recipient and to explain the evolution of the feature of the producer that is its cause. Examples are upright posture in herring gulls, teeth-baring in dogs, and "alarm calls" in vervet and Campbell's monkeys. Drawing on various empirical sources, Kompa argues that signals may to a certain extent be learned, flexibly and even intentionally produced.

One key feature that may distinguish symbols from signals, she claims, is that the former don't function so as to directly influence behaviour, but to alter features of the recipient's mind. Another candidate is "displacement," that is, a symbol's use to pick out objects not immediately present to the senses. Kompa's central question concerns the preconditions of such forms of representation. She rejects the hypothesis of the genesis of language as a form of grooming-at-a-distance, i.e. gossip (Dunbar), and the theory that it may have developed out of a musical or prosodic protolanguage that facilitated mating or mothering (Mithen, Falk). Instead, she follows proposals of Bickerton and Tomasello, according to which language came into being in the context of hominins' attempts to recruit conspecifics for tasks such as scavenging. If this is correct, then humans' linguistic capacities are essentially tied to the fact that their life form requires modes of cooperation that are neither necessary for other species whose members are individually better able to fend for themselves, nor possible in species without capacities for shared intentionality. The cooperation necessary has two levels, first the behavioural cooperation required to accomplish tasks necessary for survival, and second the mental alignment required in order that producer and recipient both take the vocalisations of the former to be relevant for both their and the other's interests.

On the basis of this narrative, Kompa rejects the claim that meaning is essentially determined by norms: some rudimentary forms of symbolic reference plausibly

developed in mutualistic interaction prior to, and as a precondition of, the establishment of standards. Such reference does, she thinks, require a feature that will become
the object of a pragmatic principle by means of which we guide our production and
interpretation of implicit meaning within an established system of language, i.e. relevance. Grice's maxim of relation—be relevant—was, however, not plausibly in play at
the dawn of linguistic meaning, as the agents were only discovering the significance of
relevance and had no option but to try to establish it.

Although, then, Kompa rejects the claim that normativity has to be in place for
there to be meaning, she does, like Searle and Lewis, assume that language, once established, is at least generally a conventional practice. That is, she assumes that a stable
semantics is dependent on linguistic conventions. Stable meaning, she claims, should
be thought of as what Lewis calls a "coordination equilibrium," that is, as a way of
solving a problem of mental alignment relative to which no agent would have been
better off had any single agent acted differently. Such coordination equilibria were
plausibly established by repeated precedent, as a result of which a particular solution
became salient, taking on the status of a standard to which everyone is motivated to
conform as long as the others also do so. This, she assumes with Lewis, makes linguistic conventions "normative" in the sense that the relevant agents believe that they
all ought to conform. She adds that the norms should be understood as prudential,
because, unlike in the moral case, compliance is in the immediate interests of agents.
This is why non-compliance is likely to trigger ridicule or embarrassment, as opposed
to indignation or punishment.

In Chapter 13, "The Normative Nature of Language," the ethnolinguists **N. J.
Enfield and Jack Sidnell** argue for a far more intimate relationship between language and norms. According to Enfield and Sidnell, social norms play two decisive
roles relative to language.

The first concerns the level of everyday linguistic interaction. Conversational
exchanges, they argue, are structured by norms, such as those concerning the appropriateness of asking and responding to questions. The authors distinguish social
norms from laws in a manner that, up to a point, parallels that developed by Mertens.
Above all, they see the guiding role of the relevant kinds of informal normative
structures as having three features. First, it is subliminal, i.e. it is unnoticed, so that
the resultant behaviour surprises no one, even if it isn't explicitly expected. Second,
it is, as they put it, "abliminal," i.e. its failure is noticed and is remarked on. Third, it
is inference-vulnerable, such that its absence generates inferences meant to explain
that absence.

These latter two conditions are clearly weaker than any that specify the triggering
of Strawsonian reactive attitudes, although in some contexts comparable reactions do
come into play. Nevertheless, according to the authors, the relevant norms still generate "obligations" and "duties," "rights" and "entitlements," and are thus more than

merely prudential norms. Enfield and Sidnell see talk of obligations as justified by the central role of accountability in linguistic exchange. Speakers can, for instance, call each other to account for not answering a question, for answering a question not posed to them, or for asking an inappropriate question. Faced with inappropriate or a lack of appropriate moves, the pressure to accountability leads to further responses or explanations. And speakers appear to take it that they have "duties to themselves" to choose words that are referentially correct or appropriate to particular kinds of interactive contexts. Moreover, Enfield and Sidnell claim that the norms regulating sequences of questions and answers are in some sense specific to this particular form of linguistic interaction. Although they are a particular kind of social norm, they are not reducible to any non-linguistic strictures, such as those that regulate politeness or etiquette.

Enfield and Sidnell do not only claim that the pragmatics of everyday linguistic interaction are regulated by norms; they also, more controversially, claim that these norms are the source of meaning, understood as the topic of semantics: what is sometimes called conventional or codified meaning. The basic notion of meaning the authors work with is that of Peirce, who insisted on the crucial character of the concept of an "interpretant," the understanding of a sign that allows its object to be picked out by the sign's users. According to Enfield and Sidnell's version of this view, norms of accountability tie speakers to intentions to refer to entities characterised by certain properties; moreover, they equally bind listeners to corresponding understandings. The authors take it that it is the binding character of the norms at work here that leads to a stabilisation of meaning in the form of conventions. They argue for this thesis by describing various scenarios in which agents appear motivated to enforce referential conventions and in which it appears that the rights to do so are themselves in turn specified by relevant norms.

Enfield and Sidnell thus propose a competing account of the constitution of conventional linguistic meaning to that offered by Kompa. Both see the decisive task as the explanation of meaning's stabilisation. But whereas, in Kompa's model, such stabilisation is a result of the natural emergence of a coordination equilibrium, Enfield and Sidnell see social norms as the stabilising factor. Moreover, where Kompa sees pre-conventional meaning as pre-normative, grounding in the causal requirements of relevance in cooperative interaction, Enfield and Sidnell see pre-conventional structured cooperation as itself regulated by social norms. How strongly the two models are in competition here is, however, perhaps not so clear, because, whereas Kompa is interested in a phylogenetic explanation, Enfield and Sidnell's interest is in the perpetual remaking of linguistic meaning in the ongoing process of social interaction.

In Chapter 14, the linguist and philosopher **Anne Reboul** poses the very basic question "Can There Be Linguistic Norms?"—a question which she argues should be answered (almost completely) in the negative. Although Reboul's position appears diametrically opposed to that of Enfield and Sidnell, this results in part, although by no means entirely, from her narrower characterisation of both the generic concept of a norm and the more specific concept of a linguistic norm. Unlike both Enfield and Sidnell, and Kompa, Reboul takes it that noticing unexpected behaviour and forming explanatory inferences in view of such behaviour are insufficient for talk of norms, which are present only when deviance is generally sanctioned. Moreover, she is concerned to draw a clear line between social norms that influence linguistic behaviour and linguistic norms in a narrower sense. The latter would be norms specific to language that regulate only the production and interpretation of utterances. She combines these characterisations with the specification of a further feature that is generally uncontroversial within discussions of linguistic normativity, if not within the broader discussion of the normative animal thesis, namely that any structure worthy of being labelled a norm satisfies NA3 (see chapter 1, section 2.3), according to which it has a human, more specifically a social origin.

Reboul goes on to discuss three kinds of candidates for linguistic norms that would fulfil her characterisations. The first, which concerns syntactic and semantic structures, is rejected for reasons which, she argues, follow from the uncontroversial idea that norms are at core criteria of correctness. Correctness criteria which, as such criteria, explain behaviour that satisfies them, would, so it seems, need to work via choice on the part of the relevant agents and, even where compliance is automatic, at least be accessible in a way that would allow the agents to give them explicit and accurate formulations. This is the challenge to explain the intentional character of semantic and syntactic "rule following," a challenge she believes cannot be met. Where ex-post appraisals of linguistic behaviour are brought to bear, these, she adds, express commitments to social hierarchy rather than any true beliefs about the relevant semantic or syntactic compositionality.

A second area in which it may seem that linguistic norms are at work concerns the pragmatic standards orientation to which enables the production and understanding of implicit meaning. Here, Reboul begins by rejecting the claim that Grice's conversational maxims should be understood as norms. Although these seem to be principles to which agents do have access, it is implausible, she claims, that they could have a social origin, at least an origin in social deliberation, as they appear to be universal. Moreover, because of the flexibility of their criteria, the maxims, she thinks, also appear not to satisfy a condition according to which norm addressees should not be unable not to comply (cf. chapter 1, section 2.2). In general, she takes it that Gricean explanations work with overly demanding psychological processes, processes that implausibly take place in every spontaneous everyday interpretation of implicatures. In contrast, the neo-Gricean account conceives at least lexically triggered implicatures as default processes, which, because they work at the sub-personal level, cannot, she—in contrast to Enfield—believes, be explained by orientation to norms. Reboul herself favours the post-Gricean view developed by Sperber and Wilson, according to which all understanding works according to the economic principle that cognitive costs be minimised and benefits maximised, where the relevant calculations take place below the threshold of processes accessible to intentional thought. Reboul cites empirical studies which favour the post-Gricean account for implicatures that have no specific lexical trigger. She argues, however, that, even if lexically triggered implicatures could be shown to be produced and triggered by use of the Gricean maxims, it would still be implausible to see the relevant processes as guided by specifically linguistic norms. Here she follows Grice in taking the cooperative principle to be a general rule guiding rational interaction, one that is neither social in origin nor enforced by sanctions.

The third area in which Reboul takes it that linguistic norms might be at work is that of lexical semantics, in as far as the referring property of words can be distinguished from reference established by compositionality. Reboul concedes that rigid designators, paradigmatically proper names, might be taken to require norms in order to do their work, for instance, norms that specify what counts as baptism and what follows from it. These are, however, the only cases that she accepts might require norms. She explicitly engages with Enfield and Sidnell's claim that speakers are accountable for compliance with linguistic conventions, a claim she rejects for two reasons: first, she believes that it is incompatible with the use of words in tropes, and second, she argues, like Kompa, that the prudential pressures toward communicative success are sufficient to explain adherence to linguistic convention. Finally, she insists that linguistic conventions are not themselves norms because they are not supported by sanctions, but ground no more than an unobtrusive practice of correction where their standards are not met. This distinction parallels that made by Mertens relative to conventions and norms in general.

Hanjo Glock's Chapter 15, "The Normativity of Meaning Revisited," homes in on the third area discussed by Reboul, marshalling a series of arguments for the claim that there are semantic norms that are constitutive of lexical meaning. The concept of a norm with which Glock operates here is that of a general standard that provides agents with reasons for intentional action and against which actions can be assessed as correct or incorrect. For this concept Glock uses the terms "norm" and "rule" interchangeably. The norms at issue are the conventions that specify the meaning of particular words, whether through explicit or ostensive definitions, or by means such as exemplification or colour charts. Conventions in turn Glock understands as shared arbitrary rules or norms. According to Glock, then, lexical normativity is constituted by rules that explain the meaning of words, thus providing speakers with reasons to use those words in certain ways, to avoid and criticise other uses, and allowing them to move via substitution or inference from one claim to another. His strategy in the chapter is to discuss objections to various features of this basic claim.

Unlike Mertens, Kompa, and Reboul, Glock rejects Lewis's definition of convention, both because it requires attitudes of implausible complexity and because conventions need not be solutions to coordination problems. The decisive feature of conventions he sees as their arbitrariness, that is, the fact that other norms would have been feasible in their place. This is obviously true of linguistic meaning rules. Whether such rules may have been established as coordination equilibria, in spite of the fact that such a function is no part of the definition of convention, is not discussed by Glock, although he does, like Kompa, see conventions as coming into being through the entrenchment of regular forms of behaviour.

As Glock takes conventions to be shared rules, he discusses arguments, primarily stemming from Davidson, according to which language use or communication can be successful without any such common standards. Against the claim that linguistic regularities are conformed to for mere prudential reasons, he presses the distinction between a rule's normative status (compare the convention to drive on the left in Britain) and agents' reasons for conformity, where the latter don't undermine the former. In the face of the claim that linguistic conventions are unnecessary for linguistic communication, he concedes that the concept of language is too vague to allow a definite answer. Although, then, the preconventional use of symbols one might call "linguistic" may have been possible, the unique role that language plays for humans is, Glock argues, tied to the fine-grained character of the thoughts that require linguistic conventions.

Independently of whether linguistic conventions are shared in any substantial sense, Glock also discusses widespread objections to the claim that such conventions are norms, an objection sometimes put in terms of the claim that, whereas norms are regulative rules, semantic conventions, like the rules of games, are merely constitutive. As such, they don't tell anyone what to do, but only what counts as a particular kind of move.

A key question here is what counts as "telling someone what to do." To the strongest interpretation of this idea, formulated in terms of all-things-considered obligations, Glock objects that our thought has space for pro tanto obligations. However, antinormativists have maintained that the alternative, understanding semantic conventions as providing the minor premise in practical inferences that yield hypothetical imperatives, is no reason to think of conventions as normative. This is because all sorts of descriptions concerning ways and means of doing things can play exactly this role. Here, Glock replies that, unlike mere descriptions, constitutive rules appeal to a normative practice in the context of which certain prohibitions and entitlements are in place. Without such normative constraints, the counts-as premises in the relevant practical syllogisms would not hold.

Moreover, such counts-as explanations are themselves clearly normative. According to descriptivist accounts, a standard that names the conditions that have to be met for a performance to count as correct merely provides a set of descriptive conditions. Against such views Glock insists that standards provide grounds for the correction of moves or utterances that don't meet those standards. This is entailed by the fact that relevant standards are standards of correctness, not merely redescriptions. This in turn ties in with the fact that, unlike what has been suggested by Davidson and others, meeting the standards is not merely a matter of speaking truthfully. Glock illustrates this non-equivalence with examples of the difference between falsity and linguistic incorrectness, a distinction that in the case of lexical meaning comes down to the difference between facts, on the one hand, and understanding, i.e. the grounds an agent takes herself to have for a term's application, on the other.

For Glock, the action-guiding role of norms and, a fortiori, linguistic conventions is decisive. He sees them as fulfilling this role by providing reasons for action, including action critical of actions that aren't adequately guided by those norms. As such, Glock's model has to confront the claim that, in the majority of cases of linguistic action, no explicit thought is expended on such norms. Glock's claim here is that linguistic agents must be potentially aware of the relevant norms, a potentiality he claims is given when fairly weak conditions are satisfied. Strong conditions that might be met would involve the agents either being able to formulate the rules if prompted or at least to recognise such formulations. A weaker, but still sufficient condition would consist in the capacity to explain certain performances as "the done thing." Glock even thinks that non-linguistic creatures may see certain forms of behaviour in terms of correctness standards, as manifested by behaviour that sanctions deviations. If this is true, non-linguistic hominins may have acted in line with implicit rules prior to, and conducive to the development of language.

PART II

Social Norms

3

There Ought to Be Roots

Evolutionary Precursors of Social Norms and Conventions in Non-Human Primates

Peter M. Kappeler, Claudia Fichtel, and Carel P. van Schaik

1. Introduction

The evolution of life in permanent groups has been one of the major evolutionary transitions (Maynard Smith and Szathmary 1995). This fundamental change in so-cial environment necessitated the concomitant evolution of behavioural mechanisms to ensure group cohesion and coordination as well as to mediate inter-individual conflict and cooperation. The group-level properties of animal societies that emerge from patterns of the underlying dyadic social interactions among group members characterise their social structure (Hinde 1976). The combination of various outcomes of patterns of affinitive, affiliative, and agonistic interactions has been classified into broad categories, which vary in their relative degree of despotism, nepotism, and tol-erance (Sterck et al. 1997). Thus, the social structure of an animal society captures the essence of how individuals in different species interact with each other. In human societies, social norms provide an additional kind of grammar for social interactions in that they specify rules about social interactions in many different contexts (Bicchieri and Muldoon 2011). The main aim of this chapter is to explore the notion that the behavioural and cognitive constituents of human social norms have equivalents or precursors in our closest living relatives, the non-human primates.

The social system of a species can be decomposed into three interrelated, but heu-ristically distinct, components (Kappeler and van Schaik 2002). The social organisation describes the size, composition, cohesion, and genetic structure of a social unit; the mating system summarises patterns of mating and reproduction; and the social struc-ture characterises the emergent patterns of social interactions among individuals that vary in several factors, including age, sex, kinship, dominance, personality, and condition. The majority of species can be characterised by a particular social system, notwithstanding intra-specific flexibility in one or several of its components (Kappeler et al. 2013; Snell-Rood 2013; Kamilar and Baden 2014). Closely related species can have very similar social systems, as for example most macaques and baboons (Kamilar and Cooper 2013; Thierry 2013), but speciation can also be associated with significant and sometimes radical changes in social systems, as evidenced by the living members of the genera of Great Apes (Watts 2012). Generally, and compared to other traits, primate behaviour actually exhibits comparatively little phylogenetic signal (Kamilar and Baden 2014).

In addressing species differences in social systems, Chapais (2013) has pointed out that it is unlikely that all components of a social system arise simultaneously at every speciation event. Instead, evolutionary change in social systems is more likely stepwise, cumulative and based on exaptations. Comparative studies among closely related taxa can therefore help to identify evolutionary origins and modifications of particular components of social systems, such as social norms and their constituent elements. In this particular case, comparative studies can help to decide whether social norms are an example of uniquely derived human traits, or whether they have functional predecessors or even equivalents in other taxa with which we share common ancestors (Cummins 1998).

Even though patterns and processes of social evolution are so fundamental and general that the comparative net could be cast much wider to explore this particular question (see, e.g. Claidière and Whiten 2012), our closest living biological relatives, the mammalian order *Primates*, provide the obvious and most interesting taxon for such a comparative approach because features of their life history, behavioural flexibility, social complexity, and cognitive capacities set them apart from most other animals. First, compared to other mammals of the same body size, primates live on average longer, begin reproducing at a later age, and produce smaller litters (usually singletons) that enjoy extensive parental care (van Schaik and Isler 2012). Second, these relatively slow-paced life histories are correlated with the evolution of larger brain size, for which energy is freed up by this reduction in growth and reproductive rates (van Schaik and Isler 2012). Third, because larger brain size is generally associated with increased cognitive abilities (Deaner et al. 2007; Reader et al. 2011), non-human primates may be more likely than most other mammals to be predisposed towards cognitive mechanisms, such as a theory of mind, that might be required for the evolution of social norms. Fourth, the more than 400 species of living primates exhibit much more variation in their social systems than other mammalian orders, including complex societies with several hierarchical levels, nested neighbourhoods, or fission-fusion dynamics (Aureli et al. 2008; Grueter et al. 2012; Kappeler 2012). The size and complexity of a society appear to be reasonable prerequisites for the evolution of coordinating mechanisms such as social norms. Fifth, the combination of advanced cognitive abilities, social complexity, and long developmental times may have selected for mechanisms promoting behavioural flexibility, which is pronounced in primates (van Schaik 2013; Kamilar and Baden 2014). Behavioural flexibility provides the necessary versatility to respond to sudden and short-term changes and challenges in the social environment, including dynamic collective rules. Finally, primates also generally exhibit high levels of social tolerance that may be required in this context (Burkart et al. 2014).

In our exploration of equivalents and precursors of social norms in non-human primates, we first characterise social norms in humans and distinguish them from related processes in order to derive essential behavioural elements that can be operationalised and studied in non-verbal species such as primates. We begin this quest by identifying dyadic precursors that serve to regulate interpersonal relationships among primates. Next, we explore behavioural, cognitive, and emotional mechanisms of individual primates that could potentially play a role in the generation, maintenance, and extinction of social norms. Interactions with third parties also may be relevant in this context because they provide insights into underlying socio-cognitive abilities. Finally, we examine behavioural contexts in which social norms and related collective phenomena occur in primate societies in order to identify potential functions, and hence, selective forces promoting them.

2. Human Social Systems and How They Are Organised

2.1. Human Social Systems

Modern human societies, especially of WEIRD, i.e. Western, Educated, Industrialised, Rich and Democratic, people (Henrich et al. 2010), are socially highly complex, with every individual being embedded in a concentric hierarchy of social units, ranging from the nuclear family over neighbourhoods or communities to national states. In addition, most individuals are also members of multiple functional groups like a company or school, the fire brigade, an academic committee or a football team, each with its own organisation and rules. Because traditional hunter-gatherer societies, which represent the social system of 95% of our species' history, live in less complex core units (Hill et al. 2011), much of modern humans' social complexity may have, evolutionarily speaking, very recent origins. However, because traditional forager societies also exhibit social network structure beyond their core band (Hamilton et al. 2007; Apicella et al. 2012), a comprehensive appreciation of human social diversity ought to benefit from a recapitulation of the major social transitions in recent human history. The reason this perspective is relevant is that norms may only come into being or become significant in populations of a certain size and structure, highlighting the key point that we can only expect to find precursors, rather than fully fledged norms, in non-human societies.

Until about 13,000 years ago, all humans lived in bands consisting of an average of 28 adults (range 5.8–81.6) belonging to one or a few extended families (Hill et al. 2011). In these small groups, as in today's traditional societies, everybody knew everybody else, collective decisions could be made in face-to-face meetings with all parties involved, and there was no (need for) political leadership (Diamond 2012). Once the group size exceeded several hundred individuals, social organisation diversified along kinship lines, and several clans made up a so-called tribe. Everybody may or may not have known every other member of the tribe personally; Dunbar's number of about 150 social relationships that humans are supposed to be able to manage, based on their neocortex size, may well define the practical upper limit of this ability (Dunbar 1992; but see de Ruiter et al. 2011). However, each member knew each other at least through reputation or hearsay. Most tribes today function without strong political leadership and make collective decisions in inclusive meetings (Diamond 2012).

At the next level of organisational complexity, tribes grade into chiefdoms, which consist of thousands of members. Chiefdoms arose in response to the transition from hunting and gathering to agricultural food production, and thus posed novel social challenges due to the impossibilities of collective decision-making and personal knowledge of all members of a chiefdom. Hence, chiefdoms have recognised leaders with high social status, proto-bureaucrats who handle administrative tasks, as well as shared ideologies and social identities that facilitate distinction between members of the same and other chiefdoms (Diamond 2012).

Finally, once population size exceeds thousands (going up to > 1 billion in today's China), most people within these so-called states can no longer know each other personally. Many more social regulations and enforcing institutions are necessary to keep states operational, and decision-making is conferred to one or a small group of leaders, who rely on executive powers to carry out their decisions, and on a variety of specialised bureaucrats who administer them (Diamond 2012). Thus, certain rules for organising human social behaviour can be associated with or a priori are excluded from certain types of social systems.

2.2. Rules for Social Behaviour

Given this perspective on human history during the Holocene, it is likely that legal rules, which specify directives for many practical contexts and procedures of the everyday life of WEIRD people in great detail, and which may always have been imposed by political leaders, have been in existence only since the first states emerged about 3500 BC (Diamond 2012). Some legal rules converge with moral codes, such as those stipulating that killing or stealing are unacceptable behaviours, which have other and older origins (see van Schaik and Burkart, Chapter 7 in this volume). Conventions constitute a less formal and less explicit set of collective rules orchestrating social behaviour. They are characterised by arbitrary and variable contents that vary geographically, as well as temporally, between and within different societies (Rudolf von Rohr et al. 2011). They are therefore assumed to be cultural constructs with limited biological input. However, several studies have indicated the existence of similar group-level outcomes in various animal species, suggesting the existence of functional precursors of social conventions in other primates and other mammals, as well as other vertebrates (Claidière and Whiten 2012; van Leeuwen and Haun 2014).

In the study of animal conventions, an influential operational definition held that "an individual displays a particular behaviour because it is the most frequent the individual witnessed in others" (Perry 2009, 706). Other definitions focused more on motivational aspects: "a powerful tendency to discount personal experience in favour of adopting perceived community norms" based on "an intrinsic motivation to copy others, guided by social bonds rather than material rewards" (Whiten et al. 2005, 739). Because conventions are therefore sometimes seen as a sort of custom driven by group pressure, which is only influenced by the number of individuals performing a particular behaviour, rather than their identity, authority, or reputation, conventions also have been characterised as majority influences (van Leeuwen and Haun 2013). Based upon an earlier distinction by Deutsch and Gerard (1955), Claidière and Whiten (2012), and van Schaik (2012) independently pointed out a useful functional distinction between informational and normative conformity. Accordingly, informational conformity is concerned with accuracy and the search for information about reality (utility), whereas normative conformity is concerned with social interactions. In empirical animal studies, however, it is often difficult to separate majority influences from other social influences (van Leeuwen and Haun 2014).

The product of these processes is indistinguishable from traditions. Traditions, as used in animal behaviour, are long-lasting behavioural practices shared among members of a group that are unlikely to have emerged from non-social mechanisms (Whiten et al. 1999; Perry and Manson 2003; Hopper et al. 2007). Traditions can be specific to a particular group or to several groups in a population (Whiten et al. 1999; Luncz et al. 2012), can persist over years or decades (Luncz and Boesch 2014; Schnoell et al. 2014) or perhaps even millennia (Mercader et al. 2007), and can arise not only through conformity but also through any other process that produces local homogeneity, such as individual evaluation of the relative utility of several cultural variants. In most cases, it will be impossible to distinguish traditions from conventions in the narrower sense of being produced by conformity. Moreover, if conformity turns out to be very common, the two concepts may merge altogether.

Social norms are distinguished from conventions, but the differences are subtle. Social norms also promote behavioural homogeneity at the group level, but they are based on an internalised normative component that entails a sense of oughtness, rather than on the copying of a conspecific's action, and this normative component also generates social expectations by bystanders (Horne 2001). Bicchieri and Muldoon (2011) have also argued that, in the case of conventions, there is a strong overlap between the individual's self-interest and the interests of the community that support the convention, whereas compliance with social norms is almost never in the immediate interest of the individual who has to conform. Social norms and conventions are based on informal understandings, which sets them apart from legal rules and orders, which depend on asymmetries in social power and (the threat of) punishment (Sunstein 1996).

Social norms can and have also been distinguished from moral norms. In contrast to moral norms, social norms are conditional, i.e. deviation is not unconditionally sanctioned, and they have a dynamic component because they depend on local agreements and may rise and fall in usage accordingly.

To complicate matters further, there are social regulations concerning a particular behaviour that involve several or all of these mechanisms simultaneously. For example, incest is punished by natural selection because of its deleterious effects, and it is subject to moral and social norms, as well as conventions and traditions (called taboo in this case) that are additionally formalised by legal rules. We therefore agree with Bicchieri and Muldoon (2011) that the semantic vagueness surrounding the concept of norm is common to all social constructs, and—we may add—not entirely satisfactory.

This semantic vagueness and the corresponding difficulty in operationalising behavioural processes are particularly problematic when we are faced with the challenge of studying rules for structuring social behaviour in non-verbal animals. Even in humans, it is not sufficient to describe the behavioural pattern, but, to assess the existence of a norm, "it is important to ask people not just what their personal normative beliefs are, but what they expect other's normative beliefs to be" (Bicchieri and Muldoon 2011). Crucially, it is possible to ask people these questions. Now imagine the challenge for the proverbial scientifically curious Martian ethnographers arriving on Earth to study the social behaviour of the ubiquitous naked apes whose communicative channels are closed to them. They would thus be unable to do what sociologists, psychologists, and social anthropologists are doing all the time: to ask their subjects about the nature and function of widespread or even generally accepted social rules.

If our Martians were keen observers and identified regularities in social interactions that can be observed and quantified, they would be facing the formidable practical problem of teasing apart the different possible causes of the observed behaviour. In analogy to Tinbergen's famous four questions in ethology (Tinbergen 1963), which have recently been amended to include questions about animals' awareness (Bateson and Laland 2013), there might be several correct answers to the question "Why does individual X (not) exhibit behaviour Y?" To explain the extreme rarity of incestuous behaviour among humans, for example, one could provide a sufficient explanation based on the Westermarck effect, a genetically controlled mechanism of sexual imprinting that decreases sexual attraction between individuals who lived in close domestic proximity before sexual maturity (Rantala and Marcinkowska 2011). However, the same outcome might be achieved and explained by either a moral norm, a local tradition, a convention, a social norm, a law—or, to make it worse for inductive empiricists, a combination of some or all of them (which is actually the case in this example in most societies). This absence of access to the process that produces the pattern is the core problem faced by students of animal behaviour interested in evolutionary precursors of homogeneous collective behaviour, with the alleviation that laws can be excluded a priori.

Because we are limited in our inference of the cognitive, emotional, and motivational abilities and states of non-human animals by methodological constraints, this task is not trivial—perhaps even impossible. Researchers are limited to measuring physiological variables, such as heart rate or activity of certain brain regions, and observable behaviour patterns. The latter can be based on observations of natural interactions, ideally of animals in their natural habitat, or on experiments that provoke measurable outcomes. However, many previous studies, especially experimental ones, reporting apparent examples of conformity to majority behaviour were premature because study subjects had no opportunity to copy the majority (because only one demonstrator of a novel behaviour was initially trained), or because there were no opportunities to forgo individually acquired behaviours, or because alternative explanations could not be excluded with certainty (van Leeuwen and Haun 2013, 2014).

As noted earlier, in humans, norms cannot simply be identified based on the observation of a recurrent, collective behavioural pattern (Bicchieri and Muldoon 2011). Only when we observe widespread convergence of normative expectations can the existence of a norm be inferred (Bicchieri and Chavez 2010). Some have even argued that norms are just shared expectations and not behaviour itself (Homans 1961), which would make observational studies irrelevant. Focusing on these shared expectations, it can be argued that a basic feature of norms of any kind is that deviations are met with disapproval or even sanction, in animals as well as humans. This behavioural response, also called punishment in the animal literature (Clutton-Brock and Parker 1995), can come from second parties (those immediately affected by actions of first party), or even by third parties (uninvolved bystanders) (Rudolf von Rohr et al. 2011). Systematic recordings or experimental provocation of punishment would therefore constitute indirect evidence for the existence of collective expectations, provided all other potential explanations for this behaviour can be excluded (Clutton-Brock and Parker 1995; Cant 2011; van Leeuwen and Haun 2014). In cases where there is not enough behavioural freedom for affected parties or bystanders to vent their frustration at the norm violation, it might be possible to measure some relevant physiological responses, although this approach may already push the limits of practical feasibility of animal experimentation. Cognitive constructs, such as identification and internalisation, which constitute additional key defining elements of social norms, are even more challenging to measure in animals.

A final practical problem in animal studies of collective behavioural phenomena consists of partitioning and explaining inter-individual variation. Looking at both sides of the coin simultaneously, we see both behavioural regularity and deviations thereof, at the level of the individual, the group (i.e. individuals within groups), the population (i.e. among groups in a local area), and the species. Because it is impossible to study all individuals of a species, the assessment of social regularities will necessarily be influenced by sample size. Moreover, the question of how representative a sample is raises further questions not only about the power of a study, but also about the natural levels at which collective behavioural phenomena occur, which, in turn, may provide insights into their underlying mechanisms and functions.

Two methodological approaches may be useful in dealing with these questions. First, studying the behaviour of animals that disperse between groups may reveal the nature of between-group variation in social customs. Second, cross-fostering studies provide an opportunity to distinguish between social customs that are invariant components of species-specific behavioural repertoires and those malleable by socialisation.

In conclusion, we think that, at the current state of knowledge, social norms in animals are impossible to operationalise, and, hence, that it is most conservative to postulate that they cannot be inferred with the currently available methods. Empirical studies of animal social behaviour have revealed patterns of behavioural homogeneity, however, and they can be attributed to one of two causes. In the remainder of this chapter, we ignore one of them, namely stable species differences in social behaviour, which are largely genetically controlled. Instead, we focus on reports of intraspecific behavioural conformity for which genetic control can be excluded, i.e. conventions or traditions, and review their potential function and underlying mechanisms. Before we turn to such social mechanisms operating at the group level, we visit their likely evolutionary precursors, i.e. the behavioural regularities characterising dyadic social interactions.

3. Digging for the Roots: Dyadic Precursors of Group-Level Phenomena

As argued in the preceding, because it is unlikely that such a complex, functionally integrated set of behavioural, cognitive and emotional mechanisms that contribute to human normative behaviour arose instantly de novo during the early evolution of *Homo* (whether this happened only in *H. sapiens* or already in the first representatives of our genus or even one of their ancestors is another interesting question in itself), they must have emerged from simpler mechanisms that were available in the form of exaptations. Assuming such a shift in function of relevant traits points towards regulators of dyadic social relationships as the most promising candidates for such building blocks. Dyadic social relationships emerge as properties of repeated interactions between individuals that recognise each other individually and remember their interactions (Hinde 1976). Because of the salient combination of life history traits distinguishing primates from other mammals (see earlier discussion), their societies exhibit a level of social complexity that is matched by only a few other taxa, and therefore offer promise for finding functional precursors of mechanisms underlying human conformity.

Importantly, patterns of social relationships are not just a neutral epiphenomenon of random interaction; a growing number of analyses based on long-term field studies have demonstrated substantial fitness consequences of social relationships (Kappeler and Watts 2011). Specifically, individuals characterised by above-average frequencies of affinity, affiliation and mutual support, which are said to have strong social bonds, enjoy greater reproductive success, higher infant survival and greater longevity, and these effects are independent of dominance rank, which confers additional fitness benefits as a function of social interactions (Silk 2007, 2012; Silk et al. 2009, 2010; Schülke et al. 2010). Thus, the mechanisms underlying dyadic social relationships have long been under strong natural selection in the primate lineage. Here, we can only focus on three relevant aspects that ought to reveal insights about ancient building blocks of human conformity: bonding mechanisms, punishment and dominance hierarchies.

3.1. Social Bonding Mechanisms

First, social bonds are variable in quality, which in turn can be broken down into three dimensions: value, which characterises the individual benefits afforded by the relationship; compatibility, which characterises social tolerance relative to other dyads; and security, which refers to the predictability of repeated interactions between partners (Cords and Aureli 2000; Aureli et al. 2012). Predictability, i.e. the extent to which memories of the integrated previous interactions with a particular individual generate reliable expectations about future interactions, is of key interest for the present purpose: It generates expectations about the behaviour of others in particular contexts, which are an essential element of social norms. Moreover, violation of expectations may provoke either an emotional response that may guide future interactions with the same individual (Schino and Aureli 2010), or an immediate aggressive response, which has been variously characterised as punishment, coercion or strong reciprocity, i.e. a propensity to impose behavioural sanctions on others (Clutton-Brock and Parker 1995; Fehr and Fischbacher 2004b).

Agonistic interactions also offer opportunities for bystanders to become involved in dyadic relationships. Third parties may influence the quality and maintenance of dyadic relationships of others by directing either affiliation or aggression at either the aggressor or victim. This type of third-party intervention has multiple functions and is widespread among primates (Aureli et al. 2012). Importantly, it provides the simplest mechanism with which individuals interfere in a corrective way in the social behaviour of others, presumably to satisfy their individual expectations and interests. Thus, basic features of dyadic social relationships of primates and other mammals, including social expectations, emotional and behavioural responses to violations of expectations, and third-party interventions, are widespread. It is eminently plausible that selection co-opted them for similar functions at the group level.

3.2. Behavioural Sanctions

Violations of individual expectations about the behaviour of others in a particular context are functionally associated with behavioural and emotional mechanisms that play important roles in human conformity. We speak of punishment among animals when "individuals (or groups) commonly respond to actions likely to lower their fitness with behaviour that reduces the fitness of the instigator and discourages or prevents him or her from repeating the initial action" (Clutton-Brock and Parker 1995, 209). Punishment is widespread, and may consist of actual aggression or the threat thereof (Cant 2011; Cant and Young 2013), also leading to coercion or negative pseudoreciprocity with similar effects (Raihani et al. 2012). It has been studied most intensively in the context of explaining the evolution of cooperation (Raihani et al. 2010, 2012), but it also plays a role in other social contexts, including the establishment and maintenance of dominance relations, the establishment of mating bonds and in the parent-offspring conflict.

Despite the anthropomorphic shorthand, punishment is not contingent on mental state attribution and awareness about the consequences of the punishing act because it can be considered as a kind of negative direct reciprocity (Bshary 2010). Seen from this perspective, punishment is very similar to tit-for-tat reciprocity, whose only cognitive requirements also include individual recognition and basic memory, and which differs from punishment only in that costly responses to others' behaviour can also be beneficial to the recipient (Bshary 2010).

If the punishing act is performed not by the recipient of the initial act but by a bystander, the triadic interaction can be called third-party punishment, sometimes also called "policing"—a term referring to the outcome of this type of third-party intervention. Some scholars distinguish between policing and third-party punishment because policing involves a neutral, non-aggressive intervention (Flack et al. 2006; Rudolf von Rohr et al. 2012). Obviously, the functional outcome may be the same. Yet another use of the term "policing" is for when workers in eusocial insects destroy the eggs laid by other workers. But in this case, the action is more like dyadic punishment, because the punisher derives an immediate, rather than indirect, benefit (Ratnieks and

Reeve 1992). Regardless of terminological issues, the presence of these various forms of punishment and policing shows that basal behavioural mechanisms required for modifying the future behaviour of others are already well established in vertebrates from fish to primates.

In humans, punishment and policing, just like other types of social interactions, are associated with, or even potentiated by, powerful emotional responses that also have precursors or equivalents in non-human primates (de Waal 2011). Social transgressions or other inflictions of fitness costs elicit anger, which is embedded and conserved neurophysiologically across mammals (Fessler and Gervais 2010). Behavioural responses to unfairness, which have been studied in some primates (Brosnan and de Waal 2014), may be underpinned by anger or an emotion derived from it. The subjective perception of anger is perhaps also involved in motivating third-party interventions, but as with most emotional responses of animals, their physiological underpinnings are very difficult to measure with sufficient ecological validity in freely interacting animals in wild conditions.

In humans, individuals may sometimes experience shame as a result of their actions that elicit punishment or policing by others—an emotional response that may also contribute to the stability of social norms. Because shame is associated with postures and behaviours that serve to appease an opponent, such as gaze avoidance and stooped postures (Tracy and Matsumoto 2008), its evolutionary roots have been linked to appeasement behaviour in animals (Fessler 2007). Accordingly, a subordinate, who appraises herself as occupying a lower social position, may experience proto-shame in an encounter with a dominant in which the status difference is relevant, and this emotion and the related appraisals and attitudes have phylogenetic origins across mammals and perhaps beyond (Fessler and Gervais 2010). Attitudes have been characterised in this context as "durable, hierarchically organised representations of previously appraised traits and relational outcomes that potentiate differential emotional readiness toward others" (Fessler and Gervais 2010, 178). Because attitudes are updated by emotional experiences and help to regulate emotions by shaping appraisals guiding future actions, they play an important role by linking emotions and behaviour, also in non-human primates (Aureli and Schaffner 2002), and also in contexts unrelated to behavioural sanctions.

3.3. Agonistic Interactions and Dominance Hierarchies

Social interactions that involve exchanges of submissive and or aggressive signals or behaviours, so-called agonistic interactions, are widespread among group-living animals. When individuals recognise and remember each other individually, pairs of individuals will establish dominance relations based on the outcome of agonistic interactions that formalise inter-individual conflict. The establishment of individual rank relations, which lead to dominance hierarchies at the group level, is favoured by

natural selection because they reduce the costs and risks of conflicts. A dominance hierarchy is therefore an automatic by-product of dyadic dominance interactions, whose
properties entail behavioural and cognitive mechanisms that may well have been co-
opted for establishing and stabilising social norms in humans.

First, dominance relations are primarily maintained via the exchange of threat and
appeasement displays, which are functionally linked to proto-shame (see earlier discussion). In non-human primates, this emotion and the related attitude are exclusively
focused on the relative position in a social hierarchy (Fessler 2007), but in humans they
became linked to norms. Second, dominance hierarchies are a powerful mechanism
to install social order with behavioural mechanisms that do not require sophisticated
cognition (Seyfarth and Cheney 2012b). Conflicts among individual interests and
competition for resources are unavoidable costs of group-living, and any mechanism
reducing these costs is favoured by natural selection because it will enhance the probability of individual survival and reproduction (Aureli et al. 2012). In primate societies,
dominance hierarchies therefore have an important by-product function at the group
level in promoting social stability, order and cohesion, and, hence, the same function as
many social norms and conventions in humans. These effects on group cohesion and
stability are adaptive because the many benefits favouring group living are fundamentally dependent on group cohesion (Krause and Ruxton 2002).

Third, some Old World primates are characterised by dominance hierarchies that
are not only established via dyadic interactions, but also stabilised by social rules and
processes. In species with so-called maternal rank inheritance (Walters and Seyfarth
1987), adult females and their philopatric daughters form matrilines with stable dominance relations, and within each matriline, daughters rank inversely below the matri-
arch as a function of their age. How and why these rules were established remains largely
unresolved (Chapais 1995), but they are also reinforced by third-party interventions
that stabilise the status quo (Pereira 1989), because uninvolved individuals ally with
victims of aggression against lower-ranking attackers, who want to improve their rank,
but thereby threaten the stability of the overall hierarchy. Functionally, the outcome of
these interventions therefore corresponds to those established by social norms.

In conclusion, the needs and mechanisms organising the daily lives of individual primates have resulted in a suite of behavioural, cognitive and emotional
mechanisms that must have been available for our hominin ancestors to elaborate
upon after their separation from our last common ancestors from members of the
genus *Pan*. Looking back in time from the modern human perspective, we can consider them precursors.

In the final section, we focus on functional contexts promoting the evolution of
social norms that may also have precursors among non-human primates, after first
reviewing some of the empirical primate studies that have been interpreted as suggestive evidence for the existence of social norms or conventions.

4. Social Norms in Non-Human Primates?

A number of observational and experimental studies of non-human primates have reported apparent evidence for the existence of behavioural components of social norms or conventions. We briefly summarise some of these studies here and critically evaluate their claims based on the preceding considerations and definitions. Van Leeuwen and Haun (2013, 2014) have already provided important methodological and conceptual concerns about many of these studies that we do not repeat here.

4.1. Social Rules or Norms

One of the earliest reports about a social norm in primates concerned claims of respect of property. In an experiment with long-tailed macaques (*Macaca fascicularis*), individuals obtained a valued food resource in the presence of another individual. Kummer and Cords (1991) observed that dominant individuals did not take this tube from subordinate individuals as long as the subordinates kept the tube in their hands or close to their body. If the tubes were, however, placed close to the subordinates on the ground, dominant individuals took the tubes. Because in both cases the risk of aggression was equally high, the respect of property was not absolute, and the outcome of the experiment may simply reflect the presence of simple rules of what constitutes control over access to a resource. Based on observations of mobbing of individuals attacking weaker group members, such as juveniles, the same authors also suggested that these macaques have social rules that serve to protect weaker individuals, but it is impossible to exclude the interpretation that these polyadic interactions represented selfish third-party intervention strategies.

A similar "social regularity" regarding inhibited aggression was inferred from observations that chimpanzee males did not normally use their canines in conflicts with females. However, these polyadic conflicts are also open to alternative interpretation because if the males actually bit, females vocalised more intensely and formed a coalition with another female against the male (de Waal 1991). Other types of third-party interventions involving impartial intervention of individuals in dyadic conflicts, which usually terminates the conflict, have been reported for a variety of monkeys and apes (listed in Rudolf von Rohr et al. 2012).

Food sharing provides another context where social rules have been identified. Inequity aversion was first studied in brown capuchin monkeys (*Cebus apella*). They were trained to exchange a token against a food reward: a preferred food item such as a grape or a non-preferred food item such as a piece of cucumber. In a paired experimental set-up, where two monkeys sat next to each other and exchanged the token against a food reward in turns, they exchanged the token against the reward equally often, independent of the quality of the reward, when both individuals received the same reward. However, if one individual received a high-quality reward and the other individual a low-quality reward, the individual receiving the low-quality reward stopped exchanging the token and sometimes even threw the token towards the experimenter, suggesting that these monkeys do have expectations about fairness or a sense of inequity (Brosnan and de Waal 2003). These studies have since been repeated with other species, including chimpanzees, showing that this aversion is widespread (Brosnan and de Waal 2014). They are most parsimoniously interpreted as a monitoring of exchange in dyadic relationships, rather than a preference for justice at the level of the whole group, however.

The social consequences of such aversion were reported in a study of food calls in rhesus macaques (*Macaca mulatta*), which produce these calls when they discover high-quality food items, thereby attracting group members to the resource. Individuals that discovered hidden coconuts and did not produce food calls received more aggression when discovered by other group members, consistent with the notion that these cheaters were punished (Hauser 1992). In a similar experiment with white-faced capuchin monkeys (*Cebus capucinus*), rates of food calls increased with food quality. In addition, individuals who called when they discovered food were less likely to be approached by others who were in visual contact than individuals who remained silent. Calling rate also varied in accordance to dominance status of approaching individuals; individuals who called when they were approached by higher-ranking animals were less likely to receive aggression than individuals who did not call. Thus, food-associated calls may function to announce food ownership, thereby decreasing aggression from other individuals (Gros-Louis 2004).

In the context of social interactions, a study of pig-tailed macaques (*Macaca nemestrina*) reported that infringements of dominance rules are met with social sanctions (Flack and de Waal 2007). These monkeys use a facial expression, the silent bared-teeth display, as a submissive signal. Subordinate individuals produce these displays not only in response to threats by dominants, but also spontaneously in the absence of threat or aggression, as for example, when passing by a dominant individual. Individuals that produce fewer or none of these submissive signals in peaceful contexts groom and reconcile less frequently and fight more frequently than others, excluding potential alternative explanations, such as reciprocity, temperament and proximity.

4.2. Conformity

Several primate studies have reported examples of behavioural homogeneity. First, white-faced capuchin monkeys process a particular fruit by either scrubbing or pounding it on a substrate to access their seeds, with both techniques being equally efficient (Perry 2009). During the first two years of life, young capuchins try a variety of techniques but then settle on the technique they have apparently observed most frequently. This pattern has therefore been interpreted as a case of normative conformity (Claidière and Whiten 2012), but it cannot be decided whether they followed a majority rule or used the most frequent social information (de Leeuwen and Haun 2014) to settle on the respective technique, or whether this was simply the best technique. Second, in dyadic social interactions in some groups of the same white-faced capuchin monkeys, individuals sniff at the hand of the interaction partner or insert the finger into their eye sockets or nostrils (Perry et al. 2003). These displays are suggested to strengthen the social bond of the interaction partners and were practised in some groups for only a few months and in others for years. While not constituting examples of normativity, such rituals may be instructive for reconstructing the origins of normative conformity involving arbitrary behaviours. The development of a pacific culture in one group of baboons (*Papio anubis*) after all aggressive males died within a short period of time (Sapolsky and Share 2004) indicates that normativity can have multiple origins.

Conformity was also reported for several studies of the social transmission of experimentally introduced behaviours. In a pioneering study, two dominant female chimpanzees were trained to retrieve a food reward from an artificial fruit with one of two techniques (Whiten et al. 2005). After this training session, the apparatus was presented to the whole group. Group members learned to open the fruit by observing the dominant female and opened the fruit by using the same technique. Some individuals also discovered the alternative technique and used it. However, after the fruit was returned two months later, individuals that earlier had discovered and used the alternative technique then used the technique that was more common in their group, suggesting that they conform to the majority of their group, but it has not been demonstrated that they indeed follow a majority rule. Similar experiments have since been conducted with capuchin monkeys (Dindo et al. 2009) and redfronted lemurs (*Eulemur rufifrons*), but in those cases preference for one seeded technique diminished over time (Schnoell and Fichtel 2012; Schnoell et al. 2014).

Other observations are consistent with conformity being due to copying of dominants. Thus, two groups of chimpanzees were trained to exchange two types of token for a food reward, with one type being associated with a highly-preferred food (grape) and the other one with a medium-preferred one (carrot) (Hopper et al. 2011). The dominant female in each group was trained beforehand to exchange one token for either a grape or a carrot. Group members could first observe the dominant female exchanging the tokens before they could choose one of the two tokens to exchange them for a reward. In both groups, chimpanzees took more often the token chosen by the dominant female, although some individuals in the carrot group also chose the other token, receiving the highly-preferred reward. Thus, this experiment is consistent with chimpanzees' showing normative conformity, but also with prestige-based copying.

A comparative study in which chimpanzees, two-year-old children and orangutans were given the choice to copy the behaviour of one or three conspecific demonstrators, dropping a ball into a coloured box to receive a reward, examined the mechanisms enhancing conformity (Haun et al. 2012). It revealed that chimpanzees and children, but not orangutans, more often copied an action performed by three individuals, once each, than an action performed by one individual three times, providing clear evidence for normative conformity based on majority influences.

Finally, groups of wild vervet monkeys (*Chlorocebus aethiops*) were offered two types of coloured corn; one colour was palatable, whereas the other was made unpalatable (van de Waal et al. 2013). Vervets quickly developed a preference for the palatable colour, even after the originally unpalatable colour was no longer combined with the bitter taste. Importantly, males migrating between groups adjusted their initial colour preference to the one of the new group, although they arrived with a preference for the other colour and corn of both colours was palatable. This study provides the most convincing example of conformity in animals to date. However, relying on the feeding strategy of other group members might also be due to individual interests because others might have had more experience with local food and may have had the experience that at least once in a while some of the food items were not palatable. Thus, we cannot decide whether the conformity was informational or normative. The normative interpretation would be strengthened if deviant preferences were met with disapproval (shunning or even punishment) from the other group members.

4.3. Assessment of Current Evidence

In conclusion, even though several studies reported norm-like behaviours among non-human primates, there is, as of yet, not much convincing evidence for normative conformity, perhaps also because the topic has not yet attracted sufficient interest among primatologists. Lack of interest may also reflect frustration with methodological obstacles. For instance, norms also require expectations, which are, however, very difficult or even impossible to operationalise and measure, for example because it is not trivial to distinguish between private and dyadic or more common expectations. We therefore argue that exact equivalents of human social norms are absent, viz. impossible to demonstrate, among non-human primates despite the widespread occurrence of their ingredients.

On the other hand, objective observers might make similar arguments about our fellow humans. In animal studies, what we can record are the actors' behaviours, not their intentions or motivations, allowing one to dismiss these observations as inconclusive for the continuity with human phenomena. However, the functional equivalence to the kinds of behaviours in humans should sensitise us to the possibility that they are also motivated in similar ways. After all, the motivations of humans in similar interactions will also remain hidden to all but the actors, or perhaps even to them as well.

5. Functions and Evolution of Social Norm-Like Behaviours

Although social norms in humans cannot be explained by focusing on their function alone (Bicchieri and Muldoon 2011), the functional contexts in which conformist behaviour of non-human primates might be advantageous may illuminate some of the evolutionary pressures that favoured the evolution of social norms in our own lineage. Two kinds of contexts in which copying or adopting the behaviour of others is advantageous have been proposed. First, doing what others do provides cheaper and more reliable information. Copying the behaviour of others saves time and prevents making potentially risky mistakes. Claidière and Whiten (2012; cf. van Schaik 2012) defined such reliance on the wisdom of the crowd to obtain non-social information about reality as "informational convention." Sometimes this may involve ignoring personally acquired knowledge of a superior behavioural alternative and copying the behaviour of others expressing a less effective behaviour (Galef and Whiskin 2008), but, on average, this algorithm appears to provide more benefits than costs. Second, normative conformity is based on processing of social information and functions to manage social relations (Claidière and Whiten 2012). In humans, it is based on compliance, identification and internalisation (Kelman 1958), which are challenging, if not impossible, to study in animals.

There are three functional explanations for the coevolution of normative conformity in humans that emphasise different mechanisms and processes (see also van Schaik and Burkart, Chapter 7 in this volume). The first explanation focuses on the role of punishment in cultural evolution. Accordingly, punishment is a powerful mechanism to penalise both norm violators and those who fail to punish norm violators, generating cultural group selective pressures that lead to norms being treated as extensions of the self, i.e. to the development of collective expectations (Boyd and Richerson 2009). A second explanation focuses on another proximate aspect related to the predictability of social allies. When group members compete over prospective allies, conformists are at an advantage because their behaviour is more predictable (Haley and Fessler 2005). If such coalitions enhance fitness, conformity and predictability will increase. A third view emphasises the functional context of intergroup conflict as source of selective pressures favouring group conformity (Bowles 2006, 2012). Any perceived lack of conformity to group norms will be highly visible and subject to punishment, so that behavioural assimilation is a selfish strategy that will help individuals to avoid conflict. Group-specific norms will therefore minimise perceived differences among group members and at the same time maximise those between groups. Because between-group conflict is also rife among non-human primates (Crofoot and Wrangham 2010), and because the two other mechanisms are not mutually exclusive and may be involved in this behavioural context, intergroup conflict may have contributed to the functional convergence of all the behavioural elements already present in dyadic relationships discussed in the preceding. Whether and why intergroup conflict has taken on such a powerful role in human history remains a topic for speculation at present.

Acknowledgements

We thank Kurt Bayertz and Neil Roughley for the invitation to join the "Anthropology and Normativity Group" and their inspiring meetings over the years, as well as all members of this group for discussion and helpful comments on this chapter.

4

On the Human Addiction to Norms

Social Norms and Cultural Universals of Normativity

Christoph Antweiler

1. Introduction

Social norms are psychic (cognitive or emotive) expectations about desired (as well as unwanted) behavior of people with supra-individual validity. Norms are about expected behavior in specified circumstances of recurrent social interactions and are linked to sanctions. Norms become manifest empirically in language, in behavior, e.g., in habits and *rites de passage*, or in material artifacts, such as symbols. This contribution tries to develop a cultural anthropological perspective on social norms and socialization.[1]

Social scientists are generally focused on average and regular features of societies. An anthropological understanding of culture is focused on standardized cognition, behavior, and artifacts. As an empirically oriented science, anthropology[2] studies social norms and their foundation in values and worldviews as one of its main topics. Cognitive anthropology conceptualizes culture as the knowledge enabling a person to act in effective *and appropriate* ways in her society. The crucial factor forming social

[1] Thanks go to Peter Kappeler, Karl Mertens, and the editors for constructive critiques of an earlier version, which improved the chapter considerably, and to Birgitt Röttger-Rössler for pointing me in the direction of relevant literature.

[2] For brevity from now on, I use "anthropology" to refer to cultural anthropology, in the English-speaking scientific community also called "social anthropology," "socio-cultural anthropology" (or, infrequently, "ethnology").

norms emphasized by anthropologists is enculturation via social learning. Using case studies, this chapter describes particular forms as well as cross-cultural patterns in the socialization of norms. An open question is the shares of imitative learning and emulation vs. learning by explicit teaching. Even if socialization is crucial, not all norms result from social transmission. Thus, finally, some issues where we need explanations beyond socialization are outlined.

The road map of the argument is as follows. After an introductory example of social norms, section 2 shows that a core of human culture is normal and standardized behavior and the related expectations about such behavior. This is reflected in norms being a crucial part of the general concept of culture in anthropology. More specific, cognitive concepts of culture defining culture as "models for" socially accepted action are even more inclined to emphasize normativity as the core of sociality. Here, I emphasize why both methods of anthropology, naturalistic fieldwork in single societies and cross-cultural comparison, are crucial in theorizing about norms in human societies. I conclude that anthropology can provide a bridge between deductive approaches, experimental studies, and naturalistic approaches to understanding norms among the different primate species.

Section 3 inquires into social norms and their functions for individual and collective identity as well as cooperation in humans. Social norms are conceived as generative rules for expected behavior in recurrent interaction situations. Their general function is the coordination of behavior. In typically human large and complex societies, norms function to coordinate action among people not personally known to each other. A further point discussed here concerns the ambiguities of the notion of norms as "expected behavior."

Section 4 builds on that ambiguity and considers the fact that norm systems usually include "rules for breaking rules." Anthropological studies show that rule-breaking is widely spread, but even the ways of not observing some obligations or violating prescriptions are structured along socially expected lines.

Section 5 analyzes the process of norm acquisition through social learning in a cross-cultural perspective. The general method of cross-cultural comparative research is discussed and main findings about the universality of normativity or specific social norms are reported. I show that enculturation into crucial social norms—in contrast to socialization in general—across cultures is done through consciously rationalized procedures and explicit teaching.

Section 6 demonstrates that not all social norms are explainable by socialization proper. Some norms, e.g., rules for ethnocentric behavior, are cross-culturally more easily learned than others, e.g., norms allowing peacemaking. This is already implied by the specific procedures for teaching crucial norms dealt with in section 4, which build on biotic learning preparedness. Thus a full understanding of the genesis of norms calls for a truly bio-cultural approach.

As an introduction to the topic by way of an example, here is a glimpse into the norm culture in a part of Indonesia, the culturally extremely diverse country where I am doing anthropological research. The two principally desired and expected behaviors in the dominant culture there, Javanese Culture, are avoiding conflict and showing respect to elders and people higher in the social hierarchy (Geertz 1961, 99–102; Magnis-Suseno 1981, 37–62; Koentjaraningrat 1984, 100–22, 233–51; Schweizer 1989, 244–7). To evade conflict, one should always help others and avoid quarrels of any sorts. One should not criticize anyone openly, ask directly for something, or formulate anything in a blunt way. If you lose in a collision of interests, you should not show any chagrin. According to the respect norm, everyone should accept the social rank of the other, especially of elderly and socially higher persons. This involves two specifically named norms, respect (*hormat*[3]) and submissive friendliness (*andap-asor*). The respect principle is practiced in specific forms of address, use of the appropriate speech level, and body language. The respectfulness demanded refers only to overt behavior, whereas consent is not requested. Both norms are founded in the ideal of a refined person who behaves in a controlled manner, shows no emotions, knows the Javanese language, and speaks relaxedly and gently (*halus*). If these norms are obeyed, a highly valued state of inner and collective harmony, as well as harmony with nature, called "peace and calmness" (*slamet*), is achieved. This value is based on a worldview according to which individual, society, nature, and the supernatural are intensely connected. All things have their proper place, and the person is required to act in such a way that a harmonic consonance (*rukun*) is ensured. Similar norms of respect and dispute avoidance pertain to other stratified societies of the Malay realm of Insular Southeast Asia (Malaysia, Indonesia, Philippines). Violations of these social norms trigger an emotion of shame (*malu*), which is socialized by specific means, as explained in the following. Specific social norms such as these are intimately related to the general way of life of peoples.

2. Norms as the Core of Culture Concepts in Anthropology

Why are norms crucial for understanding human cultures and their change? What is the relation between concepts of "culture," concepts of "norms," and the broader notion of "normativity"? Conceptions of culture in anthropology are proverbially diverse (Kroeber and Kluckhohn 1952; cf. Vann 2013). The broad diversity of concepts used boils down to two major views, a totalistic (holistic) view and a less comprehensive, mentalist view (Vivelo 1978, 16–19). Both concepts have a relation to norms and normativity.

[3] Italicized terms are *Bahasa Indonesia*, the national language, or *Bahasa Jawa*, Javanese language.

Most anthropologists adopt an encompassing concept of culture. Culture is conceptualized as the totality of a people's way of life. Such a *holistic* view puts an emphasis on the systematicity of culture, the interrelatedness of several aspects, and the resulting "patterns" of culture. From the perspective of materiality, culture is not reducible to material categories. Culture includes behavior (socio-facts), thoughts and emotion (menti-facts), and material products of behavior (arti-facts). Culture understood as a way of life consists of the sum of transformations of natural entities characteristic of a particular human group.[4] In short: culture is the accumulated sum of innovations (Rudolph and Tschohl 1977). Thus, in addition to non-genetically transmitted information emphasized in most biological concepts, the anthropological concept of culture emphasizes innovation. Innovations stem from individuals and may be already shared by some other living members, but per definition are not (yet) transmitted between generations.

Cultural anthropologists (even more than other social scientists and researchers in the humanities) are focused on normal behavior of individuals in a collective. The focus is on the usual variants, the habits, standards, and conventions of behavior, cognition, and its products. The core of culture is *standardized* thoughts, feelings, and actions (Hansen 2009). To put it simply: people behave as if they had spoken to each other to coordinate their behavior. Thus, culture in the anthropological view is more about norms than about values (culturally defined ideas about what is normatively right, true, and beautiful).[5]

Some of the definitions of culture within this first view are what has been portrayed as "normative definitions of culture." Culture is seen as ideals, values, and rules for living (Kluckhohn and Kelly 1945, 79; Kroeber and Kluckhohn 1952; Lull 2000, 86–9). These cultural behavioral standards are often regarded as self-evident by members of a society and thus are (probably universally) called the "normal" or "natural" ways of doing things, seeing the world, or dealing with issues. They are usually regarded as the "right" way to behave, and this already implies a normative component, an "ought."

The second and far more specific view of culture is the mentalist view. Culture is conceptualized as an ideational system as already implied in the previously mentioned "rules for living." Culture is seen as a conceptual code consisting of knowledge and beliefs used by people to interpret themselves, order the world, and make decisions.

---

[4] The German term "Daseinsgestaltung" aptly conveys this specific aspect of the *making* of existence.

[5] Like anthropology, sociology is particularly concerned with normal behavior as well. Emile Durkheim, the founder of sociology as an academic discipline, conceived *faits sociaux* as the principal subject matter of sociology. Social facts are conceived as the collective *regularities* which are independent of individual behavior. Social scientists in general are mostly interested in recurring actions, regularities of social action, patterned behavior. Furthermore they emphasize intersubjectively shared orientations or long-term social arrangements (social institutions). Their main topic is behavior which is *collectively generated* and *normatively hedged*.

Pertaining to behavior, culture is a system of rules for behavior rather than an observed pattern of behavior (Kluckhohn and Kelly 1945, 79; Goodenough 1961, 521–2; Cancian 1975; Antweiler 2015). This less comprehensive view is used most prominently in cognitive anthropology. Generalizing from the distinction between phon*etic* and phon*emic* approaches in linguistics, anthropology is interested in *etic* as well as *emic* aspects of cultures. A mentalist and emically oriented definition aims at the normative core of culture, by focusing on the actor's "conceptualization of *appropriate* behavior" (Vivelo 1978, 18, emphasis orig.). In this mentalist perspective, culture is seen as the specific knowledge of the standards enabling persons to act in appropriate ways in their society. Culture is a code or a sort of grammar, and people usually act according to this code.

Some of the current definitions of culture in anthropology (especially in US-American anthropology) are heavily influenced by mentalist concepts. They go even further by defining culture as conceptions of ways of life that are shared by members of a society (e.g., Kottak 2013, 28–9; Haviland et al. 2014, 331–2; Peoples and Bailey 2015, 23–4; Rodseth 1998 for a critique). This view is also held by some leading positions within social philosophy (e.g., Tuomela 2007, 65–82). This limitation to the shared part excludes, firstly, innovations not yet socially distributed and, secondly, other aspects of individual ways of life or private worldviews (*mazeway*, Kearney 1984). In view of the prevalent concepts of culture and the basic methods of its study, anthropology—especially cognitive anthropology—has a clear relation to normativity. Thus, even if norms are not the specific research topic, the anthropological approach is principally interested in cultural standards and thus oriented toward social norms and normativity.[6]

How does this anthropological understanding of culture relate to primatologists' and psychologists' understandings? The main misunderstanding here pertains to the different breadth of coverage of concepts of culture. Researchers in biology and many psychologists tend to understand culture merely as non-genetic transmission of information between generations (epi-genetic transmission, tradition, tradi-genetic transmission). They are primarily interested in the variants of behavior between populations X, Y, and Z of one and the same species at different locales. More precisely, it is only this part of the variation, which is taken to be inexplicable by differences in the natural environment (cf. Kappeler et al., this volume, 69, 72). Studies in "cultural primatology," what is also called "primate anthropology" [*sic!*] have shown that there are such traditions in several non-human primate species, but they do *not* claim that these are vital for the survival of the individuals.

---

[6] A corollary of this is the problem that exceptions to cultural standards or habits are often not reported or simply dismissed (cf. Mertens, Chapter 5 in this volume).

For humans, non-genetic factors are not only relevant but *inevitable* for the physical survival of the individual. Thus, for humans, culture is the principal means of biotic adaptation. Any notion of humans not including culture is *biologically* meaningless. Humans have to live culturally in a social collective, but they are not constrained to live in a specific society. It is culture in the singular sense that humans depend on, not culture in the plural sense. To survive, humans need a society, but it is not a specific society or the specific culture, i.e., the historically and locally specific collective to which they currently belong. A concept from evolutionary biology that comes close to this typical human systemic and inevitable transformation of nature is "niche construction" (Laland et al. 2000; 2012).

How do anthropologists study culture? The basic method is the ethnographic approach, where primary data are collected through fieldwork. This is an experientially rich data-gathering procedure done in natural settings. The naturalistic orientation is similar to that of ethology (comparative animal psychology) and primatology, but differs from the experimental approach of mainstream psychology (cf. Turiel and Dahl, this volume, 206-207). To give an example related to norm socialization, in anthropology, human attachment is not studied in an experimental way in the laboratory, but in real-time and real-space settings (Quinn and Mageo 2013). The strength of such studies is that they reveal the cultural context and ecological embeddedness of the subjects studied. The weakness is that the microscopic methods are less verifiable. Generalizing from the distinction between phon*etic* and phon*emic* approaches in linguistics, anthropology is interested in etic as well as emic aspects of cultures. Since the symbolic turn in the 1970s, anthropology focuses on the emics: understanding cultures from the insider's view. Due to the experiential approach of anthropology, learning norms is everyday work for anthropologists, even if socialization is not the topic under study. Anthropologists—especially if focused on the *emics*—try to learn the culture. Thus the fieldworker, especially if new to the field, is virtually a child and thus fieldwork is like a "second enculturation" (see e.g., Eller 2012, 44).

The second basic method of anthropology is cross-cultural comparison. Existing primary data from fieldwork reports are used for a secondary analysis to develop or test cross-cultural questions. This approach is used to search for characteristics shared by many or all human societies. Anthropologists have been able to establish empirically hundreds of traits shared by all or nearly all societies ("universals," "human universals," Brown 2000; Moghaddam 2002; Norenzayan and Heine 2005; Antweiler 2012a, 2015, 2016).[7] Among the most well-known of these pan-cultural similarities are incest avoidance and reciprocity in economic and social exchange. One of the

---

[7] Note that this conception differs markedly from "universals" understood as traits of all *individuals* in a species, as e.g., in Kappeler and Silk (2006).

most general phenomena linking the manifold universals is the ubiquitous tendency to rule-making. Most of the entries in lists of universals could be rephrased as saying that: "In all human societies there are rules for . . . ." Common examples are rules about proper food and accepted marriage partners. The ubiquity of rules demonstrates a susceptibility to normative regulation of thought, emotion, and behavior. The anthropologist Kate Fox puts it bluntly: "The human species is addicted to rule making" (2014, 13; cf. Chibnik 1981).

In sum, cultural anthropology provides empirical studies of norms in social interaction in collectives beyond dyads. Anthropology highlights by way of its culture concept systemic connections between different aspects and functions of norms. Furthermore, anthropology provides comparative insights into norms in societies with different environments, structures, sizes, and levels of complexity. Studies from cultural anthropology thus are especially useful to get a view into human psychic functioning worldwide—beyond WEIRD (Western, Educated, Industrial, Rich, Democratic) people. Our current knowledge of the human psyche is based on a very limited and biased basis of studies almost all done by Western researchers with Western subjects. Where comparative data are available, WEIRD societies consistently occupy the extreme ends of distributions. This makes WEIRD people often the worst subpopulations one can study to generalize about humans (Henrich and Norenzayan 2010, 63–5, 79; Lancy 2015, 184–5, 206–7).

3. Social Norms as Generative Rules

How are social norms best characterized? Social norms are ideals, rules, or guidelines that say how people ought to behave. The basic structure of social norms consists of an obligation plus a sanction plus a scope (Popitz 1980; Lucke 2014). Norms are standards of propriety and appropriateness, where compliance is expected by social actors. The typical realms of norms are sexuality, social relations, and economic exchange. Almost all known cultures in time and space include hundreds or thousands of norms. Anthropologists call the corpus of acceptable norms of a specific ethnic group an *ethos*.

Normative guidelines pertain to particular people and their desired behavior in *certain* situations. Seen in an interpretative perspective, the emphasis is on ought, should, and situations (Peoples and Bailey 2015, 30). Norms thus are not fixed musts or rights but *generative* rules for behavior under certain circumstances. Normative expectations do not refer to rare situations in new social contexts: norms concern expected behaviors in *recurring* social situations. Formally the expectancy structure is as follows: Alter A expects behavior X from Ego B within an *inter-individual* interaction. Sociological deductive theorizing formalizes this as the insight that Society A expects behavior Y from Ego B within a social relationship (Popitz 2006, 61–75). The expected behavior, the "ought," may be simply a "want" and can belong to habitual social reality and thus may be detached from particular individuals (cf. Bayertz 2010, 184–6).

Norms do not concern actual (etic) behavior or behavior assumed to be average by the members, but ideal patterns (or rules) for, and thus expectations of, the regularity of appropriate behavior (Peoples and Bailey 2015, 31). The regularity with which the expectations are held does not say anything about whether the factual behavior is regular as well (Spittler 1967, 14). A useful distinction is between ordinary and crucial norms. *Folkways* or etiquette are the norms about how things should be done. They guide everyday behavior and are followed by members of a society so readily that they are hardly aware of their existence. *Mores* are stronger norms carrying moral connotations. Mores are believed in the society to be crucial for an orderly and decent way of life (Scupin and deCorse 2006, 55; Peoples and Bailey 2015, 31). Since mores are believed to be morally significant, transgressions are sanctioned more strongly and more frequently in public. How to greet or dress may be a *folkway*, but the shameful greeting or the decent dress required for a young girl in rural Malaysia or Indonesia is a question of mores.

Norms are a part of non-material culture, but primarily are about correct overt *behavior*, and less about the right thoughts, attitudes, or values. Thus, the core of norms is mental, but the cognitive aspects are often symbolized in highly valued words and observable symbols (fine art, body adornment, monuments). This is an indication of the fact that norms are based on or at least connected to values, beliefs, and worldviews, which may be very different. To give an example, North American society has many norms referring to the notion of individual responsibility and initiative. Individuals should work for their own self-interest. The expectation for grown self-sufficient Americans is that they should not live with their adult children, and young adults are not supposed to live with their parents (Scupin and DeCorse 2006, 54–5). These norms are based on the value of individualism dominating the prevailing US-mainstream worldview. But the connection to norms is not strict: the basic norm of individualism allows for gender varieties and also for several values attached to it as an *emic* explanation. That was shown in a study comparing individualism in three New York neighborhoods (Kusserow 2004).

Norms reflect and enforce the culture of a particular community and are linked to collective identity (Cancian 1975). Despite intra-cultural diversity, there is at least a minimal acceptance of these norms within the social unit. There is widespread agreement that people ought to adhere to certain standards and that people who repeatedly fail to follow these standards face aversive reactions. This being the case, some anthropologists define norms as those ideas shared by members of a culture about the way things ought to be done (Nanda and Warms 2015, 39; Peoples and Bailey 2015, 31).

Pertaining to formal structure, norms may be informal and un-codified or formal and codified. Thus, from an anthropological perspective such rules go beyond public norms that are consciously followed or broken. Most of these rules are hidden below the surface. A bank robber is clearly behaving in a deviant way by breaking a formal law, but follows a lot of conventions unconsciously. He usually comes clothed to the bank, walking rather than crawling, utters his demands in conventional language, and makes his getaway on the right side of the street: "The man who robs a bank is, in sociological terms criminally deviant. But the anthropologist can perceive him as a routine-bound conformist as well" (Keesing and Strathern 1998, 289).

The content of social norms can thus be seen as *expected* behavioral regularities. In research about norms, it is important to establish a clear understanding of "expected" between scholars studying human animals and researchers studying non-human primates. In non-human primate societies, norms can only be clearly observed in regular behavior in recurrent social situations (Kappeler et al., this volume, 71; Mertens, this volume, 107). At first sight, in studying non-human primates, "expected" behavior can only mean behavior likely to occur *in the view of the scientist*. But the analysis of recurring sanctions (e.g., studies on "punishment") by social partners might also provide insight into social expectations of the non-human primates themselves. Among scientists studying human societies, the "expected" does not mean "likely to occur," but socially "desired." The expected way of life is related to endorsed rules and conventions. This implies that the individual has intentions and can decide between several options of action. Thus, the behavior expected is a form of intentional action. It is related to consciousness and sense-making. Thus, norms can be seen as the culturally organized ought and want, as the "grammar of society" (Bicchieri 2006).

If we speak of *social* norms, the "social" may refer to their form or their content. If the "social" is understood as content, social norms have other social beings, mainly members of the own we-collective, as their addressees. The strict sense of the term *social* norms thus would exclude behavior of an individual vs. non-social entities, e.g., handling material artifacts or acting in the natural environment. A large part of social norms is about social exchange between people of one's own society. The "social" may also refer to the distribution in a society (social as societal). That is important, as humans are not only individuals (organisms) in social populations, but persons (complexes of social relations) in *specifically* configured *social structures* (Radcliffe-Brown 1935). All human beings not only live in a social way, but also are embedded in *one* local/historical society. The existence of such a particular social structure in every society is a human universal (Antweiler 2012a, 111–6; 2016).

To sum up, norms as understood here are deontic strictures: socially or culturally generated ideas about appropriate behavior, the "ought." This understanding of norms is different from the second meaning of "norm," the descriptive or statistical norm, the greatest frequency or the average of a variable. Only the second refers to actual observable behavior. While we should always keep these two understandings apart

(Bicchieri and Muldoon 2011, 1), they are often causally related. The normative is re-lated to the normal, to normality: it is the "normal," which often is cognized, phrased, perceived, and learned as the good and right or the "natural" way of thinking, feeling, or dealing with things. It might be that it is this link which characterizes normativity as a specific primate mode compared to other animals. The following aspect of norms, meta-norms, may be specific for the human primate.

4. Meta-Norms: Rules for Breaking Rules

Despite cultures existing as shared ways of life largely governed by norms, people differ in their interests, knowledge, understanding, and beliefs. Intra-cultural diversity is a normal state of affairs, even in small societies. Beyond that, norms are often con-tradictory, so that individuals have to decide about compliance (Nanda and Warms 2015, 100). In some societies anthropologists have documented unspoken rules saying which norms must be obeyed strictly and which are more flexible. Typically there are "rules for breaking rules" (Edgerton 1985; Peoples and Bailey 2015, 33). Obeying traffic lights and vehicle lane markers in Turkey or in Rio is not regarded a necessary requirement for proper driving. These officially valid norms are perceived by actors as mere suggestions open to negotiation. The negotiations are culturally specific and themselves rule-based (Lull 2000, 86).

Norms are interpreted in situational ways in all human cultures. Some norma-tive rules have socially established exceptions and some are only loosely enforced. Edgerton describes several other examples in which rule violations are not deemed truly deviant. But these violations are patterned and themselves follow rules. An eve-ryday example from my own experience in German public traffic might illustrate this. It is usually tolerated when a car driver drives into a one-way street in the wrong direction to enter an empty parking space. This is tolerated by bystanders, if, and only if, it is the first parking space at the very beginning of the street. People would not tolerate it if the driver entered the street in the wrong direction to get a parking space in the middle of the street. The implementation of a rule in a social situation involves an interpretation of its relevance.

Powerful examples of institutionalized rule-breaking are the annual Rhenish car-nival, the carnival in Brazil, and other carnivalesque celebrations throughout the world. In these instances the "normal" norms are suspended temporarily, but they are exchanged for other norms. During carnival, usual norms are typically inverted, espe-cially rules related to gender and social status or rank. Women may act according to ways usually normative for males, poor people are allowed to behave as kings, invisible nobodies become stars. This "social inversion" is temporary, but in Brazil aspects of inversion pervade situations and settings at other times, e.g., during military parades and religious processions (DaMatta 1979). This gender and rank dimension points to a general pattern of perception and public reaction to norm violation. In general, the reactions to violations of social norms are usually related to the status of the violator. Public reaction also depends on the account of the violation given by the violator. The account-giving itself is akin to negotiation and the negotiation has its own rules (Edgerton 1985, 13–20). This aspect is highlighted if the breaking of a social norm is perceived in different cultures through media worldwide. An example is the Clinton sex scandal, to which the reactions varied enormously within the US and elsewhere, e.g., in Mexico and China (Lull 2000, 86).

We have no clear data, but it may be that rules for breaking rules are universal. Thus, rule-breaking is not unbounded but rule-based in itself. There are socially shared meta-rules for breaking rules. This aptly demonstrates that humans are primates that are hell-bent on creating social norms. There are some exceptions. Some "simple" traditional societies and even more complex traditional societies value individualism quite highly, as does traditional Thai society. This culture has been portrayed as a "loosely structured" social system. But even in those societies there are some strict social norms, e.g., of respect to elderly and of etiquette in greetings (Embree 1950; Evers 1969; Bunnag 1971). Whereas anthropologists could not, of course, find societies entirely without norms, there are some societies with very few norms. Interestingly, in these cases even these few norms are not justified by any appeal to ideals (Taude in Papua New Guinea, Hallpike as documented by Christopher Hallpike in unpublished material).

Functionally, norms fulfill the task of making behavior predictable. They do so both for other people as well as for the actor himself. The more general function is to reduce complexity in understanding other persons and in decision-making about social behavior. On the collective level, norms function as devices to get group members to conform to expectations and to obey authorities: social control. What implications does the functional importance of norms hold for behavior among individuals in human collectives?

If social norms are functionally so important for societies, they have to be obeyed. Since violations of norms are commonplace, compliance clearly cannot be regarded as automatic. There are several options and varieties of installing obedient behavior. Social control of the individual may be done either through sanctioning disobedience or through internalized social control via norm socialization. The latter often results in either habitual, less conscious norm-following behavior or in more reflected self-obligation, itself resulting in appropriate acting. Since norms are crucial for societal stability, compliance has to be socially organized or implanted in the individual, or both. Socialization or enculturation is one important and universally found mechanism.

5. Enculturation of Norms: Cultures Collaborate with the Brain

In addition to social control via punishment of deviance in adults, norms may be internalized in the brains of infants and children. The task of a society is to establish a form of internalized social control through which adult individuals make themselves conform to cultural expectations. The norms have to be made a part of their personalities (Eller 2012, 209). In anthropological studies the learning of norms by the individual is usually dealt with under the rubric child-rearing. Since Margaret Mead's pioneering 1928 study *Coming of Age in Samoa* (Mead 1971), child-rearing as a topic has played an important role in anthropology. Studies within the "Culture and Personality school" (1920s–1950s) in cultural anthropology focused on the causal effects of child-rearing on typical modal adult personalities. The specific processes of social learning have since then been studied as "enculturation" or "socialization," these terms mostly used synonymously.[8]

Enculturation is the learning of culture by children from their parents or other members of their society. Within enculturation, infants and children are provided with spatial, temporal, and other orientations, including explicit normative orientations. Enculturation begins soon after birth and may be lifelong. It is to a significant extent intended to mold behavior in later life in a way that conforms to norms. Indirectly, socialization begins already during pregnancy, and in some societies the infant is taught appropriate forms of address even before he or she has uttered its first word (Lancy 2015, 173). The main socializing agents cross-culturally are members of the household, initially in all societies the newborn's mother. Later, other household and/or family members come to play socializing roles, as well as non-kinfolk and professionals. Individual peers often play a crucial role in parenting, thus socialization is not only the transfer of knowledge between generations.

Enculturation practices involve many specific practices, how infants are held, carried, weaned, toilet trained, and nursed, how parents and other adults interact with children (e.g., with discipline or indulgence), the form of physical attention and love children receive from parents and other caretakers, how fathers are physically present and participate, kinds of behaviors that are punished and rewarded, how and by whom such sanctions are administered, methods used to teach kids basic skills, and work expectations placed on children (Peoples and Bailey 2015, 215). Enculturation

---

[8] Some authors use the term "enculturation" to emphasize the transmission of cultural knowledge from one generation to the next and thus leave out intra-generational social learning (Haviland et al. 2014, 128; Peoples and Bailey 2015, 25). Other anthropologists define "socialization" as "teaching young people norms in a society" (Ferraro and Andreatta 2010, 329), thus leaving out non-normative dimensions of socialization, e.g., learning skills or learning about environmental conditions.

typically tends to be habitual and thus imprecise, presenting no blueprint for adult behavior (Scupin and DeCorse 2006, 97). Cultural models of child-rearing are in most
cases unconsciously applied by parents or other socializing actors. Since child rearing
often is just caretaking, practices are not deliberately directed at raising ideal adults.
Instructions are often practical or situation-oriented, aiming, for example, to prevent
children from approaching a fire or a hot stove (Quinn 2005, 479).

As rare as teaching is in non-modern societies, it does occur in one area, namely,
instruction in good social manners and especially appropriate behavior vis-à-vis
kin (Lancy 2015, 172–3). Enculturation practices usually convey social norms specific for the society in question. Almost all anthropological research in childhood
and child care is particularistic, as the few textbooks and readers show (Rogoff
2003; LeVine and New 2008; Lancy 2015; cf. also DeLoache and Gottlieb 2000).
However, there are universal patterns in the ways in which cultures install norms
in children.

A rich source for universal patterns in the learning of norms are the few comparative studies of child-rearing. Some studies compare a limited set of geographically widespread and historically (almost) unrelated societies in detail, rather than
conducting broad cross-cultural comparisons (Whiting and Whiting 1975; Newman
1976; Whiting and Edwards 1988; Trommsdorff 1989; Munroe and Munroe 2001;
Röttger-Rössler et al. 2013). In a secondary analysis of field reports by anthropologists
and psychologists, Quinn (2005) compared child-rearing practices across several
non-Western societies. She reanalyzed them in a fine-grained way by close reading
and comparing them systematically.[9] Quinn's leading question is: What is it about
child-rearing that makes it so crucial for the formation of adult behavior and personality (selfhood)? Are there universal ways to raise children and, if so, *how* is child
rearing so effective everywhere in turning children into persons who know social
norms and conform to them voluntarily ("culturally valued adults"; Quinn 2005,
478, 507)?

Quinn used the concept of "cultural models" from cognitive anthropology. Cultural
models are shared cognitive representations ("schemas," "scripts"; Schank and Abelson
1977). Such default models function to make sense, interpret sensory input, and shape
behaviors. Mostly below the level of awareness and barely articulated, they are linked
to the shared acts and artifacts produced in a community. They are "automatic pilots"
that allow us to conduct our daily business while expending little mental energy
(Bennardo and De Munck 2014, 3–6).

---

[9] It should be noted that the original studies were conducted by anthropologists coming from a particularistic perspective and a concern with meaning rather than explanation. Thus, these studies were interested
in describing culturally specific models ("ethnotheories," "folk theories") and initially were not conducted
with a view to making universal claims of any kind.

One kind of such cultural models are cultural solutions to those routinely required tasks that the individual brain is ill-suited to solve. Here, the individual is usually assisted by other persons, because the task is complex, recurrent, and vital. Furthermore, the task is widespread enough within the population to make a common solution attractive. Installing social norms in the course of raising children mediates the solution to such critical, recurrent, widespread, and complex tasks in societies. A cultural model of child-rearing specifies (a) the desired kind of adults the children raised are to become, and (b) a set of practices to effectively socialize them to be the desired adult later. These ideal concepts of valued adults vary, and methods vary among communities, as the solution has to be suited to match local ecological and economic givens. Thus, they can be conceived as conditional strategies. On the basis of his account of cultural models, Quinn ties norm socialization to a conception of norms as *endogenous* products of individuals' interactions, a conception often dismissed in social science accounts (cf. Bicchieri and Muldoon's critique 2011, 1; cf. Ullmann-Margalit 1977).

Common forms of sanctioning misbehavior in children are beating, teasing, shaming, intensive staring at the child, gaze avoidance, pointing out the physical dangers of misbehaving, isolating the child from others, or leaving the child alone (Lancy 2015, 187–98). According to Quinn's reanalysis, these methods of reinforcing social norms vary in their combination and practice among the societies compared, but they share some traits: (a) experiential constancy, (b) emotional arousal, (c) general evaluation of the child, and (d) predispositional emotional priming (Quinn 2005, 480). Taken together, this limited set of child-rearing practices seems to be the main requirement of effective norm socialization.

First, norm-learning has to incorporate practices which maximize the constancy in the child's experience in learning important norms. This is achieved through regularity and repetition. This was shown exemplarily in an experimental field study on the Gusii agriculturalists in western Kenya (LeVine et al. 1994). In routine interactions, verbal formulas, like "smile, smile, smile!" are repeated, sometimes accompanied by making sounds for getting the child's full attention. The techniques are similar across societies but adapted to local traditions. In Gusii society, adults conversing rarely sit face-to-face, but side-by-side or at a 90-degree angle. Thus, mothers sometimes suddenly stop looking at their children in order to keep their attention in moments of affective display, thus marking an important juncture in interaction. The mother's averted gaze habituates the infant to be attentive to forms of behavior that will later be required of her in adult interaction (LeVine et al. 1994, 211, 213, 222; cf. LeVine and Norman 2001). In order to reach constancy, contradictory, extraneous, and diverting experiences are excluded, thus facilitating habituation or even embodiment. Besides giving implicit cues to appropriate behavior, explicit corrections of behavior are regularly administered through body language, e.g., by averting the gaze or by refraining from signs of approval, as in the unsmiling observation of a child's escapades. The measures taken are embedded in the usual cultural patterns of behavior that are regularly experienced by the children every day.

Child-rearing, secondly, includes practices that arouse strong emotions. This is done through teasing, frightening, shaming, and beating, or it is achieved through strongly praising. A common way of sanctioning children who transgress norms is to beat them. A second kind of sanction involves frightening them by referring to alleged attacks by animated beings like spirits. A common way throughout the world is to frighten the child with an adult dressed up as a ghost. Another common practice is to use foreigners—sometimes the anthropologist!—to frighten kids: "Here comes the foreigner (*bronyi*), she's going to take you away," as Quinn experienced in Ghana (Quinn 2005, 492).

The often harsh methods occur within an atmosphere of security surrounding the well-loved child. They are applied in a repeated manner and often packed in a co-narrated story into which the narrating adult includes the child. The children thus are motivated to learn and remember these normative lessons. As an example, Briggs reports detailed ways in which Inuit grandparents instill in a child a sense of belonging to the family and their values by showing intense mock-hostility towards the parents: "Your father is VERY BAAD . . . Your mother is VERY BAAD" (Briggs 1998, 127, cf. 94, 134). A related practice is to alternate abruptly between a soft and seductive timbre and a throaty tone of mock-hostility.

Thirdly, norm lessons are often linked with utterances expressing global evaluation of approved children's behavior. Approval or disapproval are themselves emotionally arousing, because they are linked to expectations of security and care held by parents or other members of the society (Quinn 2005, 491). These global evaluations are expressed through explicit labeling or demarcating: "Yes, you are a good girl." Beatings are accompanied, e.g., by saying emphatically, "This is a bad child," or signaling the withdrawal of love: "We don't want you." Learning norms involves unpleasant experiences and lessons that are abstract, complex, or otherwise demanding.

Thus, fourthly, child-rearing practices aimed at instilling norms train the child in emotional predispositions in order to prime her for subsequent learning (Quinn 2005, 502). Child-rearing goals always include norms for adequate expressions and regulation of emotional behavior. Moreover, emotions are often explicitly assigned a socializing function. Children are trained not only to adjust their behavior to norms, but also to similarly regulate their repertoire of emotions such as anger and embarrassment. Thus, Quinn's term "predispositional priming" might be substituted by *socializing emotions* to convey the socializing agency of emotions (Röttger-Rössler et al. 2013, 3–6).

An example is enculturation aimed at raising children to become a person sensitive to feeling a specific form of shame (*malu*) if, e.g., the Malay norm of respect explained in section 1 has been violated (Goddard 1996; Collins and Bahar 2000;

Fessler 2004; cf. Fessler 1995; cf. Fung 1999, 183–5 on Taiwan). This is achieved, e.g., through dramatizing narration that creates a sense of fear and vulnerability, so that the child becomes sensitive to specific sanctions applied later in life. Visceral dramatization primes the child to be emotionally sensitive to verbally stated sanctions later in life. In Minangkabau society in Indonesia and elsewhere in the Malay realm, it is common to hear people talk positively of children who can suppress anger (*marah*) and "already *know* how to feel ashamed" (*suda tahu malu*). If a transgression has become public, persons who are related to the norm violator are expected also to feel shame (vicarious shame). Thus, *malu* should be regarded as a blend of social fear with virtue (Röttger-Rössler et al. 2013, 19, 27; cf. Röttger-Rössler 2013).

The didactic function of all these affective techniques is not only to make norm socialization effective in general, but to raise motivation to learn the norms and to make the lessons lasting in their effect. The universal set of four features of effective norm socialization established by Quinn focuses on implanting norms by evoking emotions and thus using characteristics of the common human psyche. The four methods are built on different human psychological mechanisms which are used by the cultures: culture collaborates with the human brain's learning capacity in order to solve universal problems in norm socialization (Quinn 2005, 480).

The methods described in the preceding are often specifically planned, harnessed, and explicitly related to myths in instructive folktales. This may be astonishing, since even crucial parts of enculturation need no deliberate adult instruction, as reflected in the widespread (and realistic) expectation in most cultures that children learn to talk without explicit teaching (Ochs and Schieffelin 1984). But as humans differ and since the problem of norms everywhere is related to specific traditions and environments, every child-rearing community has to develop a solution to the universal problem of norm socialization (Quinn 2005, 479–80, 506). Child-rearing practices demonstrate a general insight regarding social norms. Whereas the normative orientation is universal, social norms are always related to the particulars of the natural and social environment. The particulars are linked to universal requirements and universal capacities. Whereas the substance of what they teach is immensely variable, we can expect that similarly designed mechanisms for the effective rearing of children are reinvented in any human community.

6. Beyond Socialization: Toward a Bio-Cultural Approach to the Socio-Genesis of Normativity at Supra-Individual Levels

Socialization is the principal mode of genesis of social norms at the individual level. To explain the existence and genesis of norms in societies on the societal meso- and macro-levels, we need explanations that go beyond socialization. This holds especially if norms in complex societies are to be explained. Due to limitations of space, I cannot go into sociological attempts to explain the slow and unintended historical development of collective norms or the socio-genesis of normativity in human evolution (Niedenzu 2012).

Crucial questions about norms and their genesis remain unresolved if we restrict our analysis to culturalist or conventional anthropological or sociological approaches. Other proximate and ultimate causes (Pagel 2012; Antweiler 2012b; Nesse 2013) have to be taken into account if we want to answer the following questions in depth: why is norm-orientation ubiquitous in human individuals and human societies, and why is all this socialization business needed? Why are some norms learned more easily and quickly than others (e.g., ethnocentrism and racism vs. cosmopolitan behavior or anti-racist norms)? Which other types of social learning are there beyond socialization? What is the link between preparedness, imprinting, and universals in norm socialization (cf. Bayertz, this volume, 171)? Anthropology could learn here from recent refinements in primatology (Hoppitt and Laland 2012). What constraints are imposed by organismic and systemic requirements? What factors generate cross-cultural similarities or near-universals? Universals can be generated not only through genes, but also via global diffusion, independent invention, and other factors (Antweiler 2012a, 155–85). What are the constraints on norms resulting from the sheer complexity of modern societies? What is normativity's role in human and non-human niche-construction?

To answer more ultimate questions, anthropology has to go beyond an understanding of human nature confined to traits specific to humans (Roughley 2005). We have to see human nature as including characteristics shared with other primates (Paul 2006; Meyer 2010, Boehm 2012; Sanderson 2014). Despite their tremendous variation, human societies are a variant of primate communities at the end of the day (Rodseth et al. 1991). Norms become a necessity under certain conditions: (a) the relevant organisms are egoistic but dependent on cooperation (they need sociality); (b) many non-acquainted individuals are living together (this requires that their behavior is controlled and coordinated); (c) organisms are not sufficiently determined (open programs, no strict biotic norms, in contrast, e.g., to panic reactions). These conditions are only given if certain cognitive capacities exist: only if organisms have the capacity for consciousness are they able to decide and thus pursue options intentionally. Expectations about own or others' behavior following from norms require the faculty of anticipation. In comparison, capacities for a theory of mind and empathy seem less important.

A basic conceptual challenge pervading this book is that, whereas "norm" is a core concept of the social sciences and humanities, norms (in contrast to morality) hardly belong to the conceptual toolkit of evolutionary human sciences (sociobiology, evolutionary psychology, evolutionary ecology, primatology). Even more problematic is the different understanding of "expected" in notions of norms as expected behavior. In cultural anthropology, the core of norms is seen as positively *evaluated* action which is expected *by social co-actors*. If the term "norm" is used by biologists at all, this most often refers to behavior expected by the researcher as the average or typical behavior.

The theoretical challenge, as I see it, is to analyze the causal entanglement between usual or average behavior and socially expected behavior. The basic methods problem lies in the differing empirical basis due to the different communicative abilities of the subjects studied. Whereas cultural anthropology and the humanities have a chance to approach at least a large part of social norms (as cognitions) relatively directly through language, researchers on non-human primates have to infer norms wholly on the basis of observed behavior, material traces of behavior, or materialized culture in artifacts.

5

On the Identification and Analysis of Social Norms and the Heuristic Relevance of Deviant Behaviour

Karl Mertens

A long-standing view in philosophy and sociology is that social norms are to be exclusively attributed to human beings.[1] According to this view, social norms—or even normativity as a whole—and anthropology are closely linked. Human beings—in contrast to other animals—are able to develop forms of social organisation that are guided by social (and other) norms. Recent empirical research, however, has shattered this picture. In particular, advances in primatology research have challenged the standard view according to which normativity in general, as well as the tendency towards social normativity in particular, is something specifically human.

In order to respond to the challenge posed by this new research, it seems helpful to sketch how the questions addressed in this context could be answered. The core idea seems to be easily outlined: since both our concept of normativity and our understanding of specific forms of normativity refer back to human life, we first need to clarify the idea of human normativity.[2] Accordingly, research into both humans and

---

[1] For example: "Only humans—instinctually impoverished, biologically underdetermined and environmentally determinable beings—are the bearers of social norms" (Peuckert 2010, 215; thanks to Neil Roughley for the translation). The origin of this view is Arnold Gehlen's theory of institutions. In most cases, the relevant contributors to the sociological and philosophical discussions about social norms simply presuppose that social normativity is (exclusively) a phenomenon of human societies (cf. e.g. Goffman 1971; Bicchieri 2006).

[2] This is explicitly formulated in Kappeler et al. (this volume, 67): "In our exploration of equivalents and precursors of social norms in non-human primates, we first characterise social norms in humans and distinguish them from related processes in order to derive essential behavioural elements that can be operationalised and studied in non-verbal species such as primates." This methodological decision is already made by Aristotle (cf. Historia Animalium I 1, 487a 11–4; I 6, 491a 14–23).

animals has the same starting point. But there is a difference in their focus. If we want to investigate normativity as a specific characteristic of human beings, we should try to delineate the *necessary* conditions of normativity, forming a concept of normativity that encompasses all the different kinds of norms that can be found in human life. In this context, the clarification of specific forms of normativity as they are revealed in social, moral, or linguistic norms—but also, for example, in juridical or other institutional norms—is a second step. In contrast, if we want to sketch a concept of normativity that may be successfully applied to animal research, we should concentrate on the *sufficient* conditions of normativity, if any. By reference to these conditions, we should be able to recognize whether certain animal social behaviours are guided by norms or not.[3] Since animals are not capable of linguistic expression, the desired criterion (or criteria) of normativity must be independent of the human faculty of language. An additional prerequisite is that human observers acquire evidence that animals evaluate behaviour normatively from their own point of view (and not simply from an anthropomorphic perspective, which is superimposed on them).

In line with these considerations, I will suggest that a suitable candidate providing the desired sufficient condition of normativity is the concept of sanction.[4] A sanction is a specific kind of behaviour performed by members of a social group in response to a behaviour of one or more other members that fulfils or violates the normative standards of the social group. Therefore, sanctions may consist either in forms of praise (including reward), or in forms of rejection such as disapproving, ignoring, ending cooperation, or punishing.[5] For methodological reasons, which shall be clarified in what follows, negative sanctions seem particularly useful for studies of animal behaviour. If we adopt corresponding lines of inquiry, the exploration of normativity must deal with social norms that are constitutively joined with negative sanctions—or more precisely, with the risk of negative sanctions. This terminology needs a brief explanation: A social norm in a rather broad sense is every norm that is constituted or used in social interaction. In contrast, I will use the term "social norm" in a narrower sense (as characterised in the preceding) in order to single out those special norms that require sanctions if they are violated.[6]

---

[3] The distinction between "necessary" and "sufficient conditions" should be understood in the strict logical sense of, respectively, *conditiones sine qua non* and *conditiones per quam*.

[4] The relevance of sanctions to our understanding of norms is also stressed by Kurt Bayertz (this volume, 166): "sanctions presuppose the validity of a norm."

[5] The positive and negative concept of sanction is mentioned, for example, in Goffman (1971, 95): "A social norm is that kind of guide for action which is supported by social sanctions, negative ones providing penalties for infraction, positive ones providing rewards for exemplary compliance."

[6] This understanding of social norms is also found in important sociological and philosophical contributions (cf. e.g. Goffman 1971; Miller 1997, 2001; Popitz 2006). Other authors relevant to this discussion operate with a broader concept of social norms, which also includes norms without risk of sanctions. Cf., for instance, Bicchieri and Muldoon who characterise social norms as a "kind of grammar of social interactions" which "is not the product of human design and planning" (2011, introduction). In contrast to

In the following, I would like to deal with these issues in two stages. First, focusing on social norms encountered in human societies, I am mainly interested in determining the essential characteristics, i.e. the individually necessary and conjunctively sufficient conditions, of social norms in the narrower sense defined earlier. In particular, I will examine the difference between social and other norms or rules (which are similar to social norms, but imply another relation to sanctions) (sections 1–4). Second, I will make some methodological remarks regarding the analysis of social norms (section 5) and will address the elementary question of how it is possible to define adequately the normative character of a social order in which we do not participate. Here I will identify the distinctive sign of the implicit presence of social norms which guide human societies and which might also inform the social behaviour of animals. This sign can be made particularly clear by considering social reactions to individuals disobeying or violating what is requested on a normative level.

1. Two Examples of Social Norms

Let us consider the following situation: Paul is late to meet with Paula, his wife. It is not the first time that this has happened. Thus, Paula is understandably quite angry. She clearly manifests her disapproval to Paul by complaining about his tardiness. From Paula's point of view, her anger is based on the combination of at least two conditions: first, Paul should come on time and he fails to do so repeatedly; second, Paula holds Paul responsible for his coming late, i.e. he could have done otherwise. For his part, Paul may excuse himself by mentioning circumstances that prevented him from arriving on time. For example, he could assure her: "I am very sorry about my late arrival, but my boss held me back for an important order." Naturally, this will not be the end of the story. For instance, Paula could blame him for his inability to say "no" to his boss, adding that there should be something more important than his work and his boss, namely herself, his wife, etc.

Another example: Philippa and Philip are invited for dinner by their friends Paul and Paula. Paul has prepared a delicious soup which has already been placed on the table. In order to put the main course in the oven, he shortly leaves to go to the kitchen while Paula and Philippa are talking. After a hard day, Philip is quite tired. Thus, he is not very interested in joining the conversation, and he is ravenously hungry. So, immediately after sitting down, he takes a few spoons of soup. In this situation we would expect that someone, probably Philippa, will rebuke Philip because of his impoliteness.

Both situations share some important features. They present violations of norms, more precisely: of social norms, which govern social behaviour in a particular society.

"social constructs" like "conventions" or "descriptive norms," Bicchieri understands social norms as "norms that emerge through the decentralized interaction of agents within a collective" (Bicchieri 2006, x).

Additionally, the reactions of the involved persons converge: in both cases we have forms of social disapproval. Of course, both examples would have to be altered if they took place in other social or cultural contexts. Standards of punctuality and customs of eating are extremely different from society to society, from culture to culture. But regardless of the society and culture in question, there are almost always some norms that define the frames of punctuality or socially acceptable behaviour during a dinner. One should note one notable difference between the relevant norms in our two examples. Whereas punctuality seems to be a norm more or less valid only in certain parts of the world, like Central and Northern Europe, North America, and Japan (Payer 2009, 162), the norm requiring that persons invited to a dinner should wait for a signal from their host before starting to eat seems to be more widespread. In any case, it is difficult to imagine societies in which the second type of deviant behaviour would not be subject to reproach at all. Even in cases where people meet for dinner without being invited by someone (at least by someone who takes part in the dinner), they regularly communicate by means of words or gestures about the beginning of the meal. If someone does not take part in this communication—e.g. by starting to eat when his or her plate has been served, without paying attention to the others—he or she would be regarded as an impolite person.[7]

At first glance, the chosen examples seem to be inapt to guide the question of how to approach the (possible) normative dimension of animal groups or societies, because in the cases sketched in the preceding the disapproval concerning the norm-deviant behaviour is verbally expressed. However, a closer look reveals that this objection is misleading. Even in human societies—for which the faculty of speech certainly is a constitutive condition—the verbal blame of a norm-deviant behaviour is only one instrument of social reaction, and in certain cases a rather weak one. This becomes clear if we slightly modify the original examples. For instance, suppose that the person repeatedly arriving late is a superior who is intentionally delaying meetings with staff. In the second example, suppose that the participants of the dinner are not acquainted with one another (for instance, they are new colleagues from different cities). In these new cases, perhaps nobody would express any verbal disapproval or refutation. What the participants say may even conflict with their attitude towards a person who ignores

---

[7] This seems to be a globally valid norm, comparable to the norm that people who meet should greet one another (cf. Goffman 1971, 73ff.; cf. Mertens 2013). However, there are forms of meeting that do not necessarily involve being introduced to or greeted by other persons present (e.g. a concert, a lecture or a play); similarly there are also forms of coming together in order to eat (like a quick lunch in a canteen at the working place) which do not imply the norms at play in dinner invitations or in cases of dining together by mutual agreement. But these cases are rather instances of individual actions in a social context: sitting next to each other with someone and eating your lunch in a canteen does not constitute an example of "eating together" (understood as a collective action). It would be interesting to ask whether personal greeting before a dinner is a reliable signal implying the norm that the dinner should only start after a certain kind of agreement about the beginning of the meal.

or violates a social norm.[8] However, supposing that the social encounter is not episodic, and that the respective group is (or becomes) part of an enduring social world in which the persons are involved,[9] the behaviour towards the person who does not follow the respective social norm will change. Perhaps the members of the group mutually show their disapproval by nonverbal facial expression or gestures. Especially when a person repeatedly behaves in a norm-deviant manner in a given situation, the other group members will try to avoid further situations which provoke or encourage such behaviour. In the worst case, they will, if possible, simply not attend further meetings or dinners with the norm-violator. This will be obvious in the case of persons of the same social status. But even persons who are socially subordinate to a norm-deviant superior have options for responding or even retaliation consistent with their subordinated status (for an interesting example see Spittler 1967, 43f.). In short: even in human societies, the reactions to a norm-deviant behaviour are not purely verbal but essentially demonstrated by a corresponding social behaviour.

2. Social Norms versus Conventions, Customs, and Moral Norms

In order to establish a broad consensus on the conceptualisation of social norms, I will follow the lead of two authors who deal with social norms in different theoretical contexts: Heinrich Popitz, a sociologist inspired by maxims of phenomenological analysis (Popitz 2006), and Seumas Miller, an analytical philosopher (Miller 1997 and 2001, 123ff. [enlarged version of Miller 1997]). Their characterisations of social norms fundamentally converge and even supplement each other in some essential points:[10]

(1)   Social norms generate regularities in social behaviour (cf. Miller 1997, 211, 223; Popitz 2006, 78ff.).

It is important to explain more accurately how social norms generate regularities. Here we may distinguish between, on the one hand, behavioural regularities, which are

---

[8] Cf. Spittler (1967, 17f.) who highlights that, in order to discover social norms guiding a collective behaviour, one should be sceptical about the linguistic utterances given as answers to questions about the validity of accepted norms. This also seems to be a good heuristic maxim in analysing the social norms which persons in the previously mentioned social situations follow.

[9] In order to evaluate how a social group's reactions towards a non-accepted behaviour guide social norms, it makes sense to focus on more fixed social relationships rather than on transient social groups in which the interest to enforce a social norm is weaker (cf. Spittler 1967, 23f.).

[10] In the following passage, I try to combine the considerations of Popitz and Miller. The sequence is nonetheless focused on the key ideas of this chapter and departs from Popitz as well as Miller where necessary.

explained in terms of further descriptive features of the agents or contexts, and, on the other hand, regularities that result from rules or norms.[11] Examples of the former are natural laws or basic social interactions (like the anticipatory behaviour of pedestrians accidentally heading towards one another in a crowded street) (cf. Goffman 1971, 5ff.). Examples of the latter may be the social behaviour that is performed by people following rules (like traffic rules, rules of etiquette, etc.). Whereas regularities of convergent social behaviour may merely be stated, rules or norms confront agents with pressures of "must," "ought," or "should" (Hart 1961, 8ff., esp. 9f.). Thus, norms or rules are reasons for performing actions of a certain type and avoiding actions which are not compatible with the relevant rules or norms. This implies that deviant behaviour is possible in principle. Whereas a wrong description of mere regularities provides a reason to correct the description, rules which are not followed provoke protest, correction, or punishment. With this terminology in mind, it is important to emphasise the normative character of social norms:

(2)   Social norms set standards that generate public reasons for special types of required social behaviour in the light of the fact that divergent behaviour is possible in principle.

Relying on a rule or a norm is a public affair. As a matter of principle, we never decide about such rules on our own—as we can say following the lead of Wittgenstein and Winch (Wittgenstein 1953; Winch 1958). Rules or norms are only available in a society which prescribes how to do something correctly or adequately. This can be noticed in the case of norm-deviant behaviour because every kind of rejection of behaviour for normative reasons implies a reference to a social awareness, manifested in the behaviour of the respective social group. This is of principal methodological relevance, particularly if we ask whether there is a normative dimension in animal behaviour. For, to address this question, we first need to take into account the behaviour of the whole group. This is the reason why we cannot state that a particular behaviour is non-compliant to a normative order if we only investigate forms of individual rejection of a behaviour. Protests, disapprovals, or even punishments *can* be expressed and performed from an individual point of view (an individual person or animal protests against the behaviour of another person or animal). However, disobeying or violating a rule or norm implies that every individual protest is governed by the awareness of the group.[12] As a consequence, for heuristic reasons, in order to capture the dimension of normativity, it

---

[11] The following clarification of the concepts of "rule" and "norm" follows Glock 2010, 91f.; see also Antweiler (Chapter 4 in this volume, section 3) and Glock (Chapter 15 in this volume, section 2).

[12] That a (moral) ought requires "the will of a social group," is also stressed in Bayertz (this volume, 163).

is essential that we observe the social behaviour not only of second parties as "those immediately affected by actions of a first party," but also of third parties as "uninvolved bystanders."[13]

Now it becomes clear that the examples I have given need to be more extensively described if we want to take them as paradigmatic for social norms. Thus, it is characteristic that Paula, for instance, may complain about Paul's repeated lateness when she talks to her friend Philippa. Similarly in the second case, we could develop the situation a little bit and imagine that the hosts, Paul and Paula, or Philippa will talk about the incident later with uninvolved friends and express their indignation at Philip's behaviour. Gossiping is certainly a good indicator of the presence of effective social norms.

The public dimension is a necessary condition of social norms. It provides social expectations which can be expressed through the following interactive, temporal, and evaluative aspects:

(3)   The conformity of the behaviour performed by individual members of a social group at least partly depends on the norm-compliant conduct of the other members of the group. (Miller 1997, 211)

(4)   The regular and repeated behaviour of agents in compliance with a social norm sets important standards for how social agents act, insofar as the latter are geared to the expected behaviour of other persons in the future. (Popitz 2006, 76)

(5)   In addition, the expected behaviour is socially desirable, while deviant conduct is socially undesirable. (Popitz 2006, 81)

These five aspects, however, are not distinctive or specific characteristics of social norms, because they are largely shared with conventions or customs. Customs as well as conventions are likewise rules or norms producing regularities of social actions. In establishing the fact that people typically perform certain types of behaviour in certain corresponding situations, customs and conventions create a space of expectable and desirable social behaviour which is anchored in norm-compliant conduct within a social group or even in a whole society.

---

[13] Cf. on this distinction Kappeler et al. (this volume, 71), who rely on Rudolf von Rohr et al. (2011). However, Kappeler et al. also stress the difficulties in interpreting third-party interventions. In their contribution they come to a sceptical result. The importance of "third-party norm enforcement," "third-party punishment," or "impartial indignation" is also argued for in Chapters 6, 7, and 11 in this volume by, respectively, Schmidt and Rakoczy, van Schaik and Burkart, and Roughley. Regarding the existence of normative attitudes in the social behaviour of non-human primates, Schmidt and Rakoczy also draw a negative conclusion.

If we follow David Lewis, *conventions* can be considered as rules which solve problems of coordination when agents have to organise cooperative actions:[14] How should one go through a narrow door (e.g. in an elevator)? How should I buy a loaf of bread? What is the right way to start a football match? In each of these cases, there are fairly simple strategies for initiating cooperation. To pick up an example of Lewis: it may be a convention that in the case of a disrupted phone call the caller takes the initiative for the second call while the called person waits (cf. Lewis 1969, 5, 11f., 43f.). Whereas conventional rules in Lewis's sense can be reconstructed as rational answers to coordination-problems, there are other rules determining social behaviour which are socially accepted and followed for merely factual reasons. One sub-group of these rules are *customs*. The reason to follow a custom is just that we are part of a society in which the respective custom has to be accepted. For instance, in various societies and cultures certain holidays are celebrated in quite different ways. The established holidays and the forms of celebrating them certainly do not solve problems of coordination. Nevertheless, there are norms which set standards for such holidays and celebrations that require adequate behaviour on the part of the members of the respective society. Insofar as they are characteristic of a particular society (perhaps established and preserved for a long time), they become a signifi-cant part of the social and cultural identity of this society. However, it is important to emphasise the arbitrariness of customs as well as of conventions. As "shared, arbi-trary rules"[15] they have emerged in the horizon of—theoretically possible but not realised—alternatives.

Against this background, one might try to sketch an important difference be-tween conventions or customs on the one hand and social norms on the other hand: Following a custom or a convention implies a social awareness of alternative possibilities which is part of the social praxis. If someone acts contrary to convention or custom, she does something that she should not do. For example, she might not take into account the previously mentioned convention of calling again if a phone call is disrupted; or she might not use the cutlery for a dinner required by the custom of a specific society or culture. However, not following the respective convention or custom—particularly if this happens unintentionally—will be regarded by the other participants as a behaviour that could be acceptable within another social framework.

---

[14] Lewis 1969. It should be mentioned that this concept of convention is quite specific. Glock rightly states that "[t]his account does not capture what we standardly mean by a convention." And he continues: ". . . many conventions, for example some rules of etiquette and custom, do not solve problems of coordination" (Glock 2010, 92). Therefore, I want to distinguish between Lewis's concept of convention on the one hand and customs on the other hand, which are examples of a broader concept of conventions as analysed by Glock.

[15] Glock 2010, 94; cf. Turiel and Dahl, (this volume, 202-3), who distinguish judgements about contin-gent conventions from judgements about moral obligations.

Therefore, a person who somehow acts against a conventional or customary norm is simply corrected or reminded of the expected and desired way of acting. In contrast, someone violating a social norm will not merely be corrected or reminded to act in the desired way: her behaviour will rather be a matter of more or less explicit social blame, disapproval, or even punishment. In a certain way, it seems no exaggeration that in the case of violating a social norm, the social awareness of alternative possibilities is missing.

This difference between social norms and social rules like conventions or customs becomes clearer if we turn back to the reactions towards deviant behaviour we sketched earlier. Paula is angry about the tardiness of Paul not because Paul has broken what could be conventionally or customarily expected from him in a specific society. Paul's lateness is an affront to her as his wife. His behaviour does not manifest the kind of respect he owes to his wife. Therefore, she does not merely remind Paul of a convention or a custom. Rather, she stresses that Paul is obliged to act otherwise to her and that their relationship as husband and wife depends on this. Similar considerations apply to the second case. Starting to eat without any explicit signal from the host is not a mere ignorance about the usual way a dinner starts (which would be comparable with the lack of knowledge of how to use the appropriate utensils). Again, the failure implies a more fundamental lack of the respect that a guest should show to his host or that dinner companions should show one another. What is violated in both cases has a strong normative meaning. It is something which must not be done *at all*.

Hence it is necessary to mark the stronger obligational force of social norms in contrast to rules which are due to conventions or customs.[16] Concerning this point, we may consider a sixth feature which is discussed in the literature about social norms:

(6)   The normative dimension of social norms is experienced as a strong obligation.

In this context Miller states that the involved agents "believe or feel that they ought to, or more often, ought not to, perform the actions prescribed, or proscribed, by the norm" (Miller 1997, 211). In order to describe this experience of obligation, Miller characterises social norms—with reference to H. L. A. Hart—as "norms with (felt) moral/ethical or quasi-moral/ethical content" (Miller 1997, 211; cf. Miller 1997, 223; cf. Hart 1961, 86f.).

The normative force of social norms is felt as a particular obligation comparable to a moral obligation. It does not entail requirements merely contingently, i.e. in virtue of a society which is aware of possible alternative social orders. Social norms rather

---

[16] If we are interested in terminological fine-tuning we could differentiate between weaker and stronger normative obligations by distinguishing "rules" and "norms."

apply to the central order of a particular society. Therefore, acting against social norms is tantamount to an affront to the core of a society. As a consequence, such an affront generates strong feelings against persons who behave in a norm-deviant manner.

However, characterising this experience by reference to moral feelings is somewhat misleading. Social norms need to be further distinguished from moral norms. Paul's tardiness and Philip's behaviour at the dinner table are not moral issues but cases of a social upset. What is the difference? Moral norms imply that the required orientation of behaviour is independent of the social status of a person. Even if they refer to a particular social, cultural, or historical situation, moral norms claim to provide universal guidelines for acting and forbearing, equally applying to all members of the social group, society, or culture (for this claim of moral orientation see Mackie 1977, 83ff.; cf. Baier 1958, 195ff.). Keeping promises or telling the truth and even not betraying members of one's own criminal group (when we also speak about moral norms concerning a particular group) are requirements which are independent of the particular social status of the addressed persons. In contrast, social norms are essentially related to specific social roles; they are only valid with regard to the concrete status and relationship between social agents and do not claim indiscriminate universal validity for all members of a society. For instance, the requirement of punctuality does not equally apply to situations of waiting between persons standing in the relationship of a married couple and persons standing in an official or professional relationship. We treat a delay in waiting for the doctor differently than arriving late to a private meeting. Furthermore, the sketched social norm of waiting for the host's signal before starting one's meal depends on the respective social roles of host and guest. And even when there is no social disparity between a host and his guests, social norms governing the beginning of a common dinner take into account the role of participants in that dinner.

Whereas moral norms must be observed universally by everyone in a particular society (or even by all humans), social norms have to be followed in accordance with the agent's social role in a particular social and cultural context. Hence violating or shirking moral obligations may be understood as acting against an order which is collectively shared. Since moral acting is required from everyone (or at least from every member of a particular society), violations of moral norms will be criticised by everyone who is sensitive to moral obligations, even including the person deviating from the norm. In contrast, obligations of social norms only concern social role expectations. Therefore, even if social norms imply socially strong commitments, from an individual's point of view, distancing oneself from social norms is easier than from moral norms. Whereas the agent may distance herself from a social norm even if she outwardly adheres to it, this is not really possible in the case of moral norms. Following a moral norm as such entails the inner affirmation of the individual acting according to the norm.

Therefore, although the requirements of punctuality and being invited to a dinner may also imply moral questions concerning *mutual* respect or acknowledgement required from every member of a society, as social norms they are founded on differences among social roles in a particular society and culture. In the first of the previously sketched cases, punctuality is considered in relation to the social role of "being a husband," whereas in the second case politeness is considered in relation to the social role of "being a guest invited for dinner." Regarding these considerations, we may add a further condition for social norms:

(7)   Social norms tend to preserve the central order and hierarchy of a given society.

The reference of social norms to social roles is one of the main reasons which may explain conflicts between different social norms. Let us return to the example of Paul and Paula. Suppose further that although he is frequently late, Paul's lateness is unintended. Rather, Paul is to be held responsible for his tardiness as a consequence of his acting, more precisely: as a result of a particular failure. Somehow, Paul ought to have taken the possibility of coming home late into account when he decided to stay longer at work. In not doing so, he ignores a social norm, according to which he should have acted otherwise. By excusing himself for his late arrival, Paul obviously acknowledges the validity of the respective social norm. However, by mentioning the request of his boss to stay until the work is done, he refers to a competing social norm ruling the situation in question. He denies that his action is to be judged in the light of the social norm on which Paula is relying. In the conflict between arriving on time for the private date with his wife and the professional demands of his employer, he deems the latter as the one which has to take precedence.

The example clearly shows that different social roles are governed by different social norms with corresponding conduct expected in the respective areas of social action. Therefore, social norms often provoke conflicts for agents who are involved in different social interactions and subsequently bound by different commitments. These conflicts confront agents with the possibility that the refusal to do something which is expected in a particular field of action will lead to corresponding social reactions. Since agents are involved in many social roles, conflicts between social norms are necessarily predestined (Popitz 2006, 68). These conflicts are neither avoidable nor determinable by a clear hierarchy of social norms because such a hierarchy does not exist (Popitz 2006, 73f.). Instead, agents have to manage the task of making decisions which—although social roles are internalised and habituated (Popitz 2006, 73f.)—can be only reached by repeated acts of situational preference. Quarrel and strife, as well as discussion of the socially required behaviour, suggest that agents do not (and even cannot) simply execute what is required by social norms. Instead, they have to make decisions in social situations and in communication with others. This proves that the order created by social norms is flexible in application.

To go even a step further: on the one hand, social norms tend to establish expectable social interactions, thereby providing a stable and reliable order. On the other hand, this social order is changeable and always open (cf. Miller 1997, 225f.). In this regard we have to take into account two different possibilities. First, cases of conflicting social orientations like those sketched in the preceding show that the openness of the social order may be based on the orientation towards different conflicting social norms, when one violates one social norm by preferring a competing one. Second, there is also the possibility of modifying or reshaping the framework of normative rules themselves. For example, unprecedented social norms concerning the communicative availability of staff members have been established in the work sphere due to the increasingly widespread distribution of mobiles and smartphones. Meanwhile, there are many jobs bound up with quite strict requirements regarding the handling of emails or phone calls while not at one's place of work which are absolutely incompatible with the previously established practices concerning letters and phone calls.[17]

3. The Risk of Sanction as a Characteristic Feature of Social Norms

Up to this point our discussion has focused on the question of what is expressed in the forms of social blaming and disapproval towards violations of social norms. The previous considerations have shown us that the obligations of social norms that we feel and the corresponding social pressure to conform to them must both be understood through negation, i.e. by considering cases in which agents act against social norms. After all, the strong feeling of obligation and the social pressure to act in accordance with social norms is the consequence of a society which punishes everybody who acts against them. This is the key insight in the explanation of social norms provided by Popitz, which can be summarized as follows:

(8)   Actions governed by social norms are connected with the risk of sanction.

Deviations from the norm encounter the readiness of other participating agents to sanction the deviants. These sanctions may be realised in quite different ways, ranging

---

[17] To give another example: in the fifties and early sixties of the last century, a social norm in Germany prohibited unmarried men and women from living together under one roof. This social norm was ignored by many individuals and groups, especially by the younger generation in the sixties and in the following decades. As a consequence, this social norm has almost completely disappeared nowadays.

from a mere criticism or verbal blaming to stricter punishment like denial of further cooperation, etc. (cf., for example, Popitz 2006, 83ff.). As a consequence, the reference to sanctions distinguishes social norms from social rules like conventions or customs (cf. Popitz 2006, 69).

The previous characterisation of social norms has underscored their functional meaning. *First*, they provide social agents with expectations regarding the future behaviour of other agents. Thus, social norms make situations predictable and give agents confidence in their behaviour. Due to them it can be expected that desirable conduct is effectively performed by other agents. Social agency is only possible at all if social interactions of a particular kind can be reliably counted upon. Because of social norms, agents have good reasons to assume that an unfinished action which has already been initiated—or an action that should be done—will be carried out in the future. Without these expectations, a society would be, as Popitz states, "a queuing society" (*eine schlangestehende Gesellschaft*). Popitz gives the following explanation: "If nobody were to risk relying on assumptions about what other agents are going to do, social activities would have to be postponed until the man in front has done his part. Obviously, this would be an extremely slow society" (Popitz 2006, 77, own translation). For many actions it is necessary that others do certain things in advance in order to make these actions possible at all. In these cases reliability is crucial. For instance, if Paula has a date with her husband Paul, she must be confident that Paul will appear at the agreed place on time. Punctuality requires agents to act in such a way that others who are affected can count on those actions. Deviations meet with disapproval, provoking anger and perhaps imperilling future cooperation. These reactions show that social norms apply to a social sphere which has to be protected in a special way.

Second, if the former characterisation were sufficient, the distinction between social norms and conventions or customs would merely be a difference with respect to the forms of guaranteeing and enforcing the particular social behaviours. In this case, we would have to state that social norms in principle pursue the same social aims as conventions or customs, only by other—more precisely, by stronger—means. However, this view does not capture the specific character of social norms. The readiness to respond to norm-deviant behaviour by sanction effectively demonstrates a deeply anchored awareness that infringement of social norms endangers the stability of the society in an eminently severe way. Social norms are grounding principles for a society. They tend to stabilise the space of expectable behaviour which is constitutive for a society. Particularly they require respect for and acknowledgement of the obligations connected with the specific social role or status of interacting persons which are regarded as essential to society. Social norms thus tend to preserve a given social hierarchy. Because of this, a behaviour which is incompatible with a social norm is not merely corrected—as happens with behaviour violating conventions or customs.

In contrast, someone who violates a social norm manifests a personal deficit belonging to the agent herself. Therefore, sanctions eventually apply to a person who behaves in a norm-deviant way.

4. Social Norms versus Institutional Norms

Following the path laid out in section 3, the risk of sanction can be seen as a decisive condition of social norms. However, this condition is only a necessary one. This becomes clear if we compare social norms with institutional norms, which are also connected with the risk of sanction. As Popitz and Miller demonstrate, there are different forms of sanctions in the case of social norms and in an institutional context. To quote Miller once more: In contrast to institutional norms, social norms ". . . are not, qua social norms, explicitly formulated; nor do they, qua social norms, emanate from any formal authority or have any formal sanctions attached to them" (Miller 1997, 211). Therefore, we can introduce a further condition:

(9)   In the case of social norms there is no institution that guarantees the compliance of the relevant agents.

Paula, for instance, is not able to extort punctuality from Paul. She may criticise or reprimand him; she may show her anger and even break up the relationship with him. However, there is no institution which lets her force him to act in a certain way (possibly even against rival obligations felt by him). Neither is there any institution which makes it possible to enforce the norm that the guests should wait for the host's signal to start eating. In other words, normative requirements are not institutionalized. Institutional norms, in contrast, are linked to an authority that represents and enforces social obligations independently of individual desires.[18] Only by relying on an institutional context—above all in the sphere of law—is it possible to enforce the normatively desired actions and to punish forms of deviant behaviour.[19]

For instance, the requirement of punctuality is institutionally fixed in the work sphere and can be judicially enforced by sanctioning non-compliant conduct. When, for example, a person regularly shows up late for work, warnings, penalties, or even dismissal support the norm with force. In comparison with such institutional norms, the mere risk of social sanction seems relatively weak. However, without such an

---

[18] The institutional anchoring of norms requires a central authoritative body to which the exclusive use of sanction is confided for the sake of defending social norms (cf. Popitz 2006, 70). The frequently mentioned example of a social norm, left-hand or right-hand driving, is—due to its judicial enforceability—better regarded as an instance of an institutional norm.

[19] It should be mentioned that the relationship of a married couple comprises aspects of both a relationship governed by social norms and a legal relationship connected with institutional obligations.

(admittedly weak) risk of sanction, social norms would be nothing more than mere conventions or customs.

These considerations are important also in characterising the bearer, i.e. the subject of social norms. While, like laws, institutional norms are created, modified, or revised by the power of a legislative authority, social norms are developed and conserved by social practices that shape the respective norm through corresponding sanctions. Therefore, in the case of deviant conduct, the social pressure involved is neither organised nor formalised but is executed by the spontaneous reactions of individual social agents.[20] However, this setting has to be properly understood: it is the social group, even society itself (rather than its individual members) which collectively protects the observance of a social norm. Thus, the anonymous social collective is the bearer of social norms. As Miller points out, "the attitude of disapproval within the social group is . . . a collective attitude, rather than a mere aggregate of individual attitudes."[21]

If we consider the final condition (9) independently of the other eight conditions, we have merely a further necessary condition. For example, customs and conventions don't require institutions that enforce norm-compliant action. However, if we take the lack of institutional authority together with conditions (1) to (8), that provides us with sufficient conditions.

5. The Holistic and the Individualistic Account of Social Norms

In the final part of this chapter, I would like to make some remarks on the methodological decisions that are connected with the analysis of social norms. I will argue that we need both a holistic and an individualistic account of social norms. The following considerations are also intended to address the question of how to recognize norms (and particularly social norms) in the behaviour of animal groups.

Normally, we do not explicitly talk about social norms, but are rather just aware of them in the background. We do what has to be done when we act together; we are reliable partners in social cooperation; we are honest; we arrive on time; we know how

---

[20] Cf. Baier 1958, 127ff. Baier discusses the opposition between law and social norms with key concepts which are partially connoted otherwise in my contribution. He does not use the notion of social norms; however, what he explains in the context of considering "custom" corresponds to what I am characterising as social norms.

[21] This proposal has to be distinguished from what is called "social approval theory." While this conception locates the normative force of social norms in subjective interests to avoid social pressure, the normative force as sketched here does not depend on a subjective motivational context; rather, it is a norm which is "anonymously" available in a society. This consideration aligns with Miller (1997, 217ff., esp. 219ff.) Miller (1997, 223): "I conclude that the social approval theory fails to do justice to the collective character of the attitudes of approval and disapproval constitutive of social norms."

to behave when invited to dinner and we do not talk about confidential conversations in public. In this respect, social norms are mostly implicit and unobtrusive; they are effective but anonymous structures, taken for granted by individual agents. We do not decide, either deliberately or merely intentionally, to follow the normative obligations; we just do it because social norms are part of the unreflected order of the life-world governing our individual behaviour.

Since social norms are typically assumed unconsciously, they have to be considered from a collective or holistic perspective, providing a top-down analysis of social life that moves from the social whole to its parts. From such a perspective, we can explain, for example, the social behaviour of individuals by recourse to general structures of social life, like rules, norms, institutions, etc. As Martin Hollis has pointed out, there are two variations of this analysis (cf. for these and the following considerations Hollis 1994, 1ff.; 94ff.; 142ff.). On the one hand, we can analyse the effectiveness of social structures from an objective third-person perspective. In this case, we talk about social mechanisms, functions, and systemic structures which constitute social phenomena and govern social processes. To characterise this theoretical attitude Hollis uses the classical concept of "explanation" (*Erklären*). On the other hand, we can also take up the holistic or collective approach by speaking as social agents immersed in the processes and phenomena examined. In this attitude, we refer to holistic structures like rules or norms—and we do this as agents who are able to "understand" (in the terminological sense of *Verstehen*) social structures.

The fundamental problem for both varieties of the holistic account is that the analytical approach is opposed to the typically non-thematic, anonymous and even unconscious character of social structures in general and of social norms in particular. Thus, for methodological reasons, it is necessary to find a way to focus on something which otherwise would not be a focal point in our normal lives: How can we make explicit what is mostly implicitly at work in our everyday life? In answering this question, I would like to emphasise one point which has been addressed several times in my foregoing considerations: We become aware of the structures of our social world in general—and of the social norms guiding our cooperative actions in particular—by deviant cases, i.e. when something does not function as usual, when something goes unexpectedly wrong. Disruptions of normal conduct attract our attention and indirectly demonstrate the ordinary functions of the rules and norms guiding our social world. Therefore, these cases are of particular heuristic interest when it comes to analysing social norms. Hence, the collective and anonymous features of social norms become especially visible if we take a closer look at deviant cases of social behaviour.

It is noteworthy that the situations which make us aware of the normative force of social norms call attention to the norm-contradicting power of individual actions. In general, social norms are violated, but also developed, modified, or abandoned in social interactions by individual agents. Thus, social norms turn out to be changeable. As we have seen in the preceding, the analysis of such processes depends on examining social phenomena by recourse to individual agents and their behaviour. This may be a reason for what we could call an individualistic account of social norms, because it refers to individual agents. Following once more the lead of Hollis, we can state that individualistic accounts analyse social events and phenomena by using a bottom-up model (cf., also for the following, Hollis 1994, 1ff.; 115ff.; 163ff.): they assume that individuals and their actions are primary social facts. As with the holistic approach, two varieties of individualism may be distinguished here. Depending on the methodological attitude, we may pursue (i) individualistic explanation (*Erklären*) or (ii) individualistic understanding (*Verstehen*): Whereas (i) takes individual acting as an event to be described from the objective third-person perspective, adherents of (ii) are interested in social action from the point of view of the agents' experience. Accordingly, the social processes resulting from individual conduct are either (i) a kind of mechanism in compliance with natural or economic laws or (ii) a result of individual acting that is understandable only because we are ourselves deeply entrenched in the sphere of action.

Even if actions are governed anonymously by social norms, the analysis of these norms requires that we take into account the fundamental fact that human agents are individuals. As sketched earlier, this comes to the fore especially when agents are pulled in two directions by conflicting social norms—or when they become aware of the social pressure to do something in opposition to their individual preferences. In these cases, agents may deliberate about what to do and retain the option to act against the social expectations. Since there are always some individual agents who do not act in the way prescribed by existing social norms, these can be developed, modified, or revised. In other words, the norms themselves are subject to change. But also the survival of a social norm requires that individual agents adhere to it, either because they have internalised the corresponding way of acting or because they bow to the pressure it exerts.

However, if we try to examine social conduct based on the core concept of individual acting, neither of the individualistic accounts mentioned in the preceding, i.e. (i) and (ii), are capable of elucidating the meaning of the normative force in question. For instance, if we discuss the scene between Paul and Paula in an individualistic way, we could only sketch the sources of a quarrel that is provoked by the different individual interests and their partial (and mutual) disappointment either from an objective third-person perspective, or from the perspective of the participants in social acting. But in order to characterise the specific kind of criticism, blame, disapproval, and anger involved, we must refer to the normative social context for a married couple's social relationship. Otherwise, we could at most demonstrate that the interaction between Paul and Paula is based on an agreement between these two persons. But the disappointment is not simply a frustration about the collapse of an individual aim or about the ignoring of a private agreement between two agents; it is rather the

disappointment about the failure to comply with an expectable, socially fixed, principally reliable, and required norm belonging to the role of a husband.

In this context, Miller discusses Margaret Gilbert's famous example of "walking
together" as a paradigmatic case of a joint action and points out a basic problem.
His criticism focuses on the assumption that acting together provides a normative claim which Gilbert expresses as follows: "As long as people are out on a
walk together, they will understand that each has an *obligation* to do what he or
she can to achieve the relevant goal. Moreover, each one is *entitled* to rebuke the
other for failure to fulfil this obligation" (Gilbert 1990, 6). In contrast to Gilbert,
Miller considers several interpretations for the source of the normative force, eventually stating that they all fail to prove that the normative meaning in question
results from commitments based only on the joint action. Miller discusses three
possibilities: First, if the two persons walking together are friends, the normative
meaning "is generated by the personal relationship of friendship" (Miller 1997, 214).
Second, the normative obligation could follow from their job (for example, both
are police officers) (cf. Miller 1997, 215). Third, "there may in fact be a social norm
of politeness which requires people not to break with one another's company
without explanation."[22] In summary, Miller states that all of these options demonstrate that the source of normative obligation cannot be found in the joint action
of the two involved persons.

What strikes me here is that again, the forms of behaviour that deviate from expected
and acceptable social norms are of particular heuristic relevance. Such cases demonstrate that an approach which traces normative significance back to the commitments
of individuals cannot adequately analyse social norms.[23] In particular, their specific
normative force cannot be captured by an analysis of interaction between individuals
because the forms of criticism and disapproval are social sanctions that presuppose a
normative order which itself cannot be based on merely personal interactions. The
requirement of social norms is essentially anonymous and exceeds in principle the
individual springs of action.[24]

To summarise: the foregoing considerations are intended to show that a sufficient
analysis of social norms has to combine both the collective and the individualistic
account. This is due to the fact that the dependence of social norms on interactions
between individual persons, as well as the constitutive meaning of an anonymous

---

[22] Miller (1997, 215). Gilbert's attempt to sketch the sources of obligations and rights in dyadic interactions
is also critically discussed in Steinfath (this volume, 181ff.).

[23] Another argument against such an approach to social norms is demonstrated by Jon Elster (1990),
who stresses that social norms are not a matter of self-interest by pointing to social norms of revenge as an
example. Cf. Miller (1997, 218). See also Bicchieri and Muldoon (2011, sect. 2).

[24] That social norms are bound up in a form of collective intentionality is also pointed out in the initial
remarks in Schmidt and Rakoczy (this volume, 122f.).

normative framework, are particularly conspicuous when agents modify the norms governing social interaction—or even act contrary to them. Therefore, in looking at deviant cases it becomes obvious that both the individualistic as well as the holistic account are insufficient if they are used alone.

Taking into account these reflections on human normativity, we may ask whether the behaviour of animals, as understood through empirical ethological research, is guided by rules that accord with those discussed in the preceding. Empirical research in this area has to take into account both aspects: the behaviour of single members of the animal group or society and the holistic structures which their behaviour follows. Just as in the case of human conduct, deviant behaviour of animals is of particular heuristic relevance.

We can first revisit our earlier suggestion of the holistic account in the context of animal behaviour: namely, in animal behaviour a normative order could be effective without individual animals' being explicitly aware of it. The norm will only be clearly registered if an individual's norm-deviant behaviour provokes special kinds of sanctions. These sanctions must be structurally distinguished from merely individual disapproval or counteraction. Therefore, the reaction to a non-compliant behaviour must be public; this means that the reaction of the social group realises (or at least assents to) the sanction against the deviant. This is why the investigation of third parties' behaviour is of fundamental importance.

Such investigations certainly do not produce a methodological problem if we examine animal behaviour from an objective third-person perspective, i.e. if we approach social structures of animal research from the standpoint of a detached observer. In contrast, if the investigation of normativity were obliged—for methodological reasons—to consider understanding from a first- or second-person perspective as well, we would seem to reach the limits of empirical research into animal normativity. However, this need not be the case if we further explain and broaden our usual anthropocentric concept of understanding. One possible strategy could be sketched in accordance with proposals rooted in Anscombe's analysis of action and intention: namely, to approach behaviour or action from an agent's perspective is to refer to the intentional stance, i.e. to assume that a given behaviour is guided by a particular intention of the involved individuals. However, as a result of the problematic implications of what is called the introspective or private account, we cannot have recourse to the agents' experience or awareness of intending or willing—especially if connected with the concept of particular volitional acts (cf. Ryle 1949, 62ff. [chap. 3]; cf. Anscombe 1957). From an analytical point of view, therefore, to speak of intentional attitudes like "intending" or "willing" does not presuppose a methodologically privileged access to the intentional experiences of an individual; hence to call a behaviour "intentional" is only a linguistic reference, a kind of description of this behaviour (Anscombe 1957, all above sect. 4, 7ff.).

This is an important point, especially if we turn to the intentions of animals. Following the analytical account, we are able to talk about intentional attitudes guiding human or animal behaviour without needing to know what it is like to have an intention or will from the respective agent's point of view (cf. Bayertz, Chapter 8 in this volume). In so doing, we make animal behaviour understandable to us. This is no illegitimate anthropomorphism if we assume that such ascriptions are not arbitrary but must be evaluated in view of their suitability for a specific structure of animal behaviour. This evaluation of animal behaviour is also available for humans because we at least partly inhabit a common life-world and share some basic experiences with animals. Following this line of argument, we can, at least in principle, understand animal behaviour to a certain extent, namely as far as we share some elementary types of intentional behaviour. If this is true, we are not confronted with unsolvable methodological problems if we ask whether the interaction of animals is guided by norms.[25]

[25] I am very indebted to David and Therese Cory, who corrected my English text. In addition I am much obliged to Jörn Müller and Michela Summa for their critical remarks and helpful linguistic corrections of this chapter. Moreover, I am grateful to Neil Roughley and the other contributors to this volume for their instructive critique of a previous version of this chapter.

6

On the Uniqueness of Human Normative Attitudes

Marco F. H. Schmidt and Hannes Rakoczy

1. Introduction: The Descriptive and the Normative

All animal species, including humans, are subject to physical laws and evolutionary processes—things that are the case in a causal universe (i.e., descriptive facts). For instance, antelopes are threatened by predators, such as lions; humans cannot fly, but walk upright; and chimpanzees are mostly frugivorous and live in groups. But humans are special in that they are not just "causal animals." Humans also "ought" to do certain things, such as standing in line at the grocery store, accepting Euros as currency in some countries, or refraining from hurting one another.[1] It is undeniable that humans (understand themselves to) have rights and obligations, and create their own "laws"—social norms—to regulate and give meaning to socio-cultural life. In other words, humans are also "normative animals," and this is an essential aspect of human existence that cannot simply be argued away (Sellars 1963a). Not only that, many would contend that norms have played a key role in the evolution and maintenance of human cooperation, collaboration, social institutions, and culture (Fehr and Fischbacher 2004a; Boyd and Richerson 2005; Boyd and Richerson 2006; Gürerk et al. 2006; Chudek

---

[1] Note that according to some accounts, even phenomena at the individual or functional level are normative in some sense (e.g., entailing some sort of success or failure). Theorists discuss the normativity of meaning and intentional content (Kripke 1982; Wright 1986; Wedgwood 2007), such that, for instance, mental states are subject to rules of rationality and justification (e.g., beliefs "aim" at truth and can be evaluated via epistemic norms as justified or unjustified, Engel 2011; Wallace 2011a). For some, even biological functions are to some extent normative (Millikan 1990). Here, we focus on practical normativity (in particular, social norms) and its relevant deontic notions (e.g., "ought," "right," "wrong," obligations, and entitlements).

and Henrich 2011). Thus, shedding light on the ontogenetic and phylogenetic roots of human normativity is of vital interest not only for its own sake, but also regarding our understanding of major human "achievements," such as social order and organization at small or large scale, cooperation and collaboration among genetically unrelated strangers, or upholding (but also changing) group-wide values. In this chapter, therefore, we will review empirical work on the ontogenetic emergence of normativity in human children and on the phylogenetic question of whether there is evidence that our close living primate relatives (focusing on chimpanzees) have the capacity to understand normativity. We will argue that so far, there is no convincing evidence that non-human primates understand normativity or develop normative attitudes toward their conspecifics' actions. Hence, the proposal based on empirical grounds is that humans are, to date, the only normative species on Earth. Before looking at pertinent empirical work, it is important to lay out how we can construe normativity and delineate normative and non-normative phenomena in order to understand what it would take for a creature to be granted normative attitudes and thus be dubbed a genuine normative animal.

2. Key Aspects of Normativity

Most fundamentally, normativity requires capacities for intersubjectivity or *shared (collective) intentionality*, that is, the ability to share attention and mental states (e.g., intentions, goals) with conspecifics and thus to engage in shared intentional activities (Sellars 1963a; Gilbert 1989; Searle 1995; Meijers 2003; Tuomela 2007; Bratman 2009; Schmid 2009; Searle 2010; Schweikard and Schmid 2013; Carassa and Colombetti 2014).[2] The standard definition of social norms[3] reveals why collective intentions are so central to normativity: social norms prescribe or proscribe certain actions under certain circumstances for a given group of people (which might encompass a few to virtually all rational agents) and thus regulate everyday social interactions (Hechter and Opp 2001). That is, norms are collective phenomena that transcend individual perspectives, opinions, and non-collective mental states, such as individual beliefs, goals, and desires—they give agents reasons to act in certain ways independent of their particular interests or desires (Searle 2001). So it is not about what individuals

---

[2] Scholars disagree, however, as to where to locate normativity, that is, whether shared intentional acts inherently involve normativity (e.g., obligations and entitlements) or whether normativity is typically a result of shared intentional acts, potentially even instantiable only through language use (for overviews of different positions, see Schmid 2009; Schweikard and Schmid 2013). For the current purposes, however, the crucial point is simply that a creature needs to be able to share intentions in order to have or develop normative attitudes.

[3] In this chapter, we use the terms "social norms" and "norms" interchangeably and as umbrella terms that comprise all kinds of practical norms, many of which will be introduced further in the following.

intend, want, or desire, but about what "we" (as a group) do and do not do in a certain context.

Importantly, norms set *standards* of what counts as appropriate behavior in a given situation (Popitz 2006). This means that there is some level of abstraction or detachment involved insofar as a normative creature—an individual who is not isolated, but participates and shares intentions in a group of agents—would be able to assess (not necessarily explicitly or reflectively) a concrete act in the here-and-now in light of some "ideal" act, practice, or principle (Winch 1958; Pettit 1993).[4] Thus, we have the *possibility of error*—an action can be right or wrong according to some standard, and taking a normative attitude toward conspecifics' actions essentially means treating their actions as right or wrong (Wittgenstein 1953; Brandom 1994, 1997).[5] This also implies that the existence of alternative forms of behavior is central to normativity (in contrast to causal necessity where alternatives, such as choosing not to obey the law of gravity, are precluded). For some norms, often dubbed *conventional norms*, alternative forms of behavior would be equally possible and thus these norms are arbitrary (e.g., driving on the right vs. left side of the street); for other norms, however, alternative forms of behavior would physically be possible, but still be considered wrong (normatively speaking), due to the non-arbitrariness of these norms. For instance, prototypical *moral norms* pertain to issues of well-being, justice, and rights (Turiel 1983; Scanlon 1998; Roughley, Chapter 11 in this volume), and so it is not an arbitrary choice whether or not to harm others. The same logic applies to norms of instrumental rationality: agents should take the most efficient means to reach their ends (Korsgaard 1997), although other means are, of course, physically possible.

Closely related to the idea of a standard is the feature of *generality*. Norms prescribe or prohibit certain acts not just episodically, but in general, for all relevant agents and in analogous circumstances (e.g., shopper A, shopper B, shopper C, etc., should stand in line not just in grocery store A, but also in grocery store B, grocery store C, etc.). And so a normative creature would be able to take an impersonal perspective, make an inductive leap, and realize that she is merely one agent among many equivalent agents. That is, norms apply to oneself just as they apply to others (Nagel 1986). Norms, such as standing in line, often apply in one context (e.g., at a grocery store), but not in another (e.g., on a dance floor); norms are hence usually *context-relative*. Perhaps the

---

[4] See Roughley (this volume, 234–236) for an account of moral normativity in which a creature would assess an act in light of an "ideal" (emotional) attitude toward the concrete act observed.

[5] Of course, taking a normative attitude toward others' actions is itself prone to mistakes and thus subject to assessment, which might lead to an infinite regress. This is, however, an ontological issue about the nature of norms in general, and solutions have been proposed, for instance, by Brandom (1994), who opts for a third way between what he calls "regulism" (norms as propositionally articulated rules) and "regularism" (norms as mere non-normative behavioral regularities), the idea of norms and normative attitudes being implicit in social practices.

most distinctive feature of normativity is its "oughtness" or *normative force*: we "ought" to perform certain actions; we have normative expectations about what people (in our group or even beyond) ought to do in certain situations (Tuomela 2007; Chudek and Henrich 2011). Obviously, these expectations are not purely cognitive, but come with motivational force, not to describe the world, but to bring about certain states of affairs in the world. Therefore it has been proposed that descriptive expectations have a mind-to-world direction of fit, whereas normative expectations have world-to-mind direction of fit, a contrast that applies to beliefs (mind-to-world) and desires (world-to-mind), too (Searle 1983; Wellman and Miller 2008; Schmid 2011; Christen and Glock 2012). Finally, people apply sanctions (e.g., express disapproval) when others violate norms, and thus they *enforce* norms—at least partly because they are committed to their group's norms and value them as ends in themselves (Parsons 1951; Münch 1987; Sripada and Stich 2006; Rossano 2012; Schmidt and Tomasello 2012). Crucially—and this point is related to the possibility of error, the generality, and the normative force of norms—agents enforce norms even as disinterested third-party observers (Fehr and Fischbacher 2004a, 2004b).

Considering the preceding key aspects of normativity, we can state that a normative animal—an animal with normative attitudes—would be a creature that demonstrates an understanding, at minimum, of the following: normative force, generality, and the possibility of error. It becomes clear that the mere following of norms (or imitation of actions) is inconclusive; for a creature might just like to act in similar ways as others or desire to avoid sanctions, not at all understanding that actions can be right or wrong according to some norms. Much better evidence for a creature taking a normative attitude toward others' actions is third-party norm enforcement, since it reveals that the creature understands actions as subject to assessment and evaluation in social interactions (Brandom 1994, 1997).

3. Normative Attitudes in Human Children

Much historical and more recent research on children's understanding of normativity (in particular, morality) focused on epistemic aspects, that is, on children's knowledge about morality and different types of norms—typically investigated via interview methods (e.g., asking for children's explicit judgment of norm transgressions in hypothetical stories). Jean Piaget (1932) and his follower Lawrence Kohlberg (1969) characterized children as developing in stage-like fashion from irredeemably egocentric creatures that focus on their idiosyncratic needs (and follow norms to avoid sanctions by authorities) to genuine moral creatures that reason autonomously and objectively. More recent work, initiated by Elliot Turiel and colleagues (Nucci and Turiel 1978; Turiel 1978; Smetana 1981; Turiel 1983) found that young children's knowledge about different social domains (i.e., moral, conventional, and personal) is much more profound than previously thought. This work showed that by three to four years of age, children reliably differentiate between known conventional norms (that serve to sustain social order and organization, e.g., dress codes or classroom behavior) and known moral norms (i.e., issues of well-being, justice, and rights). For instance, children understand conventional transgressions as less severe, dependent on authority, narrow in scope, and less deserving of punishment than moral transgressions (Nucci, Saxe, and Turiel, 2000; Smetana, 2006; Turiel, 2006; for reviews, see Killen and Rutland, 2011; Turiel and Dahl, this volume, 202-203).

Here, however, we are interested in children's ability to exhibit normative attitudes in social interactions and thus whether they would engage in third-party norm enforcement when others violate norms in their presence. Theoretical reasons for this approach are, as explained earlier, that (i) normative expectations aim to fit the world to the mind, not to merely represent the world correctly, so active third-party norm enforcement is well-suited to get at a creature's normative expectations and understanding of the normative force of norms; (ii) the mere acting in accordance with norms leaves open whether a creature has normative attitudes toward actions or develops such attitudes in social interactions (Brandom 1994, 1997); and (iii) an evolutionary approach calls for adequate comparisons of human children and non-human primates, and third-party interventions (which could also be non-linguistic) are a good candidate for this purpose (in contrast to, e.g., interview methods).

4. Enforcement of Conventional Norms

The first experimental investigation of young children's spontaneous third-party enforcement of norms was conducted by Rakoczy, Warneken, and Tomasello (2008). Young children learned simple rules of solitary games; thus the focus was on conventional norms. More specifically, the norms in question can be called *constitutive norms* as they constitute new forms of behavior that did not exist prior to the norm. The formula used for creating these new social facts (i.e., games) is "X counts as Y in context C" (Rawls 1955; Searle 1995, 2010)—for instance, "This move counts as checkmate in the game of chess." And if these constitutive norms are generally accepted by a group of people in their practices, they have normative implications, such that participants of a certain practice ought to treat X as Y in C (Searle 1995, 2010). Constitutive norms are typically contrasted with another type of conventional norm, that is, *regulative norms* (or coordinative norms) which regulate already existing behaviors (e.g., table manners regulate eating or traffic rules regulate driving; Searle 1995). In Rakoczy et al.'s (2008) study, two- and three-year-old children were given the opportunity to spontaneously intervene against a puppet who committed violations of constitutive norms in the context of simple games. An adult demonstrated a game using normative language and new verbs (e.g., "This is how daxing is done"), and thereafter, the puppet announced that she was going to dax as well. However, she performed a different action, which, as had been explicitly made clear by the adult beforehand, was a violation of the constitutive norms that had been introduced. The three-year-olds, and less explicitly also the two-year-olds, criticized and reprimanded the puppet—often using generic normative language, such as "This is not how it is done. One must do it like this."—but they did not intervene when the puppet announced that she would show the child something (without referring to the game of daxing) and performed the very same action. Children's third-party enforcement of constitutive norms thus provided evidence that they did not just prefer one action to another, but that they took an impersonal perspective and understood the underlying normative force and generality of the norms, such that they applied them to other participants of the social practice in appropriate ways.

As mentioned earlier, another important aspect of norms (especially conventional norms) is their context-relativity. For instance, kicking a ball is totally fine in the context of a soccer match, but not when playing tennis. Rakoczy, Brosche, Warneken, and Tomasello (2009) assessed whether young children understand that constitutive norms are binding in certain contexts only. In one context (at one table) a certain game action was correct, but not in another context (at another table). Three-year-olds (but not two-year-olds) understood the context-specificity of these conventional (constitutive) norms; that is, they intervened against third-party game rule violations only when an action was inappropriate in a given context.

Another norm-governed activity is pretense (Currie 1998; Rakoczy 2008a). Participants in a pretend game take on certain roles and act as if, for instance, a banana were a telephone (i.e., object substitution), thus treat X as Y in context C analogous to other constitutive norms (Rakoczy 2008a). Rakoczy (2008b) tested children's normative understanding of pretense. Two- and three-year-old children were shown simple pretend actions, for example, treating an object as a knife in a pretend game. Children protested when a puppet pretended to eat the object that was supposed to be a knife in the game context, but not when she pretended to eat an object that was designated as a carrot. A follow-up study found that three-year-olds (but not two-year-olds) are able to switch between different pretend identities in two game contexts. For instance, a yellow stick may count as a toothbrush in one game at one location and as a carrot in another game at a different location (Wyman et al. 2009). What these findings suggest is that at around three years of age children understand something about the context-relativity of conventional norms—that certain conventional activities are prescribed in some contexts but not in others.

5. Normative Learning

What mechanisms are at play when children learn norms? It is important to look closely at children's norm acquisition, for instance, to understand better how quickly children pick up norms and how rational, systematic, and selective they are in deciding on what to learn from whom. In one study, three- and four-year-old children watched an adult and a peer model performing two alternative game-like actions (Rakoczy et al. 2010). Children at both ages were found to preferentially imitate the action performed by the adult. Importantly, children also understood the action presented by the adult as the prescribed way to do things: they protested when a puppet deviated from the action the adult had performed (i.e., the puppet performed the action the peer had demonstrated), but not when the puppet performed the adult's action. In another study, Rakoczy, Warneken, and Tomasello (2009) found that young children from age four selectively learn rule games from reliable over unreliable models and, crucially, that their learning aims not just at satisfying preferences, but at realizing normativity: they applied the acquired conventional norms to a third-party puppet who deviated from the action the reliable model had demonstrated.

The studies discussed so far involved some kind of explicit teaching and the use of normative language (e.g., "This is how we play the game of daxing") to make clear what the norms were. In everyday social interactions, however, children (and adults) frequently have to infer whether an act is normative from subtler, social-pragmatic cues. Therefore, Schmidt, Rakoczy, and Tomasello (2011) asked whether young children at age three would attribute normativity to game-like actions that are neither explicitly taught for their benefit nor introduced with normative language. When children incidentally observed an adult perform a game-like act with cues of intentionality and recognition (i.e., she immediately recognized some objects and acted as if she knew "the rules of the game"), children nevertheless attributed normativity to the action and later protested against a third-party puppet that performed an alternative action. They did not infer normativity, however, when the adult performed the action as if she were inventing it on the spot (i.e., the adult incidentally found the objects in a room and looked at them curiously not recognizing them as something known), even if the adult invented the action in a pedagogical context for the child's benefit. Schmidt et al.'s (2011) finding suggests that, contrary to the recent "natural pedagogy" account (Gergely and Csibra 2006; Csibra and Gergely 2009; Csibra and Gergely 2011), young children do not mainly use ostensive cues (e.g., eye contact) to interpret a modeled action as generic. Rather, it seems that young children consider both the social-pragmatic context and the intentionality of the model when attributing normativity to an act or not. Since children in this study jumped to normative conclusions so quickly, it is even possible that their threshold for attributing normativity is very low early in ontogeny and that they have a propensity to "promiscuously" impute normativity to others' intentional actions, just as they impute purpose to objects and others' actions and minds more generally (Kelemen 1999; Kelemen 2004; Schmidt et al. 2011). This "promiscuous normativity" might be akin to children's over-imitation, that is, the tendency to copy actions that are obviously causally unnecessary to reach a goal. In fact, recent research suggests that there is a normative component in children's over-imitation—that is, one reason why children over-imitate seems to be that they think that this is just the way things should be done. In one study, three- and five-year-old children learned instrumental actions (necessary to achieve a goal) including unnec-essary acts (irrelevant in terms of goal achievement) performed by an adult (Kenward 2012). When a third-party puppet omitted the unnecessary acts, children protested, even if the puppet reached the instrumental goal. In another study, researchers had three- and five-year-olds observe a model perform instrumental (necessary to produce some effect) and unnecessary acts (Keupp et al. 2013). In one condition, the model introduced the whole action sequence as a game (e.g., "daxing") thereby suggesting that it is subject to conventional norms. In a second condition, the model stressed the goal (i.e., the effect) of the action sequence (e.g., "ringing the bells"), thereby fo-cusing on instrumental—not conventional—aspects. Children protested more against a puppet who omitted unnecessary acts in the conventional condition than in the instrumental condition, which suggests that they construed these irrelevant acts as binding, presumably because they are part of a conventional activity.

In sum, these findings suggest that young children are eager—sometimes overeager—to identify actions that are subject to social norms. They learn norms via mere inci-dental observation of intentional actions without any normative language involved. And they learn norms selectively and rationally taking into account social-pragmatic cues, such that they prefer to learn from competent and reliable persons.

6. Further Contexts and Aspects of Normativity

Another important domain of normativity is artifact use. Artifacts are built for a purpose and there are appropriate ways to use them. With respect to this normative dimension of artifact use, Casler, Terziyan, and Greene (2009) found that two- and three-year-old children learned familiar and new artifact functions and then protested when a third-party puppet deviated from the demonstrated appropriate way to use the artifacts. Language use is of course subject to normativity, too. One can make errors in describing the world, or in acting on the world as prescribed. Rakoczy and Tomasello (2009) found evidence that three-year-olds understand that speech acts have different "directions of fit" (Searle 1983) and can thus be used correctly or in-correctly: for instance, assertions describe the world (mind-to-world direction of fit) while imperatives are used to change the world by getting someone to do something (world-to-mind direction of fit). Accordingly, three-year-olds took into account the underlying normative structure of assertions and imperatives in correcting a commentator who asserted that an actor was performing a certain action (although that was not the case), but they protested against the actor, if she was not doing what the commentator told her to do using imperatives. In a follow-up study, four-year-olds were found to understand the normative structure of future-directed speech acts (Lohse et al. 2014): that is, they recognized that a speaker made a mistake when her prediction ("A will do X") did not come true, whereas an actor made a mistake when she did not follow an imperative that had been given earlier by a speaker.

Another interesting context in which children can demonstrate their understanding of normativity is the autonomous emergence of norms without any interference of authorities. Many norms—in particular, conventional norms—are introduced or socially constructed among equivalent participants of a social practice (Piaget 1932). A recent study by Göckeritz, Schmidt, and Tomasello (2014) looked at children's spontaneous norm construction without any adult interference in an instrumental task with interdependent roles: triads of five-year-old children had to work together on an apparatus in order to achieve a common goal (obtain some rewards). Children created their own norms for coordination (akin to regulative norms introduced in the preceding), and they transmitted these norms as objective to novice peers (i.e., using generic normative language, e.g., "One should do it like this!").

7. Enforcement of Moral Norms and Rights

Perhaps the most prominent type of norm is moral norms. As explained before, prototypical moral norms are about things like people's welfare, justice, and rights (Turiel 1983; Scanlon 1998; Roughley, Chapter 11 in this volume), and thus often prohibit the causation of harm without reason. Moral norms are considered important for the maintenance of human cooperation, because they are a means of suppressing immediate self-interest (Sripada 2005; Joyce 2006; Krebs 2008). Typically, the violation of moral norms is a serious issue (Turiel 1983), and unaffected bystanders show strong emotional reactions (Nichols 2004), so one might say that moral norms carry more normative weight than other norms (Rossano 2012).

Recent work has found that young children's enforcement of norms is not confined to conventional activities or instrumental acts. Three-year-old children also protest and reprimand violations of moral norms, for example, against harming others by destroying or throwing away their property (Rossano et al. 2011; Vaish et al. 2011). An important aspect of moral norms (in particular those against harming others) is that they are usually understood as being wide in scope and hence applicable to basically all rational agents (Turiel 1983; Korsgaard 1996; Scanlon 1998). However, conventional norms (e.g., constitutive norms that govern games) are narrow in scope and thus applicable only to those who have agreed to them, be it voluntarily or just indirectly by becoming a member of a social group (Searle 1995; Kalish 2005; Diesendruck and Markson 2011). How to best construe the distinction of moral and conventional norms is a highly debated topic. Social domain theorists have argued, backed by an enormous body of research, that children (and adults) make judgments in, and navigate through, conceptually distinct knowledge domains of morality and convention (Nucci, Saxe, and Turiel 2000; Smetana 2006; Turiel 2006; for reviews, see Killen and Rutland 2011; Turiel and Dahl, this volume, 202-203). Others have, for a variety of reasons, questioned the validity of this distinction. One objection points to cross-cultural variation as to what counts as "conventional" or "moral" (Shweder et al. 1987). Another criticizes the very specific content used to study responses to transgressions (e.g., harmful actions that are common in school contexts; Kelly et al. 2007). Still others argue that a distinction that is based on differential emotional involvement is more pertinent, according to which some transgressions elicit strong feelings (e.g., norms prohibiting harm, but also disgusting actions), while others come with less emotional involvement (Haidt et al. 1993; Nichols 2002; Nichols 2004; Haidt 2012).

Irrespective of this debate, it is evident that prototypical moral and conventional norms are likely to be considered different at least regarding some dimensions. In a recent study, Schmidt, Rakoczy, and Tomasello (2012) investigated how young children understand the scope and normative force of paradigmatic moral and conventional norms. Three-year-old children modulated their norm enforcement according to the type of norm and the group membership of the transgressor: for moral norm violations (i.e., destroying another's property without any obvious reason), they protested equally against in-group and out-group perpetrators, but for conventional norm violations (constitutive norms governing simple rule games), they protested more against in-group members versus out-group individuals, which suggests that children recognized that conventional norms are limited in scope to members of their own group and that group members can be expected to respect them.

The studies reported so far focused on norms as agents' obligations to perform certain acts. People, however, have not only obligations, but also rights or entitlements to act in certain ways (Helwig 1997; Killen and Smetana 2006)—and these rights are mutually recognized and supported or granted by the group or institutions (Feinberg 1980; Searle 2010). Entitlements are special normative phenomena in that they are inherently associated with obligations by others. Entitlements thus create normative constraints on others' conduct (Hohfeld 1913, 1917; Rainbolt 1993; Searle 2010). For instance, when a right-holder is entitled to perform some action, others are obligated not to interfere with the right-holder's entitlement (to perform that action). Young children's understanding of entitlements was investigated in different contexts in a recent study (Schmidt et al. 2013). Three-year-olds defended a right-holder's entitlements (e.g., to use a toy) against a second party who threatened the right-holder's entitlements—they protested against the second party and, for example, gave the right-holder the toy back. Interestingly, children even enforced second-order entitlements, for instance regarding ownership where only an owner is entitled to entitle others to use her property.

Taken together, the research reviewed suggests that young children develop normative attitudes toward a variety of different acts in different contexts. They enforce social norms as unaffected third parties, suggesting that they take an impersonal perspective regarding norms and understand something about the normative force and generality of norms. Importantly, from early on they enforce norms in context-relative ways and take into account different social-pragmatic cues when deciding whether others' actions fall under normative assessment or not. Hence, early in ontogeny human beings start developing into normative beings and care about upholding shared standards, which suggests some attachment to their cultural group beyond strategic motives (Rossano 2012; Schmidt and Tomasello 2012).

8. Normative Attitudes in Our Close(st) Living Primate Relatives?

Given the key aspects of normativity (normative force, generality) outlined in the preceding and the argument put forward earlier that "norm" following or imitation are insufficient candidates for indicating the existence of normative attitudes, the natural starting point for hints of normative attitudes in our living primate relatives (in particular chimpanzees, but also monkey species) would be social interactions in which non-human primates have the opportunity to intervene even though they are unaffected third-party bystanders.

One phenomenon that deserves closer inspection is conflict management in non-human primates. When conflicts in social groups of macaques or chimpanzees occur, individuals—who are *prima facie* not directly involved—sometimes "police" or intervene in fights, potentially with the evolutionary function of stabilizing group life and perhaps also of increasing individual fitness (Flack, de Waal, et al. 2005; Flack, Krakauer, et al. 2005; Flack et al. 2006; Rudolf von Rohr et al. 2012). Regarding macaques, it has been suggested that not only impartial interventions (which are relatively rare), but also partial interventions (agonistic support of non-kin subordinates), should be considered as policing in the broad sense, since they are not only beneficial to the individual, but also to the group, leading to fewer group conflicts (Beisner and McCowan 2013). Thus, it is an open question what role impartial interventions play that occur rather infrequently. Furthermore, it is mainly high-ranking animals that intervene in third-party ways (at low cost as retaliation is unlikely given their power), which creates doubt as to the possibility that these interventions are accompanied by psychological attitudes that are of interest for normativity. Regarding chimpanzees, policing behavior is rare and is performed by dominant individuals, too (Rudolf von Rohr et al. 2012).

Thus, more generally, it is unclear whether high-ranking individuals intervene because they are afraid of losing their dominant position or because they see an opportunity to demonstrate their power or achieve mating benefits. Moreover, without experimental control, it is hard to tease apart normative attitudes and simple dislike. It is important to show that individuals intervene in third-party ways not only because they dislike an act (which might be one reason), but because the act is "wrong" (according to some norm). There is, however, an experimentally controlled study on impartial third-party interventions (i.e., punishment) in chimpanzees. Riedl, Jensen, Call, and Tomasello (2012) gave individuals the opportunity to punish a "thief" who stole some food either from themselves (second-party theft, self-interest involved) or from a third-party victim (third-party theft, no self-interest involved). Punishment consisted in pulling a rope to release a trapdoor, so that the thief lost the food. Dominant individuals punished the thief, but only when they were affected (second-party theft; see Jensen, Call, and Tomasello, 2007, for similar findings), and they showed more "anger" (e.g., threats and displays) toward thieves in cases of second-party versus third-party theft. This suggests that (dominant) chimpanzees do not exhibit normative attitudes when they are harmed in such contexts, but rather negative attitudes like anger or frustration based on preferences and the non-fulfillment of individual goals.

Another important context to explore is social learning. Chimpanzees have behavioral traditions and thus culture, broadly speaking, as these traditions vary between different regions which do not necessarily vary in their ecology (Whiten et al. 1999; Whiten et al. 2005; Whiten et al. 2007; Price et al. 2009; Luncz et al. 2012; Luncz and Boesch 2014). So there is evidence for the transmission and persistence of certain behaviors in chimpanzees, but it is disputed whether this amounts to social learning or can be explained by individual learning mechanisms or genetic differences between groups of chimpanzees (Tennie et al. 2009; Langergraber et al. 2011). A recent study suggests that stable between-group differences are at least partly a result of chimpanzees possessing a bias to copy dominants (Kendal et al. 2015). As explained earlier, such copying behaviors are inconclusive as to whether normative attitudes are in play—more conclusive processes of social control and third-party sanctioning have not been documented yet.

A final natural context in which normative attitudes might arise is one of resource distributions, in particular, if individuals understand such a context as a social situation in which it is not only of relevance what "I get," but what "I get" as compared with what others get. Thus, a sense of fairness or equality (in terms of equal treatment) might be involved (Rawls 1971; Feinberg 1974; Sen 1992). Recent research has found that humans develop a sense of fairness early in ontogeny during the second year of life (Geraci and Surian 2011; Schmidt and Sommerville 2011; Sloane et al. 2012; Sommerville et al. 2013)—infants expect resources to be allocated equally among recipients, and these fairness expectations are interrelated with infants' own tendency to share goods altruistically (Schmidt and Sommerville 2011). Sarah Brosnan and colleagues studied inequality aversion in capuchin monkeys and chimpanzees using a paradigm in which two individuals could exhibit equivalent effort (handing over a token to an experimenter) for receiving a reward (Brosnan and de Waal 2003; Brosnan et al. 2005; Brosnan et al. 2010). However, one individual received a reward of high value (e.g., a grape) for exchanging the token, while the target individual received a reward of low value (e.g., a carrot or cucumber) for the token. The question was whether the target individual would refuse to take the low-value food. These studies found mixed results, with monkeys and male (but not female) chimpanzees refusing unequal "offers" (Brosnan and de Waal 2003; Brosnan et al. 2010), and with between-group differences in chimpanzees as to whether they reject low-quality food at all (Brosnan et al. 2005). Bräuer, Call, and Tomasello (2009) tested chimpanzees, bonobos, and orangutans in the same token-exchange paradigm, but added an important control condition in which the high-quality food was merely present (but nobody received it), thus controlling for the possibility that individuals just expect to get better food rather than making social comparisons. The authors found that apes did not reject unequal offers when their partner had received better food—the small group of bonobos refused unequal offers when their partner was given high-quality food, but this effect was not statistically reliable. In sum, these mixed findings do not allow for drawing conclusions regarding whether chimpanzees or monkeys show inequality aversion (see also Bräuer and Hanus 2012). It is important to note that, even if there were clear evidence for systematic social comparisons, this would not directly be indicative of normative attitudes, as rejections could be based on disappointment or frustration due to the violation of descriptive expectations ("I will get what she got") or non-fulfillment of desires ("I want what she got"), rather than normative expectations ("I should/deserve to get what she got"). Nonetheless, more studies on refusal behaviors in social contexts are required as more conclusive findings might hint at important phylogenetic intermediate steps toward normative attitudes (e.g., via simple forms of egocentric indignation or resentment; see Roughley, this volume, 229-233).

Another important task that has been used comes from experimental economics: the ultimatum game. This is a two-player game in which a proposer makes an "offer" on how to divide some resources (e.g., an offer of $20 out of $100), and a responder can either accept the offer (thus both get their share of the proposed split) or reject the offer (both get nothing). A creature sensitive to fairness would reject (highly) unequal offers, although this would be "irrational" if the ideal model is a *homo economicus* that maximizes his payoffs. Human adults typically reject offers below 20% (Camerer 2003), suggesting sensitivity to fairness. A behavioral version of the ultimatum game has been used to test chimpanzees (Jensen et al. 2007a; Proctor et al. 2013) and bonobos (Kaiser et al. 2012). In all studies, apes did not seem to be sensitive to fairness, as they almost never rejected unfair (non-zero) offers, but only zero offers—which suggests that apes do not focus on social aspects, but rather on whether they receive at least "something."

Together, these findings on policing, social learning, and fairness suggest that non-human primates are not (yet) creatures with normative attitudes, but rather "socio-causal animals" with an intricate individualistic psychology that allows for pursuing individual goals and benefits and for regulating social behaviors and (power) relationships leading to stable forms of group living.

9. Concluding Remarks

We started out by separating the normative from the descriptive. It is a (descriptive) fact that humans have peculiar "oughts" that govern their conduct on a group level in impersonal ways and build the basis for human cooperation, social institutions, and culture. The research reported here suggests that it does not require a protracted process of socialization for human children to develop normative attitudes toward others' and their own actions. Rather, from around two to three years of age, human children begin enforcing different kinds of norms when third parties violate them. And so they develop an understanding of the normative force and generality of norms, treating relevant actions as subject to assessment and as tokens of a given type. It is of particular note that young children might have a tendency to overgeneralize adults' intentional actions and thus rapidly attribute normativity even in non-pedagogical contexts of incidental observation. Crucially, children also appreciate the context-relativity of many norms and apply them accordingly.

The apparent lack of normative attitudes in our close living primate relatives with respect to the three promising contexts reviewed (conflict management, social learning, fairness) should not detract from the immense cognitive and social capabilities of apes and other social animals that all exhibit a rich group life. It might merely be that important prerequisites for normativity, in particular, shared intentionality and joint attention, are not present in non-human primates, and that they are thus more like "socio-causal animals" that focus on statistical regularities, fulfillment of their individual goals, and conspecifics' mental states (at minimum their perceptual states) in competitive, rather than cooperative, contexts (Hare and Tomasello 2004; Call and Tomasello 2008; Rudolf von Rohr et al. 2011; Rakoczy and Schmidt 2013; Rakoczy et al. 2014; Tomasello 2014). Certainly, definitional and conceptual issues of how to conceive of normativity or morality are always a challenge. Thus, an evolutionary perspective on morality with a focus on behaviors that may be adapted to animal group life (e.g., leading to evolutionary stable strategies) may identify moral systems in a broader, functional sense, which is nevertheless informative for understanding proximate mechanisms and the genesis of human normativity (Alexander 1987; Flack and de Waal 2000; Machery and Mallon 2010; Baumard et al. 2013; van Schaik, Burkart,

Jaeggi, and Rudolf von Rohr 2014; Kappeler et al., Chapter 3 in this volume; van Schaik and Burkart, Chapter 7 in this volume).

The crucial adaptation of the hominin lineage which paved the way for developing normative attitudes might therefore have been a novel form of intersubjective sharing, namely abilities to share attention, intentions, and emotions based on a suite of special social-cognitive skills and cooperative motivations (Tomasello et al. 2005; Tomasello 2014). Whether these new social-cognitive and motivational capacities evolved in the context of cooperative breeding (unique among apes; Burkart, Hrdy, and Van Schaik 2009; Hrdy 2009), in the context of obligate collaborative foraging among interdependent hominins (Tomasello et al. 2012), or yet another context, is an open question (see Dubreuil, 2010, 87–8, for an argument favoring foraging contexts due to a relatively later onset of cooperative breeding in hominins). Nevertheless, these new abilities of engaging in shared intentional activities (e.g., group hunting and ritualistic practices) plausibly allowed our hominin ancestors to overcome an individualistic perspective on the world (with descriptive expectations and, e.g., disappointment in the event of non-fulfillment) and to gradually take a more collectivistic perspective with formerly descriptive expectations transmuting into local normative expectations about each other's behavior (Schmid 2009; cf. Carassa and Colombetti 2014). This transformation might have been possible given that shared intentional actions as such might involve normativity (obligations and entitlements) or bring about normative consequences for the participants involved (Gilbert 1989; Gilbert 2000; Schmid 2009; Steinfath, Chapter 9 in this volume). Moreover, the intersubjective sharing of intentions introduced the possibility to deviate in a "public" social context: any participant of the joint activity could detect "anomalies," realize the non-attainment of shared goals (and causes thereof), and, importantly, experience that all participants' acts are subject to reciprocal assessment. This process may then have given rise to the emergence of group-wide normative attitudes leading to new forms of group living, and shaped subsequent human phylogeny and ontogeny in dialectical ways, thus contributing to the evolutionary success of the hominin lineage and to the gradual formation of human cultural and institutional reality.

Acknowledgements

We would like to thank all contributors for the insightful discussions in Münster and the valuable comments on an earlier version of our manuscript. Special thanks go to Kurt Bayertz and Neil Roughley for organizing and structuring this exciting project.

PART III

Moral Norms

7

The Evolution of Human Normativity

The Role of Prosociality and Reputation Management

Carel P. van Schaik and Judith M. Burkart

1. Introduction

In today's world, we often have to learn to comply with arbitrary rules, suggesting that normativity is a recent cultural invention made after we began living in complex, large-scale societies that arose as we developed rational solutions to new problems of coordination and conflicts of interest. However, these kinds of problems are not new, but are in fact known to have been fundamental to the human foraging niche for a very long time. We therefore suggest that the notion of normativity is old and arose in the context of human morality. Morality is all about proper social conduct and is therefore normative, given the accepted definition of norms as social regularities whose violation invites sanctioning (see Opp 2015; Roughley, Chapter 1 in this volume). Thus, there is no morality without normativity. This perspective implies that other forms of normativity, including social norms and conventions, arose secondarily, building on the ability to be normative in the moral sense.

Darwin (1871) was the first to suggest an evolutionary basis to morality and its normative side. Although the evolutionary approach was long dismissed, it is currently in ascendancy. First, moral psychology has shown the critical role of moral emotions in reaching moral judgment (Prinz 2007), even when it might initially appear that moral reflection was involved (Haidt 2012). These findings should toll the death knell for any approach that assumed morality was a recent cultural invention, entirely built upon reason and passed on to the subsequent generations by patient conditioning. Second, studies of the ontogeny of these preferences and biases show they often arise before one can reasonably assume a major effect of cultural influences on behavior (Bloom 2013). The evolutionary account can also readily accommodate cultural influences.

We will therefore consider human morality an adaptation. More specifically, we argue that it evolved to enable the unique cooperation underlying the ancestral human foraging niche. We will begin with a description of this niche and the everyday morality that underlies it, focusing on its two main components (prosociality and norm compliance), and explain its relation to our unique, highly interdependent, foraging niche as shown today by the last remaining nomadic hunter-gatherers.

Clearly, human morality did not evolve from scratch. Other animals with social bonds or collective action, perhaps especially primates, also have social obligations, part of the regulatory apparatus to maintain and service these bonds (Kappeler et al., this volume, 73–75). We will therefore look for the key differences between human and animal morality, paying special attention to the role of third parties. These differences are also found in the proximate regulation of morality and especially its normative side. It concerns the social reach of norms: from second-party enforced "norms" in dyads to third-party enforced norms in groups or even species. We will suggest that the emergence of effective language subsequently greatly extended the social reach of reputation and thus expanded indirect reciprocity to include all members of the community, even those hardly known to each other, and simultaneously increased the effectiveness of norm enforcement by third parties. We will use these insights to understand the cultural influences on human norms, and speculate that moral norms are the source of all human normativity.

2. The Human Foraging Niche

Scholars sympathetic to the idea that human morality has some evolved core may nonetheless have trouble recognizing this core, because the lifestyle of virtually all people today is remarkably different from the lifestyle of mobile foragers, which is most representative of the conditions in which human sociality has evolved. This lifestyle is also remarkably different from the lifestyle of the extant great apes (Watts 2012), and gradually evolved over a period of approximately two million years until the origin of agriculture a mere 10,000 years ago. Understanding the hypothesis presented in the following requires that we briefly summarize this lifestyle based on recent literature (Johnson and Earle 2000; Hill 2002; Marlowe 2005; Kaplan et al. 2009; Marlowe 2009; Hill et al. 2011; Moffett 2013).

Mobile foragers live in bands of an average of 25–30 people of all ages and both sexes who share a camp. Camps are moved multiple times per year. Bands of the same macro-band, also called a community, regularly exchange members. The community has a shared language, which is often unique. Total community size ranges in the hundreds or at most a few thousand. All foragers form pair bonds that are socially recognized (i.e., marriage); usually, they are freely formed or dissolved. Polygyny is allowed but rare.

Men mainly hunt, fish, or obtain honey, whereas women mainly gather: the sexual division of labor. For both sexes, their foraging activities may be coordinated or synchronized, and most of the time they are therefore cooperative in at least some sense. Depending on their technology and the prey species, men may hunt in groups or alone. The food obtained by men, in particular the meat from larger animals, is shared widely with other families in a camp. Gathered food is mainly shared within families. Collective actions are also common, ranging from moving camp to managing habitats through fire or damming a river to poison and collect fish. Raiding enemy groups is also collective. Overall, sharing and joint activities strongly reduce starvation risk.

Major decisions are made collectively, sometimes after long discussions. The social system is egalitarian, with the majority of men jealously preventing one among them from emerging as leader, except transiently in times of war. Men gain status by being generous.

Parents, but also many others, prominently among them grandmothers, look after babies and young children. Children are free to play and roam, and gradually learn their skills. The foraging niche is so skill-intensive that women reach peak foraging efficiencies (yields per unit time) in their mid-twenties, whereas men do so about a decade (or even more) later.

We hypothesize here that morality is an adaptive set of behavioral predispositions for prosociality and norm compliance, which evolved to support this uniquely derived form of human cooperation.

3. Human Morality and Its Function

Morality is a code of conduct prescribing proper actions. Ultimately, morality serves to keep a cooperative society from falling apart. Morality is also normative: if someone violates the code of conduct, this has social consequences from direct partners or third parties. The two major components are therefore prosociality and norm compliance. They correspond closely to the two moral domains proposed by Haidt (2007, 2012).

Nothing in this description implies that morality should be unique to the human species, given that norms are broadly defined to include both explicit and implicit social rules, and that social sanction may come from dyad partners or third parties. Thus if formulated this broadly, there is no reason to deny morality to nonhuman animals, especially the well-documented primates (de Waal 2006; Kappeler et al., Chapter 3 in this volume). This implies that we must identify what makes human morality, including our normativity, different from that of animals.

Following Darwin (1871), van Schaik et al. (2014) and Tomasello (2016) hypothesize that human moral behavior serves to maintain the lifestyle of nomadic foragers, which is uniquely cooperative among animals. At the dyadic level, it involves exchanges in both direct and indirect reciprocity, and at the level of bands or communities, it involves coordinated joint activities or even synchronized collective action. Human morality, then, serves to support this cooperation and interdependence, by maintaining the stability of the sharing networks of dyadic reciprocity, indirect reciprocity, and collective action against collapse due to free riding, and so prevent the otherwise massive fluctuations in food intake, which would inevitably lead to starvation. Since subsistence ecology is culturally variable in humans, including mobile foragers, cultural variation in the content of moral norms and of realized moral preferences is entirely compatible with this hypothesis (cf. Hauser 2006; Monroe et al. 2009).

Table 7.1. Core functional contexts (first column) in which the major human moral behaviors (second column) used to appear. The moral behaviors are regulated by a rich set of proximate mechanisms and emotions. Some of these functions, behaviors, and proximate mechanisms are also present in nonhuman animals, in particular the ones toward the end of the table.

Functional Context	Behaviors	Mechanisms (+ Emotions)
Cooperative breeding	Provisioning mother and offspring Babysitting Teaching	Proactive prosocial motivations steep reactive prosocial motivation (empathy)
Cooperative hunting and gathering	Adult food sharing	Allocentric inequity aversion
	Receiving help when needy	Concern with reputation (sensitivity to audience)
	Coordinated collective action (hunting, gathering)	Shared intentionality ($\rightarrow$ coordination, synchrony); preference for conformity, homophily ($\rightarrow$ synchrony)
Raiding (warfare)	Raids on other groups, defense against them	Various mechanisms above; plus within-group bias in relevant emotions
Social bonds (pair bonds, male-male bonds)	Reciprocal exchanges	Gratitude, guilt, shame, as well as cheater detection
Incest avoidance	No mating with relatives	Sexual aversion toward relatives
Parenting and family support	Protect and support biological kin	Strong kin-bias in relevant emotions

3.1. The Content of Folk Morality

Here we briefly present the outlines of human morality and its major functional contexts in which it appeared historically (Table 7.1). Today's folk morality, i.e., the behaviors that most humans would consider moral, still largely reflects these functions, which are a mix of old (ancestral) and new (derived).

The first two functional contexts are cooperative care for offspring and interdependent hunting and gathering, together called foraging: individuals help (provision, care for) immatures and those adults who have established and maintained a good reputation. Being cared for in case of need is a key requirement in an ecological niche characterized by interdependence on a variety of time scales (Hill and Hurtado 2009). A good reputation is essential for this (for review, see Hrdy 2009; Marlowe 2010). Reputation is enhanced by both prosocial preference and group-level norm compliance: people are nice to those with good reputations (Milinski 2006). These two contexts are derived in humans relative to great apes, but cooperative breeding is also present in callitrichid monkeys, with similar consequences (Brügger et al. 2018; Burkart, Brügger, and van Schaik 2018).

In coordination, two or more individuals perform different but complementary actions, and thus share a common goal; these individuals may, but need not be, in close proximity. Coordination makes the sexual division of labor possible, but also underlies the specialization and trade seen among more recent sedentary human societies. Synchrony refers to the simultaneous performance of the same or complementary actions in close proximity, and is thus a key requirement for collective action during some forms of hunting, gathering, processing, shelter production, raiding, etc.

The third entry, concerning the functional context of raiding (an opportunistic form of warfare; Wrangham and Glowacki 2012), is probably more pronounced in humans than in all other primates, with the possible exception of chimpanzee males.

The other entries in Table 7.1 illustrate some aspects of morality that are probably more widely shared with other species, and thus phylogenetically older. Thus, the fourth set, linked to social bonding, is patchily distributed among primates (Silk 2012). In humans, within-sex social bonds are found in both sexes, perhaps more so among adult males, as in chimpanzees. Humans also show clear pair bonds, which are found in various taxa (Dunbar and Shultz 2007) but not in great apes. The fifth functional context, inbreeding avoidance, is quite widespread. It is especially useful to include it here because the aversion to mate with relatives is well documented among many primates, and also seen in humans (Pusey and Wolf 1996; van den Berghe 1983). The final context refers to obligations to protect and care for offspring and close relatives, which in humans are a basic aspect of folk morality (in that bad parents are disapproved of).

The plausible presence of moral preferences shared with other animal species is a strong argument in favor of evolutionary continuity. Indeed, there may well be additional moral preferences that are shared, for instance an aversion to infanticide (Rudolf von Rohr et al. 2011; van Schaik et al. 2014). However, evolutionary continuity inevitably also suggests that each species will have a unique subset of preferences (and the range of individuals to which they are applied). The list of Table 7.1 may thus not be complete, but it serves to remind us that everyday morality is about more than being prosocial.

All these moral tendencies are prosocial, in that they benefit other members of society, often at some immediate cost (but with a long-term net benefit) to the actors. There is also a second major component of morality: Haidt's (2007, 2012) loyalty to the group, expressed in norm compliance. Social life inevitably contains elements of both cooperation and competition. Morality is therefore essentially about restraint: not reaping benefits even though they are within reach. A moral system based entirely on prosocial motivations is unlikely to be stable without some pressures to refrain from harvesting immediate selfish benefits that end up harming society. Thus, moral norms are needed because humans have a psychology with both selfish and prosocial tendencies, and have incentives to behave selfishly (free ride) if they can do so undetected. More formally, they are needed whenever two conditions are met simultaneously: (1) *interdependence*: societies in which reliable food sharing or coordinated collective action is essential for fitness, and thus individuals, including dominants, need each other; and (2) *conflicts of interest*: there is an incentive to exploit others or free ride on their efforts.

4. Mechanisms Underlying Human Morality

4.1. The Non-Normative Elements

The prosocial element of morality involves proactive giving, sharing in response to requests or signs of need, and a tendency toward equal or equitable outcomes. The prosocial motivations producing these behaviors are at the core of human morality, serving to maintain the unique form of direct, and especially also indirect, reciprocity, as well as coordinated and joint action.

Prosocial motivations underlie friendships and pair bonds, and our obligations to our friends and spouses are part of everyday morality. These bonds are similar to those found in nonhuman primates (de Waal 2006; Massen et al. 2010), and parsimony argues for shared mechanisms in the servicing of these social bonds in nonhuman primates and humans alike.

Vitally important for receiving help from others is a good reputation. People partly represent this function of reputation in the form of a psychological goal, being explicitly concerned about their reputation. Even in modern states this concern is generally seen as legitimate, as shown by laws allowing individuals to sue others for slander.

Indeed, reputation management already starts at an early age in humans (Rochat 2012), and is partly subconscious, as shown by a variety of experiments in which humans show a high sensitivity to the perceived presence of an audience, which elicits greater proactive and reactive prosociality (Haley and Fessler 2005; Bateson et al. 2006; Burnham and Hare 2007). Incidentally, such audience effects on prosociality are not found among chimpanzees (Engelmann et al. 2012; Nettle et al. 2013), and are thus almost certainly derived in humans, consistent with the virtual absence of indirect reciprocity in nonhumans.

Privileging these motivations over others is especially important because they often occur in situations of low situational urgency, where signals of need may not be present, whereas other competing selfish stimuli (the temptation) are immediate and strong. As a result, we generally do the right thing, except in cases of unusual hardship (and thus a strong motivation toward the selfish goal) or where the situation is perceived as carrying an unusually low risk of detection. The latter is achieved by our high subconscious sensitivity to the possible presence of an audience.

Another important motivation to uphold the fair sharing of large food items, e.g., a mammalian carcass acquired to be divided among group members, is our sense of fairness, also known as advantageous inequity aversion, i.e., an allocentric aversion against receiving more than others. Among animals, we tend to see some form of so-called disadvantageous inequity aversion (egocentric), especially in those species where individuals form social bonds with non-relatives (Brosnan 2013; but see Bräuer and Hanus 2012; van Schaik 2016). However, the advantageous version, where ego protests when alter receives a smaller share than seems fair to ego, is unique to humans (Fehr and Schmidt 1999).

Turning now to joint actions, we see two distinct behavior patterns: coordination and synchrony. Coordination is based on trust and therefore fundamentally on the same underlying mechanisms as reciprocity and indirect reciprocity discussed in the preceding. Tomasello et al. (2005; Tomasello 2009) argue that both synchrony and coordinated action require as an underlying motivation the active preference for having a common goal, i.e., shared intentionality (see also Schmidt and Rakoczy, Chapter 6 in this volume). There is no conclusive evidence for it in nonhuman animals, but this may be more due to the absence of a satisfactory operational definition that would allow us to definitively rule it in or out among nonhumans than to its actual absence. For instance, Boehm (2018) and van Schaik and Burkart (2018) both suggested that raiding chimpanzee males show all the hallmarks of shared intentionality.

Synchrony may in part be produced by the chameleon effect or mimicry, which refers to the tendency to adopt the postures and gestures used by a partner during social interaction (Chartrand and van Baaren 2009), and which has a mutually enforcing effect on social bond strength: people who show mutual mimicry like each other more, and people who like each other show more mimicry. This phenomenon is part of a more general homophily, the preference for being behaviorally similar to dyad partners (Haun and Over 2013), which in the dyadic context may also be expressed as over-imitation and reflects (but perhaps also contributes to) the strength of the social bond.

Empirical evidence abundantly shows that synchronized action, such as marching or joint dancing, singing, or music making is not only intrinsically rewarding but also produces mutual trust and thus the feeling that one is a member of a supportive alliance (Fessler and Holbrook 2014). It therefore elicits a willingness to engage in joint tasks, including joint aggression toward out-groups (Wiltermuth and Heath 2009). Thus, liking and synchrony interact and mutually reinforce each other.

The strong between-community hostility shown by humans also requires a strong within-group bias in all relevant moral emotions. There is extensive evidence for our moral parochialism in everyday interaction, as vividly confirmed by a formal study in a tribal society (Bernhard et al. 2006). This bias corresponds to Haidt's (2012) loyalty domain.

For all these actions, the evidence is exclusively or overwhelmingly from humans, but the remaining ones are widely shared. In humans, inbreeding avoidance is known to develop automatically based on experience-expectant inputs during early immaturity (the so-called Westermarck effect), and is therefore close to what one might call innate. Interestingly, in humans it is accompanied by strong emotions, both on the side of individuals who are directly involved and on the side of outside observers (Fessler and Navarrete 2004). People also feel that parents have an obligation to care for their children, that adult children should care for their aging parents, and that siblings should support each other. As a result, there is a kin bias in many moral emotions, such as empathy or proactive prosocial motivations, or greater forgiveness of norm violators, and so on. Kin bias belongs in the category of moral behaviors in humans as well, because it is accompanied by strong feelings of duty and obligation, and society also expects this (a normative element).

Overall, then, all these moral actions are founded upon clear motivations, often experienced as strong emotions by the actors. However, the actors can also observe these emotions in their fellow group members and use these observations to evaluate their reliability. This is where normativity comes in.

4.2. The Normative Element

Sticking to a society's rules for proper conduct, be they in direct or indirect reciprocity in dyads or in coordinated or joint actions by multiple actors, is not just governed by these prosocial preferences. Behavioral regularities can be recognized as being norms when violations are sanctioned in some way. Indeed, both internal (the urge to comply) and external (avoidance and punishment) motivators regulate our motivation to comply with moral norms.

Arguably the safest tactic to maintain a good reputation and avoid sanctioning is to have a strong intrinsic motivation to engage in proactive prosociality. If the costs of discovery are exceptionally high, one does better to avoid temptations altogether than to weigh the risks each time, and perhaps make a mistake. However, this function need not be mentally represented. Selection has therefore assigned a high priority to these prosocial moral emotions, experienced as a sense of high urgency or sense of duty. Thus, its function may reflect the damage due to loss of reputation, which is extremely high, because a good reputation is vitally important to a forager, and regaining it may require inordinately more effort than gaining it in the first place. The potential loss of reputation that would result from violating the norm usually far outweighs the opportunity cost (and thus fitness loss) of not violating it. This asymmetry may make it adaptive to possess strong internal drivers and not rely too much on external drivers.

An additional, but overlapping intrinsic motivation besides a strong prosocial motivation and reputation management is to actively seek out, and conform to, norms. This is expected given the presence of culturally variable local norms in humans. It is known that children do this (Over and Carpenter 2009; Schmidt and Rakoczy, Chapter 6 in this volume).

On the external control side, people are expected to be forever alert to the presence of free riders or cheaters (Cosmides et al. 2005). We may therefore have a tendency to stress cheater detection more than praising the prosocial contributors: gossip is more often malicious than positive. This tendency may be adaptive as well. The cost of missing beneficial acts by a person with a good reputation may be negligible compared to not noticing inappropriate selfish acts by someone with an otherwise good reputation. In fact, one would expect people to be especially keen on identifying norm transgressions when there is a suspicion that someone's good reputation may be undeserved.

The second component of the external control of norm compliance is avoidance of free riders, and thus exclusion from future cooperation, or even punishment by either damaged second parties or third parties. These kinds of sanctions are the most interesting aspect of normativity, so we will examine them in detail in the next section.

We wish to end with a note on moral emotions. Emotions can be regarded as the subjectively experienced side of what can be more objectively described (in ethological terms) as motivations (or more colloquially as "drives"). Moral behaviors often have a strong emotional feel to them, which serves to give them a higher priority than competing motivations. This is not only true for the behaviors serving to uphold reputation. For instance, many people feel strongly that one should care for one's relatives, while simultaneously avoiding inbreeding with them (although contemporary moral philosophers rarely consider this aspect of morality). The evolutionary approach predicts that the strength of a particular moral emotion should be correlated with the negative impact on fitness when a norm violation is found out. Perhaps independently, the strength should also increase with the strength or likelihood of temptation. We do not know of any test of this prediction, but it is a strong test of the evolutionary approach.

5. How Human Morality Is Different: The Third-Party Perspective

To provide background for the discussion of who engages in norm enforcement, it is useful to examine the possible players. Players can be directly involved as actor or first party (A in Figure 7.1) or as recipient or responder, or second-party (B), but also may be a third party. Third parties, however, come in several varieties: they can be a non-involved fellow group member, with a social bond to B (C) or without any bond to A (D–F), or more generally, can be a completely uninvolved, out-group third party (K–Q).

The role of third parties is strongest by far in humans (Burkart, Brügger, and van Schaik 2018). People experience anger when witnessing norm violations and have an urge to punish the transgressors if they can do so without incurring too high a cost and even if the transgressors are in-group strangers (Henrich et al. 2006). Indeed, they tend to derive satisfaction from it (de Quervain et al. 2004). Such punishment is intrinsically linked to the importance of indirect reciprocity and its mechanism: reputation (although reputation is uniquely important in humans, it may rely on older mechanisms; Anderson et al. 2013; Kawai et al. 2014). In indirect reciprocity, in-group

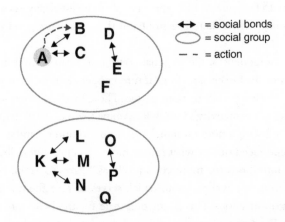

Figure 7.1. The role of third parties (C–Q) in human morality. A's actions toward B may provoke responses from various partes: B, who is directly involved (second-party); C–F, who are uninvolved in-group bystanders; and K–Q, who are uninvolved, out-group bystanders. The response of in-group bystanders may also depend on their social bond with A: thus, C may respond differently than D–F.

third parties, C, observe interactions between others and decide, based on their evaluation of these interactions, whether or not to engage in cooperative interactions with
A in the future. If the role of C is important, we must expect that selection led A to
include C's responses into A's behavioral decisions. As a result, even the emotions that
at the proximate level are internally generated and directed at second parties may have
ultimately (over evolutionary time) been co-shaped by third parties.

   Although nonhuman animals may well have emotions similar to the ones we consider moral when it comes to the first- and second-party perspectives (thus including
those involved in social interactions), evolutionary continuity breaks down in the third-
party perspective. We know of no animal species in which third parties disapprove of
others' actions, such as inbreeding or inadequate parenting, although opportunities
to do so would abound. However, infanticide by males (van Schaik 2000) may be an
exception to this rule, as suggested by the general commotion accompanying such
acts, perhaps because no one remains totally unaffected by this. Yet even in this case,
a recent experiment by Rudolf von Rohr et al. (2015) suggests that any moral disapproval is limited to within-group third parties. Although individual chimpanzees were
far more interested in watching video clips involving total strangers engaging in infanticide than other activities (hunting, male displays, or grooming and nut cracking),
they did not show any differential signs of distress relative to these events. Likewise,
chimpanzees do not show contagious yawning, considered a sign of empathy, when
watching video clips of yawning strangers, whereas they readily do so when exposed
to clips of group members (Campbell and de Waal 2014). Perhaps, their hostility toward strangers interferes with empathy, and thus moral judgment.

   Humans are different. In our species, even uninvolved third parties that belong to
a different group (K–Q in Figure 7.1) tend to have evaluative judgments of A's action
toward B, especially if they involve serious harm (although they can be more easily
suppressed than in-group responses). This indicates the presence of collective (i.e.,
impartial) norms, which are almost certainly absent among all animals. Thus, we generally disapprove of inbreeding, even if it involves total strangers (although our own
experience modulates this response; Fessler and Navarrete 2004). This is consistent
with the presence in our species of a preference for abiding by the general, impartial
rule, without regard to the individuals involved.

   Third-party in-group disapproval varies across societies. In foragers and perhaps
other small-scale (face-to-face) societies, disapproval is in the form of dyadic (second-
party) shunning and gossip (Marlowe 2009). The shunning reduces the trespasser's
opportunities to free ride, and the gossip harms his reputation. In both ways, the
trespasser will have trouble finding cooperation partners, and will become isolated.
However, foragers are also likely to engage in restorative behaviors such as reconciliation. When actual punishment occurs, it is often collective, reserved for the rare cases
where particularly bad (violent) repeat norm violators are expelled or even killed

(Boehm 1999, 2012). In large-scale societies, however, regular third-party punishment is common (Fehr and Fischbacher 2004). Its absence in chimpanzees (Riedl et al. 2012) confirms it is derived relative to great apes.

Many consider such individual third-party punishment to be altruistic in both the psychological sense, in that the punisher intends to help specific victims or society at large, and the biological sense, in that it apparently reduces the punisher's fitness. Indeed, because third-party policing of any kind can evolve through individual selection only under very restrictive conditions, especially in large groups (El Mouden et al. 2010), "altruistic punishment" is often considered the key explanandum in models of group selection or cultural group selection (Boyd et al. 2003). Nonetheless, it is likely that those who seemingly unselfishly uphold the society's moral norms actually are those who stand to benefit significantly from this activity, either indirectly, through reputation enhancement (dos Santos et al. 2010), or directly due to disproportionate benefits and/or negligible costs, as in punishing animals (Raihani et al. 2012), or as institutionally appointed norm enforcers (Baldassarri and Grossman 2011).

In sum, in most species sanctions are mainly by second parties, those directly affected. In a few species, we may see responses by third parties, perhaps because they are indirectly affected. But only in humans do we see explicit disapproval of norm violations by third parties, often even outside their own group, suggesting the presence of truly collective, agent-neutral norms. Nonetheless, humans still tend to show a parochial element to attitudes toward norm violations, consistent with cultural variation in norms.

Having established the role of third parties as the key difference between human and nonhuman morality, we can now ask how and why this difference arose.

6. The Evolutionary Origins of Human Normativity

The presence of sanctions that threaten the loss of reputation reflects the importance of interdependence in shaping human normativity: directly or indirectly, third-party influences have been critical to its evolution. When all players have a good reputation and stick to the cooperative norms, indirect reciprocity in human groups looks just like indiscriminate cooperation—the classic altruism of multilevel selection models (Wilson 2015). However, it can only afford to look like this because players have good information about potential partners, which in turn leads these potential partners to avoid free riding and thus avoid incurring sanctions.

The origin of our strong tendency toward indirect reciprocity may go back to the origin of full-blown language. Plausible estimates put the emergence of modern language at approximately half a million years ago (Dediu and Levinson 2013). Once language was sufficiently developed, it had two main effects on indirect reciprocity.

First, language's main social use (gossip; Dunbar 1996) greatly expanded the number of possible partners on whom players would have enough information to judge whether they would make reliable partners for indirect reciprocity. Without language, one can really only rely on information as first or second party, or as third party in those social interactions one can directly observe. This obviously limits the scope of indirect reciprocity. Second, communities could now engage in a moral dialogue, in a process of mutual challenges and justifications, which then inevitably favors the formulation of more general and impartial norms, from an impartial perspective (cf. Tomasello 2016). The same process can also readily produce cultural variation in the content of social and moral norms. These two processes turned macro-bands or communities into socially cohesive cooperation networks.

If individuals have an explicit preference for the impartial rule, this is an expression of justice. Justice is the normative (third-party) version of the individual-level preference for fairness. The prediction therefore is that non-linguistic species will necessarily lack aspects of justice, such as practices relating to desert (Christen and Glock 2012).

7. Cultural Variation and Normativity

The evolutionary approach to normativity is not incompatible with the presence of major cultural variation in behavior, including normative behavior, because one major adaptive strategy is phenotypic plasticity or behavioral flexibility. In various primates, this flexibility is culturally supported (Whiten 2012; van Schaik 2013). In the case of food selection and diet, for instance, we see major cultural variation in food-processing techniques, including technologically supported techniques (Sanz et al. 2013) and geographic variation in diet (Bastian et al. 2010). Obviously, such cultural elaborations of adaptive human behavior are especially pronounced in humans (Richerson and Boyd 2005).

Among modern societies, moral norms show remarkable variation, as do the underlying moral intuitions (where intuitions are realized emotions, as modified by experience). Historically, however, this may not have been as pronounced. Among foragers the content of morality is fairly uniform (Hill 2009), as predicted by the evolutionary hypothesis: the social problems are approximately the same everywhere. Even so, even among foragers, social organization changes dramatically upon adopting a more sedentary lifestyle (Keeley 1988), and one can postulate similar changes in the underlying moral intuitions. The even more massive social changes following the invention of food production and the consequent changes in the nature and size of human societies (Diamond 1997; Kaplan et al. 2009) must have led to even more culturally induced variation in moral intuitions, in tune with the nature of the societies produced.

Cultural variation is strongly enhanced by the presence of the urge to comply with local moral norms. Thus, moral emotions, although they historically have a core

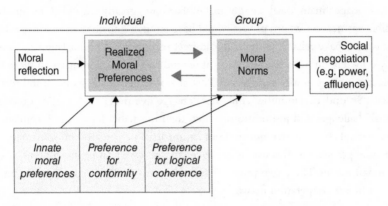

Figure 7.2. The interaction between the biologically based moral preferences and various processes (social and individual—cognitve) channeled through moral norms to produce the realized moral preferences. Moral preferences and moral norms together produce moral action.

context and are elicited by a core set of stimuli, are malleable and may expand (or perhaps even shift) their content. Figure 7.2 illustrates this process. It shows how innate moral preferences (the primary emotions) are modified into realized moral preferences (the moral intuitions people have) under the influence of a variety of internal and external (social) processes.

It is easy to see how this malleability to cultural influences could have arisen. Children are very good at sensing moral norms and internalizing them (Schmidt and Rakoczy, Chapter 6 in this volume). The very existence of this process implies that the contents have always been somewhat variable in humans, despite the presence of an innate core. Its presence therefore made it easy for new content of moral norms to be added, and old content to be abandoned, when people adopted new forms of subsistence and social organization.

The tension between innate moral preferences and the preference for norm compliance means that only a limited number of moral norms may be truly culturally universal. This outcome is relevant to the debate as to whether we should expect such universal moral norms (see Turiel and Dahl, Chapter 10 in this volume). Interestingly, even moral norms that show a patchy distribution often still involve strong emotions, as shown by the strictly policed rules of some religions.

8. On the Origin of Other Standards and Conventions

Humans are normative animals. Indeed, human social organization has a fundamentally normative dimension, and developmental research has revealed that even small children understand this (Rakoczy and Schmidt 2013). This fact suggests that moral norms are the oldest form of normativity, which arose as soon as language had become sufficiently precise, and that social norms (local rules subject to sanctioning, such as rules regulating school attendance) and conventions (arbitrary rules subject to sanctioning, such as etiquette or certain traffic rules) owe their existence to our normative minds extending the application of normative judgments to recently evolved domains outside morality, linked to living in complex societies with extensive divisions of labor. This idea may provide the most convincing explanation for the fact that some people respond to violations of conventions, such as etiquette, with great indignation.

9. Conclusions

In light of a clear evolutionary foundation to morality, the evolutionary approach should help us to provide a plausible account for both the adaptive function and the origin of normativity. We developed the argument that all morality, human or non-human, is normative, because in the many species that form dyadic social bonds we see elements of partner control, or at least partner choice (which selects for adequate cooperative attitudes; Schino and Aureli 2017). However, only in humans do we see moral norms that apply systematically to third parties, in some cases even including total strangers (especially when moral reflection is involved). The reason, we propose, is that human cooperative networks became extended toward less familiar individuals or even in-group strangers, whose reputation could be evaluated through gossip. In societies where gossip determines one's fate, it tends to keep everyone honest. This extension could only have arisen after human language had sufficiently evolved to allow such evaluations to reach any and all. Language led humans to negotiate local refinements of broader norms. A child's tendency to actively deduce the local moral norms (rather than wait to have them delineated through opprobrium) makes it easier to adjust to local norms that arose culturally through innovation and negotiation. This tendency thus made it possible for moral norms to become fine-tuned to local conditions. Finally, we argue that moral normativity provides the foundation for the application of norm reasoning into non-moral domains, including conventions. Thus, our tendency to follow rules in all walks of life arose as a byproduct of our evolved preference to recognize and follow moral norms, because they were the cornerstone of our cooperative foraging niche.

Acknowledgments

We thank Hanjo Glock and the other participants in the workshops in Münster on which this book is based for valuable discussion, and the organizers (and editors of this book), Kurt Bayertz and Neil Roughley, for bringing us all together.

8

The Emergence of Moral Normativity

Kurt Bayertz

I fully subscribe to the judgement of those writers who maintain that of all the differences between man and the lower animals, the moral sense or conscience is by far the most important. This sense . . . is summed up in that short but imperious word "ought," so full of high significance.

—CHARLES DARWIN (1871, 70)

1. The Content of Morality and Its "Form"

1.1 Behaviour

For a long time, anthropological interest in morality stemmed mainly from the belief that it (together with reason and language) was an indication, if not proof, of the uniqueness of human beings: human beings can be moral, whereas animals cannot. From an evolutionary perspective, this assumption is questionable for it seems to presuppose a sharp dividing line between human beings and animals, and in so doing to suggest that human morality did not evolve naturally, but was (literally or metaphorically) God-given. Those who are not willing to postulate such a miracle have no choice but to assume that morality evolved in some way, and this in turn presupposes that there must have been some kind of precursor for it in the animal kingdom. Empirical research has in fact identified some such precursors; particularly relevant, of course, are the corresponding findings in primates, our closest biological relatives. The now extensive literature on this topic names various related phenomena, such as parental care, cooperation between relatives and non-relatives, asymmetric assistance, peaceful resolution of conflicts by third parties, and inequity aversion (for an overview, see Brosnan 2014). Even though some of these findings are debatable or require further specification, many authors do see them as sufficient evidence of the existence of at least some kind of morality—let us call it a "protomorality"—in non-human primates and other animals. Accordingly, human morality did not originate all of a sudden, then, but has deep phylogenetic roots.

From a philosophical perspective, the underlying conception of morality is an obtrusive issue, of course. We can only speak of "protomorality" if we have an adequate conception of (fully developed) human morality. The methodological reason for this is obvious: to the extent that we wish to identify the behaviour of animals as a precursor to or "building block" for human morality, we require criteria which will enable us to filter out the relevant elements from the complex repertoire of behavioural patterns in animals. These criteria result from our conception of (fully developed) morality; let us call it "morality" *tout court*. Whilst protomorality precedes morality chronologically, the methodological order between the two conceptions is reversed: we require a conception of morality in order to identify protomorality.

A brief glance at the previously mentioned literature reveals that an explicit conception of morality is not always given; instead, authors tend to work with implicit conceptions centring around the assumption that morality is to be viewed as a particular type of *behaviour*. This is easily recognisable from the empirical phenomena mentioned earlier. An immediately consecutive second step then characterises this behaviour more precisely as altruistic, cooperative, or prosocial. Sometimes emotions which can be regarded as proximate triggers of such behaviour (e.g. empathy) are also included. This focus on a particular type of behaviour[1] is easy to explain, especially when the protomorality of animals is under investigation. Since scientists cannot ask animals questions, their crucial source of information is actual behaviour (cf. Kappeler et al., this volume, 70f.). Not even concomitant emotions are directly observable, meaning that they have to be inferred. Only when we turn to human beings and their morality do we have speech as an additional source of information, through which we can then acquire more knowledge about the motives and reasons behind an observed behaviour.

Although there are compelling reasons to concentrate on behaviour when addressing protomorality, it would be premature to take this as inducement to define human morality as altruistic or cooperative behaviour. Such a definition would capture one important feature, it is true, but it would also be too broad and simultaneously too narrow. On the one hand, types of altruistic and cooperative behaviour exist which are

---

[1] To give some examples: "in our evolutionary perspective, moral interactions are a subset of cooperative interactions" (Tomasello and Vaish 2013, 323); and "we regard morality as the expressed behaviour, the part most easily measured" (van Schaik et al. 2014, 67). Brosnan opens her paper (Brosnan 2014, 85) with the question: "Is moral behaviour unique to humans?"

not moral: we just have to think of the "altruism" of suicide bombers or of cooperation between criminals. On the other hand, morality constitutes far more than certain
types of behaviour. We use the expression "morality" to refer to a system containing
numerous elements other than behaviour, roughly divisible into four groups: firstly,
the emotions, attitudes, characters, and virtues of the moral agents; secondly, the norms
and ideals pursued (or not) by the agents in their actions; thirdly, evaluations of the
actions or individuals through praise and admonition; and, fourthly, the justifications
for such evaluations or moral norms. This list should sufficiently underline the insight
that morality does not reduce to the sum total of prosocial behaviour.

If this is accurate, the continuities at the behavioural level so emphasised by some
authors are less significant than might appear at first glance. Focussing on behaviour
depicts a far shorter and smoother transition from protomorality to morality than is
the case if we take a more complex conception of morality as our basis.

1.2 Form

One might argue that even if morality does not coincide with behaviour (of a particular kind), behaviour does still represent its core; and that the relevance of this core
does not decrease just because some other elements are included as well. It cannot
be overlooked that all elements within moral systems refer directly or indirectly to
actions. More precisely: they aim at either the prevention or the promotion of actions.
The evaluations which we make of actions, for example, are precisely intended to
encourage or discourage such actions; they therefore have a *practical* purpose, in other
words, that of steering actions or behaviour.[2] All elements within moral systems ultimately serve such a practical purpose. It cannot therefore be a case of casting doubt
on the significance of behaviour for morality, but far more of paying attention to the
specific manner in which morality refers to behaviour. Morality does not primarily
concern a person *doing* something in particular; but it does always concern the idea
that a person *ought* to do something (or not).

Whenever something is referred to as "moral," an essential characteristic is that it is
obligatory. Or, to put it another way: an essential feature of morality is that it is *normative*. Accordingly, in order to be classified as "moral," any element within a moral
system must display two characteristics: (i) It must have a certain "content." There is
no room here to discuss this content in more precise terms. Disregarding the objection
mentioned in the preceding, I shall here fall into line with the predominant definition whereby a feeling, a norm, a judgement, or an action is to be classified as "moral"
and recognised as an element within the moral system if it is altruistic, cooperative, or
prosocial (in a sense still to be more closely defined). (ii) This prosocial content must

---

[2] In this text I make no distinction between "action" and "behaviour."

assume a certain "form": it must be *binding, mandatory*, or *obligatory*. Here we come to the normative dimension of morality which I shall address in more detail in the following.

The terms "content" and "form" highlight two aspects of morality which are analytically easy to distinguish, and yet closely connected. Firstly, the two aspects do not occur separately. Form does not exist without content. There is no ought per se, but only ever ought in connection with something; it is always a content of some kind which ought to be done. Secondly, form does not determine content in every respect. On the one hand, the content of an "ought" need not be moral, but can also be, e.g. legal or religious; on the other hand, an "ought" can have different moral contents, as is shown by the mere fact of historical and cultural diversity regarding morality. Nevertheless, form is, thirdly, not compatible with every type of content; for example, impossible actions cannot be represented in the content of an "ought."

The starting point for this chapter is, therefore, that we can only attain an appropriate conception of morality by taking into account content *and* form. With regard to content, this should be fairly indisputable: one cannot understand what morality is if one does not know its content. But what about "form"? Maybe this is merely "packaging" for the content; and maybe this packaging can be ignored without any great loss.

But this is not the case. Content *as moral content* does not exist without the form of normativity. Normativity is the *necessary* form for moral content. This becomes clear when we remember that morality fulfils a certain social function. Through it, the behaviour of individuals is to be steered in a particular direction: they *ought* to perform certain actions and refrain from performing others. Here it is assumed that individuals would not perform or refrain from performing these actions by themselves, or at least not with enough certainty. This results from the fact that moral actions are, from the point of view of content, generally taken to be altruistic or prosocial; as such, they are not always in the immediate interests of the agents. Individuals are to do something regardless of whether or not they actually want to. This exactly explains the normative form of morality. Morality necessarily *demands* a certain type of behaviour because a structural tension exists between this behaviour and the self-interest of the individuals. This is also the reason why moral normativity is often accompanied by insistence. Moral norms do not merely "recommend" or "request" a certain behaviour, they "categorically"[3] demand it.

This is true, by the way, not only of behaviour, but also of evaluations or emotions. If a certain judgement is morally correct, then this judgement *ought* to be passed

---

[3] Here this term is not meant in its special Kantian sense; it is only supposed to underline the particular "strength" of the moral ought. Authors such as Sidgwick (1874, 6f., 26) also use it in this way.

by all those finding themselves in the same situation. And the same is true of moral emotions: it is not just a case of whether somebody is empathetic, but also and in particular of whether that person *ought* to be empathetic and behave empathetically. In the following I shall not go any deeper into evaluations or emotions, concentrating instead on actions.

The following deliberations are based on the assumption that normativity is not a phenomenon at the periphery of morality, but one of its essential features; and that consequently every theory of morality has to provide an understanding of this characteristic. If this is accurate, an evolutionary or historical theory of morality cannot concentrate exclusively on content, but has also to provide an interpretation of the genesis of its "form": it has to make the genesis of moral normativity comprehensible. In the following I would like to make a few proposals in this regard.

1.3 Different Normativities

What, then, do we understand by the *normativity* of morality? In everyday contexts we say without hesitation that somebody "ought to" or "has to" or "is obliged to" do something; and usually our conversational partners understand what this means. Nevertheless, an explicit explanation is anything but obvious. This is true not only of our everyday awareness, but also for the empirical sciences, including evolutionary approaches to morality. So far, the latter have largely concentrated on the content of morality, only rarely analysing its normative form. Darwin, at least, seemed to sense the relevance of this phenomenon when he wrote: "I fully subscribe to the judgement of those writers who maintain that of all the differences between man and the lower animals, the moral sense or conscience is by far the most important. This sense [. . .] is summed up in that short but imperious word 'ought,' so full of high significance" (Darwin 1871, 70). But he failed to provide any suggestion as to how this "imperious word" was to be understood. Only very recently has a more intensive assessment of the normativity of morality as an issue begun to emerge (Rudolf von Rohr et al. 2011; Kappeler et al., this volume, 77ff.; van Schaik et al., Chapter 7 in this volume). In this regard, evolutionary and anthropological research still has a long way to go.

Philosophical ethics has also had difficulties finding answers to this question. Across broad stretches of its history, it has not even noticed the existence of a question which can and must be asked. Immanuel Kant was probably the first to recognise "ought" as a central *explanandum* of ethical theory formation; and it is no coincidence that the term "duty" (indicating normativity) plays such a major role in his ethics. Since then, more attention has been paid to this question in the literature, so that today we have at our disposal a series of answers which—as is usually the case in philosophical works—harshly oppose one another. I would like to name six of these theories of moral normativity (TN):

TN₁ *Divine command*: The oldest and historically most influential of the six stems from an age in which no difference was made between morality and religion. It states: "ought" is what God wishes. This interpretation is an obvious choice in Jewish-Christian influenced cultures because the latter historically attached importance to a list of norms starting with the words: "Thou shalt . . .". The *Decalogue* is probably the most memorable source for the assumption that "shalt" or "ought" is a synonym for "commanded by God."

TN₂ *Rational will*: The theory that moral normativity must be interpreted as the volition of God was viewed and rejected by Immanuel Kant as an expression of a "heteronomous" moral consciousness. In his theory, he replaced divine will with human will; albeit not the subjective and random will of an arbitrary individual, but the general and rational will of mankind. In Kant's own words: "for this ought is actually a willing that holds for every rational being, on the condition: if reason were practical in it without hindrances" (Kant 1785, 449). Christine M. Korsgaard (1996, 102, 117) has taken up the Kantian approach in recent years and has attempted to develop it further.

TN₃ *Sanction*: Another interpretation assumes that moral normativity derives its sense and meaning exclusively from the threat of punishment or the promise of reward. Disregarding divine punishment for now, it proposes that moral normativity be identified with *social* sanctions which (potentially) succeed violations of norms. This is the direction taken by theorists like Thomas Hobbes (1651, 246), Arthur Schopenhauer (1840, 478f.) or Ernst Tugendhat (1984, 73).

TN₄ *Sense of obligation*: Whereas the sanction theory resorts to external authority, other philosophers have identified moral normativity with an internal authority: the conscience or the "sense of obligation" (Prichard 1912, 9) which we have acquired following successful moral socialisation. Accordingly, "ought" is nothing other than a *feeling* of having an obligation.

TN₅ *Logical property*: Based on the conviction that philosophical access to the morality issue necessarily takes place via language, Richard Hare advocated the theory that "ought" is a logical feature of moral language: that "of entailing at least one imperative" (Hare 1981, 21).

TN₆ *Rational justification*: Finally, a view exists whereby "ought" is to be grasped as an implication of ethical justification. The fact that I "ought" to act in accordance with a certain norm then simply means that this norm is well justified (Habermas 1998, 35). In other words: something which ought to be done is practically rational.

This list is not exhaustive but it does give us an idea of the variety and heterogeneity of the philosophical approaches to moral normativity. I shall not go into the answers listed here in any detail. They are all unsatisfactory, and yet they all draw attention to important aspects which in a theory of normativity need to be taken into account. They offer a *first* condition of adequacy for an explanation of normativity such as I shall be proposing in the following sections. Such an explanation should not ignore the wealth of relevant philosophical insights; far more, it should pick up on insights which have been gained and incorporate them within an ideally coherent overall picture. In the following sections I shall therefore return to the philosophical interpretations of "ought" mentioned earlier and attempt to clarify the contributions they can make to a theory of moral normativity.

A *second* condition for such a theory is that it should be "naturalistic" in a weak sense of the word. On the one hand, it should survive without metaphysical assumptions such as those underlying (TN₁), making "ought" comprehensible within the natural world. In addition, it should be "naturalistic" in the sense of being compatible with the findings of the empirical sciences: not only should it not contradict these findings, it should also demonstrate productive connections with these findings. This is particularly true of psychology, the social sciences, and evolutionary anthropology.

This plea in favour of an alignment with the empirical sciences should not, however, trigger an expectation that a satisfactory conception of ought can be gained on this basis alone. A *third* condition of adequacy is required: such a conception should be non-reductionistic and non-biologistic. Even if such a conception has recourse to biological roots of morality and normativity, at the same time it should plausibly show that—and how—the "moral ought" was able to break free from these roots (at least partially), establish itself as a *cultural* phenomenon, and develop *historically*. Not only do the evolutionary origins of morality have to be explained, but also its further cultural development.

2. The Volition of Others

2.1 *Volitions*

Of the theories of moral normativity listed, the first two are very promising in their approaches. The divine command theory has the advantage of making plausible in very simple terms what it means that somebody ought to do something. It views "ought" as a relationship between two subjects, one giving the other a reason to behave in a certain way through his will. The problem with this theory lies in the fact that it views the volitional subject as a power from beyond, thus introducing a metaphysical element which is superfluous for our understanding of the moral ought; superfluous because we are already familiar with structurally similar relations from our everyday lives. They are to be found, for example, when parents make their children perform certain actions, or forbid them to perform others; the children are to do something because the parents want it. There is therefore no reason to see ought as a genuinely theological idea which loses all meaning outside the God-mankind relationship, as maintained by Arthur Schopenhauer (1840, 477f.) and later Elisabeth Anscombe (1958, 4f.). The phenomenon of moral "ought" does not have an essentially theological dimension; it is an everyday and, in this sense, natural phenomenon for which we have to find a natural explanation.

Kant had already taken a step in this direction when he interpreted the practical ought as volition, while at the same time distancing himself from the theological interpretation of volition. But his approach also remains unsatisfactory, for two reasons. Firstly, for Kant morality is a question of the inner integrity of the individual. Accordingly, he views ought as a subject-*internal* relationship between the individual as an empirical, natural being (Kant: "homo phaenomenon") on the one hand, and as a rational being (Kant: "homo noumenon") on the other. The essentially intersubjective, public, and social character of morality in general, and of the moral ought in particular thus disappears. This leads directly to a second problem. By making a strict distinction between the "homo phaenomenon" and the "homo noumenon," Kant expels the moral ought from the world of empirical, natural human beings and catapults it, if not into a transcendental world, then certainly into an ideal world of reason. It is then difficult to see (a) how it is supposed to make an impact from one world to the other, in other words how natural human beings can be morally obligated; and (b) how the moral ought can have developed in evolutionary terms.

If we wish to hold on to the fruitful idea that the moral ought is to be grasped as a kind of volition, we will have to go beyond Kant and remove it from the ideal world of reason, transplanting it into the empirical world—more precisely, the intersubjective world. This is exactly the approach of Hans Krämer (1992, 47), who insists that moral "ought" presupposes not only subjects, from which it originates, but also addressees, to whom it is directed. "Ought" is accordingly always the flipside and counterpart of the volition of the other. In this sense, ought always presupposes correlative volition and refers back to it. Krämer's proposal can be summed up in the following formula, in which A and B stand for random subjects and z stands for a random act or omission:

[1]   A *ought* morally to do z = B *wants* A to do z.

We shall see that this formula goes too far and therefore requires correction. Nevertheless, it opens up the prospect of a natural explanation of moral normativity which is also capable of integrating the findings of the relevant empirical sciences.

But what is this "volition" from which "ought" originates? I shall use this expression to denote conative attitudes which display the following three attributes: (a) they contain a reference to a state of the world which the attitude's bearer believes could be produced by acting; (b) this state of the world is evaluated (not necessarily consciously and explicitly); (c) the attitude's bearer is motivated to perform actions which promote this desired state of the world. This characterisation is broad enough to include conative attitudes of animals. For our context, only those attitudes are relevant which refer not to states of the world in general, but to other individuals and their actions. The expression "expectation" is often used for such volition in the literature: B expects A to do z. Provided that the term is not being used to signify mere prediction, its meaning is equivalent to that of "will," where this is directed at other individuals and their behaviour. Wherever "will" or "volition" is used in the following, the term "expectation" could be substituted.

It is obvious that the biological fitness and well-being of an individual depends not only on his general environment, but also on the fellow members of his species and their behaviour. For early ontogenesis, during which the individual relies on parental care, this is particularly obvious. But in later phases of life as well, individual fitness can be promoted or hindered by competition, conflicts, or cooperation with fellow members of the species. Animals and human beings will therefore try to influence the behaviour of fellow members through facial expressions, gestures, or vocal utterances (Krebs and Dawkins 1984; Maynard Smith and Harper 2003). In such cases, the communication has an *imperative* character: B signalises his will to A, and A is to follow it. We can assume that the significance of imperative communication in social animals is more marked than in other species; in the former, interactions between individuals are more frequent than in solitary animals.[4] We can also assume that the significance of imperative communication increases to the same measure as genetic behavioural control decreases. The larger the scope for individual behaviour, the harder it becomes for fellow members to predict, and the more motivation there will be for the latter to try to influence behaviour. In addition, the possibilities for influencing other individuals through imperative communication increase if their behaviour is not comprehensively programmed.

2.2 Groups

However, the proposal that the moral ought has to be understood as the *volition of others* is too strong and too undifferentiated. If we interpret Fido's scratching at the door as "Fido wants to go out," then [1] would result in this scratching generating a moral obligation on the part of his mistress to open the door. This would obviously be absurd. And this cannot just be because Fido is a dog. Nor does the mere fact that starry-eyed Harry *wants* a date with his pretty colleague Sally mean that she *ought* to go out with him; she has the option to decline politely without violating an obligation. This is intuitively plausible and is already suggested by a closer look at [1]. For not only can Harry want something from Sally (the agreement to a date), but also Sally

---

[4] In this context, findings about communication between great apes (usually chimpanzees and bonobos) growing up in captivity and their human caretakers are informative: nearly all the communicative acts of the apes recorded by Tomasello and his colleagues were requests for objects or actions, in other words had an imperative purpose (cf. Tomasello 2008, 34–8 and 249–56).

can want something from Harry (to be left in peace); the conflicting volitions would in this case cancel each other out. In succinct terms, it cannot be correct that an arbitrary instance of volition constitutes an ought; and certainly not a moral ought. The proposal that an ought should be understood as a volition of others therefore requires further qualification.

We are now on the trail of the additional conditions which must be fulfilled before an ought can emerge from a volition: we must be clear that the idea of a selective interaction between two individuals is the product of an abstraction. Among social creatures, *every* interaction occurs against the background of, and on the basis of, communal life. Just as there are no totally isolated individuals, each interaction between individuals takes place in the direct or indirect context of the group. This is true of our closest biological relatives, but in particular of our own species. However far we go back in the history of our species, we will never find individuals living in total isolation in the manner postulated by Rousseau. Over tens of thousands of years, our ancestors lived in small groups. A close biological relatedness between the members of the group was characteristic of their lifestyle, as was a highly egalitarian character of their social structure and a strict agreement in their customs. In addition, close cooperation dominated during child-rearing and while hunting and gathering. In contrast to the situation among other primates, a considerable proportion of the overall group participated in these cooperative activities, sometimes even the majority of group members (van Schaik et al. 2014).

On our quest for the volitions which lead to the formation of moral normativity under such conditions, the first condition they need to fufill is their occurrence in *repeated* interactions between members of the group. Secondly, it seems necessary that they are found in the context of interactions where the individuals concerned have not just the same goal, but a *collective* or *shared* goal. They therefore require a mutual behaviour facilitating the achievement of this goal. The relevant volition, then, cannot be reduced to volitions of the individuals concerned. As conative mental states, volitions are bound to the mental activities of individual living organisms, it is true; but they can be shared by several individuals and thus pass from being individual states to being genuinely collective ones. We then encounter the phenomenon of a "collective intentionality" or "shared intentionality" (Searle 1995, 23–6; Tomasello et al. 2005). For this there seem to be foundations in human nature that not only have a phylogenetic impact, but also are empirically traceable in ontogenesis (cf. Schmidt and Rakoczy, Chapter 6 in this volume).

The first specification of [1] then states: what A morally ought to do is essentially determined not by the will of a random individual B, but by the mutual and collective will of several individuals, in other words, by the will of a social group G:

[2]   A ought morally to do z = group G wants A to do z.

As regards both their content and their extension, the relevant volitions are directed to the group. Their contents concern the functioning of the group and actions of its members that support such functioning. Under the conditions dominating at the beginning of the development of the human race, there was little room for the idiosyncratic volitions of individuals. Since survival crucially depended on the functioning of the group, the (collective) will of individuals was in all probability primarily directed at just that. What they wanted from each other was thus (a) cooperative behaviour in the production of food, in the rearing of children, in defence against external enemies, etc.; as well as (b) a behaviour which caused as few conflicts within the group as possible. What individuals mutually want in this situation is therefore prosocial behaviour. When the functioning of the group is at stake, the (collective) will of individuals is naturally directed at its members and remains limited to them. At first, any obligations beyond the group therefore do not arise. This group relativism is unavoidable as long as the traffic between members of different groups remains selective, and consequently no stable mutual will between groups can form.

If these deliberations are accurate, moral normativity enters the world as an integral component of a collective will aimed at the functioning of the community in question. Put another way: moral normativity initially coincides with social normativity. Any differentiation between the two does not begin until much later; and there are strong indications that this process has still not reached an end today. I shall address some aspects of this differentiation in the following.

2.3 Institution

We can imagine that several individuals might come together ad hoc, develop a common goal and a collective will directed at this goal, but then separate again once the goal in question has been achieved. In such cases, however, one would not wish to speak of the formation of (maybe moral, maybe social) normativity. This forces us to make a further explicit qualification going beyond [2]. It consists in a stability of the collective will which is more than temporal, and which in turn presupposes independence from any factually involved individuals. Metaphorically, we can also say that the collective will of individuals must take on a more solid aggregate state in order for normativity to emerge: it has to have solidified into a custom, a tradition, a convention in order to generate an ought. As I would put it, it has to be *institutionalised*. The second specification of [1] emphasises this institutional stabilisation of the common will:

[3]   A ought morally to do z = an *institutionalised* volition of the group exists that A do z.

There has been an in-depth debate among philosophers and social scientists about the concept of institution and its distinction from related terms such as "custom" or "convention" (cf. Searle 1995; overview in Miller 2014), but I cannot go into that debate in any detail here. What should be mentioned, however, are three basic features of institutions which are relevant to our context.

Firstly, institutions are related to human actions in two ways. On the one hand, they are *products of* human actions; and of actions which cannot be traced back to any genetic programming. In this sense, institutions are "artificial" or "cultural." On the other hand, they *consist in* human actions; they are patterns of human behaviour. Although some institutions have a material exterior (e.g. a building), their continued existence is essentially bound to activities of living human beings; and their existence ends when those corresponding activities end. This assumption of "artificiality" should not cast doubt on the finding that animals also have regular behaviour patterns which cannot be traced back to genetic programming; but it should be clear that instances of cultural institutions in the animal world remain very limited.

Secondly, institutions are characterised by their temporal stability; they are enduring patterns of behaviour. This does not rule out the possibility that institutions can change and develop. But it is most particularly connected with the abovementioned independence of institutions from *certain* individuals and *individual* actions. Institutions tend to continue existing when certain individuals leave or join. To this extent they even take priority over certain individuals in that they assign roles to them and control their actions within these roles.

For this reason, institutions are essentially normative; this is their *third*, and for us their most important, characteristic. Two points should be emphasised here. Firstly, the temporal stability of institutions means that the normativity resulting from them is not ad hoc or changeable. They do not prescribe certain actions for certain individuals; rather, they control the behaviour of individuals in a general (if not universal) manner. Secondly, they guarantee compliance with their norms through reward and punishment. In the literature there is a controversial debate about whether or not sanctions are a necessary feature of institutions, and whether therefore *all* social institutions are linked to a practice of sanctioning. What we can establish is that such a link always exists when (a) the institution in question fulfils important, maybe even vital functions for the group in question and its members; and when (b) the concept of sanction is understood in a wide sense so as to include negative and positive, formal and informal sanctions, e.g. the gain or loss of a reputation.

This of course suggests a close connection between normativity and institutions; and I would like to reinforce precisely this conclusion. If normativity, as [3] claims, is the "institutionalised will" of a group, then it is a social institution; at the same time, however, institutions are essentially normative. Therefore "normativity" is not reduced to "institution"; both terms refer to different aspects of the same phenomenon and are mutually explicable. This is at least true of social, including moral, norms; it can remain open for now whether or not it is true of all types of norms, e.g. logical norms.

2.4 Sanction

The previously mentioned sanctions merit more detailed attention. A family of philo-sophical theories (TN$_3$), which even today is still very influential, strongly underlines the significance of sanctions and then goes one step further by *identifying* moral nor-mativity with the existence of a sanctioning practice. This is one step too far, how-ever. Let us imagine an individual D who inflicts harm on another individual E; E reacts by acting in a similar manner towards D. Is this a sanction? One could say so, of course, but it should not be overlooked that two different cases can be in play here. In the first, E is simply reacting to the harm inflicted on him by D; this is a "nat-ural" retributive reaction which is completely explainable through recourse to the personal interests of E. It is impossible to see where the relationship between such a reaction and normativity could exist; let alone that such a reaction could constitute normativity. In the second case, a relationship to normativity does exist. Here, too, the harm inflicted by D might play a role in E's counter-reaction, but another factor is involved as well. The act by D is simultaneously evaluated according to a standard of correctness and consequently classified as "wrong." Only then does E's act go beyond a natural counter-reaction and gain normative substance. However, it does so not by constituting normativity, but rather by affirming it. In a word: sanctions presuppose the validity of a norm.

The reversal of the conceptual relationship between sanction and normativity, as postulated by (TN$_3$), has far-reaching implications: if sanctions presuppose a norm, then something in them comes into play which transcends the relationship between D and E. The more D's actions towards E are perceived not only as the infliction of harm, but also as violation of a norm, the more likely it is that the sanction can also be performed by a third party. Violation of a norm is then not just a matter between D and E, but a matter for the entire community in which that norm is valid. D's action now not only affects E, but also F (and any number of others); consequently, it is not only E who has a reason to sanction D, but also F.

In human societies, such sanctioning by third parties is not only a theoretical possi-bility, but a widely practised reality. Independently of organised sanctions (e.g. through the judicial system), violations of norms are punished by neutral third parties. Such behaviour cannot be explained, or at least not directly, through the personal interest of the punishing party, especially since, by intervening, the latter risks coming into conflict with the norm violator and incurring a disadvantage. Far more, we must as-sume that this punishing behaviour is based on a commitment to preserve the norm in question. Violations of norms are then no longer viewed as a problem between two individuals, but as a problem affecting the whole group. For this reason, individuals react to the violation who are not themselves impacted by it; the group reacts as a whole. It is not completely clear whether such a practice of third-party punishment exists in non-human primates; in the literature there are different views on this point (Riedl et al. 2012; Rudolf von Rohr et al. 2012). In any case, the practice is rare and is only conducted by high-ranking males (Rudolf von Rohr et al. 2012, 6f.). Amongst human beings it also seems to have been a late development. There were rudimentary signs in small foraging bands; but only when larger societies emerged, ones not built primarily upon relationships between relatives and direct reciprocity, did a general practice of punishment for norm violations develop (Marlowe 2009; Henrich et al. 2010; Guala 2012). The path was a long one and only embarked upon with the transition to sedentarism and the formation of advanced civilisations approximately 12,000 years ago.

The practice of third-party sanctioning of norm violations has a marked tendency to become separate from particular individuals, as is characteristic of the institutionalisation process. When the sanctioning itself is sanctioned, this tendency reaches a whole new level, for example, when those who sanction norm violations gain a good reputation, through which they can recommend themselves as cooperation partners in the future; in contrast, those who choose to ignore or tolerate the violation of a norm gain a bad reputation. Individuals are no longer at liberty to turn a blind eye to norm violations. This practice of sanctioning (non-)sanctioners tends to establish itself in particular where larger societies replace smaller communities, and where through progressive division of labour indirect forms of cooperation gain a greater relevance. Against this background, *formal* sanctions through specialised state organs can also ultimately emerge. In short: what was initially undifferentiated social normativity begins to become differentiated into mores, law, and morality.

If we draw up an overview of the emergence of the "form" of morality as outlined so far, it appears as a process which starts by involving individuals who want something from other individuals in certain situations. This volition is initially an individual, mental, and thus internal state. Some of these volitions are genuinely collective in nature: they are aimed at goals crucial to survival which can only be realised together. On the basis of such volitions, a collective practice emerges which achieves temporal stability in customs, traditions, and institutions. The individual, mental, and thus internal states take on a temporally permanent external form, achieving (relative) independence from individual persons.

3. Exteriorisation and Rationalisation

3.1 Exteriorisation

This shift from the internal to the external is similar to the production of material tools. At the beginning of the production process is the internal state of individuals: their needs, their intentions, the knowledge of how these intentions can be realised, and the practical skills required to do so. Biologically pre-given organs serve as an aid. In order to dig holes, animals and humans initially use their relevant biological attributes, especially their hands. In a second step, these bio-logical attributes can be backed up or replaced by objects from the outside world which have either been stumbled across or sought especially. Now holes are no longer dug with human hands, but with a stick or a flat stone. Such objects can be fashioned and adapted to a particular purpose. In doing so, the available knowledge and skills flow into the objects themselves and characterise their design. In this third step, the original biological function of the hands, coupled with the knowl-edge and skills necessary for the finishing process, assumes an extracorporeal and extrabiological existence. What originally were primitive tools can now be altered and perfected. Simple shovels for digging holes emerge. Over correspondingly long periods of time they are developed further to become elaborate shovels and ulti-mately motorised diggers.

In the 1920s, Paul Alsberg characterised this process as "body liberation" (Alsberg 1922, 46 passim); what he meant was the separation of function and body: function materialises extracorporeally. In animals, such a separation can only be found to a very limited extent, and the French palaeoanthropologist André Leroi-Gourhan spoke of the "uniquely human phenomenon of exteriorisation of the organs involved in the carrying out of technics" (Leroi-Gourhan 1964/65, 257). The consequences of this exteriorisation are far-reaching:

(i)   Tools can now be transferred from one individual to another; they can continue to exist after the death of their constructor and still be used by his successors. They become independent of their creator, a super-individual possession which can be passed on via a second, non-genetic line of inheritance.

(ii) Through their extracorporeal existence, the knowledge and skills materialised in a tool can be accumulated from one generation to the next. Tools can now be improved step by step, as changes are made from one generation to the next. At the outset this occurred very slowly; later the development of technology accelerated and became emancipated from the mechanisms and temporal horizons of biological evolution (Leroi-Gourhan 1993, 130–9).

(iii) Biological adaptation of human beings to their given environment is replaced, at least in part, by transformation of the tools required. The human hand can remain unspecialised, whereas the functions detached from it, found in a spade or hammer or pliers, become ever more differentiated and ever further developed.

(iv) Through the continued generation of material artefacts of this kind, there emerges within the natural environment an artificial environment in which humans live. It detaches itself ever more clearly from the natural environment, a process which in biological terms counts as niche construction (cf. Laland and O'Brien 2011). This new environment is "artificial" not only in the sense that it is man-made, but also in the sense that human intentions, knowledge, and skills are materially stored inside it. New individuals are born into an environment which offers them the chance to acquire these stored intentions, knowledge, and skills (cf. Sterelny 2012).

For our present context it is important to add that not only practical functions like digging can be exteriorised, but also mental functions like memory, e.g. through writing. This was emphasised early on by both Alsberg and Leroi-Gourhan; in the more recent literature, some related aspects have been discussed under the label "extended mind" (Clark 2008). If mental contents and processes are not limited to the brain, but can be wholly or partially outsourced to the surroundings, then the same is also true of the volitions mentioned earlier. In the latter case, however, the result is not exteriorisation in the shape of an independent material object, but in a stable pattern of behaviour, i.e. a social institution. Ignoring for now any differences which might exist between these two kinds of exteriorisation, in one crucial respect they are analogous: in both cases, mental states, abilities, or functions initially bound to the biological constitution of an organism become detached from that organism and assume an extracorporeal existence.

One particularly important medium for the exteriorisation of mental states is propositional language. It facilitates the explicit communication and generalisation of collective volitions. Obviously, the emergence of language brought with it a considerable increase in the abstraction and generalisation of thought. The linguistic meaning of an utterance clearly presupposes detachment from its immediate context, and at the same time furthers that detachment. Once they have emerged, we use linguistic expressions in accordance with a general meaning already established within the community of speakers. Semantic independence of linguistic utterances from their situation makes it possible to speak about absent (e.g. past or future) matters or objects, as well as abstract matters. For our purposes, it is crucial that this also makes it possible to formulate general norms and abstract values. The medium of language is therefore not restricted to the role of a neutral container; rather, it generalises and decontextualises volitions. This process later continues with the emergence of writing. According to Goody, scripturality has promoted the formation of ethical universalism: "In written codes there is a tendency to present a single 'abstract' formula which overlays, and to some extent replaces, the more contextualised norms of oral societies." (Goody 1986, 12) The institutionalisation of the collective will described earlier was most probably promoted through its linguistic communication; and later differentiation processes, including the formation of separate legal systems, are inconceivable without language and writing.

3.2 Interiorisation

Even though the cultural world is a product of exteriorisation, and even though this includes a certain "emancipation" from our biological and mental existence, there cannot, however, be a complete detachment from biology and psychology. Let us first look, once again, at material artefacts. The mental content projected onto them by their creators and materialised within them would be "extinguished" if the artefacts were to be completely dissociated from human actions. These actions are a potential contained within the artefacts which only exists for as long as it can be tapped into. In the long term, there can therefore be no exteriorisation without *interiorisation*. All the individuals involved in the development and use of certain artefacts will sooner or later die and be replaced by new ones. To these new individuals, the artefacts are just as pre-given as random natural objects: they are encountered as an external reality and have to be appropriated so that they can be accessed and their mental content activated. The prerequisite for this is a learning process, in the course of which individuals have to acquire the knowledge and skills embodied in the artefacts. Collectively and historically exteriorised contents have to be individually interiorised in order for them to remain "alive." The further the cultural process progresses, the more comprehensive the extracorporeal, cultural heritage becomes and the more complex and longer the ontogenetic learning process becomes through which new individuals absorb this heritage and keep it alive.

In an analogous way, all of this is also true of social institutions, including the moral ought. Unlike artefacts, institutions do not have a material existence separable from their use. As we have seen, they are stable patterns of behaviour and exist simply *in* the behaviour of individuals. The existence of institutions thus depends on individuals entering the group in question for the first time, appropriating the contents exteriorised there and assimilating them in their behaviour. This occurs within the framework of socialisation, and it is no coincidence that it is a particularly complex process in human beings. The behaviour of social insects towards both their environment and fellow members of their species is genetically programmed; they carry the "rules" of their behaviour inside themselves from the outset and therefore have little to learn. In higher animals, the need to learn is more marked. And ultimately, in human beings, who enter the world with comparatively sparse genetic behavioural determinants, it is significantly more marked. Here the learning phase within an individual biography is much longer than that of our closest biological relatives. All human societies make a significant effort to socialise each new generation (cf. Antweiler, this volume, 94ff.). In the course of human history, this socialisation process has become longer and more complex as an ever increasing amount of accumulated exteriorisations has to be interiorised.

It is not my intention to suggest that human individuals enter the world as a blank slate. Their biological equipment includes characteristics and skills which are advantageous for life in a culturally marked environment. Thus, human beings appear to have a special preparedness for recognising and imitating social norms; a preparedness which is not found, or at least not to the same extent, in other biological species (cf. Schmidt and Rakoczy, this volume, 134f.). The protomoral behaviours of primates summarily mentioned at the beginning of this chapter also indicate the existence of biological foundations for moral behaviour. The same is true of moral feelings (cf. Roughley, this volume, 219ff.) and of the ability to distinguish between social and moral norms, which is seemingly marked from very early on (cf. Turiel and Dahl, this volume, 202ff.). In this sense, one can say that roots of morality are to be found in human nature.

These roots are not strong enough, however, to give the morality tree the stability it requires. The tree (to remain with this image) is exposed to the bracing wind of self-interest, initially mild but later a stiff breeze. Even if biological dispositions do exist towards prosocial or moral action, this does not rule out the existence of counter-dispositions. As hinted at earlier, it remains a fact that it is not always in the direct self-interest of individuals to adhere to moral norms and that doing so demands sacrifices of them, at least sometimes. Here there is a disanalogy to many other social norms. A clear example is provided by linguistic norms: since human beings have an interest in having their linguistic utterances understood by their addressees, there is no temptation to violate linguistic norms (cf. Kompa, this volume, 261). In the case of moral norms, this is different; here individuals do not always have a personal interest in adhering to them. On the contrary: the function of morality consists in limiting the pursuance of (direct) individual self-interest.

Due to this latent tension between morality and self-interest, a certain level of social pressure always has to be built up in moral communities to promote conformity with moral norms. This pressure is exerted by sanctions, as already mentioned. In addition, socialisation aims to anchor all valid norms (the institutionalised and exteriorised volition of the community) deeply within the individuals, allowing them to become a motivating force. In this way, biologically inherent moral feelings are reinforced and complemented by the "conscience" as an internalised authoritative body. Provided that moral socialisation has succeeded, the moral ought is then represented from the inner perspective of the agents as a "sense of obligation" (Prichard 1912); and provided we adhere to this perspective, (TN_4) offers a plausible interpretation of the moral ought.

And yet the inner perspective is not the only one, and ultimately not the decisive one. From the point of view of the community, a reduction of ought to a "sense of obligation" is not acceptable. The members of the community *ought* to act morally even if they do not have this "sense of obligation" (maybe due to failed moral socialisation). One can *have* a certain obligation without *feeling* obligated. To this extent, the moral ought is independent of all internal states of individuals, from their moral feelings, their conscience, and their "sense of obligation." Even if there has to be a kind of emotional and intellectual "sounding board" for the moral ought in human nature, its origins are not internal. The moral ought is an "external," social reality.

3.3 Distance

That, from the perspective of the individual, the origins of the moral ought appear external is a fact that has motivated some theorists to brand it a foreign body which takes the individual by force. They interpret the (not always gentle) practice of sanctioning both during and after socialisation as a homogenisation mechanism intent on taking individuals and pressing them into a normative corset; a resulting "sense of obligation" would then be the product of social trimming.

Indisputably there is always also an inherent element of "heteronomy" in morality, and ought seeks to limit our decisional freedom. It is a deficiency of the Kantian interpretation of the moral ought (TN_2) that it fails to acknowledge this element of "heteronomy." All the same, the trimming accusation falls short in several respects. It is based, *firstly*, on an incorrect presupposition that the "essence" of human beings is interior, is given by nature, and can only be clouded by external social influences. The exteriorisation theory states, to the contrary, that the experiences, knowledge, and volitions of preceding generations are stored in cultural achievements, including morality, and that they can therefore be acquired by newly arriving individuals at each stage. The latter are not only saved from having to repeat these experiences; they are most especially equipped with behavioural possibilities which they only have at their disposal because they are at the (temporary) end of a long line of generations. At birth, individuals do encounter a social reality into which they have to integrate; but at the same time, a heritage is put at their disposal which makes them capable of performing certain actions in the first place.

Secondly, all individuals profit from the moral restrictions imposed on their actions because morality also restricts the actions of other individuals. By providing individuals with a certain level of protection, here too morality makes certain actions possible.

In our context, a *third* point particularly needs to be emphasised. The "foreignness" with which the exteriorised volition of others is encountered by individuals creates a *distance* which can become the starting point for a reflective and critical stance towards the volition. Our species has, of course, some specifically intellectual skills which facilitate reflection and criticism; at the same time, however, the external nature of morality and the social institutionalisation of the ought also make it easier to apply these skills in practice. It should be clear that the actual scope for application depends on numerous factors which cannot be discussed in any detail here, e.g. the level of education possessed by the society in question or the scope for political freedom within that society. Fundamentally, however, we can establish that the possibility of distancing oneself from pre-given institutions, including the moral ought, is one of the characteristics of the human life form.

The fact that this possibility of distancing oneself is an integral element of the human life form is easily illustrated by taking a look at moral socialisation, which takes place on two parallel paths. On the first, morality is handed down by example and by imitation; the other path involves explicit instruction, i.e. instruction conveyed by language. This second path is of interest because it is, firstly, specific to the human species and, secondly, makes the possibility of distancing oneself particularly transparent. The option of questioning or contradicting is built into the structure of linguistic communication from the outset. Even if the actual scope of doing so can be limited by other social factors, linguistically formulated norms (like other linguistic utterances) permit conversation, discussion, or controversy concerning the communicated contents. Even children can ask why they ought to do certain things and refrain from others; and among adults there is also what today many like to call "discourse." On the first, indirect path this option obviously does not exist. To the extent that moral socialisation takes this path, there is an option *not* to follow a set example, but not the option to ask questions or to contradict.

Asking questions means demanding *reasons*. A discourse does not consist simply in countering one assertion with another, but in criticising or defending previous assertions on the basis of reasons. One of the characteristics of linguistic statements is that they are made with a claim to correctness or validity and therefore in principle (not always at that moment) both require justification and allow for it. From the outset, norms therefore exist in a double sphere: in a sphere of causes, to the extent that their genesis can be explained causally, and in a sphere of reasons. This sphere of reasons will depend on the worldview of the group or community in question, and it will change as this worldview changes. Over long periods of time, mythological or religious justifications of morality were customary and were viewed as sufficient. From today's point of view, some of these justifications might appear bizarre; but it is not a case of how "good" reasons used to be or are now. What is crucial is (a) that behaviour which is mutually expected and desired by individuals can become the object of conversation and reflection; (b) that in the process reasons come into play; and (c) that with them a connection is made between morality and the overall worldview.

3.4 Reasons

This brings us to a stage of moral development far removed from its origins. We do not have to explain when this stage began historically; what is clear is that it was reached with the first advanced cultures. Individuals now no longer lived in small, egalitarian groups, but in socially differentiated, hierarchically ordered societies. The legitimation requirements on moral norms grow with the evolution of larger societies, in which moral expectations not only emerge on the part of individuals who know each other well, but also on the part of individuals who are strangers to each other. Larger societies render norms and ensuing obligations more important, yet at the same time also more problematic than before: what individuals are now expected and consequently obliged to do becomes independent of personal relationships.[5] For this to work, sanctions are absolutely necessary, but not sufficient. People have to *believe* that they have obligations and ought to do something; and this presupposes that there are shared beliefs to the effect that such obligations exist, as well as why they should be obeyed. Together with other mechanisms, religious systems have played an important role in this context.

Once cultural development has advanced far enough, thinking about the content of morality and the reasons for its binding nature can grow beyond everyday contexts and become methodically reflected. Religious systems or philosophical theories can emerge which aim at justifying actual valid norms. And more: theories like this not only can formulate reasons for or against the validation of norms, they also can question the criteria deeming the appropriateness of these *reasons*. Thus metatheoretical discourse becomes possible, negotiating predominantly linguistically formulated contents and claims, which are no longer directly connected to the institutionalised patterns of behaviour underlying them, and even less to the volitions of individuals underlying that behaviour.

Theorists who are professionally involved in such metatheoretical discourses might then react as if the moral ought were a logical feature of moral language itself (TN_5) or as if it only came into the world through practices of justification (TN_6). But what could the sources be which feed the normative authority ascribed to language by the first of these theories? Or do we wish to postulate the existence of an inherent normative power? Better not! But a constructive approach to this theory would be to interpret what it declares to be a "logical feature" as actually the linguistic sediment in a long historical development which had its starting point in the externalised and institutionalised will of human subjects; in other words, to interpret it as an "exteriorised" volition. Identifying moral normativity with rational justification is a claim with a similar status. This theory cannot be accurate for the simple reason that, in the long early phase of moral development, rational justifications hardly played a role of any importance; in this phase there would then also have been no obligations. But (TN_6) is accurate to the extent that it insists that, in the long term, the moral ought

---

[5] In this point, the small groups of prehistoric foragers were closer to the social forms of our closest relatives in the animal kingdom. "The morality of apes' social interactions—individuals inhibiting their immediate self-interest in favour of others—is governed mostly by their personal relationships; that is to say, individuals form prosocial relationships with others based on a kind of attitudinal reciprocity that develops as each individual helps those toward whom they have formed a positive attitude (precisely because they have helped them in the past). Individual's actions thus reward those with whom they have a positive relationship and fail to reward, or even to punish, those with whom they have a negative relationship. Much human morality is based on this kind of attitudinal reciprocity as well, especially with family. It is just that humans have developed some other moral motivation and mechanisms in addition" (Tomasello and Vaish 2013, 236f.).

also depends upon it being plausibly justifiable to individuals. But this does not mean that the ought is rooted (alone) in these justifications. Instead, it seems more appropriate to assume that a socially established practice of justification can have an influence on what individuals want from each other. Although (TN_5) and (TN_6) fall short as explanations of the moral ought, their central messages can easily be integrated within the theory outlined here.

4. Summary and Conclusion

First: The starting point for the deliberations in this chapter was the assumption that an adequate understanding of morality cannot be attained if the only thing taken into account is the behaviour of individuals. A one-sided focus on behaviour leads (a) to an underestimation of the complexity of (developed) moral systems and (b) to an overemphasis on the continuity of moral development. In particular, what needs to be taken into account beyond the prosocial content of morality is its normative "form," resulting from the specific function of morality. The latter consists in controlling the behaviour of individuals. Normativity has been discussed comparatively rarely in the ethical literature, and what discussion there is has remained unsatisfactory to the present day.

Second: In a second step, a proposal was then outlined, according to which the moral ought results from the volition of the members of a group; but naturally not as the result of arbitrary volition. The origin of moral normativity is rather (a) a shared, collective volition which (b) is directed at the members of the community, (c) is stabilised by custom and tradition to become an institution, and (e) is reinforced by sanctions. There is, therefore, a close connection between moral normativity and institutionalisation; through the latter the ought achieves a relative independence from the individuals involved. The moral ought is exteriorised volition.

Third: From the point of view of content, volition/"ought" first refers to the elementary biological interests of individuals, which can only be safeguarded through a functioning community. The moral ought therefore initially coincides with the social ought. Only much later, following the emergence of larger societies, do morality and the normativity associated with it begin to crystallise out of the totality of social obligations. In the further course of history, the circle of "objects" to which moral obligations are bound increases; parallel to this, the content of morality becomes ever more distinct from the ought of mores, religion, or laws. This process of differentiation is accompanied and reinforced by the formation of special moral reflection and justification procedures.

Fourth: According to the deliberations laid out here, morality has strong biological roots. Its history begins in the animal kingdom, but then increasingly emerges from it, becoming more and more a cultural process which partially emancipates itself from biological imperatives. The emergence of moral normativity marks one of the crucial thresholds in this emancipation process: protomorality becomes morality. It is an essential element in the transition from pre-human to human life forms, from nature to culture. This is its anthropological relevance. Whatever else he/she might be, the human being is a normative animal.

Fifth: Although, according to these considerations, moral normativity is grounded in the volition of human individuals, it cannot be reduced to it. As institutionalised volition, it is a genuinely social and cultural phenomenon; and as exteriorised volition, it is a non-biological reality existing outside individuals. To put a fine point on it: it is a good example of how the "essence" of human beings is not primarily internal. It is located (at least in large part) outside individuals and their bodies: in the normatively impregnated niche which humans create for themselves in the shape of culture.

Sixth: From a meta-ethical point of view, these considerations answer the question of the ontological status of norms and normativity. Accordingly, norms are social institutions, and normativity is a feature of these institutions. Those who like "isms" may characterise the interpretation presented here as a variant of ethical realism. It asserts that the moral ought is a genuine fact and, as such, an element of reality: a social fact and a part of social reality.[6]

---

[6] Translated into English by Sarah L. Kirkby.

9

Joint Activities and Moral Obligation

Holmer Steinfath

1. Morality and Moral Obligation

Discussions of morality and moral normativity suffer from a lack of an uncontested notion of morality. As a first approximation, I take morality to be an informal social institution, a set of social norms. The point of this informal social institution is to regulate the interactions between all members of a community in order to reduce the amount of evil or harm suffered and to avoid damaging conflicts of interests (cf. Gert 2005, ch. 1). Moral norms are taken to be binding on everyone in the relevant community. They are supposed to govern the actions of people across various areas of life; in this respect they are among the most general norms in a society. At the centre of morality lies the idea of moral obligation. I don't believe that moral obligations exhaust the sphere of morality. But I assume that they form the core of every morality, and that talk about moral "normativity" has its clearest application with respect to moral obligations.

Roughly speaking, someone is morally obliged to do or omit something if all members of his moral community can justifiably demand from him that he does or omits the action in question. Demanding something from someone is a rather serious affair, and it is analytically connected with blaming. If someone does not do what he is obliged to do and what others can justifiably demand from him, others are justified in blaming or punishing him. This way of understanding moral obligation was put forward by John Stuart Mill, among others. In an often-cited passage of the last chapter of *Utilitarianism*, Mill claims that we "do not call anything [morally] wrong, unless we mean to imply that a person ought to be punished in some way or other for doing it" (Mill 1861, ch. 5, 184). He adds that the punishment in question includes reproaches of one's own conscience; it does not have to be executed by law or by the opinion of others—two further forms of punishment Mill mentions. A group of recent writers has rephrased Mill's basic idea, focusing on Mill's emphasis on blame as an appropriate reaction to the violation of moral duties (see e.g. Brandt 1979, 163–76; Gibbard 1990, 41; Skorupski 1999, 137–59, esp. 142; Tugendhat 2001, 163–84; Darwall 2013b, 40–51; Wallace 2013, 161). Thus, Stephen Darwall writes: "What it is . . . for an action to be morally obligatory and its omission to be morally wrong, is for it to be something whose omission would warrant blame and feelings of guilt, were the agent to omit the action without excuse" (Darwall 2013b, 43). Disagreements in details notwithstanding, I share the general approach to moral obligation favoured by Mill, Darwall, and many other writers.

Given this approach, my aim is a deeper exploration of the structure of moral obligations. More precisely, I will try to elucidate the interactions and relationships between persons in which moral obligations are rooted. Intuitively, we incur moral obligations by being part of a social community and forming social bonds with others. But whereas social bonds are also characteristic of the life of many non-human animals, morality seems to be an exclusive feature of human groups. If so, there must be something special about our social life that helps to explain why moral considerations pervade our interactions with others to such an extent. In order to contribute to a solution of this puzzle, I will highlight some important structural similarities between moral obligations, on the one hand, and genuinely joint and common activities uniting two or more human beings, on the other. Though I will argue that shared intentionality and joint actions are not sufficient for moral obligation, I believe that they are the key for a better understanding of the binding force of moral obligations. My approach is an attempt to clarify conceptually and (in a broad sense) phenomenologically how and why our doing things together with others are typically intertwined with moral obligations. I do not aspire to make a contribution to evolutionary conjectures about the origins of morality. However, some of my considerations bear a striking resemblance to hypotheses on the evolution of human social life.[1] They might therefore help to support or to modify such hypotheses. In turn, they could certainly profit from empirical findings in evolutionary and developmental psychology. I will hint at some of these findings in the course of my argument.

Let me add one further preliminary remark on moral obligations. I believe that there are several distinct forms of moral obligation, but I will concentrate on just one form, namely "directed" or "relational" moral obligations. These are examples of a kind of normativity I call "dyadic." I focus on these obligations because it is widely supposed that they are bound up closely with joint activities and common practices. My first step will be to analyse the abstract structure or form of dyadic obligations

---

[1] I am thinking especially of the work of Michael Tomasello (cf. Tomasello 2014).

(section 2). I will then illustrate the connection between these obligations and joint activities by three examples (section 3). On the basis of the given examples, I will then discuss the dispute between Margaret Gilbert and Michael Bratman concerning the question of whether (and in which sense) genuinely joint activities are constitutively normative phenomena (section 4). I shall deny that joint activities are inherently laden with obligations and entitlements. However, I believe that we can sketch a smooth transition from joint activities to a form of morality (section 5). Full-blown moral normativity presupposes a group of more than two people, but the normative structure of a moral community mirrors the way in which people relate to each other in typical joint activities. I end with tentative comments on the prospects of a plausible transition from group-moralities to a universalistic and egalitarian morality to which we now adhere (section 6).

2. The Form of Dyadic Moral Obligation

Where I use the term "dyadic" moral obligations, others prefer to speak of "bipolar" obligations or normativity (Darwall 2013a, 20–39).[2] Nothing depends on this purely terminological difference. Like other forms of obligation, the dyadic form is a general form of obligation or normativity that does its work not only in the realm of morality. For instance, a dyadic deontic structure plays an important role in theories of legal claim-rights (cf. Hohfeld 1913; Hart 1961), it is characteristic of parts of private law (Weinrib 1996), and the concept of dyadic normativity might even be applied to games and conventional norms (Thompson 2004). While these variations are interesting, I will concentrate on the moral case.

The general form of dyadic obligations can be captured in sentences like

(1)   X has a duty to Y to A, or

(2)   X owes to Y to A.

The crucial part of these sentences is the variable "Y." There is someone, namely Y, to whom X owes something, namely to A, i.e. to do or to omit something.[3] X does not have an obligation *period*, but rather an obligation *to someone*, that is to Y. His obligation is directed towards or related to Y—hence the aforementioned talk of "directed" or "relational" duties. Conversely, Y has a claim, an entitlement, or a right against X, namely that X does or omits A. In my understanding of dyadic obligation, there is no obligation or duty of X to Y without a corresponding claim or right of Y

---

[2] Darwall follows with his terminology Ernest J. Weinrib (cf. Weinrib 1996) and Michael Thompson (cf. Thompson 2004).

[3] I take X and Y to be individual persons, but the variables might stand for groups or institutions as well.

against X. Dyadic obligations, or the dyadic normativity of which they are part, display a characteristic correlative structure. Dyadic obligations generate a particular normative order "in which each party's normative position is intelligible only in the light of the other's" (Weinrib 2012, 2).

The structure of dyadic obligation is well reflected in nuances of reactive feelings and attitudes that Peter F. Strawson emphasized (Strawson 1962). If I have wronged you, thus violating a duty to you and a claim of yours against me, you are warranted to resent me. Others might be justified to feel indignation towards me, but that is not the same as resentment. Whereas resentment is a personal reactive attitude, indignation is, in Strawson's stipulative use, an impersonal reactive attitude related to the harms others do to others, not to me. The special standing that the victim has against me in dyadic normativity implies that he is warranted to resent my action, and me, in a way in which no one else is. And if there is room for forgiveness, then it is my victim—and he alone—who has the normative standing to forgive me. Likewise, the potential victim normally has the normative power to waive his right, a power that, once again, he alone is allowed to exercise. The correlativity that is constitutive of dyadic obligation implies what Stephen Darwall calls a particular *individual* authority on the part of the claim-holder against the obligor (Darwall 2013a, 23, 27), an individual authority to demand respect of one's rights and as a person. No third party has this kind of authority.

I take the correlativity of dyadic obligations as irreducible to its two poles. You cannot build up the correlativity of duty and right by just combining the duty of the obligor and the right of the claim-holder. As we have seen, duty and right don't exist independently of each other. The poles of the normative relation between obligor and claim-holder fully depend on the relation itself. They can only be understood through the relation between them (Weinrib 2012, 1).

An example for a dyadic moral obligation is the duty to keep one's promise. If I promised you to help you with your move, I am normally obliged to support you when you move. Conversely, you normally have a claim against me that I keep my promise.[4] The correlativity of this and other dyadic obligations is not a trivial formalism. On the contrary, it is highly interesting from a theoretical point of view. The correlative logic defies consequentialist reconstructions. Absent special circumstances, it is morally wrong to break a promise I gave to you, but it is not wrong because of the bad consequences that my not keeping my promise might have for you or the community. The moral wrongness of breaking the promise is more immediate. It is wrong not to keep my promise because not keeping it means disregarding a justified claim of yours, a claim you have obtained directly through my giving a promise to

---

[4] The qualification expressed with "normally" in this and the antecedent sentence is necessary because one may argue that coerced promises or promises to perform immoral acts are not binding.

you. In breaking my promise I directly and immediately disrespect your claim that corresponds to my duty. We cannot understand the obligation that is generated by a promise additively, i.e. by considering first the interests of the promise-giver and then the interests of the promise-taker. A consequentialist might pursue a two-level strategy and argue that the whole practice of promising has good consequences overall. Yet the internal logic of dyadic obligations escapes a consequentialist interpretation. In this respect, these obligations are "deontological" duties.

3. Dyadic Obligations and Joint Activities

If we took the correlative duties and claims of private law as our paradigm, we could consider dyadic obligations as highly artificial devices of the law of institutionally advanced societies. But dyadic obligations of a moral kind have their natural home in familiar pre-institutional cooperative activities and practices. Something like these obligations and claims is part of our everyday life and deeply influences how we relate to each other. Once there is a normative vocabulary available, dyadic obligations and claims result almost inevitably from specific, but pervasive interactions between persons. Three examples may help to illustrate this hypothesis.

The first example is the example of walking together. It stands for countless activities that we can engage in with another person. It was Margaret Gilbert who made the example of walking together prominent in the literature on shared intentionality (Gilbert 1990). Though I will criticize Gilbert's analysis in the next section, I think that it has an undeniable intuitive appeal. We can take Gilbert's approach as a useful starting point that has to be modified and corrected in further steps.

According to Gilbert, two people genuinely do something together only if their interaction manifests a normative structure that exhibits precisely the correlativity which I have just explored. Take Gilbert's protagonists Jack and Sue who genuinely walk together instead of accidentally walking side by side. And imagine Jack suddenly draws ahead leaving the exhausted Sue behind. In this situation Sue could react in various characteristic ways. To quote Gilbert:

She might call out "Jack!" with a degree of impatience. She might catch up with him and then say, somewhat critically, "You are going to have to slow down! I can't keep up with you." In both of these cases she rebukes Jack, albeit mildly. She might not do this, of course, but it seems that, . . . failing special circumstances, her doing so would be *in order*. In other words, it seems that in the circumstances Sue is *entitled to rebuke* Jack. We would expect both Jack and Sue to understand that she has this entitlement.

The existence of this entitlement suggests that Jack has, in effect, an *obligation* to notice and to act (an obligation Sue has also). Particular acts Jack might perform in fulfilling his obligation to rectify matters include stopping and waiting for Sue to catch up, slowing his pace, smiling encouragement, asking if she is getting tired. These are the kinds of thing we expect to find if one party realizes he has drawn ahead of the other. Though he may not be obligated to do any one of these things, he is obligated to do something along these lines. The point can also be put in terms of *rights*: each has a right to the other's attention and corrective action. We would expect those out on a walk together to *realize* that they have the obligations, and the rights, just noted. (Gilbert 1990, 3)

It should be obvious that the obligations and entitlements that Gilbert believes to be necessarily implied in joint activities can't be explained additively combining the separate interests of the partners of the joint activity. Thus, Jack's obligation does not arise directly out of his own intentions and interests, and it does not arise out of the intentions and interests of Sue, either. Gilbert claims that "*the obligation is such that Jack's failure to perform entitles Sue to rebuke him*" (Gilbert 1990, 5, emphasis orig.). I interpret this as Gilbert's way of saying that the obligation in question is a dyadic, correlative obligation. According to Gilbert, the interlocking obligations and entitlements she mentions are direct implications of the joint activity of walking together. Just by walking together, Jack and Sue obtain correlative duties and rights. And if Jack ran away without any excuse or explanation to Sue, he would do something wrong, but not because his betrayal might have harmful consequences for Sue. It would be wrong because it meant denying a legitimate entitlement of Sue's.

The second example is relationships based on mutual trust. It would be worth pursuing the important question as to whether all genuinely joint activities presuppose trust between the partners of these activities (on trust, cf. Baier 1995). Trust is certainly essential for close relationships like friendship and love, but without any trust social life in general would be far more complicated and fragile, if possible at all. In any case, I think that mutual trust generates particular normative bounds. If I trust you, and you respond positively to my trust, I would be entitled to blame you if you betrayed my trust. Mutual trust generates correlative duties and rights on the part of the trusting agents. Again, barring special circumstances, the trusted person has the duty not to disappoint the person who trusts him. And if he were to let the trusting person down regardless, he would acquire new derivative obligations like the duty to beg pardon for his omission or duties of compensation.

The third example can probably be interpreted as a variation of the first. It is the example of talking together or speaking *to* one another, and not just *at* each other. I have in mind especially conversational forms of joint deliberation that build upon, and aim at, the exchange of reasons about what is true and what should be done. Philip Pettit and Michael Smith argue that deliberative exchanges in which "people claim to direct one another's attention to reasons that are relevant to what they should think or do" (Pettit and Smith 2004, 157) are governed by constitutive rules. According to Pettit and Smith, at least many of these rules have a moral and deontological character. What they write is reminiscent of Habermas's ethics of discourse:

The existence and the accessibility of these constitutive rules mean that people who enter into deliberative exchange must disclaim, as a matter of common knowledge, any attitude or action that runs counter them. Thus no one can aspire to deliberate with someone without being taken to rule out deception, coercion, intimidation, or infidelity to commitments undertaken. . . . To set out to deliberate with someone is to announce or present oneself in a certain guise: as a person who can be expected to honour the constraints associated with deliberative exchange. (Pettit and Smith 2004, 166)

As I see it, Pettit and Smith are right that joint deliberations constitute a common practice and that this practice is in turn partly, but not exclusively, constituted by rules. They are also right in claiming that others can rebuke me when I violate the rules of the deliberative practice, while I am participating in this practice. However, Pettit and Smith go wrong in suggesting that my violation is wrong only because I am breaking the rules constitutive of the practice of deliberative exchange. They model this practice on games like chess, and they believe that someone who does not communicate sincerely makes a normative mistake similar to someone who moves the bishop in a manner reserved for the knight. But that in itself would not be a good reason to rebuke the other person. There is in fact a deeper reason for blaming people when they violate the constitutive rules of deliberative exchange. This reason lies once again in the fact that the agent who does not sincerely communicate his beliefs in a joint deliberation thereby violates a legitimate expectation, claim, or entitlement of the person he tries to deceive. This entitlement originates, or so it seems, directly from the common practice itself and only indirectly from the rules that are constitutive of that practice.

4. Gilbert and Bratman on the Normativity of Joint Activities

Even if the examples given were sufficiently suggestive, we would still need a deeper explanation of how dyadic obligations and rights take root in joint activities and common practices. I shall presuppose that joint activities like walking together, being part of a relationship based on trust, and conversations, especially in the context of joint deliberation, do in fact have a normative structure of the indicated kind. Sceptics doubt that the protagonists of Gilbert's example of walking together have obligations and entitlements at all (cf. Bittner 2002).[5] They claim that they would be astonished if they were blamed because they quit a joint activity suddenly and without excuse. But I assume that such doubts express a general unwillingness to accept obligations of any kind whatsoever. Such scepticism seems contrived; it does not take the phenomena

---

[5] Gilbert responds to Bittner's challenge in Gilbert (2014a, 53–5).

seriously. However, the rejection of outright scepticism does not foreclose the possibility that there are joint activities without correlative obligations and entitlements, or that these normative features are at least not constitutive of joint activities. In contrast to Gilbert's claim that people genuinely do something together only if their interactions include correlative obligations and entitlements, such normative implications might, instead, be a regular addition to joint activities.

I have already indicated that I will not follow Gilbert's analysis. Nevertheless, it is a particular strength of Gilbert's theory that it pays special attention to the correlativity of obligations and entitlements that are so often part and parcel of joint activities. Gilbert presupposes a unique and irreducible mechanism that immediately creates interdependent duties and rights. The pertinent device is that of "joint commitments." In the example of walking together, Jack and Sue are, according to Gilbert, jointly committed to walking together, and *thereby* they acquire a normative standing towards each other—a standing that is constituted by correlative duties and claims. The normative positions of both ground, *inter alia*, the right to rebuke or blame the other should he or she unilaterally quit or disturb the common endeavour. A joint commitment cannot be rescinded by one person alone but only together, or so Gilbert argues. Gilbert offers some interesting observations on the ways in which a joint commitment might come into existence.[6] But the phenomenon itself is something that she takes to be a primitive feature of our social life. In this perspective, it is our ability to form joint commitments that enables us to enter the sphere of the normativity of reciprocal obligations and claims. And if this normativity is thought to distinguish human beings from other animals, it would be our capacity for joint commitments, perhaps in combination with other abilities, which separated us from other creatures. Thus Gilbert delivers both an elegantly simple and extremely wide-ranging theory of the foundation of sociality and social normativity. There are, however, reasons to doubt the cogency of her approach. I will mention three objections, though I won't develop them in any detail.

The first objection articulates the impression that the explanation of all genuinely joint activities through joint commitments seems to paint a picture of our social life that is too voluntaristic. A joint commitment is either the same as, or akin to, a joint will. But more often than not we just find ourselves to be part of a relationship or a common endeavour without any act of will or consent. I have to admit, however, that I am not sure how voluntaristic the notion of "joint commitment" is meant to be understood. In her more recent writings, Gilbert tries to dispel doubts that she adheres to a voluntaristic view. Yet she acknowledges that some of her formulations are apt to

---

[6] Gilbert discusses the formation of joint commitments in many places of her work. Thus she claims that it suffices for the emergence of a joint commitment between two persons when both express their "readiness" to be jointly committed and do this on the basis of "common knowledge" (cf. Gilbert 2014b, 196).

provoke a voluntaristic reading (cf. Gilbert 2003, 53f.).[7] The problem is that one simply cannot tell how similar a "joint commitment" and a common will are intended to be, because Gilbert conceives of joint commitment as a primitive phenomenon that eludes further analysis.

In any case, despite Gilbert's disclaimer, a voluntaristic reading of her approach is not far-fetched. Gilbert shares the widespread assumption that obligations and claims have to arise out of something like a voluntary act, or an endorsement, or an acceptance of those who are normatively bound by obligations and claims. In this respect she belongs to a broadly contractualist tradition. Contrary to versions of contractarianism in the Hobbesian tradition, Gilbert tries to ground the normativity of joint activities not in singular acts of approval from each party of the activity, but in a common will—or, for that matter, in a joint commitment. At this point, the second objection comes into play. I very much doubt that obligations and rights could have ever been created by the joint activity of just two persons. Normative notions like those of a special "standing" or "authority," or of being "obliged," or of having a "right," imply a claim to objectivity or being objectively justified that seems to presuppose a social community of more than two people. It seems that these notions require normative standards that can only be intersubjectively constituted in a broader community.[8] For the time being this objection must sound dogmatic. But I will come back to the general point to which this objection draws our attention.

The third objection has repeatedly been pressed by Michael Bratman.[9] Bratman construes several examples of activities that seem to be genuinely joint activities, yet do not necessarily imply the normative structure that Gilbert describes. Now, Gilbert would certainly dispute most or all of Bratman's examples. But I think there is at least one field of joint actions that is apparently not constituted by correlative duties and rights, and that is the field of interactions of small children either with other children or with adults (cf. Schmidt and Rakoczy, Chapter 6 in this volume). Even in this case, we are faced with the notorious problem that children as we know them have always already been socialized into a culture that uses normative notions all the time. However, it seems not so difficult to conceive of a joint project of a small child with another person which is a genuinely joint action, even though the child does not yet have a command of a suitable normative vocabulary. Gilbert would perhaps reply that correlative obligations and entitlements can be in place without an apt normative language. Still, it is quite difficult to make sense of correlative norms without a fitting normative vocabulary. Obligations and rights define a normative status that apparently

---

[7] Gilbert hopes that her notion of "readiness" to be jointly committed is less liable to be understood along a voluntaristic reading (see note 6).

[8] For a similar observation see Mertens, this volume, 117ff.

[9] For a summary of his view, see Bratman (2014, esp. ch. 5).

cannot be created without a deontic language or equivalent symbolic devices (cf. Searle 1995).

When they are put in this way, these objections are presumably not decisive. But let us have a look at Bratman's alternative view. Discussing this view will help us to formulate an alternative to Gilbert's theory of joint commitment on our own. For Bratman, joint actions are constituted by a complex structure of interlocking individual intentions (cf. Bratman 2014, esp. ch. 4). In the walking example, I intend that we walk together and you intend the same (i); we both intend that our intentions are realized through our respective intentions (ii); our intentions include similar intentions with respect to meshing "sub-plans" that are essential for successfully walking together (iii); we each believe that if the intentions of each in favour of walking together persist, we will walk with each other by way of our suitable intentions (iv); we also each believe that there is interdependence in persistence of our intentions (v); an interdependence which in fact exists (vi); all this is common knowledge between us (vii); and our shared intention to walk together leads to our walking together "by way of public mutual responsiveness in sub-intention and action that tracks the end intended by each of the joint activity by way of the intentions of each in favour of that joint activity" (viii).[10] Bratman's core idea is that such a structure of interlocking intentions suffices to create a shared intention and action that comes to more than an elaborated strategic interaction, while it does not necessarily generate mutual obligations. Once our intentions are connected in a suitable way, we have all that we need in order to say that *we* do something together. The relevant first-person plural is supposed to be not a primitive notion, but something built up from the sketched web of intertwined individual intentions and activities. Bratman does not deny that such a web can be enriched and even transformed through obligations and entitlements of the kind that Gilbert emphasizes. But in his opinion, these duties and claims do not inhere in every genuinely shared intentional action. Instead, Bratman believes that there is another kind of normativity which is indeed constitutive for shared agency, namely a kind of *rational* normativity. Bratman thinks that the way in which our intentions relate to each other in shared agency imposes a "rational pressure on me, as time goes by, to fill my sub-plans in ways that fit with and support yours as you fill in your sub-plans" (Bratman 2014, 108). This pressure is supposed to be derived from a rational demand for coherence and consistency. These demands, in turn, are thought to be essential for the web of interconnected individual intentions that Bratman places in the centre of his theory. Elucidating these normative implications, Bratman writes:

---

[10] I take the last clause—"the mutual responsiveness condition"—from Bratman (2014, 103). The other elements of Bratman's analysis of shared intentions are slightly changed and abbreviated formulations used by Bratman (2014) and related papers (cf. Bratman 2014, 84, 103).

Rational pressures on me to be responsive to and to coordinate with *you* are built into my *own* plans, given their special content and given the demands of consistency and coherence directly on my own plans (demands that are a part of the planning theory of individual agency). And similarly with you. . . .And if one or both of us fails to be appropriately responsive to the other, while continuing to be participants in the shared intention, we have an explanation of the sense in which there has thereby been a rational break-down. (Bratman 2014, 108)

I don't have space to comment on all aspects of Bratman's intricate view of shared agency. I do believe that he succeeds in identifying a way of practically relating with others that is neither purely strategic nor necessarily laden with mutual obligations. Still, I doubt that the structure that Bratman isolates lies at the heart of those interactions which are so readily converted into something normative or moral. On the basis of Bratman's account, it must seem almost mysterious that dyadic obligations and entitlements pervade our social life to such an extent. In his view, these duties and claims are somehow accidentally attached to joint actions like walking together. Of course, it is open to Bratman to explain pragmatically why we might tend to invest common activities with moral or quasi-moral norms. He could, for instance, suggest that activities like walking together are so important to us that we became interested in backing them with normative standards and principles, consequently strengthening these standards and principles with suitable informal or institutionalized sanctions. For reasons such as these, we may have invented a social norm to the effect that any member of a joint enterprise like walking together may blame any other member for acting contrary to the common endeavour. Yet this way of supplementing joint actions with obligations and entitlements seems to be too "external." For one, we would need a further explanation as to how the envisaged social or moral norm could bind the partners of the joint activity. We would need a binding-mechanism that could fulfil the function that Gilbert ascribes to joint commitments. Moreover, we would have to search for formulations of standards and principles that would not only explain how those who are doing something together are obligated to fulfil their roles in the common project, but would also explain why each of the participants *owes* his contribution *to* the other. In other words, we would need an explanation for the correlative structure of the normativity of joint actions. Given the current form of his theory, I cannot see how Bratman could plausibly meet this requirement.

In a less abstract way, the limits of Bratman's approach come to the fore when we ask how people normally react when their partners in a joint activity change their mind and quit the common project without any excuse or explanation. On the basis of Bratman's reconstruction, there would be room for rational criticism. In Gilbert's example of Jack and Sue, Sue could accuse Jack of being inconsistent or behaving irrationally when he suddenly draws ahead. But without moral principles that are added to the practice of walking together, she could not justifiably blame Jack for his inattentiveness, if we followed Bratman's line of argument. However, even in the absence of moral principles, rational criticism does not seem to be our first and most natural reaction to divergences from a joint project. On the contrary, it can be quite rational to quit or to exploit a common endeavour, at least if "rational" means something like "maximizing one's interests."[11] The fitting response is the attitude of resentment highlighted by Strawson. We resent the other for being uncooperative or neglecting what is necessary for our common success.[12] And I think that *via negationis* this resentment points to a sense of "we" or "us" that Bratman fails to capture.

At a first glance, the invocation of Strawsonian resentment takes us directly back to Gilbert's account. But contrary to a widespread misinterpretation of Strawson's remarks, resentment as such is not a genuinely normative reaction (cf. Deigh 2011a and Roughley, this volume, 229ff.). It is simply not the case that resentment conceptually presupposes a kind of normative or moral authority to demand something from someone else, as, for instance, Stephen Darwall and Jay Wallace have claimed (cf. Darwall 2006; Wallace 1996). Strawson rightly argued that resentment is a personal reactive attitude that is a natural reaction to the perceived ill will or lack of goodwill of others in their dealings with me. Yet in resenting the other for putting our common project in danger, I do more than just expressing that I don't like what the other does. Resentment is a natural reaction to the ill will or lack of goodwill of the other *insofar as I see him as a partner in a common endeavour, or as a participant of a shared practice, or just as a member of my group.* In this respect, resentment implies a kind of recognition of the person whose action I resent. I cannot resent someone whom I believe to be a sociopath or someone whom I deem a complete stranger from another tribe which I believe to be inferior to my own group. Ill will or lack of goodwill as such does not suffice to elicit reactive attitudes like resentment. As Strawson has put it, these attitudes express a "participant stance." This stance is only available to those who are part of a "we" or at least believe themselves to be such a part.

The particular sense of being a part of a "we" that I have in mind is presumably a pre-reflective and pre-intentional sense, and a sense children gather at a very early

---

[11] I guess that Bratman would not deny that it can be rational to abandon unilaterally a common project. In the passage quoted in the text, he seems to speak of a "rational break-down" only under the condition that both of us *continue* to be participants in a joint intention. This situation is modelled on forms of weakness of the will in the individual case, not on considered changes of one's intention.

[12] This line of thought gains further support from developmental studies with children. An anonymous referee drew my attention to the fascinating experimental work on the developmental origins of commitment by John Michael and his colleagues. They have convincingly shown that even children at the age of two react with protest when their partners in a joint action behave uncooperatively (Michael and Székely 2018). However, I think that Michael and colleagues tend to interpret the protest of children too quickly as forms of *normative* protest. They impute normative attitudes like normative expectations, a sense of commitment, and a sense of obligation to very young children in a manner that is structurally similar to Gilbert's approach, and thus falls prey to the objections raised against Gilbert. Still, we can use their work and similar studies in order to question Bratman's rationalistic theory.

stage (cf. Schmidt and Rakoczy, Chapter 6 in this volume). That does not necessarily mean that it is a simple achievement, not requiring further psychological capacities. Perhaps we need a kind of empathy, the ability to put oneself in another's shoes, in order to see the other and oneself from the perspective of the first-person plural (cf. Roughley, this volume, 230ff.). But empathy can be a pre-reflective mechanism, too. In any case, I am not sure that we always need to invoke such an ability. Apparently, children react quite early with something like Strawsonian resentment when their partner in a common enterprise quits their project without any sign of excuse or re-gret (Tomasello and Vaish 2013, 4.1–4.25). In resenting the other, they express that they are disappointed that the other has unilaterally severed the bond between them. It is an empirical question what kind of psychological structure has to be in place to be able to react in this manner. However, it seems to be rather unlikely that in order to be able to feel resentment, children need the complex psychological apparatus on which Bratman relies in his planning theory of shared intention.[13]

This still leaves open how exactly we should understand the basic sense of unity, or being part of a "we," that we are after. In fact, I don't have the conceptual resources to provide a strict analysis of the kind of first-person plural in question. I believe that we are dealing with a primitive phenomenon. While primitive, this phenomenon still has a characteristic structure. Negatively speaking, the relevant "we" does not, as it were, swallow its members, i.e. me and you in the typical two-person case. I am still aware (at least dimly) that I am an individual with his or her own perspective, and I am aware that the same holds true for you. But as partners we have a role that cannot be under-stood apart from the unity that we are forming together. In a way that is structurally equivalent to what I have claimed for correlative obligations and entitlements, the relation between us cannot be built up from independent poles. There is not first an "I" and a "You," who somehow have to come together to form a "we"; "I" and "You" rather are derived from the "we"-relation whose poles they are. One might speak of a special I-You-mode as an irreducible form of referring to us.[14]

In some respects, the picture that evolves from these considerations on the "logic" of resentment comes close to Gilbert's view, without collapsing into it. Gilbert rightly thinks that there is a special bond uniting you and me in a joint activity. But this bond is originally not a genuinely normative bond. It is rather an emotional bond, the vi-olation of which triggers the emotional reaction of resentment. And as this reaction normally affects the other towards whom it is directed, it exerts a kind of pressure on the other to continue with our common project. My resentment and your being affected by it reveal that we normally feel bound by our joint activity. If you fail to

---

[13] Bratman responds, to my mind unsuccessfully, to this challenge in Bratman (2014, ch. 4.9).
[14] Cf. suggestions Michael Thompson has made in an unpublished lecture entitled "I and You."

comply with our project, I will be disappointed, and I will also be puzzled. I will see your deviation from our common course as a kind of defect, or as something that needs explanation. I will have to struggle to understand your behaviour as it does not fit who we are, i.e. partners or, so to speak, co-authors of our story. Perhaps one could characterize this nexus as a weakly normative connection. However, this normativity falls short of the strongly normative language of "obligations" and "rights" on which Gilbert insists.

5. The Path to Morality

If these reflections are on the right track, Gilbert's direct derivation of mutual obligations from joint activities is blocked. At the same time, we have found a pre-normative structure of joint activities that bears similarities to Gilbert's view. So how do we get to the correlative normative structure with which we started, and how do we get there without denying the insights that can be derived from Gilbert's analysis? Focussing on the reactive attitude of resentment, we can rephrase this question by asking how resentment may become a genuine normative reaction.

I have already criticized the attempt to get to the normative level of duties and rights *just* by referring to moral standards and principles to which joint activities are then subjected.[15] I certainly do not want to deny that we need such standards, and considering the deficiencies of Gilbert's view, such standards cannot emerge from the dyad of "I" and "You" alone. They will have to come from the larger community whose members we are (cf. Mertens, this volume, 117ff.). But in order to bind us, these normative standards have to be connected in the right way with the primarily emotional bonds at the heart of joint activities and special relationships. This cannot be achieved by a functional analysis of norms that merely highlights their social role, e.g. their contribution to the stability of joint activities and special relationships. Functional accounts investigate norms from an external, third-person perspective. But the normativity of norms is always in the eye of the beholder. From a first-person perspective, normativity enters the scene via the idea of justification.[16] Once people start to ask each other why on earth they treat each other in the way they do, they are on the path to normativity and morality. And it is the idea of being justified that transforms resentment into a genuinely normative reaction. Resentment becomes a

[15] Similar to my approach, Facundo M. Alonso seeks a middle-ground between Gilbert and Bratman (cf. Alonso 2009). Still, his view is, or so I would argue, too close to the functional reference to moral standards that I criticize.

[16] Other authors would instead refer to normative reasons. That might be a purely terminological choice, but I think that "justification" is the better term.

normative reaction at the moment when the resenting person is justified, or believes herself to be justified, in resenting the other for what he has done to her.

Again, contrary to what Gilbert suggests, the idea of justification, or being justified, cannot emerge just between the two of us; it obviously needs language, which changes the game entirely, and it needs more than two to create a framework for justification. When I believe that I am justified in resenting what you have done to me, I generalize or objectify—at least implicitly—what has happened between us. First, I will think that everyone would justifiably be resented if he did to me what you have done. And second, I will presuppose not only that am I justified in blaming you, but also that others could or should do the same, though I will, at the same time, insist that I have a special standing against you that reflects the particular pre-normative bond between us. In this way, my personal reactive attitude of resentment will become the correlate of the impersonal reactive attitude of indignation in Strawson's sense mentioned in section 2. In this way, my initial resentment will be converted into a more complex attitude. In the case of joint activities, I will still resent you personally for, say, quitting our common project without excuse. I will see our relationship as disturbed, and will be disappointed that you have deserted me. Yet in addition, I will blame you for having violated a norm, a norm that, to my mind, should be acknowledged by everyone, or each member of our broader community. Accordingly, we get a normative structure with two layers. First, we have the layer of special correlative obligations and claims between you and me as partners in a joint activity. This layer mirrors, as I have said, the pre-normative relationship between us which is presupposed in the personal reactive attitude of resentment. But in order to become full-blown obligations, our special obligations have to be embedded into a second layer of mutual and general norms that bind all members of the moral community.[17]

I cannot judge whether this structure resonates with a phylogenetic or ontogenetic development from dyadic interactions to the ability to form a more impartial perspective of the group as a whole.[18] Such a development is at least conceivable, however. Two closely connected processes come to mind. The first one leads to a kind of deepening of the relationship in a joint activity. If I go for a walk with someone, or speak to him, or do something together with him, I will soon see him not only as this particular partner in this particular joint activity, but as an agent with his own point of view. It seems to me that in each joint activity there is an element of recognizing and respecting the other person as an agent like oneself. This recognition and respect can then help to underpin the moral respect that lies at the heart of moral obligations and

---

[17] This analysis is similar to Darwall's conception in Darwall (2013a).

[18] Tomasello speculates that our social life has evolved from "joint intentionality" to "collective intentionality" (cf. Tomasello 2014).

claims proper. The second process which I can imagine leads to an abstraction from the specific context of a particular joint activity. We learn how to walk together with, or to speak to, not just this individual person, but more or less everyone in our society, or everyone with whom we share certain capacities. Especially in larger societies, there are innumerable daily encounters with alternating others, encounters that exhibit the correlative structure that I have tried to elucidate. In ways that would deserve further elaboration, we learn to see each other as members of the moral community, and not just as partners in this or that activity.

However, there are still problems to solve. I am thinking especially of a deep implication of our starting with joint activities in order to better understand the structure and possible emergence of morality. While I reject Gilbert's claim that joint activities are genuinely normative phenomena all the way down, I believe that those common endeavours which are so readily connected with correlative obligations and rights do indeed bind us. As I have explained, they bind us emotionally, and just because of what it means to do something together. We are normally puzzled when the other party fails to sustain our common activity. At the bottom of our doing something together lies a kind of relational unity. As I have repeatedly argued, this unity is reflected in the normative structure of dyadic obligations, which are in turn embedded in a more impartial morality. But this reconstruction suggests that the binding force of dyadic obligations and also that of general moral obligations not only strengthens the original bond of common activities and relationships, but presupposes this bond just as much. In fact, this is already implied by Strawson's approach to normativity through the analysis of reactive attitudes. Reactive attitudes are "participant attitudes" that are essentially characterized by "involvement or participation with others in inter-personal human relationships" (Strawson 1962, 9; cf. Darwall 2013a, 22). They conceptually require a kind of social unity or community. We can only react with resentment or indignation against a person that we deem one of us. Now, it is not difficult to imagine a sense of unity binding the members of a small group together, say a group of hunter-gatherers (cf. Kappeler et al., this volume, 66-76). They know each other and they share a common lot. But how could we model our modern universalistic and egalitarian morality on this kind of group morality?

6. From Group Morality to Modern Morality

Of course, one might doubt that there is such a thing as "the" modern morality. However, we can witness rather widespread agreement with respect to basic human rights, and this is a distinctive feature of modern morality. Thus, each human being is supposed to have, for instance, rights not to be killed against her will, not to be physically hurt, not to be humiliated, and to have a minimum of means for a decent living. These rights can be understood in different ways, but I think it is plausible to conceive them as claim-rights which all human beings have against all others.[19] Understood in this way, they fit well into the correlative structure with which we started. Here we have a single right that generates a duty in many persons, but each such duty is separately correlative to the right that generates it, and vice versa (cf. Weinrib 1996, 123). But even if this pattern constitutes the core of modern morality, as I believe it does, it is still not obvious from where human rights and their corresponding duties could derive their binding force.

Surely, many of us are committed to human rights. They are firmly convinced that there are things which should not be done to human beings. Some things are just out of the question for them. However, even if all of us had such convictions, we could not, merely for this reason, justifiably *demand* action from each other in accordance with these convictions. We may, for instance, believe that we should help each other given certain circumstances. Yet converging on such a belief does not suffice to be *bound* to each other in such a manner that we can claim that we *owe* our help to each other. I would not contradict myself if I admitted that it would be a good idea to help you or that I have good reasons to offer you my help, yet denied that I am obligated to help you or that you have a claim against me to receive my support. In order to explain obligations, especially dyadic obligations between us as human beings, we need a binding mechanism, a mechanism which really binds us together, and which can then be strengthened by correlative obligations and rights.

Does justification do the trick? It is certainly very important that we can justify the step from a group morality to a universalistic morality of human rights. And I think that group moralities tend to come under pressure with respect to justification. Once societies become larger, more anonymous, and are characterized by high mobility and myriad interactions between strangers and semi-strangers, it becomes increasingly arbitrary to exclude people from basic moral considerations. As members of complex societies, we normally don't share a very substantive identity. Quite often, we will face situations in which we encounter each other not in this or that role, but as vulnerable human beings, or as agents with their own point of view. And if that is the case, it can become difficult to justify why we should respect only some human beings, instead of all who are vulnerable or rational agents. Still, I don't see that the supposed impossibility of justifying the exclusion of some human beings from moral considerations can ground an obligation to respect them morally.

For a satisfying explanation of the binding force of universal moral obligations we need an equivalent to the group-identity and common lot that unify smaller communities like bands of hunter-gatherers. A similar intuition has motivated

---

[19] I will neglect the significant fact that human rights are often addressed not to individuals but to institutions like the modern state.

some moral philosophers to draw a close analogy between morality and personal relationships like friendships. These display a deontic structure that is characterized by reciprocal duties and expectations. Thus, Jay Wallace has suggested that we should "interpret moral rightness essentially by reference to a distinctive ideal of human relationship," i.e. a "relationship of mutual regard, or mutual recognition, or mutual consideration and concern" (Wallace 2013, 161).[20]

Thus actions would be morally right if their performance is necessary for one to stand in relations of mutual recognition with all of one's fellow agents, and morally wrong if doing them would render one unable to enter into relationships of this kind with some other person. (Wallace 2013, 161)[21]

This is unquestionably an attractive ideal, and I agree with Wallace that this ideal shapes very much the way in which we nowadays think of morality. However, an ideal of human relationships still cannot bind us, and bind us reciprocally, in the way in which a relationship can when it is already realized and part and parcel of our daily interactions. If at all, an ideal can generate correlative obligations and rights only for those who genuinely share this ideal. It cannot bind those who adhere to different ideals, even if these different ideals are ill-founded.

In the end, I think we have to admit that the universalistic and egalitarian morality that most of us consider their own is still something to be achieved, not something already given. The ideal of a universal relationship of mutual recognition will generate universal correlative obligations and rights only when we will have formed a worldwide community of mutual interrelations and a common identity. Everyone can judge for himself how close we have already come to realizing such a community, and how far we have still to go.[22]

---

[20] Contrary to what is suggested in the preceding text, Wallace has criticized the close analogy between personal relationships and morality in a recent article of his (cf. Wallace 2011b). To my mind, this criticism creates severe tensions in Wallace's general approach to morality, especially to his emphasis on "bipolar" obligations, but I cannot go further into this problem.

[21] Wallace's account is inspired by Thomas Scanlon's contractualism (cf. Scanlon 1998, esp. ch. 4).

[22] I thank all members of the group "Anthropology and Normativity" for their helpful comments on previous versions of this chapter. I owe special thanks to Neil Roughley for his encouragement and to Mario Brandhorst for helping me to improve my English.

10

The Development of Domains of Moral and Conventional Norms, Coordination in Decision-Making, and the Implications of Social Opposition

Elliot Turiel and Audun Dahl

In this chapter, we discuss norms from the perspective of psychological functioning and its development. In our view, however, to examine norms from the psychological perspective it is imperative to ground psychological study in definitions of the norms in question. And we do mean norms in the plural because one of our central premises is that it is necessary to draw distinctions among different types of norms. Such distinctions are necessary because individuals reason about social norms and form systematic patterns of judgments about different norms with varying functions, meanings, and goals. That individuals reason about social norms—and more generally about social relationships, systems of social organization, and cultural practices—means that they evaluate and sometimes oppose existing practices. The general thrust of opposition in a historical context was captured by Gregory Vlastos (1962, 31) in asserting that "[t]he great historical struggles for social justice have centered about some demand for equal rights: the struggle against slavery, political absolutism, economic exploitation, the disfranchisement of the lower and middle classes and the disfranchisement of women, colonialism, racial oppression." Hence a second central premise of our perspective is that there are complex connections between cultural practices reflecting systems of social organization and their acceptance or opposition by individuals. Opposition includes demands for equal rights and struggles for various aspects of justice.

1. Distinctions among Norms

Lawrence Kohlberg (1971), who did a great deal to further theory about and study of moral reasoning, provided useful examples of distinctions between norms or different types of uses of the term "should":

> Moral judgments, unlike judgments of prudence or aesthetics, are grounded in objective, impersonal or ideal grounds. Statements like "Martinis should be made five-to-one," "that's the right way" involve "good" and "right" but lack the characteristics of moral judgments. We are not prepared to say that we want everyone to make them that way, that they are good in terms of some impersonal ideal standard shared by others. (Kohlberg 1971, 215–16)

Kohlberg used this example to point to how norms can be fundamentally different epistemologically and to illustrate that people use terms like "ought" and "should" in different ways. They conceptualize moral obligations differently from preferences of taste or prudence or aesthetics.

These propositions were based on the assumption that individuals reason about norms and, in the process, are able to make differentiations regarding their functions. Development involves the construction of ways of thinking through children's interactions and relationships in varied, multifaceted environments. Such psychological perspectives on development are concordant with certain philosophical views regarding human reasoning, choice, and morality. As succinctly put by Nussbaum (1999, 71), "human beings are above all reasoning beings, and . . . the dignity of reason is the primary source of equality." Similarly, Sen (1999, 272) asserted that "[i]t is the power of reason that allows us to consider our obligations and ideals as well as our interests and advantages. To deny this freedom of thought would amount to a severe constraint on the reach of our rationality." Philosophers, going back to Aristotle (Nicomachean Ethics), have maintained that there is need to distinguish among norms, including between moral and conventional norms (Lewis 1969) and between constitutive and regulative rules (Searle 1969). Psychological research over many years in several cultures demonstrates that by an early age children make judgments about morality (defined as entailing substantive concepts of welfare, justice, and rights), which are distinct from their judgments about social conventions (defined as uniformities coordinating interactions within social systems through shared expectations; Turiel 1983).

Before we elaborate on our approach to norms and development, we consider alternative approaches that do not distinguish moral from other norms, and that de-emphasize the role of reciprocal social interactions in the development of normativity. We then first consider the construction of different domains of judgment early in life, and then in later life. This is followed by discussion of connections between emotions and reasoning, decision-making in the context of the application of different domains of judgment in multifaceted situations, and social opposition and resistance, in everyday life, that might connect with the types of historical struggles noted by Vlastos.

2. Alternative Psychological Approaches

The example of matters of taste in martinis may seem self-evident and its difference from moral oughts is one that many would accept—and there may be acceptance of differences between moral norms and norms of prudence and aesthetics. In the psychological literature, however, there is less acceptance of the idea that there are distinctions between moral norms and norms of a conventional type in systems of social organization or in cultural practices. Indeed, in some approaches it is maintained that there are no such differences since moral norms constitute societal conventions that individuals come to accept. If, as proposed in such approaches, children develop morality by internalizing the norms transmitted by adults who had, themselves, learned to accept those norms (Freud 1930; Skinner 1971; Kochanska 1994), the content of morality is dependent on established conventions. What matters in such approaches has little to do with the types of actions themselves but much to do with how circumstances (e.g., the ways rewards and punishments are administered) result in habits or compulsions to act in certain ways. A similar perspective was taken by the cultural anthropologist Ruth Benedict (1934), among others, who asserted that there is a great deal of variation in what might be considered fundamental moral values, as an example, in the "matter of taking a life" (such as killing by custom one's first two children; a husband's right to life and death over his wife; a duty to kill parents before they are old). She viewed these variations as non-random since cultures were integrated. Recent formulations of integrated cultural patterns have been proposed around two types of more or less homogeneous orientations labeled individualist and collectivist, usually associated with Western and non-Western cultures (Shweder and Bourne 1982; Markus and Kitayama 1991).

In direct contrast with internalization explanations, others have proposed that humans have innate, biologically preprogrammed moral abilities. The abilities proposed to be innate, or to emerge independently of specific experiences, include empathy, moral judgments, altruistic helping, and various normative intuitions (Bloom 2012). In articulating a nativist position, Hamlin (2013, 191) writes that "at least some aspects of human morality are innate. From extremely early in life, human infants show morally relevant motivations and evaluations—ones that are mentalistic, are nuanced, and do not appear to stem from socialization or morally specific experience." Propositions about innate or experience-independent moral abilities have been based on empirical data with infants and primates (see Bloom 2012; Hamlin 2013), the presumed evolutionary fitness value of morality, and observed regularities between different communities (Haidt and Joseph 2008).

A fundamental difficulty in evaluating claims of innateness and experience-independence is that the central concepts are typically not clearly defined (if defined at all). Contrary to what one might expect, "innate" is usually not taken to mean "present at birth." Bloom defines innate as "[not] gotten into the head by means of the extraction of information from the environment" (Bloom 2012, 72). Using a somewhat different definition, Hamlin (2013, 186) uses "innate" to describe capabilities "that emerge in the absence of specific experiences, such as (among others) being helped or harmed in particular ways/situations, observing others be similarly helped or harmed, or being explicitly taught which acts are right." For either of these definitions, it is not clear how one could determine whether a given capacity is innate. Consider for instance the notion of "specific" or "morally relevant" experiences. How should one determine which experiences count as "specific" or "morally relevant"? By most accounts, morality regulates all social interactions; so any social interaction is in principle morally relevant. Since infants would not survive without social interactions, it seems inconceivable that morality would develop in the absence of relevant experiences.

Perhaps because of the difficulties of determining which capacities meet the criteria for innateness, arguments for nativism often proceed by way of negating socialization or internalization views (Dwyer 2006; Hamlin 2013). The underlying logic is that if children's experiences are insufficient to explain the emergence of moral judgments, these judgments must be innate (Dwyer 2006). However, this inference—from negating socialization to affirming nativism—disregards a third class of theories of moral development: constructivism.

Constructivist explanations differ from nativist and internalization explanations, emphasizing development through reciprocal interactions with the environment—interactions that do occur in the first two years of life. In the constructivist view, children develop moral judgments through direct experiences of harming, being harmed, helping and not being helped, and observing others in such activities from early in life. (More details about this in the following; also see Turiel 1983, 2002, 2015; Smetana 2006; Turiel and Gingo 2017). It is proposed that children's moral judgments do not develop in the absence of experiences, nor that development is due to direct teaching. Piaget (1954, 1985), Werner (1957), and many others have extensively discussed the constructivist view of development. Piaget's position is succinctly summarized with regard to a different domain of thought as follows: "It is a great mistake to suppose that a child acquires the notion of number and other mathematical concepts just from teaching. On the contrary, to a remarkable degree he develops them himself, independently and spontaneously" (1953, 74).

Apart from the problems of determining which of infants' capabilities are "innate," we also question whether the empirical data demonstrate moral abilities in the first year. The differences between infant and adult judgments or abilities are rarely discussed (see Dahl 2014). In one paradigm, infants are shown a neutral puppet trying to open a box. The prosocial puppet helps the neutral puppet open the box, while the antisocial puppet closes the box (Hamlin and Wynn 2011). Preferential reaching for the prosocial puppet differs from the judgments of older children and adults in several ways. For instance, infants show a *relative preference* for one puppet over another. In contrast, developed moral judgments rely on categorical distinctions between what is all right and what is not all right that apply also to one's own actions (murdering someone is generally wrong no matter one's preference, and no matter who is doing it). Hence, attribution of moral judgments to infants in the first year of life seems premature.

Other arguments for biologically preprogrammed moral abilities have relied on similarities between norms in different communities ("universality") and on the presumed fitness value of morality (Haidt and Joseph 2008). For instance, the general prohibition against harming others appears to be both useful for the survival of the species and endorsed by most or all human societies. To be clear, the question is not whether the human genome has evolved in a way that allows morality to develop: Clearly, genes do allow development of morality (just as genes allow use of iPhones and control of space crafts). The question is whether genes endow people with specifically moral abilities arising independently of morally relevant experiences. As stated earlier, we do not think findings on early development support this nativist proposition.

Neither universality nor fitness value provide compelling evidence for such preprogrammed moral abilities. The inferential leap from universality of a characteristic to biological preprogramming of that characteristic is made on the assumption that genes are roughly the same whereas cultures differ across the world. This inference is problematic because there are many invariant features of relations with the environment that could help explain why most humans develop a morality. For instance, nearly all children spend a large amount of time interacting with other people. (By analogy, most children learn about the sun, not because they have a preprogrammed "sun module" in the brain but because they happen to spend many of their waking hours under a large shining object in the sky.) Insofar as both certain genetic features and certain cultural-environmental features are similar across different communities, we cannot infer that only one of them (the genetic features) contributes to cross-cultural similarities in basic moral judgments (it is probably both). We also note that fitness advantage is also not evidence for innate or preprogrammed moral abilities, since not all characteristics that promote survival are biologically preprogrammed (see Gould and Lewontin 1979).

Our arguments here are against biological predetermination of morality, not against the obvious fact that biological processes are involved in development of morality. Short of embracing a Cartesian mind-body dualism, it would seem that psychological processes must have biological and physical correlates (even though the relation between psychological and biological concepts may well escape precise determination). For instance, the experience of seeing one person hit another must be accompanied by some neural activity in the retina, the thalamus, and the occipital lobe (among other places, see Gazzaniga, Ivry, and Mangun 2013). However, as shown by developmental biologists, biological processes develop in continuous interaction with the environment (Gottlieb 1991; Spencer et al. 2009). The environment of the organism influences even the expression of genes. Such evidence poses difficulties for the claim that morality is biologically predetermined, and even for the view that "predetermined" is a useful concept in developmental psychology and biology (Lickliter and Honeycutt 2010).

In the following sections, we present a constructivist account of how children develop moral and other norms. The constructivist approach proposes that children construct thinking about distinct types of norms and understandings by inference, limit-testing, negotiations, and compromises, and through their attempts to make sense of the norms and events they encounter in social interactions (Piaget 1932; Kohlberg 1971; Turiel 1983). It is also proposed that there are morally relevant circumstances and activities that are shared and that start to be experienced at early ages. Many direct actions and social interactions are part of most children's lives, including those revolving around collaboration, helping, sharing, sympathy, and equal distribution (for a summary, see Tomasello and Vaish 2013).

3. The Beginning Construction of Norms in Infancy and Toddlerhood

We, therefore, propose that construction of thinking about norms in the social realms begins in childhood and continues into adolescence and adulthood. In this regard, it is useful to consider what is known about social interactions and the construction of norms in the first two years, and the ages by which we can confidently say that children form judgments about the domain of morality that are distinct from their judgments about the domain of social conventions. (Currently, less is known about those years than later years). First, a few studies have found that caregivers provide domain-specific justifications in the second year (Smetana 1984; Dahl and Campos 2013). However, given children's limited linguistic abilities at this age (Fenson et al. 1994), these justifications may not be understood by children. In contrast, nonverbal emotional communication is not dependent on linguistic understanding and may therefore be particularly important for communicating norms to young children (Kochanska 1994; Dahl, Campos, and Witherington 2011). Mothers are especially likely to respond with sternness or anger to harmful acts against others (moral), fear or worry to prudential transgressions, and warmth or laughter to pragmatic (that is, those involving inconvenience, such as purposeful spilling) transgressions in the second year (Dahl et al. 2014). These emotional reactions have been documented both in mothers' self-reports and in their vocal responses to transgressions in the second year. These differentiated vocal responses may help young children to notice qualitative differences between moral and other norms even before they can understand verbal explanations for these norms.

Children do become increasingly aware of others' expectations in the second year, but seem motivated to violate, not only adhere to, these expectations. Dunn (1988) provided observational evidence that, late in the second year, young children anticipate the prohibition of caregivers to do something known to upset their sibling. The children were often amused by the prospect of receiving a prohibition, and showed awareness of a norm (i.e., knowing that a norm is endorsed by others), but do not necessarily endorse the norm (i.e., agree that a particular norm should generally be adhered to). Relatedly, there is no evidence that children show negative self-evaluations after violations until around the second birthday or that they reliably protest others' violations against a third party until the third year of life (Cole et al. 1992; Schmidt and Rakoczy, this volume, 130-1).

Communication of norms, via linguistic and non-linguistic means, likely informs children's understanding of others' expectations and possibly whether these expectations are based on moral or other considerations (Dahl et al. 2014; Smetana 1984). Signals from others could also help draw children's attention to the consequences of their acts, for instance the suffering of others (Hoffman 2000). Yet, communicative signals cannot by themselves make children endorse the communicated expectations. For instance, children do not simply accept parental prohibitions, but critically evaluate them (Nucci and Weber 1995). We propose that children's judgments about moral and other norms rather stem from a consideration of the purpose served by those norms, for instance the protection and promotion of others' well-being or the coordination of play and other social activities. The development of a norm against harming others illustrates the specificity of such processes.

The general prohibition against harming others is of fundamental importance to interpersonal relationships and societal functioning. Yet, most infants hit, bite, and kick others in the second year of life, sometimes without provocation or anger (Dahl 2016). Developing a norm against harming others requires two things (see Dahl and Freda 2017). First, infants must become aware that hitting, biting, and kicking actually cause harm to others. Signals of pain will likely help children realize this process, as will their own experiences of being harmed (Wainryb et al. 2005). Second, infants must actually become concerned with not causing pain to others. Although some argue that rudimentary empathic abilities are present at birth (Hoffman 2000), clear signs of concern upon observing signs of distress in others remain rare even early in the second year. In the first half of the second year, mothers report that, after harming someone, infants were about as likely to respond with positive affect (e.g., laughing) as with empathic concern or prosocial (e.g., comforting) behavior toward the victim (Zahn-Waxler et al. 1992). At the end of the second year, children responded to distress with empathic concern or prosocial behavior more than half the time. It is around this time that harmful behaviors (especially unprovoked ones) decrease, signs of self-evaluation become evident, and children express negative judgments about moral and conventional norm violations (Smetana and Braeges 1990; Dahl 2016).

It follows from a domain-specific account that increasing consideration of the well-being of others is not the only source of children's judgments about norms. Judgments about property rights may arise as children experience the need to have predictable control over toys and food. Attention to prudential norms can arise through direct experience with pain, for instance after falling off a couch. Children's strong interest in participation and cooperation create other potential sources of norm endorsement, for instance by showing them the need to coordinate cooperative activities (Göckeritz et al. 2014).

4. Beyond Early Childhood: The Formation of Distinct Domains

As already noted, the research findings show that beyond toddlerhood—at least by the age of four to six years—children form distinct domains of judgment. Using substantive definitions of moral, conventional, and personal norms, a large number of studies conducted during the past 40 years in several cultures have demonstrated that young children form moral judgments about welfare—and in more rudimentary ways about justice and rights—and that they form judgments about other domains, including the social conventional and arenas of personal choice (comprehensive reviews are provided by Turiel 2002, 2006; Smetana 2006). Distinguishing morality from other domains reflects that individuals think about social relationships, emotions, social practices, and social order, and that thinking about morality has features distinctive from thinking about other aspects of the social world. Individuals also form judgments about social systems, social organization, and the conventions that further the coordination of social interactions within social systems (Turiel 1983). Conventions are a constitutive part of social systems and these entail shared behaviors (uniformities, rules) whose meanings are defined by the system in which they are embedded.

The domain of morality contrasts with the domain of convention in that morality is not defined by existing social arrangements or by standards agreed upon in a community. Moral prescriptions are characterized as obligatory, generalizable, and impersonal insofar as they stem from concepts of welfare, justice, and rights (Turiel 1983). For example, it is wrong to hit others because it causes harm. In contrast, social conventions are tied to an understanding of social organization, social systems, and uniformities in social organization. Because there is generally more than one possible form of social organization, social conventions are arbitrary and alterable, unlike moral norms. The distinctions among domains do not entail simple discriminations made by individuals among categories; each domain constitutes a complex configuration of thought.

The configuration of thought within the moral domain has been displayed through research presenting children with actions entailing physical harm (e.g., hitting others, pushing them down), psychological harm (e.g., teasing, name-calling, hurting feelings), and fairness or justice (e.g., failing to share, stealing, destroying others' property). These acts were depicted to study participants as intentional and as resulting in negative consequences to others. Assessments were made of the criteria by which thinking within each domain can be identified (referred to as criterion judgments). It has been consistently found (for reviews, see Turiel 2002, 2006) that children and adolescents judge that moral issues are obligatory, not contingent on authority dictates, rules, or consensus (e.g., that the acts would be wrong even if no rule or law exists about it), or on accepted practices within a group (e.g., the act is wrong even if it were acceptable practice in another culture). Judgments about moral issues, based on these criteria (criterion judgments), are connected with *justifications* based on preventing harm, promoting welfare, fairness, and rights (Turiel 1983, 2002).

However, judgments in the conventional domain are linked to existing social arrangements, and contingent on rules, authority, and existing social or cultural practices. Justifications for judgments about conventional issues are based on understandings of social organization, including the role of authority, rules, and customs. The domains of thinking are reflected in judgments about actual events experienced by children (Turiel 2008a), as well as in interviews about hypothetical situations. Research with younger and older children also shows that social interactions and communications are, in important respects, different for the moral and conventional events.

All the findings support the hypothesis that children construct moral, conventional, and personal understandings through distinct types of social interactions. Children's everyday social experiences involve participating in and observing events of several types, including what people say to each other, expressions of feelings, and concerns with how others will react. Children participate in events that involve, as examples, people harming or helping each other, sharing or failing to share, excluding or including others, treating people equally or unequally. Thus, the violation of moral norms generally has direct consequences to persons, whereas the violation of conventions and acts within the personal domain do not (Turiel 1983).

5. Emotion and Thought as Interrelated Features of Morality

The domain perspective on social interactions is based on the proposition that children have an active role in the interactions, and reflect on the type of event, including those with caregivers. Through these interactions, children develop judgments about the well-being and rights of others. An integral part of the developing moral judgments is what some emotion researchers have referred to as "concerns" (Frijda 1988). Frijda defines concerns as relatively stable dispositions to prefer certain states of the world (Frijda 1988, 351). If a person makes a moral judgment about the wrongness of hitting someone, the person is simultaneously saying that he would prefer that the hitting not take place. The moral reaction to hitting is not *merely* a preference: People prefer many things that have nothing to do with morality, for instance the success of a sports team. However, the preference for the hitting not to take place is necessary for the judgment to be a moral one. That is, if the person says that hitting is wrong but does not care the least whether the hitting takes place, he is by our definition no longer making a moral judgment (and is perhaps just reporting that hitting is commonly judged as wrong by others). As we argue in the following, the fact that most people are concerned with morality—and that they do care about the things they judge as morally wrong—is essential to understanding the relation between emotions and moral judgments.

It has been incorrectly claimed that theories in the structural-developmental tradition (including those of Piaget 1932 and Kohlberg 1971) fail to recognize a role for emotions. Those critiques, however, take a particular position on morality and emotions; namely, that for the most part moral judgments are based on intuitive, emotional responses (Greene et al. 2001; Haidt 2001; Haidt and Joseph 2008). In some theories there is agreement that moral judgments are typically, or often, formed in the following manner: People perceive a situation, which elicits an emotional (positive, neutral, or negative) reaction, which leads to an intuitive judgment about the situation.

In this chain of events, reasoning processes are relegated to trying to explain ("rationalize") the judgment after it has been reached. As an example, Haidt, Björklund, and Murphy (2000) report that people sometimes cannot come up with any justification for their judgment, a phenomenon they refer to as "moral dumbfounding." Non-rational and unconscious processes, it is claimed, lead people to form similarly non-rational moral judgments that are more or less impenetrable to thought processes and that are influenced by morally irrelevant features such as the disgusting smell of the room in which they are making the judgments (Schnall et al. 2008; for critiques of the emotivist-intuitionist view of moral functioning, see Turiel 2010).

In order to determine the role of emotions in moral functioning it is necessary to define emotions and emotional phenomena. We believe the lack of definition has been a source of much confusion about the role of emotions in morality. Ironically, researchers proposing that emotional processes dominate the generation of moral judgments rarely define emotion. Emotional processes are reduced to those involved in so-called emotional intuitions (Haidt and Bjorklund 2008) which can be manipulated by quick emotion-induction procedures (e.g., a disgusting smell or good odor; Schnall et al. 2008) and which people are unable to justify (Haidt et al. 2000).

Methodological critiques aside (e.g., Jacobson 2012), these "emotional intuitions" constitute but a small portion of most people's emotional experiences. Many emotional reactions pertain to events of personal relevance that (1) cannot be evoked by the presentation of standardized emotion-inducing stimuli in a laboratory (Campos et al. 2011), and (2) can be readily justified by the person. Imagine, for instance, receiving the news that your child has been brutally beaten up during a peaceful demonstration, rushing to the hospital, and learning that your child has suffered only minor injuries. In this case, highly intense emotional reactions would be accompanied by a clear awareness of why these reactions were occurring (see Bonanno and Keltner 2004).

We define emotions as the appraisal of events as relevant to our concerns and our reactions to these appraisals (Frijda 1988; Lazarus 1991; Nussbaum 2001; Moors and Scherer 2013). Appraisals are the person's evaluations of encounters with the environment with respect to his or her concerns (Lazarus 1991). According to this definition, people have emotional reactions when events are interpreted (appraised) to impact the fate of things important to them, be it health, the people in close relationships, or a favorite sports team. As we argued earlier, moral judgments contain a particular set of concerns, namely concerns about rights, fairness, and the well-being of individuals.

Concerns—like those embedded in moral judgments—are central to the elicitation of emotions, but they are not themselves emotions. This distinction may seem subtle, but it is nonetheless crucial. Most people always maintain that it is generally wrong to hit others, and accordingly always prefer no harm to harm, other things being equal. Still, they do not have a continuous emotional reaction to hitting. Emotional reactions occur when events are appraised as relevant to those judgments and their accompanying concerns. It is upon seeing one person hitting another that people may be morally outraged (insofar as they judge this particular act of hitting as wrong). Emotions follow from the constellation of events, appraisals, and concerns, including the concerns that form part of moral judgments, and not from the concerns alone.

In the view we are proposing, emotional reactions usually operate in concert with moral thought, not in competition with it (Nussbaum 2001). Plainly put, emotions occur when people judge particular events as morally good or bad because people care about moral issues. Morally abhorrent actions like those contributing to the Holocaust elicit both strong condemnation and negative emotional reactions, while morally exceptional acts like those of Gandhi and Martin Luther King Jr. receive moral praise and inspire what might be called moral awe.

There is also a second way in which emotions are relevant to morality. While emotional reactions often reflect *developed* moral judgments about particular events, emotional experiences and emotional signals also contribute to the *development* of moral judgments and their accompanying concerns. For instance, the painful experience of being harmed and the empathic reactions to seeing others suffer are likely contributors to children's endorsement of the general prohibition against hitting others, as this endorsement is based on the awareness that hitting is painful for the victim (Turiel 1983). Wainryb et al. (2005) reported that school-age children generally have strong emotional reactions both to being hurt (e.g., sadness) and to hurting others (e.g., remorse). Through such emotional experiences, children learn about the consequences of one's action on the well-being of others.

In sum, we propose that emotion and thought are two interrelated features of individuals' orientations related to morality. They reflect similar moral considerations, and they influence each other in bi-directional ways (appraisals lead to emotions, and emotions inform subsequent judgments). Insofar as people make moral judgments about the well-being and rights of others, people will think about those considerations and have emotional reactions when they encounter events relating to those considerations. When dilemmas arise, for instance faced with the decision of whether to sacrifice one person to save five (Greene et al. 2001), the conflicts are not between emotion and reason but struggles about contradictory moral goals: violating the value of the sacredness of life by taking a life in order to assert the value of life by saving a greater number of lives. Research has shown that people indeed think hard and feel strongly about both sides of the matter, which is why they find the decision so difficult to make (Dahl et al. 2018).

6. Processes of Coordination in Decision-Making

Earlier we outlined the criterion judgments associated with each of the domains, including judgments about rule contingency, authority jurisdiction, and common practices. These criterion judgments are part of distinct configurations of thought within each domain that include their justifications or reasons (e.g., welfare, fairness, and rights versus social organization, rules, and authority) for evaluations of acts and the criterion judgments. Such domains of thinking, however, do not mean that all social situations are simply to be identified as within a domain. Social situations can include features associated with the different domains—as well as different aspects of a domain (e.g., welfare in conflict with rights, or welfare in conflict with trust). Moreover, since thinking is not static but flexible and reflective, varying features of social situations are perceived and taken into account in the process of decision-making. Therefore, decision-making often involves coordination of different and sometimes conflicting moral considerations and goals and other social considerations and goals; decision-making can also involve coordination between different moral goals. The process of coordination involves weighing and balancing the different considerations and drawing priorities when coming to conclusions within the parameters of social situations (Turiel 2008b).

Several examples of how decisions involve coordination have been investigated in research assessing between- and within-domain considerations. We begin, however, with an example of research that was not interpreted in terms of domains but should be; namely, the well-publicized experiments by Milgram (1963, 1974), in which participants were placed in situations where they were instructed by an experimenter to administer increasing levels of electric shocks (which were not real) to another person (who was an accomplice of the researcher) in the guise of the learning of word associations. Participants were told that it was a study of the effects of punishment on learning and memory.

In the initial experimental condition, the experimenter gave instructions directly to the participant, who was in the same room, while the supposed learner, who had been strapped to the electric shock apparatus, was not visible but was within hearing range in an adjacent room. In that condition, it was found that approximately 65% of participants continued administering the shocks to the end of the scale in spite of sometimes loud protests from the victim (learner).

The title of Milgram's book (1974), *Obedience to Authority*, conveys the way the experiments are frequently construed: that large numbers of people obey authority even when commanded to inflict severe pain on another. Such a construal fails to consider that the experimental situations included multiple components that participants may have attempted to take into account. The most obvious are considerations of inflicting physical pain on another in conflict with adhering to the instructions established by the goals of the experimenter conveyed to participants in the context of exhortations to continue the experiment because that is what is required (Turiel and Smetana 1984; Turiel 2002). Milgram's (1974) descriptions of the details of what occurred in the experiment (presumably not measured) indicate that most participants, regardless of their ultimate decision, were experiencing conflict about the two considerations (e.g., even when continuing to administer the shocks, participants displayed a good deal of anxiety and would stop to tell the experimenter that the "learner" was in pain and danger, that the experimenter should see if he was all right, that he did not want to harm the learner). This constitutes one type of evidence for the proposition that participants were attentive to both considerations and that they were weighing and balancing the two.

A second type of evidence comes from the findings of different experimental conditions in the program of research (Milgram 1974). In some conditions the location and proximity of the person receiving the shocks were varied in ways that increased the salience of the harm (e.g., the learner was in the same room; the participant was told to place the learner's hand on a shock plate). In other conditions the place and role of the experimenter were varied in ways that decreased the apparent significance of the scientific enterprise and the role of the experimenter (e.g., instructions given by telephone; authority delegated to someone who was not part of the team of researchers). In most of these other conditions, the large majority of participants decided to stop shocking the learner and thus defied the experimenter's instructions (for more details, see Turiel and Smetana 1984; Turiel 2002).[1]

If we also put into the mix the decisions of the researcher (i.e., Milgram) and those who assisted him in carrying out the studies, the levels of analysis of coordination become more complex. As pointed out by Baumrind (2013), Milgram engaged in deception by placing newspaper advertisements to recruit participants that stated the study was on memory and learning. Those choosing to participate were deceived again by Milgram and his associates (i.e., experimenter and learner) when they were told face-to-face that the study was on learning and memory, that the person given the role of learner was another study participant, and that they would be administering electric shocks (all falsehoods). The researcher's acts of deception were based on the decision that deceiving others should be given less priority than the goals of a scientific enterprise on what were regarded as important questions of whether people obey authority in carrying out acts that inflict physical pain on others. Consequently, both the actions of the researchers and the study participants involve coordination of moral goals (preventing harm), honesty, and the role of authority in achieving scientific goals.

Research on honesty or trust has yielded results demonstrating that such processes of coordination are at work in many situations. Honesty is particularly interesting with regard to coordination because it is often assumed that it is an obviously moral good that ought to be consistently maintained. However, honesty is not always straightforward and does not necessarily dictate the moral course of action in a straightforward way. For instance, some philosophical discussions centering on Kant's contention that it is always wrong to lie (Bok 1979) have considered the example of someone passing a bystander who is soon thereafter asked by a murderer where his intended victim has gone. It has been argued that in such a situation the moral prescription to save a life should take precedence over the moral prescription to tell the truth and that there is even a moral obligation for the bystander to engage in deception.

---

[1] Our analyses of the findings of the Milgram experiments show that, on the one hand, preventing harm is a consideration on the part of participants and that in several circumstances they do give priority to it, but that, on the other hand, participants' concerns with rules, authority, and the scientific goals are also part of the decision-making process and that they do sometimes give priority to those considerations over preventing harm. It is precisely these types of analyses of domain conflicts, which have been part of our theoretical formulations (Turiel 1983; Turiel et al. 1987; Turiel and Smetana 1984; Wainryb 1991), that critics like Kelly et al. (2007) fail to recognize or acknowledge. They have asserted, instead, that we take the position that any type of infliction of harm would be judged as wrong regardless of laws or authority dictates (which would be a blatantly wrong position given views on such matters as self-defense, spanking by parents, or capital punishment). The situations used by Kelly et al., which pitted authority dictates against harm, have parallels in the Milgram experimental situations with comparable results. They also pitted spanking on the part of school authorities with the pain inflicted. As has been more deeply analyzed by Wainryb (1991), judgments about the act of spanking take into account the intent and goals (e.g., to benefit the child's learning or development) of the person in authority in the context of assumptions about reality (which we refer to as informational assumptions) about the effectiveness of the act toward the desired positive goals.

Research with children, adolescents, and adults has found that judgments about honesty and deception are coordinated with other considerations (Perkins and Turiel 2007; Turiel et al. 2009; Gingo et al. 2017). For example, a study with adolescents showed that they give priority to some moral and personal goals over maintaining honesty (Perkins and Turiel 2007). It was found that the large majority of the adolescents judged it acceptable to deceive parents when they directed acts considered morally wrong on the grounds of preventing injustice or harm. The majority also judged that deception was justified when parents directed personal choices judged to be within the adolescents' legitimate jurisdiction. By contrast, the large majority judged that it is not acceptable to deceive parents when they give directives about prudential acts because of parents' legitimate authority to place such restrictions. Similar processes of coordination occur in adults' decisions about deception in marital relationships involving differences in power. For example, in situations posing a conflict between honesty and physical and emotional welfare, most adults gave priority to welfare over honesty (Turiel et al. 2009).

Other research on concepts of rights and of social inclusion with children and adolescents lends support to the proposition that coordination between different social goals is central in decision-making. In coordinating different considerations, individuals sometimes uphold rights and at other times subordinate rights toward the goals of preventing harm or promoting community interests—as also documented by several large-scale public opinion surveys of adult Americans (Hyman and Sheatsley 1953; Stouffer 1955; McClosky and Brill 1983). Research in several cultures into the judgments of children and adolescents has shown that they endorse freedoms of speech, religion, and literacy as rights in response to general questions and in some situations. However, in some situations they also give lesser priority to the expression of these rights when they are in conflict with other moral considerations, such as physical harm (Helwig 1995, 1997; Turiel and Wainryb 1998; Day 2014). A similar pattern of findings was obtained in research on concepts of the fairness of social inclusion (Killen et al. 2002; Horn 2003). Children and adolescents judged exclusion based on race or gender as wrong, but they also judged exclusion to be acceptable when in conflict with other considerations like the legitimacy of achieving group goals (e.g., in sport or academic competitions).

The findings from all these studies show that conceptual distinctions and coordination are part of processes of social decision-making. It could be asked, however, if these findings do not simply reflect a distinction between abstract and concrete judgments; that the findings actually reflect a failure of individuals to apply their abstract judgments in concrete situations. We believe that would be an incorrect interpretation of the findings. People do hold abstract judgments about harm, rights, trust, and honesty, but they also hold abstract judgments about social conventions and the personal realm. All those judgments can be brought to bear in concrete situations. It has been found, for example, that in some situations judgments about honesty and trust were primary. In situations involving conflicts with other moral goals or with perceived personal goals, judgments about honesty were taken into account and applied but were subordinated to the other goals. Rather than a simple distinction between abstract and concrete judgments, the findings are that in many situations more than one type of judgment is applied—in some cases resulting in the assertion of honesty and in other cases in assertions of the necessity to prevent harm or oppose restrictions on personal choices at the expense of honesty.

7. Social Opposition and Moral Resistance: Flexibility of Thought in Normativity

In coming to some of the decisions about honesty and deception, the adolescents and adults took into account disparities in power and control. For example, in the study with adolescents, fewer of them judged deception of peers acceptable than deception of parents for the morally relevant and personal issues. The difference between how adolescents perceive the acceptability of deception of parents and friends points to another element of the coordination of different considerations in social and moral decision-making. Deception of friends is considered less acceptable because such relationships are seen as based on equality and mutuality, whereas relationships with parents involve greater inequality in power. It should be kept in mind that adolescents make distinctions among realms of jurisdiction of persons in positions of authority since they accept the legitimacy of parental authority in some domains but not in others. Younger children, too, maintain differentiated conceptions of the legitimate jurisdiction of persons in positions of authority. Research conducted in the United States and Korea shows that children are critical of authority when they dictate or promote actions that violate moral norms (Laupa et al. 1995; Kim and Turiel 1996; Kim 1998).

These findings point to a contradiction in the term "moral norms." Common definitions of the word "norm," including some listed in the *Oxford English Dictionary*, refer to standards of behavior accepted and binding to all members of a group or community. When defined as "shared standards," the term "norm" does not accurately depict how people think about maintaining honesty or adhering to relations of power and authority, because moral decisions are not always shared among members of a group. As noted, individuals within a group do not think it is always right to be honest or obedient and, moreover, do not necessarily agree when they are obliged to be honest or obedient. We have seen, for example, that people often judge that the "norm" of honesty should be violated when it conflicts with welfare or when it serves goals of maintaining fairness. Similarly, adherence to authority (such as parental authority) is seen as sometimes subordinate to fairness and the achievement of legitimate personal choices. Thus, it is necessary to distinguish between common expectations about social practices in a particular group, which may be normative in the sense of seeming to be common, and individuals' judgments about common (and uncommon) practices, and moral decisions involving the application of moral judgments, which are normative in the sense of being evaluative, and may or may not be shared by other members of the group. In many communities there are groups (such as those based on gender, social class, ethnicity, race) that are subject to unequal practices, but which are not accorded the same protections against harm, and are denied rights. It appears that in such communities the group's supposed shared norms are not applied to everyone. Here we see a discrepancy between the idea that norms can be defined as shared behaviors and the idea that substantive norms of welfare, fairness, and rights are based on acceptance and agreement.

Moreover, this type of discrepancy is clearly evidenced in research on the ways people think about cultural practices involving inequalities connected to differences in power within social hierarchies: The norms (common expectations) of a group can be negatively evaluated (a normative judgment) by members of that very group.

Inequalities due to different positions on social hierarchies involving power relationships are common to many cultures, but there are cultural differences in the groups that occupy such positions and in the extent of inequalities reflected in practices. A clear example is gender inequalities within social hierarchies. Many patriarchal societies, for instance, have clearly defined roles of dominance for males and subordination for females. Cultural practices in those societies place restrictions on many activities of females and grant males a good deal of control (Abu-Lughod 1993; Wikan 1996; Nussbaum 2000; Turiel, 2002).

Psychological and anthropological studies have examined how females in patriarchal cultures think about and react to inequalities in cultural practices. The psychological research, conducted in the Middle East (Wainryb and Turiel 1994), India (Neff 2001), Colombia (Mensing 2002), Benin (Conry-Murray 2009), and Turkey (Guvenc 2011), examined how adolescent and adult males and females think about roles in the social hierarchy and how females evaluate cultural practices that grant control to males over females in many activities—such as regarding educational and work opportunities, recreational pursuits, choices of dress, and, more generally, decision-making in the family. The findings showed that males and females are cognizant of practices granting greater autonomy, independence, and power to males than to females. However, it was found that there are two salient critiques of cultural norms. One is that females value autonomy for themselves, too, expressing desires for greater freedoms and independence—goals they perceived difficult to attain. Secondly, the majority of females judged many of the practices entailing inequalities to be unfair.

Corresponding findings were obtained in ethnographic research in poor neighborhoods in Cairo (Wikan 1996) and in Bedouin villages in Northwest Egypt

(Abu-Lughod 1993). These studies show that women act in overt and sometimes co-vert ways to oppose and subvert cultural norms of gender inequality. For example, Abu-Lughod described how women used deception to avoid practices like arranged marriages and polygamy. Such actions were based on the judgment that the practices were unfair. A woman in Abu-Lughod's (1993, 238) study put it as follows:

And this business of marrying more than one wife—I wish they'd change their views on this. It is the biggest sin. The Prophet—it is not forbidden but the Prophet said only if you treat them fairly. But a man can't, it can't be done. Even if he has money, he can't. As a person in his thoughts and his actions, he can't be fair. He'll like one more than another.

This woman's reasoning about the norm of polygamy (applicable to men, not women) provides a good example of recognition of different and conflicting norms and the perceived need to coordinate them. She was aware that polygamy is a long-standing cultural/religious norm, but she also gives priority to considerations of fair-ness. Her prescription is that the norm be altered for reasons of fairness given that she said they should "change their views on this" because it cannot be done in a fair way.

8. Conclusions

On the basis of findings from research in psychology and other disciplines, we have attempted to show that questions about norms must include analyses of how people reason. In reasoning about social interactions, societal systems, and cultural practices, individuals draw substantive distinctions among different types of norms. We have focused especially on two central types of norms—moral and social-conventional. Moreover, the flexibility of human reasoning means that norms and prescriptions of how one ought to act are not applied mechanistically, rigidly, or in absolutistic ways. In coming to social decisions, individuals typically take into account differing features of social situations, including conflicting moral goals or conflicting moral and non-moral goals. In doing so, they weigh and balance such considerations, recognizing that priorities need to be drawn.

In our view, the centrality of reason, in conjunction with emotions involving eval-uative appraisals, has implications for explanations of the development of normativity. The development of thought and emotions involves a constructive process by which different domains are formed through a variety of social interactions. Social events and interactions of the types that occur across cultures are sources of the development of judgments about welfare, justice, and rights.

An additional and highly significant feature of human reasoning is the ability to re-flect on existing societal conditions. We discussed findings demonstrating that people do not uncritically accept cultural practices entailing inequalities and unfair treat-ment even though the practices may be normative in some aspects of the societal organizations and part of tradition supported by those in positions of power and authority. In that respect, it can be said that some cultural practices are normative collective practices and, at the same time, contested practices. The practices can be collective in that they are known generally and endorsed by some groups (e.g., those of higher status in the social hierarchy) in the culture; they are contested in that other groups in the culture (e.g., those of lower status) oppose them and covertly or overtly work toward changes. Consequently, there are both commonalities (shared norms) and differences (contested norms) in the perspectives of members of a society. Perhaps differences in perspectives, along with opposition to cultural practices, are major sources of the great historical struggles for social justice centered on demands for equal rights.

11

Moral Obligation from the Outside In

Neil Roughley

1. Introduction: Deontic Moral Judgement, Moral Obligation, and Empirical Explanation

Not so long ago, Stephen Darwall made the following, striking claim, which may appear to involve the rejection of the idea that empirical research might have any relevance for an analysis of morality:

Morality as we philosophers now understand it . . . is an essentially normative rather than empirical concept. Moreover, "morality" in this sense admits of only a singular use. There are many actual and possible *moralities* (embodied psychologically and socially), but there is only one *morality*. (Darwall 2013c, 3)

Part of what is being said here seems easy to understand: the participants in one culture may—as a result of participating in that culture—believe that there are things that are morally inacceptable that the participants in another culture—as a result of participating in that culture—believe are morally obligatory or at least acceptable. That much is empirically uncontroversial. The philosophical understanding of morality, Darwall claims, is wholly different. It works with the idea of a morality that is independent of what contents empirical individuals take, for instance, to fall under the deontic modalities. Taking morality to be normative involves taking there to be only one correct answer to at least some questions concerning what is obligatory, permissible, or impermissible.

Now, Darwall is clearly overstating his case. It's perfectly possible for a philosopher to be an ethical relativist: there are people with positions in philosophy who have argued eloquently for variants of a view according to which what is morally obligatory is relative to a culture or system of social norms (Harman 1977; Prinz

2007; cf. Bayertz, Chapter 8 in this volume). Whether they might be right or whether they could even coherently be right are questions I shall not be discussing explicitly. Instead, I develop a conception according to which there is indeed only one morality, but one which is compatible with at least some degree of cultural relativity of its content. More importantly here, I shall argue that empirical data can help us to understand, rather than undermine, this conception.

I shall assume, with Darwall, that making a moral assertion involves taking it that there is a key sense in which the truth or falsity of what you are contending is not, or at least not generally, dependent on the existence of social or cultural norms that you were socialised to accept. Take participants in a moral practice who believe that torture is impermissible. Someone's having such a belief is, of course, perfectly compatible with the knowledge that someone living exactly where they are now two hundred years ago would not have been likely to believe such a thing and that their possession of that belief now is a result of changes in social conditions and accompanying cultural discourse. Nevertheless, to believe that torture is morally inacceptable entails the assumption that, in spite of such contingencies in the belief's generation, its truth conditions are another matter. An analysis of moral obligation should contribute to an understanding of how this can be so. The analysis developed in section 3 of this chapter is offered as such a contribution.

Darwall presents the tension between two views of morality as a tension between empirical and philosophical conceptions. I take it that what he thinks of as the philosophical conception is a component of everyday moral understanding, a component that philosophy has specialised in trying to take seriously. Making sense of our everyday self-understanding is indeed a task that is peculiarly philosophical. Kant's invention of the noumenal realm is perhaps best understood as a somewhat quaint attempt to elucidate the internal perspective of agents involved in making moral claims. Kant believed that reflection on the empirical conditions of that perspective can only undermine it (1785, 24f., 38f.). Darwall himself presents a modern version of this picture when he argues that normative moral concepts constitute an interconnected system in which one concept can only be understood in terms of the other and none can be understood in terms of concepts located outside the system (Darwall 2006, 11ff.).

Although I agree that what Strawson called "connective analysis" (1992, 19ff.) can be highly illuminating, I find this an unsatisfying place at which to stop. I think, in contrast, that making sense of the internal perspective on moral obligation—both of the concepts we use and of the facts that would make claims deploying them true—involves setting these features into contact with non-moral features of our self-understanding, features that admit of empirical investigation. Our moral practice is firmly entrenched in the empirical world: it has developed phylogenetically and its preconditions have to be developed ontogenetically in those creatures that grow up to take part in it. Moreover—and this is a key assumption for what follows—the phylogenetic evolution of our capacities for deontic moral judgement and for action oriented by such judgements is implausibly taken to ground exclusively in the development of abilities to recognise pre-existent moral features of the world. In particular, it is difficult to see how the claim that morality makes *demands* of human agents, the core claim concerning the existence of moral *obligations*, could have been true prior to the point in the evolution of hominins at which they began to make demands of each other.[1]

If this is correct, the existence of at least some—deontic—moral truths looks to be dependent on features of the evolved human life form in a way that has no parallel for the truths of natural science. So there are reasons to think that the evolution of moral practices, including that of the mental apparatus on which the practices depend, went hand in hand with the development of whatever it is that satisfies the truth conditions deployed in deontic moral claims. If this is correct, we have good reasons to conceive the metaphysics of moral obligation as intimately connected to the epistemic matter of obligation's conceptualisation. It follows that, had humans evolved as animals with significantly different psychological endowments, there may not have been such a property as that of being morally obligated. Accordingly, empirical data that is evidence for alternative psychological structures either in our nearest primate relatives or in unrepresentative humans is of particular interest here.

In what follows, I shall approach moral obligation via two sets of empirical data concerning agents that are missing features which we recognise as decisive for morality. The idea is that, by identifying such determinate features *ex negativo*, we may be able to uncover what we can think of as building blocks or proto-forms of deontic attitudes. Moral obligation itself is then conceivable in terms of what makes true certain impartially regulated, counterfactual variants of these attitudes. Or so I shall argue.

The first set of data, to which I turn in section 2.1, has been delivered by comparative psychological research on what has been thought to be manifestations of inequity aversion in primates. The second, on which I focus in section 2.2, derives from research in clinical and criminal psychology on psychopaths. I argue that both sets of data present agents who, on the one hand, appear to demand certain types of action or omission from other agents, but who, on the other hand, seem not to conceptualise such demands as expressing moral rights or obligations. My claims in both cases are

---

[1] So-called debunking arguments claim to demonstrate that there is an unbridgeable gap between an evolutionary view of the development of epistemic moral capacities and a robust moral realism, which postulates moral facts that are independent of the attitudinal responses of humans (Street 2006). Street's argument grounds in the claim that an evolutionary explanation of our moral judgements depends on the survival value of their being made and believed, not on the survival value of their being independently true. My claim here is simpler, a phylogenetic descendant of Mackie's "argument from queerness": it just seems bizarre that moral demands might have been inscribed into the fabric of nature prior to the development of beings capable of making any sense of them or responding to them appropriately.

hostage to empirical details, about which there has already been a considerable degree of discussion. This is particularly true of the data on psychopaths and the conclusions that they license. Because of the various interlocking issues that have been raised, I will devote significantly more time to the relevant details of psychopathy than to my interpretation of the experiments with primates.

In section 3, I move to make constructive use of the results of my interpretations of the empirical material. I propose that the non-normative demands at work in such cases can be understood as expressions of a first basic building block of the psychological infrastructure of deontic moral claims. Such an infrastructure, I argue, requires two further elements that appear unavailable to primates and psychopaths. In section 3.1, I claim that the first is a disposition that I label "Smithian empathy," which enables the move to vicarious variants of the demands we began with. In section 3.2, I go on to argue that the decisive step to the completion of our deontic moral psychology brings in the ability to reapply Smithian empathy from an impartial perspective. The psychological infrastructure thus generated enables its bearers to develop beliefs about counterfactual, impartial, and informed vicarious demands. The formation of such a belief is, I then claim, the making of deontic moral judgements. Finally, I claim, the metaphysics of moral obligation are best understood in terms of the truth-makers for such beliefs. That is, the content of moral obligation turns out to be the content of counterfactual, informed, impartial, and sufficiently vicarious demands.

The final section of the chapter both offers a defence of the account against likely philosophical objections (section 4.1) and situates it in relation to a plausible account of the proto-deontic capacities of chimpanzees (section 4.2).

2. From the Outside: Empirical Starting Points

2.1. Approaching Moral Obligation 1: Primates and the Token-Exchange Paradigm

In *Chimpanzee Politics*, Frans de Waal claims that chimpanzee life is governed by rules of both positive and negative reciprocity. He sees a case of the latter where a female chimp attacks a male, who she had helped earlier to chase a rival, but who then didn't support her when the rival went for her in turn. Such cases, he thinks, suggest that reciprocity among chimps is governed by a "sense of moral rightness and justice" (de Waal 1998, 203). De Waal's evidence here is anecdotal in character. However, a paradigm he later initiated with Sarah Brosnan aims experimentally to pick out primate reactions that express such a sense of fairness, doing so by confronting the subjects with conditions that might violate such a sense.

In the experiments, originally done with capuchins and later above all with chimpanzees, two subjects are given tokens that they can give back to the experimenter in exchange for food, which turns out to be either a highly valued grape or a less valued piece of cucumber. In the decisive condition, the first subject is given a grape, whereas the second only gets a piece of cucumber for handing over the token. The fascinating datum here is that a significant number of the second subjects reject the less valued piece of food after the first has been given higher-valued food in exchange for the same sort of token. The failure to maximise desire satisfaction in these cases is striking. Some of the subjects accompany their rejection with vociferous and agitated behaviour that looks for all the world like a form of protest. Brosnan and de Waal interpret this behaviour as indicative of inequity aversion, that is, of a disposition to react negatively to being given less than a conspecific for the same amount of "work" (Brosnan and de Waal 2003; de Waal 2006, 44ff.).

If this interpretation were to be correct, it would pick out an important step on the way to moral obligation. It would then appear that at least some primates are fitted out with something akin to what the British sentimentalists called a "moral sense," i.e. an innate sense of the applicability of certain moral categories, in this case of fairness and unfairness. Unfortunately, there are methodological problems which cast considerable doubt on this interpretation. The most pressing problem concerns the precise ground for the negative reaction. According to Bräuer et al., the decisive independent variable is the expectation of better food on the part of the negative respondent. Whether that expectation results from seeing what a confederate gets or from some other factor is irrelevant (Bräuer et al. 2006, 2009; Bräuer and Hanus 2012, 262).

If this is right, primates don't furnish us with evidence for an innate disposition to apply anything approaching deontic categories. Assuming that this is the case, I think that the paradigm still provides us with interesting data if we are seeking a way into a participant perspective on moral obligation from the outside. This is because, even if what worries the subjects is not social comparison—that is, what they are getting in comparison with what some relevantly similar subject is getting—it seems that what worries them is nevertheless a social feature of the situation. They certainly appear to be aware that they are in a distribution situation and that the distributor is not giving them what he could give them.[2]

---

[2] If we cancel this assumption, we are left with the claim that their refusal behaviour is to be explained by their being simply frustrated at getting less than they thought they would. This is the explanation mildly favoured by Bräuer et al. (2006). A word of terminological caution is in order here. Bräuer et al. label this explanation "the food expectation hypothesis." In this context, "expectation" is a slightly unfortunate term, as we often think of "expectations" as being normative, rather than mere doxastic states. Note that "normative expectations," like demands, have to be addressed to, or at least concern, other agents, whereas purely doxastic expectations can be given independently of whether any other agents are on the scene. The relevant concept of expectation here is that of a belief state, a state with content-to-world direction of fit. If this distinction were not maintained, the food expectation hypothesis would collapse into either Brosnan's account or the intermediate account I go on to propose in the text.

But this means that the animals are expressing what looks like anger at a form of so-cial behaviour. On this interpretation, the behaviour objected to would only be social in a reduced sense relative to that postulated by the inequity-aversion interpretation. Whereas in the latter interpretation, what is objected to is how the subject is treated in comparison with how another is treated, in the less exigent interpretation, what is objected to is simply how the subject is being treated (relative to how she could be treated). If we adopt the latter reading, we are dealing with *dyadic* rather than triadic sociality.

This phenomenon of dyadic social anger seems to me in itself to be important. Its explanation will not be undemanding. The animals in question would need to see the distributor's behaviour as motivated, in particular as motivated in a way that is relevant for them. The standard of relevance is brought into play, I suggest, by the animals de-manding a certain kind of treatment. Not meeting that standard apparently looks to the primates like behaviour motivated by ill will or indifference to them on the part of the distributor. This interpretation seems particularly plausible for the dramatic cases in which the chimps throw the piece of cucumber out of the cage, the cases Brosnan calls "active refusals" (Brosnan 2006, 172).[3]

I have distinguished my interpretation of the chimps' behaviour from that advanced by Brosnan and de Waal, an interpretation that takes the chimps' demands to concern the fulfilment of a specific normative standard, one of distributive fairness. Importantly, my interpretation does not only make no reference to a particular kind of normative content; it also avoids any assumption that the chimps' demands ground in a concern with any subject other than themselves. Their purely self-concerned reactions to the non-fulfilment of those demands, particularly where their refusals are "active," look very much like reactions of resentment—as long as one doesn't understand resent-ment as involving a parallel disposition to react with comparable anger to comparable treatment of conspecifics.

---

[3] As the active refusals are relatively rare, there is a question of the extent to which the mechanisms behind the impressively dramatic behaviour presented in such cases are the same ones at work whenever the subjects refuse or reject the less valued food. If it could be shown that there is no such unitary expla-nation, my proposal might be thought to only apply to such minority cases. Note that my hypothesis has two components. The first is that we are dealing with a dyadic social response that concerns the distributor and her relationship to the subject. The second is that the subject's response is triggered by the distributor's non-fulfilment of a demand. The infrequency of active refusals doesn't cast doubt on the first component, but on the general plausibility of the second. As chimpanzee societies are hierarchical, it seems likely that their tendency to react actively may be modulated by their perception of the relative rank of the agent to whom they are reacting, here the experimenter. Whether animals refuse at all may, as Brosnan points out, be mediated by factors such as sex, rank, and relationship quality (Brosnan et al. 2005; 2010, 7ff.; Price and Brosnan 2012, 147ff.). Whether these factors influence the active or passive quality of refusals that do take place could in principle be tested. For the purposes of the structure I am interested in pinning down, it would suffice that there is a set of cases that are best explained in the manner I am suggesting.

This interpretation would require that chimpanzees possess at least a rudimentary "theory of mind" (cf. Call and Tomasello 2008), but it would still be considerably less demanding than the inequity aversion explanation. Nevertheless, it would require that the chimps (or monkeys) are disposed to demand of certain other agents that they don't display indifference towards them in at least some of their actions. The omission and the active behaviour that sometimes accompanies it would be explained by my suggestion. If the disposition to make that demand is indeed what Brosnan and de Waal have teased out, I wish to argue, they have teased out a first important building block of the psychology of moral obligation—a psychology from which the chimps are otherwise well removed.[4]

2.2. Approaching Moral Obligation 2: Psychopaths

There is a second group of agents whose psychology seems to exclude them from being bearers of attitudes that ascribe moral obligations. Psychopaths have had a considerable amount of attention in recent philosophical moral psychology (Nichols 2004, 12ff.; Kennett 2006; Prinz 2007, 42ff.; Maibom 2008; Schramme 2014), I think with good reason. They have also been studied by a number of empirical psychologists interested in moral or other-regarding motivation (Blair et al. 2009; Baron-Cohen 2011, 43ff.; Hare et al. 2012).

Psychopaths are clearly agents and appear, at least up to a certain point, to be rational agents. They also have considerable, perhaps sometimes especially well developed "mind-reading" capacities. Nevertheless, they seem to be missing a constellation of psychological and moral features that have the appearance of a syndrome. Their particular interest here results from the plausibility of an explanatory claim, viz. that their moral deficits result from specific psychological deficits. I shall focus on three characteristic human features, or sets of features, that appear to be missing, or dramatically minimised, in agents that are classified as psychopaths. The deficits are motivational, epistemic, and affective. The second of these will require a somewhat more extended discussion than the others.

It should be noted from the outset that none of these three claims is without presuppositions that may be taken to be problematic. Nevertheless, I hope to show that the claims can be reasonably argued for in a way that makes their weight clear. This will involve denying certain claims that specific views of morality might tempt one to make. Therefore, the view I will end up with will not be completely neutral between all the possible positions on various features of morality. Nevertheless, I do take it to

---

[4] Since I first presented this explanatory hypothesis, it has been subject to empirical testing, which appears to bear it out. See Engelmann et al. (2017).

be neutral between the central positions of normative ethics, as well as reconstructing key features of the everyday understanding of moral obligation.

2.2.1. Lack of Moral Motivation The first claim is that psychopaths lack moral motivation. Now, there are two ways in which this claim could be emptied of its content. One involves an overly demanding conception of moral motivation, according to which, for instance, no one is *really* morally motivated unless they act for the sole reason that they are thus being moral. Kant famously claimed that no action is genuinely good unless it is carried out with the exclusive motivation of fulfilling the moral law (Kant 1785, 13f.). He also noted, very sensibly in view of this claim, that we cannot be sure whether anyone has ever really acted morally (Kant 1785, 21f.). If this were to be true, then the claim that psychopaths lack moral motivation would not tell us very much about psychopaths compared with other agents.

The other way of emptying the claim of content would be to accept the position of certain utilitarians and certain contractarians, according to whom there is no such thing as specifically moral motivation. There are, rather, only moral norms for action, and moral judgements concern merely the question of whether those norms are met. Whatever may motivate individuals to stick to the norms might be misleadingly described as "moral motivation" (Mill 1861, 159ff.). This will be misleading because absolutely any kind of consideration may for contingent reasons end up motivating agents to stick to the relevant norms. The claim that psychopaths lack moral motivation might, then, either be empty, if moral motivation is taken to involve attitudes with a very specific, Kantian content, or false, if any motivation that leads someone not to violate a moral norm can be thus labelled. Even psychopaths sometimes avoid doing certain things that are morally impermissible.

I think, however, that we have an everyday conception of moral motivation that is neither empty nor trivially satisfied. That conception is unlikely to be monistic. It plausibly includes cases in which people perform certain acts because they believe that the act in question is the one they morally ought to perform. But it also includes actions performed for the sake of others, in which the "ought" doesn't cross the mind of the agent. In many cases of helping, saving, or protecting, an "ought" thought is going to be a thought too many. But where fairness is the central consideration, the idea that you ought to perform a certain action may appropriately carry the day even where you would personally prefer the beneficiary of the action not to benefit because you see him as otherwise morally reprehensible. However, even in such cases where concern for the specific beneficiary of one's action is not motivationally relevant, the apparent germaneness of the fairness standard grounds in the agent's appreciation of features of those subjects at least potentially affected by its application. Features that tend to be associated with agency, such as autonomy or self-respect, are candidates for the object of concern here. On an everyday understanding, then, moral motivation requires a concern for others, although that concern might not directly motivate the action in question, but instead motivate the acceptance of a standard, an acceptance which in turn regulates the action.

Thus understood, moral motivation is, so it seems, foreign to psychopaths. According to the affective cognitive neuroscientist and psychopathy researcher James Blair, psychopaths share with bearers of antisocial personality disorder the tendency to reactive aggression. Importantly, their antisocial motivational resources go significantly beyond this tendency, including also the disposition to instrumental aggression, that is, aggression that is goal-directed and planned, rather than resulting from irascibility (Blair et al. 2005, 12f.). Cold-blooded, planned violence, combined with pronounced tendencies to lying, manipulation, and irresponsibility, are the moral signature of people classified as psychopaths (Hare 1993, 83ff.; O'Toole 2008; Baron-Cohen 2011, 43ff.). The profile thus sketched looks very much like that of someone devoid of moral motivation, that is, of motivation that involves any kind of concern for others—whether for their well-being or for their status as agents. In the words of the criminal psychologist, Robert D. Hare, the behaviour of psychopaths appears "morally incomprehensible" (Hare 1993, 5).

2.2.2. Lack of, or Severely Restricted Ability to Make Moral Judgements I come to the second claim about the deficiencies of psychopaths, according to which psychopaths don't make, or have serious difficulties making, genuine moral judgements. The discussion of this claim will take up a little more of our time.

It was first advanced by James Blair, who derives its justification from four studies[5] he carried out, three in the 1990s and one in 2001. Blair applied a procedure created by the developmental psychologists Elliot Turiel and Larry Nucci to test whether subjects are able to make the distinction between moral and conventional norm contraventions (Nucci and Turiel 1978; Turiel 1983; Turiel and Dahl, this volume, 200ff.). Where Turiel's primary interest concerns the question of when children develop the ability to make the distinction, Blair applied the test to psychopathic criminals and children with psychopathic tendencies in order to see whether and, if so, to what extent psychopaths are able to make the distinction at all. His answer is that psychopaths don't make the distinction (Blair 1995, 20; Blair et al. 1995, 748) and that children with psychopathic tendencies make "significantly less of a distinction" than controls (Blair 1997, 735). Blair's results have been taken up by Shaun Nichols (Nichols 2004, 12ff.) and Jesse Prinz (Prinz 2007, 43ff.), who both see them as providing strong evidence that psychopaths don't make moral judgements.

---

[5] Presumably it's not so easy to organise the kinds of studies necessary. Nevertheless, until we have more data, the inductive basis for the following points is relatively thin.

Now, there have been objections both to Blair's interpretation of his own results and to the cogency of the distinction between moral and conventional norms as developed by Turiel and colleagues. Let us begin with the latter. According to Turiel, there are various features that cluster around judgements of moral right and wrong that distinguish them from judgements based on conventional norms. Judges—including children from the age of 42 months—take their moral judgements to generally concern matters more serious than the topics of conventional judgements; they take them to be applicable to cases in other geographical or cultural contexts, unlike conventional judgements; they see the norms referred to in judging as authority-independent, again unlike conventional norms; and they tend to see them as justified by considerations of welfare, justice, or rights, whereas they think of conventional judgements as justified by rules set up to facilitate social organisation.[6]

2.2.2.1. The "Nomological Cluster" Objection One broad objection to this conceptualisation of the distinction begins by construing the basic claim as proposing that the four features just named constitute a nomological cluster, i.e. that they manifest a lawlike tendency to occur together. In the light of this construal, showing that these features can be prised apart empirically in the judgements of adults, using precisely the same kinds of questionnaires employed in the Turiel paradigm, has appeared to pose a serious problem (Kelly et al. 2007; Shoemaker 2011, 105ff.).

However, the nomological cluster interpretation involves a misunderstanding of the basic claim of the Turiel school. The authors explicitly reckon with the fact that adult judgements of what ought to be done all in all can involve a mixture of moral and conventional—and personal—considerations (Turiel 1983, 68ff.; 114ff., 201ff.; Wainryb 1993; Helwig et al. 1995; Turiel 2015, 512ff.). In such cases, questionnaires of the standard sort are not going to get at the underlying categories. In his early discussions of examples involving "coordination" of the domains, Turiel therefore cited extensive interview material or protocols instead (Turiel 1983, 117ff., 206f.). The basic idea is, rather, to get at logical and psychological features brought into play

---

[6] See, for instance, Turiel 1983, 52ff.; Smetana and Braeges 1990, 330ff.; Turiel 2015, 506ff. There are differences of emphasis, perhaps differences in the assumed strength of the connection with morality, in the literature in this tradition. Alongside the criteria just specified, sometimes other features such as (i) categoricity, (ii) "permissibility," and (iii) "amount of deserved punishment" are named. I shall leave these aside in my brief remarks here, as (i) is not easily distinguished operationally from seriousness, (ii) is actually a modal aspect of the judgement's content, rather than a property of the entire judgement, and (iii) would be a complex feature, involving a judgement that harm, which is prima facie morally problematic, should be inflicted under specific conditions, where inflicting that harm might be seen as moral requisite or might, alternatively, be taken to be conventionally required. This last point is not only a reason why punishment deserved is an unhelpful parameter for distinguishing the moral and conventional domains. It is also a reason why using examples of punishment as probes—as Kelly et al. (2007, 123ff.) do with critical intent—is an infelicitous method for getting at the distinction.

in "prototypical" cases (Wainryb 1993, 925). The uncontextualised playground and
school examples originally used—a child pulling another child's hair or stealing her
bag compared with a boy wearing a skirt or a child leaving the classroom without
permission—were intended to make that feature of the case salient that allows its un-
ambiguous assignment to one of the domains. This also seems to justify Blair's decision to use the same "school" probes in the psychopathy experiments, both with the
children and the adults.

Moreover, pace the nomological cluster interpretation, two differences among the
parameters seem highly significant. First, it seems fairly clear that what Turiel et al. call
"criterion judgements" (concerning seriousness, generality, and authority-independence)
and what they call "justification categories" (concerning welfare or rights versus smooth
functioning of organisational mechanisms) have a different status as far as determining
whether or not we are in the moral domain. Second, for a related reason, one particular
kind of so-called criterion judgements should be seen as the decisive one.

On the first point: in various places, Turiel gives indications that he sees the justification categories as primary. Moral norms are taken to have their various characteristics "in so far as they stem from concepts of welfare, justice and rights" (Turiel 2015,
506; Turiel and Dahl, this volume, 202). I think that rather tentative remarks of this nature should be given more emphasis in order to avoid confusion of the kind illustrated
by the nomological cluster reading. Whether or not this proposal appears congenial
to researchers in domain theory, it seems to me correct: moral judgements concern
primarily specific ways others may be affected—whether in their welfare or their
rights. If the proposal is accepted, it ought also to be accepted that it is misleading to
use the expression "criterion judgements" to pick out construals of moral obligations
in terms of generality, seriousness, and authority-dependence (Turiel 1983, 52ff.). If
I am right, these features should be understood as *symptoms*, rather than as criteria for
the fact that the subject takes her judgement to concern matters in the moral domain.
The generalisability of the judgement to other cultures would then be a typical, but
no necessary feature of such judgements.[7]

2.2.2.2. Authority-Independence Thus viewed, one of the properties typically
manifested by moral judgements is more closely related to the essential feature of
the moral domain than the others: that of authority-independence. Whether or not
others are affected negatively by an action or inaction is, with few exceptions, something that does not depend on the proclamations of authority. For this reason, the

---

[7] There have been repeated disputes in philosophy as to whether morality should be defined in formal
terms or on the basis of content. Whereas Richard Hare claimed that "universality" is one of the two defining features of moral judgements (Hare 1952, 79ff.), Philippa Foot countered that this would force us to
see all sorts of absurd universal prescriptions as moral (Foot 1958/59, 84). Turiel needn't, and shouldn't, take
Hare's side here.

authority-dependence probe is, along with the justification probe, the one that should be given the most weight. Blair claims that it is this parameter that is both most important and distinguishes most consistently between the domains (Blair et al. 1995, 742, 749; Blair et al. 2001, 100; Blair et al. 2005, 58). According to his results in the psychopathy studies, psychopaths don't differentiate between moral and conventional domains along this parameter[8] and are "much less likely to justify their items with reference to others' welfare" (Blair 1995, 20; cf. Blair et al. 1995, 749; Blair et al. 2001, 808).

The relevance of the data on authority-independence has been questioned. On the one hand, it has been pointed out that authority-independence is insufficient to situate us in the moral domain, as reactions of disgust and to the breaking of religious rules will tend to have this feature (Shoemaker 2011, 106, 109). But this is beside the point if authority-independence is merely a feature that generally characterises judgements about a domain essentially circumscribed by specific types of justification. On the other hand, it has been claimed that authority-independence isn't necessary for the moral domain, as authority-relative factors can play a role in restricting moral reactions to harm, particularly as shown in cases of punishment or military training (Kelly et al. 2007, 126ff.; Shoemaker 2011, 109). But both of these kinds of case are good candidates for examples that involve not only moral, but also conventional features that have to be taken into account. Only if you believe that moral judgements are necessarily characterised by the further property of overridingness[9] must accepting the relevance of authority in certain complex adult cases involving harm entail that an understanding of the moral domain doesn't require authority-independence.[10]

[8] This claim is supported by the data, although in a way that is unexpected and requires interpretation. The psychopathic criminals didn't reverse the standard pattern of answers given by the control criminals. Rather than, as Blair expected, declaring moral norm contraventions to be authority-dependent, they characterised norm infringements in both domains as authority-independent (Blair 1995, 17). Blair interpreted this as the result of the psychopaths' desire to demonstrate their knowledge of society's rules, motivated in turn by their desire for early release, coupled with the inability to distinguish between domains (Blair et al. 1995, 749). This looks plausible, although it remains speculative.

Whereas some authors (Prinz 2007, 44; Nichols 2004, 13) have accepted Blair's suggestion, others are unconvinced. David Shoemaker, for instance, has claimed that the data support a completely different hypothesis, namely that psychopaths see ungrounded rules at work in both moral and conventional cases, being blind to the fact that rules of either sort may be situationally revoked by the authority of agents the rules protect. Just as children are protected by the rule that entails the wrongness of hair-pulling and could remove their own grounds for complaint by agreeing to having their hair pulled, the teacher is protected by rules that entail the wrongness of leaving the classroom without permission and could remove her own grounds for complaint by agreeing that no permission is needed to leave the classroom (Shoemaker 2011, 113–17). This Darwallian interpretation, which interestingly shifts the identification of the relevant authority in the moral case, nevertheless looks unconvincing. This is so because it requires the implausible general premise that what we think of as conventional rule contraventions equally involve wrongs to victims. That the teacher is the victim of such transgressions as a result of the disruption they cause to classroom decorum seems particularly implausible.

[9] Turiel rejects this claim explicitly and with good reason (Turiel 1983, 74).

[10] On punishment cases, see note 6.

Finally, it should be noted that the distinction between morality and convention may appear to be flawed not only for empirical, but also for theoretical reasons. Divine command theorists might take independence from (terrestrial) authority to be definitive of morality, but deny any conceptual connection with harm and rights. Contractarians are likely to have worries that go to the heart of the distinction, conceiving morality as itself a social institution set up to order the relationships between members of a community in ways seen as strategically rational for all concerned.

This is a point at which it should be made explicit that the argument I am developing presupposes a certain broad conception of morality, although one that I take to conform by and large to everyday understanding. Everyday understanding, I think, supports the following response to the contractarian wholeheartedly, whereas my response to divine command conceptions requires a theoretical step that will no doubt not be congenial to every person on the street.

My response to the contractarian points to his theoretical aim—that of constructing a system of norms to regulate behaviour presupposing only the motivation to maximise personal utility on the part of the participants. This is an aim that more or less explicitly leads the contractarian to set aside the morality we have and then see how near such a constructive project takes us to that morality. The answer is: not very near (Roughley 2003). There is thus a clear sense in which the contractarian is not interested in morality at all, which he tends to regard with suspicion, in as far as he takes it not to be founded on the basic principles of game theory.

In contrast, religious conceptions of morality tend to have contents that also pick out welfare and rights—alongside religious duties. This is not surprising in as far as secular moralities have developed out of religious codes. I propose that we think of such religious codes as moralities only insofar as their norms concern welfare and rights. This is obviously stipulative, as anthropologists frequently work with a formal conception of morality that uses criteria such as sanctions or importance in the social life of a society. Such a conception is, however, not that of the person on the street, and its semantics are not those of everyday judgements. I am not stipulating that "morality" should be taken to only mean "secular morality." My proposal is that, if God is involved somewhere along the line, he can only give commands that count as moral insofar as they concern the welfare and rights of his subjects. Any further commands may form a further part of the behavioural code he has given to mortals. However, only the first part should be labelled "morality."

2.2.2.3. Deontic Moral Judgements

So far in this section I have argued that the distinction between moral and conventional deontic judgements, broadly as understood in psychological domain theory, is sound. I have also proposed that we accept Blair's contention that psychopaths are unable, or at least massively restricted in their capacity, to make the distinction. I conclude that psychopaths are unable, or are at least massively restricted in their capacity, to make genuine morally normative judgements. Now, this claim cannot mean that they are incapable of forming true sentences that use deontic predicates with reference to moral matters. Psychopaths can be extremely clever and they are at least sometimes able to tell people, for instance criminal psychologists, what they want to hear.[11] The claim only makes sense if there is a difference between forming sentences about some subject matter and making judgements about that matter.

The difference, briefly, in our context is that in the second case the person is able to "go on in the same way" in new instances in which she is called on to apply deontic predicates to circumstances to which she has never observed others applying the predicates.[12] Judging that x is f entails understanding, at least up to a certain point, what f means. Note that this is equally true for individual instances of their *mis*application. False judgements are still judgements, although if someone were to be consistently wrong in the sentences they utter relative to a certain topic, we might begin to doubt whether they have any idea what they are talking about.

Imagine someone who is given a set of technical terms used by physicists in certain experimental contexts, as well as some rules of thumb of when to apply them, observes their application and learns to match the sentences uttered by the experimenters on a significant number of occasions. Imagine this is possible without having anything but the vaguest idea of what the terms might be picking out. The utterances of correct sentences, even if they had a certain reliability in the restricted context in question, would not, I submit, count as expressing judgements. This is, I suggest, analogous to the situation in which psychopaths utter sentences that apply deontic moral terms.

Phenomenological support for this claim can be found in the first systematic study of psychopathy, *The Mask of Sanity* by the psychiatrist Hervey Cleckley (1941). Cleckley writes of the psychopath: "goodness, evil, [. . .] have no actual meaning [. . .] It is as though he were colorblind, despite his sharp intelligence, to this aspect of human existence" (Cleckley 1941, 40). Although what Cleckley claims is missing

---

[11] Aharoni, Sinnott-Armstrong, and Kiehl claim to have shown that psychopaths can in fact make moral judgements: when, in their experiments, the subjects were informed in advance that other members of society judge 50% of the cases to be authority-independent, the psychopaths studied were relatively good at identifying the cases that make up the 50% (Aharoni et al. 2012). However, like Blair's results, these data also require interpretation. As far as I can tell, the psychopaths have only demonstrated that they are able to make quasi-sociological judgements about the moral judgements of others. That is very different from making the moral judgements themselves.

[12] The importance of being able to "go on in the same way" is frequently emphasised by authors influenced by the later Wittgenstein when arguing that rule following is irreducible to deduction on the basis of principles. In ethics, John McDowell influentially used Wittgensteinian considerations to argue that value judgements are non-deductive or "uncodifiable" (McDowell 1979, 57ff.), a claim that kick-started contemporary particularism. McDowell's concern is the application of "thick" value predicates such as "kind" and "fair." My concern, in contrast, is the application of what are generally taken to be "thin" deontic predicates such as "permissible" and "impermissible."

in the psychopath is an understanding of value terms, the claim seems transferable to the concepts involved in ascribing moral obligation. It is this blindness to the morally deontic (whether complete or partial) which plausibly explains why psychopaths have fared so badly on the key parameters of the moral/conventional task.

2.2.3. Lack of Specific Affective Dispositions The decisive explanatory question is now: what explains psychopaths' inability, or massively restricted ability, to make genuine judgements of moral obligation? Jesse Prinz has claimed that the cause of psychopaths' inability to make any kind of moral judgement is a third deficiency named on the psychopathy checklist, "shallow affect" (Prinz 2007, 46; 2011, 217f.; cf. Hervé et al. 2003; Kiehl 2008, 134f., 143ff.). Prinz believes that moral concepts are in general analogous to concepts of secondary qualities, their referents being part-constituted by the dispositions of humans to react in specific ways to features of the world, where the reactions in question are emotional. Independently of whether this is correct as a general moral epistemology,[13] I think there is something right about it relative to the deontic moral concepts. In what sense there is something right about it, that is, in what sense being the bearer of certain emotional dispositions contributes to the capacity to think in terms of moral obligations, will be a central question in the rest of this chapter.

First, however, we need to turn our attention to the specific types of emotions that might play that constitutive role. An indication of what those might be is provided by the two particular emotional deficits listed on the *Psychopathy Checklist*: "lack of remorse or guilt" and "lack of empathy" (Hare 1991). The co-occurrence of these two deficits is, I think, no coincidence. Moral guilt and empathy are intimately connected. It is the lack of specific mechanisms involving both that explains the psychopath's inability to make moral judgements. Or so I will be arguing.

These facts, if they are facts, would in turn help us explain the psychopathic lack of moral motivation. Lack of concern for the welfare of others is closely correlated with a lack of empathy. Lack of empathy might thus directly explain a lack of moral motivation in a series of core cases in which welfare is at stake. If lack of empathy, as I shall argue, is also an explanation for the inability, or significantly restricted ability, to make moral judgements, empathy's lack might then also provide an indirect explanation

---

[13] In view of Prinz's extremely wide conception of the moral, which includes considerations of purity and respect for social order (Prinz 2007, 68ff.), it is unclear whether the empirical evidence supports such a contention. For it to do so, we would need studies of whether psychopaths are unable to distinguish between the "morally disgusting" and "contempt for the social order" on the one hand and conventional norm transgressions on the other. Apart from the practical difficulties of carrying out such studies in societies in which the dominant "morality" focuses on either kind of value, there is a very basic difficulty of distinguishing between norms that express respect for social order and conventional norms in Turiel's sense.

of the lack of any sense that specifically moral features of others, such as their rights, matter.[14]

3. A Psychological Infrastructure for Deontic Moral Judgement

3.1. Resentment*, Smithian Empathy, and Indignation*

Let us begin by returning to the social anger that appears to be manifested in the active refusals of the chimps in the token-exchange paradigm. I remarked that we might think of their anger thus manifested as a kind of egoistic resentment. As a number of authors—in particular Darwall and Jay Wallace—have taken resentment to presuppose a deontic standard to whose apparent contravention the affect is necessarily a reaction, I will in what follows use the term of art "resentment*" to pick out the egoistic emotion I want to work with.[15] As remarked in section 2.1, not only is no norm presupposed by this reaction; it is also independent of any disposition to react with comparable anger should other sentient beings be subject to treatment similar to the treatment that triggers the affective reaction.

Resentment* is the activation of an agent's natural, affectively supported disposition to demand that others at least don't display complete indifference towards him in those cases in which he is affected by their actions.[16] This is the emotion identified by Peter Strawson in section 3 of "Freedom and Resentment" and simply labelled "resentment" (Strawson 1962, 4ff.).[17] It is what I have claimed appears to be in play in the chimps' active reactions.[18] It is also a reaction that appears to be accessible to

---

[14] On the importance of empathy for prosocial behaviour, behaviour that conforms to moral norms relating to welfare in core cases, see Eisenberg 2018; Vaish 2018; Zahn-Waxler et al. 2018. Batson argues convincingly that empathy (or sympathy) cannot be what directly motivates moral behaviour in all individual cases (Batson 2014). The argument is pretty much Kant's (Kant 1785, 13ff.), but divested of Kant's exclusivist assumptions.

[15] John Deigh has argued that our everyday concept of resentment requires no such normative presupposition (Deigh 2011b, 155–60; cf. also Steinfath, this volume, 188). He may well be right, although there can be no doubt that what people resent in the everyday sense is frequently morally impermissible action. However, the presentation of the ideas contained in this section has repeatedly provoked the claim that the everyday concept presupposes moral normativity. As the truth or otherwise of that claim is not particularly relevant for what I want to say, I simply define a concept that is at least close to that picked out by our everyday term and indicate both its proximity and (possible) difference with the asterisk.

[16] For a more precise analysis of resentment*, see Roughley (2018a, 270ff).

[17] Deigh also argues that Wallace and Darwall misrepresent Strawson in attributing to him the normative concept of resentment (Deigh 2011a, 198ff.; 2011b, 160ff.). Here he is, I think, clearly right.

[18] Picking up a remark of Strawson's, Holmer Steinfath has claimed that "resentment" presupposes an understanding that the object of one's attitude is involved in some kind of shared activity (Steinfath, this volume, 188-9). If, as Tomasello claims (Tomasello et al. 2005), chimpanzees have no access to shared intentionality, this would entail that chimps in the token exchange paradigm are inaccurately described as

psychopaths. John Deigh claims that a figure such as Bruno Anthony from Hitchcock's *Strangers on a Train* is a coherent representation of a psychopath who displays what I am calling resentment★ (Deigh 2011b, 155f.). And some of the testimonies collected by Robert Hare from real-life psychopaths and their victims appear to support the claim. A psychopathic prison inmate, asked to explain why he had beaten another inmate senseless, commented "I was pissed off. He stepped into my space. I did what I had to do" (Hare 1993, 60). In such cases the psychopath seems to see some other agent as not living up to the demands he, the psychopath, makes on that other, or on other agents in general. It is the failure to meet such egoistic standards that psychopaths then feel they can cite as justification for the extreme violence they then mete out.

Resentment★ is an appropriate starting point because, on the one hand, it allows us to isolate an attitude of interpersonal demanding that is fundamental to the human life form and plausibly in play, or at least in the background, wherever human persons interact in ways they see as subject to moral evaluation. On the other hand, it is not itself normative: it is based on what Darwall says resentment is not: a "naked demand" (Darwall 2018, 301). That is the point of beginning with an attitudinal feature that can be found in primates and psychopaths.

We now need to take steps that appear inaccessible to psychopathic agents. The first of these may be accessible to chimpanzees in limited contexts (see section 4.2 in this chapter). That first step is the move to what Strawson called "vicarious reactive attitudes" (Strawson 1962, 15ff.), that is, to affective reactions that parallel resentment★, but which are triggered by the attitude's target not meeting the demand that she not treat some third person with ill will or indifference. For the sake of easy discussion and with no claims to mirror everyday language precisely, we can label this reaction "indignation★." Indignation★ is resentment★ on behalf of a third party.[19]

The capacity that allows agents to move from resentment★ to indignation★ was described by Adam Smith in his *Theory of the Moral Sentiments* under the label "sympathy," a capacity we would more naturally designate today as "empathy." In order to avoid confusion among the various notions that are picked out by the term in contemporary debates, I will talk of *Smithian empathy*. The capacity for Smithian empathy is exercised—whether actively or automatically—where an agent "goes along with" an emotion of another (Smith 1759/90, 17, 44, 70), that is, feels it on their behalf. What these idioms precisely mean is not easy to analyse, although the phenomenon is perfectly familiar from everyday interaction. Someone who feels delight for a friend who

---

"resenting" the experimenter's behaviour. I am assuming that resentment★ grounds in a basic dispositional demand that may not have any such exacting attitudinal presuppositions, but may simply be hard-wired.

[19] The concept of indignation★ that I will develop is not really Strawsonian. This is because Strawson doesn't distinguish between various ways in which the egoism of what he calls "resentment" (and I am calling "resentment★") can be transcended. See section 3.2.

has been offered the job she has been desperately hoping to get and a father who feels worried for his daughter on the day she is sitting important exams are both playing host to mechanisms of Smithian empathy.

Importantly, what is happening here is not simply that the empathiser "catches" the emotion of the empathisee.[20] There are two reasons why this is not the decisive mechanism. First, merely feeling what another feels, even if you are aware that you are feeling it because the other feels it, is not sufficient for feeling it on her behalf. Take the couple who go on holiday in order to get some sun, but who are confronted with awful weather. He is terribly disappointed and mopes around demonstratively. Were she not with him, she would take a positive attitude to the situation, but feels his disappointment taking hold of her. She distances herself from his disappointment, declaring it to be his problem, not hers. Nevertheless, she feels it bringing her down. The identity of emotion type and content plus the causal connection clearly don't entail that she is going along with his emotion. She isn't: she's feeling it *because of* him, but not *for* him. The person who feels joy for her friend is doing exactly the opposite of distancing herself; she is taking on her friend's perspective on the matter. Feeling vicarious emotions in this way involves a kind of emotional solidarity. As Smith emphasised (Smith 1759/90, 13ff.), we value this kind of solidarity immensely and are averse to the company of those who refuse to, or are unable to, go along with our emotions.

The second reason why empathy as feeling-on-behalf-of cannot be merely a matter of latching onto another's emotion is that we can feel an emotion on behalf of another person in spite of believing that the other person isn't feeling it herself. According to Smith, empathic processes are generally set in motion not by perceiving or coming to believe that another agent is in the grip of some emotion, but by perceiving or coming to believe that she is in a particular situation. Indeed, Smith claims, "we some-times feel for another a passion of which he himself seems to be altogether incapable." Similarly, Martin Hoffman conceives empathy as involving processes whose affective results are "more congruent with" the situation of the empathisee than with that of the empathiser (Hoffman 2000, 30). Smith's examples include someone empathically feeling "anguish" with the happy sufferer of dementia and the "terrors" of a mother whose seriously sick child "feels only the uneasiness of the present instant" (Smith 1759/90, 12). In such situations the Smithian empathiser feels what she takes it the other agent would feel if she were fully aware of her situation.

Note that neither of these two ways in which Smithian empathy goes beyond the mere catching of emotions from others involves anything normative. Taking on an emotion e' on behalf of someone who is feeling e need not entail that you believe her

---

[20] For such a conception, see Slote (2010, 37f.).

feeling *e* to be appropriate.[21] And taking on an emotion that another would feel in situation *s* were they to be playing host to the relevant, activated cognitive resources does not entail that you believe the emotion to be appropriate to *s*.[22] The father who worries for his daughter on the day of her exams may have the utmost confidence in her ability and believe that she has no reason for concern. If he takes it that this is the way she feels at the moment, he can still worry with her. That can also be the case if he has paternalistically shielded her from the import of the exams for her further life, believing that she would worry too much, were she to be aware of what depends on them. In this latter scenario, the father can also worry empathically, although he believes that his daughter may, and ought to be, completely carefree as she sits down to do the papers.

Smithian empathy, then, like resentment★, is a psychological phenomenon for which humans appear to have the capacity, independently of whether they participate in a moral life form. Unlike resentment★, however, Smithian empathy is, if the Psychopathy Checklist is right, inaccessible to psychopaths, who, so it seems, don't feel *for* others.[23]

Putting these two capacities together: a person capable of resentment★ who is also endowed with the capacity for Smithian empathy is able to react with resentment★ on behalf of others. This vicarious resentment★ is directed at agents who have treated those others in ways that display at least an indifference the absence of which is demanded by the person reacting. It is this reaction that we can call "indignation★."

According to the simplest case catered for by the broadly Smithian model I am proposing, where an agent *A* performs an action φ that affects a recipient *R* and *R* resents★ *A*'s φ-ing, an observer *O* may react to the scenario by emotionally going along with *R*'s resentment★. She will normally do this after paying attention to the motives for *A*'s action, with which she may also feel a certain degree of empathy. If, on doing so, she ends up coming down emotionally on the side of *R*, she will be indignant★ at *A* (Figure 11.1).

---

[21] For the counter-claim, see Darwall (2018, 293f.). Smith himself claims that judging another's emotion as appropriate is simply to fully empathise with her (Smith 1759/90, 16ff.). I read this as an attempt to reduce judgements of appropriateness to empathic attitudinising. However, there is a basic tension in *The Theory of Moral Sentiments* between such naturalistic moves and another set of claims that appear to presuppose dimensions of normativity at points in the argument precluded by the first set. Whichever set is dominant in Smith's arguments, it is the first strand I am attempting to develop.

[22] For the counter-claim, see Slote (2010, 17).

[23] The Psychopathy Checklist doesn't specify what the empathy lacked by psychopaths consists in. However, as Smithian empathy is more demanding than other capacities generally designated by the term (cf. Roughley and Schramme 2018, 20–6), the exclusion of just about any capacity thus designated will entail the exclusion of Smithian empathy.

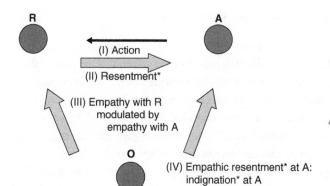

Figure 11.1. Indignation*.

We can define the concept of indignation* as follows:

O is indignant* at *A*'s having φ-d vis-à-vis *R* iff:

1. *O* is a bearer of the dispositional demand on behalf of *R* that actions be omitted which express ill-will or indifference towards *R*;
2. *O* believes that *A* has φ-d vis-à-vis *R*, where *A*'s φ-ing expresses *A*'s ill-will or indifference towards *R*;
3. *O*'s acquisition of the belief described in (2) triggers her dispositional demand described in (1);
4. (3) brings with it *O*'s vicarious experience of a specific affect directed at *A*'s φ-ing vis-à-vis *R*.

Indignation* is a state of mind of which Brosnan's chimps, even in her equality-aversion interpretation, seem incapable.[24] There is certainly no evidence that primates would display any form of social anger if one of their conspecifics were to be given less valued food for the same "work" than some other conspecific, independently of what they themselves get.[25]

---

[24] However, there is as yet no clarity on what precise mechanisms may be at work in chimpanzees who show what looks like distress and anger at attacks on infants in the community. See section 6.

[25] There is also no empirical basis for the claim that they might feel anything like self-directed anger on recognising that they have caused distress in a conspecific. Hoffman claims that, by two or three years of age, children seem capable of a primitive emotion of "guilt" grounding in empathy for distress, together with some understanding of their own causal role in bringing it about (Hoffman 1982, 300ff.). Brosnan and de Waal have argued that chimpanzees sometimes prefer to reduce inequality even where they are its beneficiaries (Brosnan and de Waal 2014). However, neither of these phenomena seem to involve the component of a—self-directed—demand that, according to the analysis I am developing here, is decisive for genuine proto-reactive attitudes. Indeed, because of its self-directed nature, guilt may, unlike resentment and indignation, not have a proto-form that can be generated without the belief that there is a relevant norm that one has contravened.

3.2. From Impartial Indignation* to Moral Obligation

Indignation* is, like resentment*, non-normative. It need only represent the reaction to an unfulfilled demand on the part of one agent and, as yet, need only concern action that negatively affects one particular sentient being. The important step here is to a type of reaction for which the being affected is no longer the agent reacting. Strawson, whose term "vicarious reactive attitudes" I have adopted, conceives the attitudes he thus describes as already "moral." This seems cogent because of his vague conception of what it might be that enables the personal reactive attitudes to transcend their status as merely personal. That vagueness is expressed in Strawson's listing of the adjectives "sympathetic or vicarious or impersonal or disinterested or generalized," all of which he seems to think can equally pick out the feature that allows such transcendence (1962, 15). However, we should take these apart. Indignation* is correctly described as either sympathetic (empathic) or vicarious. However, it need be neither impersonal, disinterested, nor generalised.

Strawson is, of course, right that moral requirements are not, qua moral requirements, addressed merely from the standpoint of individual persons. For whom and to what extent individuals demand non-indifference may be simply an expression of their subjective preferences. Moreover, their affective reactions to actions that they take to contravene their demands may depend on further individual features such as obsequiousness or aversions to certain skin hues. We think of moral requirements as independent of such features of the individuals who happen to speak in their name. We will only have reconstructed our deontic moral psychology if we have a method of guaranteeing that such irrelevant features are not in play.

I want to follow what I take to be Smith's proposal: that indignation* goes impartial. Smith proffers a suggestion as to how we can helpfully represent that process, a suggestion that famously goes under the title of "the impartial spectator." Before proceeding, let me clarify two terminological points in order to avoid certain sources of confusion.

First, talk of a "spectator" is misleading, as it encourages us to think of the non-participatory, "objective attitude" towards other agents that Strawson rightly saw as being excluded by susceptibility to the reactive attitudes. Roderick Firth's "ideal observer," who is "omniscient, disinterested, dispassionate, but otherwise normal" (Firth 1952), appears to be such a figure. What I take it Smith wants to exclude by talk of spectating is agential involvement in the relevant scenario. The standpoint he intends to pick out nevertheless remains that of someone who is emotionally involved. The mechanism of that emotional involvement is once again Smithian empathy, the same mechanism we used to move beyond the self-concern expressed in resentment*. We are now simply reapplying it to move a decisive step further away from reactions that ground in the particular concerns of the agents involved in whatever scenario is to be judged. For this reason, I prefer to talk of an *impartial empathiser*.

The second point concerns the identity of such empathisers. Importantly, we don't need to think of there being some specific, idealised god-like figure who is thus labelled. Rather, impartial empathising can be done by all sorts of people who happen not to be constrained by their interests and emotional proclivities relative to the scenario at issue and are sufficiently informed.[26] Perhaps there are cases in which there is no one available to do the job. Then the empathiser will have to be an imaginative product, but there is no reason why that should always be the case. Where the empathiser is no longer identifiable with any extant agent, the figure thus imagined is an abstraction, possibly the end-point of an abstraction process that we enter into as soon as we begin adjudicating between conflicts of interests. The fact that relevant impartial empathising can at least sometimes be performed by mere mortals is best kept in mind by replacing the definite with the indefinite article.

The proposal is that our empathic observer O now places herself in the shoes of an impartial, relevantly informed empathiser (IIE), who in turn observes the whole scenario to which O reacts and then either goes along with O's reaction or doesn't. If O takes it that her empathic resentment* at A's action would be gone along with by an IIE, then O takes herself to be impartially indignant* (Figure 11.2). Once we have completed this step, we have assembled the essential components of a deontic moral psychology. This, I shall now claim, provides us with the key to understanding moral obligation itself.

The core idea of moral obligation, understood from the perspective of a moral agent, I take to be that of being subject to a demand, where (a) that demand is issued for reasons grounding in concern for those potentially affected by the action, or action type, in question, (b) that concern doesn't reflect the interests of any particular parties or ground in ignorance of relevant facts, and (c) the demand's existence is not dependent on the existence of any human institution. In constructing our deontic moral psychology, we have embedded the idea of such demands in attitudinal structures. They are putatively expressed in what an empathiser takes to be impartial indignation*, i.e. indignation* at A's φ-ing that a sufficiently informed impartial empathiser would go along with. The metaphysics of moral obligation, then, ground in facts concerning the demands at the core of impartial and sufficiently informed indignation*. Whether there are empirical empathisers around who satisfy these psychological conditions will differ from case to case. They are not needed for there to be a fact of the matter as to how an IIE would react.

---

[26] A lot more would need to be said about both impartiality and what it is to be relevantly or sufficiently informed. A word or two about the former, negatively described attribute follows in section 4.1. The latter attribute saves us having to require omniscience, which in many cases appears unnecessary, for example, where the ways in which welfare or agency may be affected are easily determined.

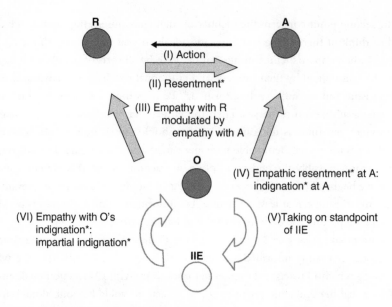

Figure 11.2. Impartially regulated indignation⋆.

On this proposal, then, what is picked out by the concept of moral obligation is essentially the object of the counterfactual indignation⋆ of an impartial, sufficiently informed empathiser in the face of some omission. The interdefinability of the deontic modalities means that impermissibility, obligatoriness, and permissibility can be understood as a matter of whether an *IIE* would be indignant⋆ at the action's performance, at its omission, or whether such a person would be indignant⋆ neither at its performance nor at its omission. Finally, we can now introduce the normative concept of indignation (without an asterisk). Indignation, thus understood, is an affective reaction to behaviour that is taken to be morally impermissible, where the morally impermissible is that to which an *IIE* would react with indignation⋆.

4. Defending and Contextualising the Account

4.1. Responses to Three Objections

This proposal will no doubt seem open to a number of very different objections. Allow me to, at least briefly, discuss three of them.

A *first* worry is that talk of an impartial empathiser is so indeterminate as to be empty and thus useless as a component of an analysis. My answer has two parts.

According to the first part of the answer, such indeterminacy is actually a virtue of the account. The account begins with the assumption that to be morally obligated is to be the addressee of a particular kind of impersonal demand and provides an explanation of this status. There is a clear distinction between there being an addressee of a demand and there being decisive reasons for the demand's deployment. It is the latter that provide the demand with content. To be obligated to perform a particular action in a particular context is to be on the receiving end of a demand for which there are specific reasons, that is, considerations on the basis of which an informed impartial empathiser reacts emotionally. How unified in type the relevant considerations are and whether they allow a certain degree of cultural relativity are questions that the account leaves open. The account thus entails that the moral obligation is one juncture at which the "traditional" distinction between metaethics and normative ethics holds up, at least up to a point.

Nevertheless, and this is the second part of my answer, the proposal is not empty, because of the importance it attaches to Smithian empathy. The criterially relevant reaction is not just whatever attitude some ideal observer might take on. Rather, it is a particular kind of affective reaction, grounding in a specific and fundamental dispositional demand and mediated by unbiased empathy. The host to this reaction is someone both able to acquire clarity on the reasons animating A, R, and O and an emotional participant in the kinds of interaction that move the agents involved. These conditions restrict significantly what can be the contents of our moral obligations. They exclude ethical egoism and any normative theory that doesn't take the weal and woe of sentient beings, the paradigmatic objects of empathy, as generating moral reasons. They may even involve restrictions on agglomeration of such reasons in view of the fact that Smithian empathy involves emoting on behalf of individuals, rather than simply taking on their emotional states.[27] This would mean that, in spite of the first part of my answer, the account is not without consequences for normative ethics.

A *second* worry about the conception advanced here might be a complaint about what may look like an unnecessarily circumlocutory trajectory via constructed emotions. Why not just go straight to impartial empathisers, someone might wonder.

This complaint goes to the heart of the epistemic and metaphysical conceptions behind the proposal. I argued in section 2.2.2 that psychopaths are unable, or are at least severely restricted in their capacity to make genuine moral judgements, and I went on to claim that this can be explained by their lacking, or being restricted in, the emotional capacities for empathy and indignation★. To move to the indignation★ of an *IIE* via resentment★, empathy, and biased indignation★ is to move through stages that must be accessible to agents in order for them to be able to make sense of the idea of the indignation★ of an impartial empathiser. The disposition to indignation★ at certain

---

[27] The account may thus block the kind of move that Rawls finds in certain derivations of utilitarianism: a move that begins with a "sympathetic impartial spectator," who fuses the desires of all persons into a coherent system, which are all then experienced as if they were his own and decided between in view of the intensities thus generated (Rawls 1971, §5, 26f.). Smithian empathy and the concept of moral obligation it structures might thus be incompatible with any such position that "mistakes impersonality for impartiality" (1971, §30, 190). Showing this would, however, require a great deal more work than can be done here.

forms of treatment of third persons is, I am claiming, a precondition of the capacity to understand what moral obligation is and of the capacity to make genuine moral judgements of permissibility and impermissibility.

The metaphysical correlate of this epistemic claim is that, were humans (or perhaps some other agents) not generally fitted out with the dispositions (or functionally equivalent proclivities) (i) to demand certain kinds of regard for themselves, (ii) to react affectively to the non-fulfilment of this demand, (iii) to empathise (à la Smith) with such affective reactions of others, and (iv) to seek an impartial standpoint from which to regulate the empathic reactions thus generated—were these not features of the human (or perhaps some other) life form, there would be no such thing as moral obligation. The psychological trajectory needs to be mapped out, in order to clarify how deeply the idea of moral obligation is embedded in our form of life. According to this construction, the metaphysics of morals is contingent, but contingent on features of our psychology that are anthropologically very basic. There are, I am suggesting, possible worlds in which there is no such thing as moral obligation. These would be worlds in which there were no bearers of the psychological properties I have been sketching.

A *third* objection doesn't concern the specific construction developed here; rather, it constitutes a challenge to any theory according to which genuine moral judgements require the satisfaction of emotional, or indeed any kind of, psychological preconditions. According to the objection, brought forward by Heidi Maibom in her rejection of the claim that psychopaths lack responsibility (Maibom 2008) and recently revisited by John Deigh (Deigh 2018, 249ff.), it is just a mistake to claim, for instance, that empathy is necessarily involved, even in the background, in making moral judgements. There are surely a significant number of moral judgements, particularly those concerning institutionally generated duties, that can be made without the capacity for empathy being in play. Deigh makes the point most succinctly by recalling Anscombe's grocer, to whom someone owes money because he has ordered potatoes, had them delivered, and received a bill. The judgement that the person is morally obligated to pay seems derivable from simple facts and to be within the capacities of just about anyone who has a basic grasp of the rules of the market—presumably including psychopaths.

The appropriate reply here emphasises that a judgement someone might make about Anscombe's grocer need not be a moral one. What we have first and foremost is an institutional duty. Whether we should think of it as also a moral duty depends, I think, on further features of the institution within which that duty is generated. It is certainly conceivable that we might be dealing with a social system of such an unjust nature that the moral quality of the duties it generates is anything but clear. But this means that the inference from institutional to moral duties depends on the satisfaction of further conditions. My contention is that those conditions are themselves empathy-sensitive: whether a system is fair can only be understood by someone capable of putting themselves in the shoes of people with various fates within the system. Someone without this capacity will only be able to judge whether the sufficient conditions for the generation of institutional duties have been fulfilled. Such a judgement should then, I am suggesting, not be construed as a moral judgement, even if it is made by using a sentence that contains exactly the same words in the same order as the corresponding moral judgement would.

4.2. Moral Obligation and Social Norms

In view of the topic of this volume, I want to conclude with a word or two about the relationship of such a conception of moral obligation to that of relevant *norms*. In order to look at this relationship, it will be helpful to take our lead from a proposal advanced by Carel van Schaik and his collaborators. The proposal presents a typology of norm-like phenomena with the aim of providing criteria for the investigation of their presence in chimpanzee populations. The candidate for a norm the authors have in mind concerns the avoidance of harm to infants, particularly in the form of infanticide. The evidence for a claim that there is such a norm consists in the behaviour of other members of the community when a relevant incident occurs, specifically "'waa' barking, persistent screaming, highly aroused individuals and even risky behaviour such as interventions and/or coalitionary defence of the mother-infant pair" (Rudolf von Rohr et al. 2011, 14). Let us leave to one side the impracticability of experimentally controlling the relevant situations and the corresponding anecdotal nature of the evidence. The crucial question raised by the authors is: what feature of moral norms would explain the fact that these forms of behaviour count as evidence that such norms are in play?

They distinguish three conceivable scenarios (see Table 11.1). In the first scenario, the reactions are simply triggered by specific cues such as the infant's screaming and are

Table 11.1 Possible Scenarios Explaining Chimpanzee Reactions to Infanticide.

	(1) Mere Regularity	(2) Proto-Social Norm	(3) Collective Social Norm
Bystander reactions on violation elicited by:	Specific cues	Empathic competence	Enhanced empathy and cognition
"Indignation"	—	Individualistic	Collective via shared intentionality
Third-party intervention	—	Via "indignation"	Institutionalised via shared "indigation"

Adapted from Rudolf von Rohr et al. (2011, 16). Alongside the omission of various features for reasons of focus, I have made four changes in order to bring the terminology into line with the perspective developed here: I have replaced the term "quasi-social norm" with the expression "mere regularity" and re-described the category named in the box at the bottom on the right. I have also put inverted commas round the term "indignation" and replaced talk of "third-party punishment" with talk of "third-party intervention." These latter two alterations aim to leave open the possibility that the items named may be present in the absence of norms. Punishment and indignation presuppose (belief in) the presence of such norms.

perhaps expressive of the "personal distress" caused by the spread of the distress of infant and mother via emotional contagion. If this is all that is going on, we have no reason to think in terms of norms. The authors call these mechanisms "quasi-social norms," which seems to me misleading. I have therefore substituted the label "mere regularity."

If the second scenario, characterised by "proto-social norms," were to be realised, "emotions comparable to indignation" would come into play. According to the model of empathy's development outlined by Koski and Sterck (2010, 43ff.) and quoted by Rudolf von Rohr et al., chimpanzees are capable of "egoistic empathy," a disposition that goes beyond mere emotional contagion, as it includes a level of emotion regulation. However, mere egoistic empathy remains self-oriented, as helping behaviour is appropriate to what the helper would require, rather than what the other needs. But perhaps, Koski and Sterck —and, following them, Rudolf von Rohr et al.—think, chimps may have some capacities that allow them to attain the next stage, that of "veridical empathy," in particular the capacity for goal reading (Koski and Sterck 2010, 51). These—tentative—suggestions may seem compatible with the claim that bystanders can understand the distress of the infant and mother. This, the authors take it, may justify talk of "indignation."

The scenario Rudolf von Rohr et al. take to be out of reach of chimpanzees, involves "shared indignation," which they construe as including reflexive cognitive representations of the fact that their own reaction to the event is widespread in the community. Here, collective intentionality—understood as constituted by reflexive, perhaps reciprocal cognitive mechanisms—is taken to be the hallmark of social norms. Even if chimpanzees should turn out to be capable of rudimentary forms of veridical empathy, van Schaik and his collaborators—like Tomasello (Tomasello et al. 2005, 685f.)—take it that they are incapable of collective intentionality, the decisive precondition of social norms.[28]

In order to situate this proposal relative to the one I have developed in this chapter, I will argue that the roles assigned to collective intentionality and indignation in the model are both pertinent and, in a way, misleading. In doing so, I hope, in conclusion, to shed some light on the relationship between moral and social norms.

First, how should we understand talk of the "emotions comparable to indignation" that would be at work in the second scenario? It seems clear that the emotion in question has to be indignation* for the following reason: according to the authors' criterion, viz. the collective sharing of the relevant attitudes, there are no "social norms" in chimpanzee communities. But indignation is an emotion that necessarily

---

[28] As the concept of collective intentionality sketched by Rudolf von Rohr et al. is less demanding than Tomasello's, it will on their construal be less implausible that chimps might fulfil the condition thus named. As passages in their chapter in this volume show, van Schaik and Burkart have becomes less sceptical as to whether chimpanzees might have the capacity for collective intentionality (cf. this volume, 143-5).

involves reference to norm violation. Interestingly, Rudolf von Rohr et al. contrast social norms with attitudinal structures in play here that they call "personal norms." These are "personal expectations of how an individual wants to be treated" (Rudolf von Rohr et al. 2011, 9). Such attitudes, they claim, are necessary preconditions for the evolution of social norms, as it is implausible that stipulations of how others should be treated might predate desires concerning one's own treatment by others. Replacing "expectations" with "demands," we have the basis for resentment★ and indignation★. I take it that talk of "personal norms" is an attempt to capture the demand-like character of the attitudes in question. The fact that the emotion in play here is indignation★, not indignation, explains why the authors feel the need to place "indignation" in inverted commas (Rudolf von Rohr et al. 2011, 18).

Rudolf von Rohr et al. and I thus agree that the chimpanzee reactions to infanticide cannot qualify as moral reactions. However, we disagree as to why this is so. They see the key deficit in the lack of collective intentionality. Now, I do agree that collections of individual attitudes that are not in some way shared are necessarily insufficient for talk of social norms. However, as I have argued, I think that the decisive step to moral obligation involves the construction of an impartial standard against which attitudes, both individual and collective, can be measured. The step to the conception of an impartial empathiser is extremely demanding, both cognitively and as regards the intentionality of the accompanying emotions. This is presumably a sufficient reason why no other animals are likely to develop morality in the full human sense.

Deontic moral attitudes—for instance, attitudes specifying the moral impermissibility of φ-ing—can, of course be institutionalised, that is, they can become the content of social norms. On my conception, this is the case where agents take it that actions of the types φ-ing and ψ-ing would be reacted to with indignation★ by an *IIE* and, perhaps for this reason, a society decides to make actions of these types the content of social prohibitions. I assume that social prohibitions function via the collective acceptance of certain kinds of attitudes and that a lack of conformity to those attitudes' contents will not infrequently be associated with sanctions of some kind.[29] The moral impermissibility of actions seems a good reason to make those actions the contents of social prohibitions. As is well known, there are problems in aligning the two systems too closely. Moreover, there are a whole set of non-moral reasons for social prohibitions.

If something like this is correct, social norms, unlike moral obligation, have no intrinsic connection to emotions. Indeed, in a formalised system of law, one might think, the less emotion involved, the better. Nevertheless, phylogenetically early versions of

---

[29] For various conceptions of the connections between social norms and sanctions, see Kappeler et al. (this volume, 71, 74-5), Mertens (this volume, 102), and Bayertz (this volume, 166-7).

human social norms may well have been proto-moral in character[30] and thus have been built up around shared reactive attitudes. For this reason, the progression represented in Table 11.1 could plausibly correspond to phylogenetic development. What I want to insist on is that the collective social norms represented in the right-hand column are not necessarily moral in character. For this to be the case, it is insufficient that patterns of indignation* are shared, and known to be widely shared. Such widely shared patterns that are accompanied and regulated by representations of impartial Smithian empathising would, according to my proposal, be social norms with moral content. One might thus label them "moral norms."

Importantly, however, this use of the expression should be distinguished from a use of the label which entails that moral norms provide intrinsic reasons for action.[31] If moral *obligation* is what I have claimed it is, then moral *norms* exist where an *IIE* would react with indignation* to actions of a certain *type*, rather than just to particular token actions. Whether this is so is, in principle, independent of whether large numbers of agents in some community are disposed to be indignant* at the performance of actions of that type as a result of mentally representing such indignation* on the part of *IIEs*. Only if we uphold this difference is it possible to make sense of the—morally important—idea that the majority of people in some community can be morally wrong. Whether there are any moral norms in the sense just explained is a matter of whether impartial empathisers would develop a pattern of the relevant reactions to action tokens of the same type *because* they are of that type.

Whether we should construe impartial empathisers as prone to react in such a patterned fashion is a fairly complicated matter that depends on questions concerning both action type individuation and the conditions of justified reactions. There are certainly difficulties in specifying action types in a way that would make it plausibly true that all actions which fall under the relevant description would invariably provoke indignation in an *IIE*. Moral norms would be true deontic propositions of a certain level of generality. However, formulating such general deontic facts has turned out to be a much more difficult endeavour than has often been imagined (Dancy 1993, 73ff.). If there are difficulties of this kind with moral norms, this means that social norms will not easily be able simply to co-opt moral contents, even where that might appear desirable. Social norms are necessarily general, as part of their purpose is the facilitation of social coordination. The implementation of social norms with moral contents is thus likely to be bound up with moral losses. But that isn't really news.

---

[30] This is the core claim of van Schaik and Burkart, Chapter 7 of this volume (cf. 152-3).

[31] According to the use of the expression that is now standard in analytic metaethics, moral norms thus understood would be necessarily "normative." On the divergence between uses of "normative" and "normativity" between this philosophical subfield and other areas of interdisciplinary discourse, see Chapter 1 of this volume, section 2.1.

PART IV

Linguistic Norms?

12

Language Evolution and Linguistic Norms

Nikola Kompa

1. Preliminaries

This chapter is an exercise in speculative anthropology.[1] It is an attempt at elucidating normative preconditions for symbolic communication. How might language (as we know it) have possibly evolved and which (types of) norms, if any, might have played a role in shaping it? After some preliminaries (1), differences between human language and non-human communication systems will be explored. I will first elaborate on the difference between (natural) signs and signals (2). In a second step, the characteristics of symbolic communication, i.e., communication by non-natural means, and its evolution will be focused on (3). The last three sections will be devoted to the question of what kinds of norms might have played a role in the evolution of symbolic language; the problem of honest communication will be addressed (4). And I will argue that

- a certain level of cooperation is a prerequisite for non-natural signs to be interpretable at all (4);
- a type of prudential norm emerges as non-natural signs acquire stable meaning (5);
- implicit communication is governed by pragmatic norms, too (6).

In order to set the stage for the discussion to follow, a tentative characterization of what language is and what a norm is will prove useful. For a first approximation, let us

[1] I am very grateful to Kurt Bayertz and Neil Roughley, who organized several workshops on the topic of the volume and gave me the opportunity to present an earlier version of the chapter at one of them; many thanks also to the other participants for valuable comments and critique. Moreover, I would like to thank Mitchell Green for inviting me to a workshop on the evolution of meaning at the Münster School of Evolution and I would like to thank him and the participants for helpful discussion. Also, I am grateful to audiences at the Universities of Zürich and Osnabrück for reading and commenting on earlier drafts of the chapter. Finally, I would like to thank Rudi Owen Müllan for proofreading the manuscript.

characterize language by some of its most prominent "achievements."[2] (i) Most obviously, language is a means of communication. Animals communicate, too. Yet human communication is much more flexible, and its expressive and creative power greatly exceeds that of animal communication systems. Human communication serves different purposes, though. John Locke (1790) has it that language is "the great Instrument and common Tye of Society" (Locke E III.I.1). According to a more recent account, the tie is strengthened by gossip, a form of semantic grooming (Dunbar 1996). Yet language is as perfect a means of inclusion as of exclusion; (only) he who speaks my language belongs to my group. For all that, we commonly communicate in order to manipulate people, to bring them to do (or think) particular things. Occasionally, we communicate in order to share information. (ii) So language helps us to acquire, but also to store and pass information. (iii) It also allows us to engage in complex cognitive and social tasks such as deliberation, argumentation, justification, modal reasoning, and make-believe. We entertain propositional thoughts and abstract ideas; recognize inferential relations between them; talk about the future and the past, possible and impossible events; make plans and write fiction. As a result, we can tell lies. (iv) Closely related, we can conjure up ideas and thoughts as we see fit, without the need for an external trigger. We can utter and understand sentences that no one has ever (heard) uttered before. Animal communications systems, on the other hand, comprise a rather restricted and mostly invariant set of signals that are meaningful in particular situations only and mostly bound to the here and now. Language freed our ancestors from those bonds. But in order to get there, they also had to become responsive to norms, or so I will claim.

What is a norm, then? In order not to prejudge the issue of whether non-linguistic creatures without (or with only rudimentary) theory-of-mind capacities are responsive to norms, I will opt for a rather lean definition.[3] Norms (i) come with correctness- or compliance-conditions; consequently, behavior can be classified into norm-compliant and deviant behavior; (ii) they guide behavior in that they generate (normative) behavioral expectations, (iii) whose non-fulfillment will commonly not go unnoticed (cf. Enfield and Sidnell, this volume, 267); and (iv) they give subjects a reason to act in a particular way that can be cited in order to justify or explain their behavior. Conditions (i)–(iii) formulate necessary conditions. Condition (iv) ought to be taken as necessary only to the extent that the idea of being given a reason to act can be spelled out in a way that does not presuppose "higher" cognitive and conceptual capacities. This is a precaution taken to make sure that animals, which lack "higher" cognitive capacities, are not *by definition* precluded from being responsive to norms. For similar reasons, to

---

[2] What are the defining features of language? The list in Hockett (1960) is useful but hardly consensual.

[3] It is important to heed the distinction between norms and norm-formulations here (cf. Glock, this volume, 299).

say that norms guide behavior is not to say that a mental representation of the norm has to be causally or psychologically responsible for the behavior in question. Note also that given (i)–(iii), those contravening a norm may be subject to correction; yet sanctions may be moderate and even altogether missing in certain cases.

Moreover, the evolution of norms is a gradual matter. We observe that others behave in particular ways. So at the beginning, there may be a behavioral expectation only, extrapolated on the basis of prior behavior (via statistical learning). It may turn into a *normative* expectation (that one ought to fulfill), due to the fact that something turns on whether it will be fulfilled (or due to prior commitments within the group or dyad; cf. Steinfath, this volume, 188). Subsequently, it may turn into a normative practice (cf. Glock, this volume, 310) and, eventually, become institutionalized (cf. Bayertz, this volume, 164ff.). This may hold good for all kinds of norms. Here I will be mostly concerned with linguistic norms, i.e., norms that govern linguistic behavior. Yet I will neglect phonetic, morphological, and syntactic norms altogether and say only very little about semantic norms; instead, I will focus on pragmatic and certain types of prudential norms that emerge as language unfolds (or so I will claim). They are a type of social norm in that they govern social interaction; they are linguistic norms in that they govern a particular type of social interaction, namely communicative action (i.e., the production and interpretation of utterances; cf. Reboul, this volume, 279). However, before we turn to the question of what kinds of norms might have emerged as language evolved, we ought to better understand at which level of communicative complexity they might come into play.

2. Signs and Signals

All animals communicate to some extent and in some sense. Some species are even able to appropriately react to alarm calls of another species (Zuberbühler 2012, 74). But animal communication systems are interestingly different from human languages. Some even say that language is uniquely human.[4] Yet as Derek Bickerton puts it, "Uniqueness isn't the issue. Unlikeness is the issue" (Bickerton 2009, 21). Language may be unique; but what is much harder to explain is why it is so unlike any other communication system. There ought to be no unbridgeable gaps in evolution; language

---

[4] Penn et al. argue that the "profound biological continuity between human and nonhuman animals masks an equally profound functional discontinuity between the human and nonhuman mind" (Penn et al. 2008, 110). Yet as they themselves point out: "The trend among comparative researchers is to construe the uniquely human aspect of these faculties in increasingly narrow terms" (2008, 110). Even Hauser, Chomsky, and Fitch distinguish a faculty of language in the broad sense (FLB) from a faculty of language in the narrow sense (FLN; comprising basically the computational mechanism of recursion), claiming that "[o]nly FLN is uniquely human" (Hauser et al. 2002, 1573).

has to have evolved.[5] Yet what could be possible non-human primate precursors of language? The challenge is thus to provide an incrementalist explanation of the evolution of language (cf. Sterelny 2016, 2018).

Moreover, suppose that there was a protolanguage; it would have consisted, arguably, of a handful of (proto)words at the beginning. Yet what could its selective advantage possibly have been? By way of reply, one might deny that the communication system that eventually turned into language was adaptive at every stage. Saltationists even claim that language came about by a single (or a few) mutation(s) (Bouchard 2013, ch. 1.4). But now suppose you were the lucky one with the mutation, thereby becoming linguistically much more skilled than all the others. How would that help when there is no one around to understand you (cf. Burling 2012, 410; Bouchard 2013, 41)? As with other traits, it seems reasonable to assume that "the main difference must and does exist in the realm of behavior and cognition" (Kappeler et al. 2010, 5).

It is more or less agreed upon that "[s]ensitivity to signals is as basic a property of life as the ability to reproduce. All organisms are able to detect signals indexing the presence of conditions hospitable to survival and reproduction" (Sinha 2014, 41). And it is common to distinguish animal signals from linguistic symbols. I suggest that we also distinguish between natural signs and non-natural signs (Grice 1957), yielding a three-fold distinction between natural signs, signals, and symbols. Symbols are clear cases of non-natural signs; signals may be in between in that they share some features with symbols and some with natural signs (Maynard Smith and Harper 2003, 3–6). The distinction has anthropological import as the emergence of symbols marks the advent of language as we know it, or so I will argue.

A *natural sign* reliably indicates a particular state of the world. According to Fred Dretske, natural signs are "events and conditions that derive their indicative powers, not (as in the case of symbols) from us, from our *use* of them to indicate, but from the way they are objectively related to the conditions they signify" (Dretske 1988, 54). Some bodily reactions may be natural signs of illness; they are causal effects of it. Those spots on someone's face may mean measles (Grice 1957, 213). If they do, they have natural meaning. It is not that the patient means something by those spots; nor has someone else given them a meaning (Grice 1957, 213–14). Nonetheless, they may be understood as signs of illness. And it is "always advantageous to understand. Any animal should be helped by understanding the noises and gestures of others, even when those noises and gestures were never intended to be communicative" (Burling 2012, 411).

But then, how do animals understand (or interpret) natural signs? According to a demanding notion of understanding only he who knows about the underlying

---

[5] Strictly speaking, it is language-apt creatures or a language faculty, not language as such, that evolved (in a decidedly biological sense of the word). Yet I am not so much interested in the purely *biological* but rather the *sociocognitive* and *normative* prerequisites of human language.

(causal) connection between a sign and what it indicates fully understands it. But there is a less demanding notion close at hand according to which understanding, basically, means reacting appropriately. What reactive behavior is appropriate will depend on what is adaptive for the reacting organism; the behavior may count as rational on a purely biological reading of "rational" (as behavior that maximizes inclusive fitness; cf. Kacelnik 2006). How to react may be learned in ontogeny or may be already part of the organism's instinctive behavioral repertoire. Consequently, while natural signs may not have evolved in order to be "interpreted," being able to react appropriately may still prove advantageous.

Next, there are *signals*. A signal has been defined as "any act or structure which alters the behavior of other organisms, which evolved because of that effect, and which is effective because the receiver's response has also evolved" (Maynard Smith and Harper 2003, 3). Others, by focusing on the manipulative use of signals and comparing them to human advertising signals, define a signal as a means by which an animal exploits another animal as tool (Krebs and Dawkins 1984, 382). Also, signals may be what Ruth Millikan calls "pushmi-pullyu" representations; they are descriptive and directive at the same time, "used to co-ordinate behavior among conspecifics. Danger signals, for example, tell in one undifferentiated breath when there is danger nearby and when to run or take cover" (Millikan 2006, 119).

Unlike natural signs, signals may, to some extent at least, be deliberately produced; and they may have evolved because they are amenable to "interpretation."[6] How do signs turn into signals, then? Signals commonly derive from movements that have no signaling function (Krebs and Dawkins 1984, 381). Herring gulls, for example, adopt an upright threat posture (vividly described in Tinbergen 1952) that is basically the same posture they would adopt in circumstances in which they actually attack their opponent. What once was a natural sign turned into a signal. Similarly, "when a dog is about to attack, for example, it bares its teeth in preparation for biting. Bared teeth have become a display that signals aggression in many mammals" (Rogers and Kaplan 1998, 17). Dogs might just have been in the habit of retracting their lips in preparation for a bite. Yet he, who saw what was coming, had a better chance of survival (mirror neurons and predictive simulation might have helped to anticipate what action was coming; cf. Rizzolatti and Arbib 1998; Hurley 2008). The dog, in turn, might begin to snarl at others simply as a means of threatening them (cf. Burling 2012, 412). Krebs and Dawkins postulate an evolutionary arms race here. "The manipulator's role is selected to alter the behaviour of others to its advantage, the mind-reader's role to anticipate

---

[6] Which mechanisms (e.g., association and statistical learning, simulation and mirroring, etc.) animals can avail themselves of in interpreting signals, understanding action, predicting behavior, and in reasoning more generally is a controversial issue that I cannot go into here; cf., e.g., Bermudez (2003) and the papers in Hurley and Nudds (2006).

the future behavior of others" (Krebs and Dawkins 1984, 401). They, arguably, employ a rather thin notion of "mind-reading" as ability to predict; yet given that manipulators abound, "real" mind-reading abilities would be nice to have, too.

Not surprisingly, there is a debate over the extent to which animal signals are learned, the extent to which they can be flexibly and deliberately produced, etc. A well-rehearsed point in the literature by now is that vervet monkeys give alarm calls in response to leopards, eagles, and snakes that differ acoustically, thereby eliciting different responses in their fellow monkeys (Cheney and Seyfarth 1990). Yet "for the most part vocal production is highly constrained" (Seyfarth and Cheney 2012a, 60). Moreover, these calls need not be produced with the intention to warn.[7] A species whose members are prone to produce alarm calls may just have a better chance of survival than a species whose members fail to produce alarm calls (Fischer 2012, 242). Also, these calls seem to be innate, as cross-fostered monkey infants, i.e., monkey infants raised by foster parents of another species, don't seem to adjust their usage if their foster parents use them differently (Seyfarth and Cheney 2012a, 61).

This has led some people to think that non-human primate vocalizations disqualify as precursors to language, exactly because non-human primates seem to have very limited control of their vocalizations. Non-human primate manual gestures, on the other hand, seem to be used much more flexibly and so to make a more promising candidate for language's primate precursor.[8] But then, the traditional picture of primate vocalization may need revising. For one thing, infant vervet monkeys still have to learn how to respond to those alarm calls (Seyfarth and Cheney 2012a, 62); that is a point about reception, not production, of course. But call production seems to be subject to audience effects, as when the epistemic situation of the recipient is taken into account (Clay and Zuberbühler 2012, 2014). Captive orangutans have even been observed to modify their signals if they haven't been fully understood (Zuberbühler 2012, 72–3). Moreover, certain alarm calls exhibit morphological complexity. Campbell monkeys give different alarm calls in response to leopards and crowned eagles. And they modify those calls with an affix "-oo" in order to generate new calls, given in response to general disturbances and disturbances in the canopy, respectively (Collier et al. 2014). As these authors note, species that combine calls in the way sketched are characterized

---

[7] Brian Skyrms, drawing on evolutionary game theory and the account of signaling systems developed by David Lewis (see the following) has it that "[n]ature has presented vervets with something very close to a classic Lewis signaling game and they have achieved something close to a signaling-system equilibrium" (Skyrms 2010, 23). He points out that "the framework also accommodates signaling where no plausible account of mental life is available" (2010, 7).

[8] Michael Corballis claims: "One argument for the priority of the manual system is that language is intentional, and the primate vocal system, unlike the manual system, is poorly adapted for intentional production" (Corballis 2012, 383). Simone Pika also points out that apes use a multifaceted gestural repertoire in recipient-specific ways (Pika 2014; cf. also De Waal and Pollick 2012). Tomasello (2008), too, defends the idea of a gestural origin of language; so does Arbib (2005a, 2005b).

by high sociality. Furthermore, there is evidence of different great-ape call-cultures. Different populations of orangutans, e.g., seem to show variations in the call types they employ, differences that cannot be attributed to genetic or ecological differences. They even seem to invent arbitrary[9] calls (Wich et al. 2012). In sum, there is a range of signals that differ in the extent to which they (or their responses) have to be learned, the extent to which they can be deliberately and flexibly produced, modified, or even invented, the extent to which they are subject to audience effects, etc.

3. The Emergence of Symbols

Symbols, it is said, are not meant to directly influence behavior but rather "to alter what is inside a listener's mind, operating in that sense in a virtual world" (Power 2014, 50). Moreover,

[c]ommunication by one animal to another about some state of the world is triadic, involving three entities, the sender, the receiver, and the world-state described. Communication between animals starts more simply, with dyadic communication involving no reference to the world, but only involving the sender and the receiver of the message. (Hurford 2012b, 377)

Yet one might ask whether signals, alarm calls for example, aren't referential, too. Don't they refer to eagles, or leopards? Or do they rather "say" something like, "Up in the trees!" or "Take cover!"?

But then, note that the "earliest words . . . would have to be used alone, apart from other words, so they could have had no syntactic properties" (Burling 2012, 410). The earliest uses of a sign for mammoths, e.g., may have been attempts at communicating something about mammoths. They may have been multi-modal, employing whatever means were available; gestures, sounds, pantomime, etc. (cf. de Waal and Pollick 2012, 87). Yet to ask whether they were referential or predicative, in the indicative or imperative mood, is, arguably, not a sensible question. For signs to acquire syntactic properties, "speakers" have to acquire the ability to distinguish different roles (subject, object), actor from action; referring (picking out an object) from predicating (saying something about it), the content of an "utterance" from its illocutionary role (whether it is a request, a warning, a description, etc.) and so on (the emergence of syntax is a huge problem that I cannot go into here).

Also, to assume that the "speaker" already had a clearly contoured communicative intention but was only lacking the linguistic means to properly clothe it is to presuppose a specificity of content that is not yet to be had. Mental and semantic content

---

[9] Arbitrariness is sometimes taken to be the hallmark of symbols. Here I stress the fact that they have non-natural and stable meaning; yet having non-natural meaning yields arbitrariness in the sense of there being no natural (e.g., *purely* causal) relation between the sign and what it indicates.

must have co-evolved. But how might it have evolved? Again, why did we get (symbolic) language while all the others seem to be content with the communications systems that they have?

Derek Bickerton has a ready answer: ". . . if humans got language, they can only have got it because they had some pressing need for it" (Bickerton 2009, 25). Bickerton's point is that language (or rather protolanguage) allowed our ancestors to construct and inhabit a new niche. More specifically, it was the high-end scavenging niche in which our ancestors no longer cracked bones to extract marrow but turned to exploiting the carcasses of large herbivores that led to the development of a protolanguage.[10] Truth be told, and as Bickerton admits, the "story to be told may be proven by future research not to have been completely accurate—it goes a little beyond what the known facts support" (Bickerton 2009, 145). Here is a slightly Hollywoodesque version of how it might have begun,

> Imagine that we're together, you and I, in this small group, eight of us, drawing breath in the scant shade cast by a thorny tree. Apart from a small rabbit-sized creature, a few lizards, and a handful or two of withered figs that we squabbled over, we haven't eaten today and it's getting on for noon. . . . Suddenly one of us lets out a shout and stands erect, pointing. . . . There, in a patch of marshy ground, lies the corpse of a huge deinotherium, a prehistoric elephant. Its hide is intact still, but other scavengers have arrived already—lionlike or tigerlike creatures, some larger than those of modern times. A pack of big protohyenas prowls the perimeter of the scene. . . . We look at one another. We break and run, you one way, I another. Nobody tells us which way to go. If one goes one way, the other goes a different way. There's nothing so few of us can do in the present situation. We need numbers, as many as we can get. And we need them now. (Bickerton 2009, 158)

Only by *recruiting* as many group members as possible do we have a chance of fighting back competitors. Recruitment may be the key to language evolution (Bickerton 2009, 132). It already brings into play an imperative, proto-normative, element; I request that you join me (cf. Bayertz, Chapter 8 in this volume). Yet it is for your own good. The niche our ancestors constructed was one in which *cooperation* would pay.[11] Competition was fierce; none of us could exploit the carcass for himself. We would all benefit from cooperation.

---

[10] When did all this happen? According to Bickerton, e.g., the advent of (proto)language would date back almost two million years (Bickerton 2009). It might have taken a while until something like language as we know it emerged. Others claim that "humans half a million years ago probably had languages structurally very similar to those on the planet today" (Dediu and Levinson 2014, 184). Still others disagree with both suggestions; it remains a controversial issue.

[11] By having constructed a niche in which cooperation would pay, they would also have constructed a niche in which honestly sharing information paid and therefore one in which language as we know it could have evolved (see the following). They engineered their environment (along the lines suggested, e.g., in Odling-Smee et al. 1996; 2003), thereby creating a selection pressure favoring language-apt creatures.

Yet once we got home in search of recruits, how could we bring the others to join us? We have to "tell" them, it seems, what is in it for them if they join us. We might do so by imitating the animal's sounds, the way it moves, etc. (Bickerton 2009, 159–60). The first "linguistic" signs would have been *iconic*, then; they somehow resembled what they stood for (Bickerton 2009, 159–60). Iconic signs presuppose mimetic skill (Donald 1998, 49), which in turn may be greatly advanced by the emergence of action simulation or mirror neurons (some authors even claim that the action-recognition mechanism that is run by mirror neurons "has been the basis for language development"; Rizzolatti and Arbib 1998, 190; cf. also Arbib 2005a, 2012; Hurley 2008, 7).

But recruitment also brings into play intentions. Yet, again, intentions and language had to co-evolve, it seems.[12] So we might imagine that, at first, those signs were only the expression of an emotion. Maybe an ancestor of ours began to imitate mammoth sounds just because he was so excited about the mammoth they had found. But to the extent that others begin to associate that behavior with mammoths, he might begin to produce it on purpose (see later discussion in this chapter), in order to recruit others, for example. Slowly, those early signs acquired a feature that many take to be a defining feature of linguistic symbols; they began to show *displacement* as they were used more and more in order to "talk" about objects and events not immediately present to the senses (Hockett 1960).[13] Still, they weren't words yet; they were not fully *symbolic*. They were used for recruitment, and meaningful in that context only (cf. Bickerton 2009, 216). How, then, did signals turn into symbols?

Firstly, they had to be used more flexibly.[14] We can imagine our ancestors beginning to use a particular sound or gesture, one that was first employed in order to recruit other group members, in different kinds of circumstances, "slowly (this could have taken countless millennia) converting it from a context-bound signal to context-free symbolic word" (Bickerton 2014, 99). Youngsters may use it in play, others in re-telling the story of how they found the mammoth; some may employ it when they come across mammoth footprints; some in trying to get others to join them in looking out for mammoths, etc. (Bickerton 2014, 218–19). Hunter-gatherers across Africa to this day seem to be prone, in storytelling, to use "the characteristic sounds of an

---

[12] I would like to thank Nicole Rathgeb and Katia Saporiti for helpful discussion here.

[13] Note that some non-human signaling systems exhibit displacement, too. Bees and ants, e.g., also have to recruit conspecifics in order to exploit food sources further away. They came up with a communication system that also carries information about objects and events not physically present. Yet their system fails to exhibit other "design-features." One other feature of language is the discreteness of its basic signaling units ("bee" means something different than "pee," for example); yet given that a bee dances faster the closer the source of nectar is that it is "talking" about, bee dancing is continuous, not discrete (Hockett 1960).

[14] As Anne Reboul has pointed out to me in conversation, flexible production has different levels. Firstly, the signal may not be automatically produced in the presence of its trigger, indicating voluntary control. Secondly, it may be produced in the absence of a trigger, yielding displacement and enabling offline-thinking.

encounter—the animal calls, thrashing of branches, departures and arrivals in prefer-ence to verbal descriptions of key events" (Knight and Lewis 2014, 302). For that to work, those listening have to be able to realize that it is make-believe.

Moreover, Bickerton has it that words came first; concepts came next. Words anchor concepts (Bickerton 2009, 208). The word "leopard," for example, binds together all mentally available information about leopards, information that will become part of the concept LEOPARD. Also, words can be voluntarily produced, and an utterance of the word can activate a representation of the information provided by the concept. Eventually, the concept can be conjured up at will; the would-be thinker thereby goes *offline*.

Online thinking occurs when an individual is involved in some specific activity, and that activity is the focus of thought. . . . Offline thinking occurs when the topic of thought has nothing to do with the thinker's current behavior. . . . To perform offline thinking both voluntary retrieval and neural linkage are essential. (Bickerton 2014, 79–80)

Drawing on work by Susan Hurley and others, Denis Bouchard claims that there is a system of neurons in the human brain that can be triggered by internal events: "These Offline Brain Systems (OBS) are triggered by representations of events themselves, and produce representations of events with no brain-external realization" (Bouchard 2013, 107; cf. Hurley 2008).

In a nutshell, the idea is that at some time in history, signs began to show displace-ment as they were used to request others to do things by at the same time informing them about things and events not immediately present. That required a certain level of cooperation that secured that our ancestors benefited from sharing information. Those signs were iconic at first (iconicity being a gradual matter, though). Yet then our ancestors began to use them in a variety of contexts and for different purposes; the signs became divorced from the situation in which they had emerged and gave way to modality-free concepts. Our ancestors began to combine, link, and entertain concepts as they saw fit; they acquired the capacity to think about mammoths whenever they felt like it and not just when one happened to be present. They began to solve com-plex tasks that required that they kept a concept in mind for a while. And they all lived happily ever after.

Bickerton's story (which builds on stories told by other people, of course) is very sketchy. It is highly unlikely that it gets many of the details right; it is probably incor-rect in many important respects, too; it may even be wholly fictitious. But at least it is a story. Moreover, any story about the origin of language has to be conjectural—given the epistemic situation we are in (note also, that for the purpose of my argument, nothing turns on what kind of foraging strategy was being pursued in the niche our ancestors inhabited back then, as long as it was one in which cooperation would pay). Here, it might help to bring into sharper focus a couple of points worth discussing.

Firstly, I take the idea of an (at least partly) iconic origin of linguistic symbols to be promising. It seems best suited to explaining how *semantic (or mental) content* came into being—given displacement. *Secondly*, the idea that language evolved in a cooperative context in order to make people do things, strikes me (and others; cf., e.g., Tomasello 2008, 2009) as plausible. Yet people were made to do things not by being made to simply causally react to the signals so produced but by being given "information" about things or events in the world (they were given "reasons," that is). That seems to best explain why they were willing to take the other one as *trying to communicate* something in the first place.

Other accounts fail on both scores. Those claiming that speech evolved as a means of grooming-at-a-distance (Dunbar 2012, 344) have a hard time explaining how semantic content could have emerged. Gossip may be a mechanism for generating reputation (Fitch 2010, 418) and the quest for reputation may help to explain why our ancestors began to give information for free more widely (also, reputation might have played a crucial role in the emergence of prosocial behavior; cf. van Schaik and Burkart, Chapter 7 in this volume). Yet while gossiping is no doubt a prominent function of language, it already requires a rather extensive vocabulary and enough to gossip about (Bickerton 2009, 28). Others defend the idea of a musical or prosodic protolanguage (e.g., Mithen 2005).[15] It might have emerged, as it did in songbirds, in order to attract mates and as a result of sexual selection; it might also have emerged as an early form of motherese (Falk 2004, 2012). In each case, only part of the population was engaged in the activity of "inventing" a language. And it also fails to explain how syntax or semantics could have emerged. Female orangutans make "come hither"-calls when retrieving their infants (Wich et al. 2012); yet not much by way of syntax or semantics has come from that so far (but then, it may be a start). That is not to deny that one of the crucial steps in the development of the characteristic human life form was taken when our ancestors turned to alloparenting, i.e., when they became cooperative breeders (Hrdy 2009).

Gestural origin theories don't face these problems. As Tomasello is eager to stress, gestures, especially those of great apes, are individually learned and can be used rather flexibly. And they can be combined to form meaningful wholes (even if apes don't do it; Tomasello 2008, 248). Pointing, moreover, may require a "referential intention." But then, "accepting modern sign as a fully adequate modality for linguistic communication makes it difficult to explain the virtually total transition, in modern humans, to spoken language" (Fitch 2010, 465). Still, as Corballis and others have pointed out,

---

[15] Charles Darwin wrote in *The Descent of Man* that "some early progenitor of man, probably used his voice largely, as does one of the gibbon-apes at the present day, in producing true musical cadences, that is in singing; we may conclude from a widely-spread analogy that this power would have been especially exerted during the courtship of the sexes . . ." (Darwin 1871, 56).

the move from gestures to spoken language would have made hands freely available for other tasks; that might have come in handy. In the end, one may venture to guess that our ancestors' first communicative attempts were multi-modal, including vocalizations, gestures, and other means available.

4. Cooperation and Honest Communication

Let us take stock. Natural signs and signals carry information. But while signals may have evolved because they do so, signs did not. Both signs and signals can be "interpreted." Yet only signals seem to have evolved as a means of influencing the behavior of others. They may be innate or learned, be more or less flexibly used, more or less deliberately produced and recipient-specific. They need not be iconic; alarm or copulation calls don't resemble what they signal. And signals may share certain features with symbols; they may, e.g., show displacement. Yet they are still bound to a particular context of use as they usually have one urgent function (for example, escaping predators). They cannot be conjured up at will (without external clues) or productively combined. These are features of symbols only; they are at our disposal (Condillac 2001 [1746]; Trabant 2008, 32). But one of the most interesting differences is that symbols have to be interpreted differently than signs or signals. They don't *reliably* indicate or signal a particular state of the world. They don't have meaning naturally;[16] yet they can be used to mean something. That is where cooperation and trust, and with them normativity, come into play. And that is why they can be used to inform others about all kinds of things.

But then, did we really "invent" language primarily in order to *honestly* inform other people? Why would we do that? The point can be succinctly put as follows: "If

---

[16] Brian Skyrms would not agree; he has it that "all meaning is natural meaning" (Skyrms 2010, 1). He draws on David Lewis's account of conventions and signaling systems (see the following) in order to explain how signals came to carry meaning or information. Lewis introduced sender-receiver games. The sender observes a state of the world and sends a signal. The receiver observes the signal and acts on it. Both have a common interest and there is one "correct" act for each state. As Skyrms explains, "signals are not endowed with any intrinsic meaning. If they are to acquire meaning, the players must somehow find their way to information transmission. . . . [W]hen transmission is perfect, so that the act always matches the state and the payoff is optimal, Lewis calls the equilibrium a *signaling system*" (Skyrms 2010, 7). Moreover, "the *informational content* of a signal consists in how the signal affects probabilities. The *quantity of information* in a signal is measured by how far it moves probabilities" (2010, 34). A signal carries information about a state if the probability of the state given that the signal was sent is higher than the unconditional probability of the state; no non-natural meaning has to be posited. But Skyrms's signals also differ from Lewis's conventions; the difference is exactly that the latter but not the former need to be (or rely on) "common knowledge" (Cloud 2014). Moreover, simple signaling systems of the Skyrmsian kind are "ubiquitous in nature. The way bacteria communicate with other bacteria and the way genes coordinate with other genes are perfect examples" (Cloud 2014, 81). Consequently, Skyrmsian signaling systems fail as a model for human language (as opposed to other animal communication systems).

information has any value, it is in the interest of no one to give it for free. And if information has no value, why are there ears ready to listen to it?" (Desalles 2014, 284). How could honest communication, and with it symbols that carry information in a non-natural way, possibly have evolved—given that they are easy to produce (cheap) and thus ought to enjoy low credibility? Oughtn't one to expect dishonest signals to abound? As Clay and Zuberbühler point out, it "is interesting in this context that dishonest signals are relatively rare, at least in intra-species animal communication (Clay and Zuberbühler 2014, 143).

One explanation would be that, as Amotz Zahavi's handicap principle has it, "receivers will only attend to signals that are physically difficult to produce and hard to fake . . ." (Clay and Zuberbühler 2014, 143). According to Zahavi's principle, "characters which develop through mate preference confer handicaps on the selected individuals in their survival" (Zahavi 1975, 205). Yet if Zahavi is right, then there simply are no cheap signals, at least not among those playing a role in sexual selection. Consequently, honest communication must have emerged in a different setting.[17]

A second explanation draws on the idea that animals avoid dishonest signaling in order not to lose reputation (Clay and Zuberbühler 2014, 143). A similar idea is promoted by Jean-Louis Desalles who points out that giving honest information may be a valuable strategy after all, as one thereby advertises that one makes a good friend. And friends are the best life insurance that one can get (Desalles 2014, 291): "conversational moves," he argues, "far from being cooperative offers, are more like competitive advertising" (Desalles 2014, 286).

Others, like Bickerton, claim that honest communication (or the lack of dishonest signaling) is best explained on the assumption that signaler and receiver share a common interest that engages them in a cooperative enterprise. On that account, a certain level of cooperation would have been a prerequisite for the evolution of language. Given that both parties benefit from sharing information and have a common interest, there would be no gain in lying (so far). Moreover, the signaler could immediately be proven wrong and lose social standing (a point highlighted in Desalles's approach, too). Tomasello also emphasizes the role of *mutualism* in the emergence of language:

Our proposal is that cooperative communication was adaptive initially because it arose in the context of mutualistic collaborative activities in which individuals helping others were simultaneously helping themselves. (Tomasello 2008, 170; cf. also Tomasello 2009; Zlatev 2014)

---

[17] Unless a signal has been deliberately produced in order to inform, the question of dishonesty—and of normativity—doesn't even arise. Natural signs are causally connected to what they are signs for; according to Dretske, indicating (in contrast to representing) is 100% reliable. That is why he can say that "[a]s I am using these words, there can be no *misindication*, only misrepresentation" (Dretske 1988, 56).

Interestingly, these considerations seem to fit in perfectly with a particular theory of how symbols acquire stable meaning that will be discussed in the following. But let's go back to Bickerton's mammoth-scenario first. Although "mammoth" need not have been among the first words that our ancestors came up with, words somehow relating to food, prey, or predators are promising candidates. As Charles Darwin pointed out,

it does not appear altogether incredible, that some unusually wise ape-like animal should have thought of imitating the growl of a beast of prey, so as to indicate to his fellow monkeys the nature of the expected danger. And this would have been a first step in the formation of language. (Darwin 1871, 57)

Suppose you try to recruit me; you request that I help you exploit the carcass of a mammoth a few miles away. You try a couple of things—gestures, sounds, and pantomime, imitating the appearance, the movements of, and the noises made by the mammoth, etc. In order to understand your behavior at all, I have to understand that what you are doing is an *attempt at communicating* in the first place, that it is a case of "signalling signalhood" (Scott Phillips et. al. 2009; cf. also Hurford 2012b, 379). I have to understand that you are not dancing, or moving and howling just for the fun of it. I have to understand that the sounds and gestures are directed at me and that they are *about* something else. You are trying to bring me to do something; but not by dragging me along but by using a sign that is about something. Slightly anachronistically, one might say that you are trying to give me a reason to join you.[18]

As long as I had been given enough other clues as to what the sign might be about, iconicity would have been dispensable. Yet if the sign had not been iconic, I would have had to understand not only *that* you are trying to communicate by means of a non-natural sign, but also *what* its non-natural meaning might possibly be. Therefore, iconicity can help explain how symbols could have become interpretable at all, as iconic signs can be interpreted—at least in part—"naturally" (Hurford 2012a, 127). Nonetheless, my interlocutor "still needs to see my gesture as *communicative* and as *relevant to our current activity*" (Tomasello 2008, 203; my emphasis). Even with an iconic sign there is room for alternative interpretations. It has *partly natural, partly non-natural* meaning. So if I am to be able to narrow down the range of interpretations, the sign better convey something relevant; otherwise I would be at a loss (and without any motive) as to how to interpret it. Yet it has to be of relevance to both of us in order for it to be interpretable. If it were only of relevance to me, why would you bother to tell

---

[18] Note that manipulation (in the sense of bringing someone to do something) and communication (as based on cooperation) are compatible, as long as manipulation is not hostile; cf. Reboul (2011).

me? If it were only of relevance to you, why would I bother to listen? (That would presuppose genuine altruism already.)

Joint communicative relevance will be generated by joint activities, shared experience, and joint purposes (cf. Tomasello 2008, 2009, 2014).[19] Joint activities, in turn, require a certain amount of trust; and they generate certain expectations as to future behavior. Moreover, I can understand what you are doing only by understanding what you are doing it for, by interpreting it in light of common purposes or interests and the expectations thereby generated. If successful, I will thereby have grasped what you meant to communicate, even if your communicative intention may not be very specific yet. For a sign to acquire non-natural meaning, the speaker will have to let the addressee "read his mind." Yet again, you will let me "read your mind" only if we are in a non-competitive, trusting context (cf. Knight and Power 2012).

In summary, in order to make your behavior interpretable at all, I have to assume that it is something relevant that you are trying to communicate, relevant to the fulfillment of a common purpose of ours. An utterance (that carries meaning non-naturally and) that cannot yet exploit conventional means is interpretable only on the assumption that something relevant has been uttered. Consequently, there will be a mutual expectation of relevance each time we understand the other one as trying to communicate something by non-conventional means (Grice 1967; Sperber and Wilson 1995).[20] I am reluctant to speak of a norm of relevance here as norm violation, i.e., communicating something not relevant by non-natural means, was no option—at least not at the beginning. Without cooperation in the form of joint activities that serve a common purpose, non-natural and not yet-conventional signs would not be interpretable. In that respect, ontogenesis seem to recapitulate phylogenesis,

> Human infants from as early as 14 month of age . . . communicate cooperatively—to share interest in things and inform others of things—and they construct and participate in joint attentional frames, which give cooperative gestures their meaning. Without a foundation in cooperative communication of this type, human language is not even thinkable. . . . (Tomasello and Moll 2010, 342)

---

[19] According to Tomasello (2008, 45–49), even great apes understand that others have purposes, yet "they have neither the skills not the motivation to form with others joint goals and joint attention or otherwise participate with others in shared intentionality" (2008, 177).

[20] Post-Griceans have it that "[e]very act of ostensive communication communicates a presumption of its own optimal relevance" (Sperber and Wilson 1995, 15). Ostensive communication consists "of making manifest to an audience one's intention to make manifest a basic layer of information" (1995, 54). And a stimulus is optimally relevant when it is worth the addressees' while to process it and it is the most relevant one available to the communicator.

5. Normative Expectations, Stable Meanings, and Semantic Free-Riding

Moreover, without cooperation, signs could not acquire anything like *stable* non-natural meaning (which is needed in order to get full flexibility and situation-independence). The situation we are facing can be described as a coordination problem. Suppose, to take an example of Lewis's, we want to meet tomorrow at noon. There are three places where we could meet. We both do not care where we meet, as long as we meet. This is a coordination problem as it meets the following two criteria. Our (relevant) interests coincide; and there will be more than just one coordination equilibrium.

> An equilibrium, we recall, is a combination in which no one would have been better off had he alone acted otherwise. Let me define a *coordination equilibrium* as a combination in which no one would have been better off had *any* agent alone acted otherwise, either himself or someone else. (Lewis 1969, 14)

How do we solve coordination problems? Explicit agreement is the most obvious way to go; if that is not an option, we can try for a coordination equilibrium that is somehow salient (Lewis 1969, 35). A precedent would fit the bill. Suppose we had been confronted with a coordination problem and reached a coordination equilibrium in the past. Now we encounter an analogous problem. We may try to solve it analogously; and so again and again, each time we encounter that type of problem. A noticeable regularity will emerge.

> Since our present problem is suitably analogous to the precedents, we can reach a coordination equilibrium by all conforming to this same regularity. Each of us wants to conform to it if the others do; he has a *conditional preference* for conformity. (Lewis 1969, 39)

Let us assume, to take the recruitment example again that eventually you managed to get me to join you in exploiting the said carcass. There might have been other means that you could have used. But given that you were successful this time, you may well use the same means again next time, the same sound-gesture combination, say; and I might do so as well (and we might both begin to use it more flexibly, too).

> Each new action in conformity to the regularity adds to our experience of general conformity. Our experience of general conformity in the past leads us, by force of precedent, to expect a like conformity in the future. And our expectation of future conformity is a reason to go on conforming. (Lewis 1969, 41)

A convention is born.[21] (Once an iconic gesture or sound is robustly associated with a particular meaning, iconicity may get lost; cf., e.g., Harnad 2012, 391). According to Lewis, conventions are a type of norm in that they are "regularities to which we

---

[21] He defines (subject to certain qualifications): "A regularity R in the behavior of members of a population P when they are agents in a recurrent situation S is a *convention* if and only if it is true that, and it

believe one ought to conform" (Lewis 1969, 97). This is so because for any particular conventional regularity R, I have reason to think that most members of my population P will conform to R and expect me to do so as well; and I myself prefer that if that is so, then I conform, too. Consequently, "I have reason to believe that my conforming would answer to my own preferences ... and to the preferences of most other members of P" (Lewis 1969, 98). That line of reasoning, in turn, gives me (and any other member of P) a reason why I ought to conform. Henceforth speakers are "held to account" for the "appropriateness" of the words they employ (Enfield and Sidnell, this volume, 268ff.).

But then, isn't conformity in the linguistic case in each member's own interest, so that they can be expected to conform anyway? Lewis contrasts conventions with social contracts. Neither are usually brought about by explicit agreement. But according to Lewis, there is an important difference between the two. In the case of a convention, the agent will prefer general conformity to conformity by all but himself. In the case of a social contract, the agent will prefer general conformity to a certain state of general nonconformity (the state of nature, so to speak) (Lewis 1969, 88–96). Why is that so? In the case of a conventional regularity, one would contravene R to one's own disadvantage; as long as the others conform, that is. This has an interesting consequence. Given that the agent prefers to conform to R on condition that all (or most) of the others do, one ought to expect there to be no *semantic free-riders*. Moral norms, on the other hand, are more like social contracts in that respect. They effectively exclude cases of general non-conformity but fail to exclude cases of free-riding. Yet if I use a word with a different meaning than that conventionally assigned to it, communication may not succeed. I run the risk of being misunderstood. That would also explain why there will be, at best, moderate sanctions in the linguistic case; people often enough inadvertently or accidentally contravene those norms. They will be met with ridicule or embarrassment rather than punishment or indignation. Deviations occasionally get corrected, but mostly in the case of children and language learners; and, most notably, not if the deviation is *obviously intended*, as in creative or deliberately idiosyncratic language usage, in which I deliberately run the risk of being misunderstood in order to reap other benefits (such as being considered witty, etc.).

Consequently, conventions bring into play a type of *prudential* norm; it is in my own best interest to conform if I want to make sure that I will be understood. That is not to deny that one might exploit the conventional meaning of an expression in order to

is common knowledge in P that, in any instance of S among members of P, (1) everyone conforms to R; (2) everyone expects everyone else to conform to R; (3) everyone prefers to conform to R on condition that the others do, since S is a coordination problem and uniform conformity to R is a coordination equilibrium in S" (Lewis 1969, 58). But then, it may be that the "substratum of conventions is regularities of behaviour that have become so entrenched and internalized as to give rise to normative expectations" (cf. Glock 2010, 92–3, and Glock, this volume, 313).

communicate something else[22]; nor is it to deny that, occasionally, one may succeed in communicating something by non-conventional means.

To sum up, there have to be mutual expectations of relevance in order for signs to acquire non-natural meaning in the first place. And prudential norms are required in order for signs to acquire stable meaning. (Whether conventions, as behavioral regularities, also give rise to semantic principles that have irreducibly normative import is debatable.[23])

But isn't he who tells lies semantically free-riding? No, as a liar intends to use the terms in accordance with their conventional meaning. He means to say exactly what he says. He wants to be interpreted accordingly. It is just that he does not believe what he says (I am focusing on typical cases of lying here). He is contravening a norm of truthfulness, though.[24] It may be classified as a moral norm. It may also qualify as a pragmatic norm.

6. Pragmatic Norms

Communicative interaction itself is a highly regulated activity, regulated by what may be called pragmatic norms. As N. J. Enfield and Jack Sidnell point out,

many social actions that are carried out through use of language come in pairs, for example requests and granting (or rejection), invitation and acceptance (or refusal), complaints and excuse (or denial), and so on. (Enfield and Sidnell 2014, 99)

Not surprisingly, children often learn words as part of a question-answer ritual that "involves turn-taking, the rituals of dialogue, the linguistic pragmatics of questioning, the mechanics of questions and answers . . ." (Lamm 2014, 271). Also, a speaker has to understand the "normative context of discourse" that determines the illocutionary force of direct or indirect speech acts; whether an utterance is a promise, a request, etc. (Lamm 2014, 268). Pragmatic norms are required to regulate *communicative* activities.

---

[22] Note that even someone using a metaphor ("man is a wolf") is using the words in accordance with their conventional meaning; it is just that she exploits the tension between the conventional meanings of the words used ("wolf" and "man") in order to get something else across.

[23] Cf. Glock, this volume, 315ff. Kathrin Glüer and Åsa Wikforss (2015a) suggest that we distinguish between meaning engendered normativity (ME), "i.e. the claim that meaning statements such as 'expression *e* means *M* for *S*' have normative consequences" (2015a, 6; § 2.1) and meaning determining normativism (MD) as "the claim that meaning is essentially such that it is (at least in part) determined by norms" (2015a, 16, § 2.2). Since I argued that signs might have acquired non-natural meaning before they acquired conventional meaning (so before there were any rules governing their application), I am inclined to reject MD. I remain neutral on the question of whether ME is correct; all I am committing myself to in this chapter is that, with the advent of linguistic conventions, certain prudential norms came into play.

[24] Some claim that it is a norm of assertion that one ought to assert only what one knows (cf. Glock, this volume, 308, for discussion).

But in the end, they may be reducible to social norms (cf. Enfield and Sidnell, this volume, 267f.; Reboul, this volume, 288).

But then there is the topic of implicit communication. Often when we communicate, we mean to get across more (or something other) than what we literally say. Semantic content underdetermines speaker meaning (cf. Reboul, this volume, 282; Kompa 2010). Implicitly communicated content cannot be read off the conventional meaning of the terms used (leaving conventional implicatures aside, if such there be). Metaphor and others tropes are cases in point; but mundane cases abound, too. Suppose you overhear someone say, "She is ready." What is she ready for, you might wonder? In trying to come up with an interpretation, you will be assuming your interlocutor to (roughly) comply with the following maxims,

> Be informative but not too prolific;
> say only what you have evidence for and believe to be true (truthfulness);
> be relevant;
> be perspicuous and brief. (cf. Grice 1967, 26–7)

You might reason as follows: "What she said is not informative enough. Yet I take it that she tries to convey something informative. What could she have meant over and above what she has said that would make her utterance informative enough?" In doing so, you would be carrying out an *inference to the best interpretation*. Pragmatic norms such as the Gricean maxims provide guidance for interpreting what is *implicitly* communicated. These pragmatic maxims are a type of prudential (rational) norm. As Anne Reboul points out, Gricean communication is a case of mutualistic cooperation (Reboul, this volume, 288). There is a mutual expectation of (and so a good reason for) compliance with the Gricean maxims, as communication aims at being understood. Happily, communicative intentions are fulfilled once they are recognized (Kemmerling 2001).

But then, at the dawn of language, signs had to acquire stable yet non-natural meaning; conventional means weren't in place yet. The second part of the first maxim, as well as the second and fourth maxim (unlike the third), will hardly have played a role back then. Given that we had no syntax and our vocabulary was rather limited, being too prolific wasn't really the problem. And without a certain specificity of content, neither truth nor *perspicuitas* was much of an issue either. We were lucky if we managed to get *something* across. Relevance (and informativeness) was our best guide. The interpretation of (non-conventional) non-natural signs, like the interpretation of implicit communication, has to rely on a principle of relevance.

Yet it is important to bear the following in mind. Firstly, pragmatic norms govern implicit communication. As soon as we avail ourselves of conventional communicative means, we are no longer bound by these norms, or to a lesser extent. Secondly, to say that there are pragmatic norms of relevance, informativeness, or truthfulness is not to deny that speakers often happen to use linguistic means in order to pursue all kinds of ignoble purposes. They have all kinds of ignoble intentions. One ought to distinguish between communicative intentions (concerning what one is trying to communicate) and other intentions (concerning what else, beyond being understood, one is trying to achieve by communicating). Communication aims at being understood. But people pursue other purposes as well.

7. Summary

We are now in a position to explain how honest communication by means of symbols (non-natural signs) might have evolved. The earliest (partly) non-natural signs were interpretable only with recourse to relevant interests and common purposes that engaged speaker and hearer in cooperative activity. Cooperation was also required for signs to acquire stable, conventional meaning, which, in turn, brought prudential norms into play. Moreover, communicative interaction is governed by pragmatic norms. Some of them may be reducible to social norms. Others govern implicit communication.

13

The Normative Nature of Language

N. J. Enfield and Jack Sidnell

You cannot prove a mere private convention between the two parties to give language a different meaning from its common one. It would open too great risks, if evidence were admissible to show that when they said five hundred feet they agreed it should mean one hundred inches, or that Bunker Hill Monument should signify the Old South Church. An artificial construction cannot be given to plain words by express agreement.

J. HOLMES (1891).

1. Introduction

We want to examine a dynamic sense in which norms play a role in language, in the following two ways:

1. Norms regulate language use in the flow of conversation.
2. Norms play a causal role in the conventionalization of word meanings.

We argue that these seemingly separate ideas are intimately bound because both are causally related to a fundamental feature of the semiotics of linguistic meaning, namely: a sign can only be said to have meaning if the sign elicits interpretants, or meaningful reactions, which "point to" that meaning.[1] We can, for example, say that

---

[1] It is also the case outside of the linguistic domain: e.g., smoke means fire, but only because when someone sees smoke they react in a way that can reveal the relation to fire: e.g., they run and grab some water, they yell "Fire!," they think "Something's burning there," and so on (Enfield 2013, ch. 4).

the English word *fruit* means what it does because we see people react as if that's what it meant. Suppose you phone me to ask if you should bring anything to the picnic, I say, "Bring some fruit," and then you respond by bringing an assortment of ripe apples, bananas, oranges, and pears. Your response provides evidence that allows me to assess whether you understand the word *fruit* in the same way I do.

The constant opportunity to test word meanings in this way is there because words occur in utterances that form speech acts in sequences of interaction. This *enchronic* frame for language usage, and for the social circulation of language, entails not only that words occur in the context of actions that are both responding to something prior and initiating something next, but also that we are always socially accountable for the choice of words we make when we construct moves in interaction (Enfield 2013, ch. 3). When we say things in conversation, people's responses, linguistic and otherwise, publicly display their understandings of what we have said (Sidnell 2014). Part of this displayed "understanding" will be an appraisal of the degree of appropriateness of what we have said. Because conversation is a socially cooperative activity, with each move we make we are *accountable* for the appropriateness of our contribution. This account-ability is a defining aspect of norms.

Here, then, is our claim. Norm-grounded accountability in social interaction is ulti-mately what regiments the conventions of linguistic meaning, proximally through the always-present possibility of holding people to account for the (in)appropriateness of their usage of a word or phrase, and distally through the aggregate effects of this pos-sibility in the historical conventionalization of form-meaning mappings in language communities (see Enfield 2014, 2015).

2. Norms

A norm is not a law. It is not written down and cannot thus be pointed to in the same way as a law can.[2] Nor is it necessarily backed up by force. Yet norms do an effec-tive job of constraining our social behavior. If a pattern of behavior is supported by a norm, at least three conditions should hold:

1. *Subliminal (the behavior is not noticed when present).* When the behavior occurs, no particular attention is drawn to it at a meta-level; nobody is within their rights to sanction the behavior or express surprise that the behavior occurred. People *subprehend* the behavior; i.e., they don't actively expect it but they are not surprised when it happens (Enfield 2013, 23 and passim).

---

[2] Certain uses of the English word *norm* are beyond the scope of this chapter. For example, the legal acts that embody policies of the European Union are sometimes referred to as "norms." These are obviously not norms in the sense we mean in this chapter.

2. *Abliminal (the behavior is noticed when absent).*[3] When the norm is violated—
when the expected behavior is missing and/or something else occurs in its
place—this can be noticed, reported or remarked upon.
3. *Inference-vulnerable (absence of, or deviation from, the behavior generates inferences).*
When the norm is violated—when the expected behavior is missing and/or
something else occurs in its place—people will assume that the person who
produced this violation had a reason for doing so; people will try to infer
what the reason was, and look for meaning there.

For example, suppose it is a sunny day, and you see somebody step outside to take
a walk. You will not be surprised if they take out sunglasses and put them on, nor will
you be disposed to sanction or question it. But if it is cloudy or nighttime and I put on
a pair of dark sunglasses, this may attract attention, and people may make inferences.
They may comment that I am just trying "to look cool"; I may offer an account by
explaining that they are "prescription glasses" and I can't see without them. Similarly
a person who wears her new shoes without removing the shop tag, or a person who
eats a croissant with a knife and fork may invite inferences: "Did she forget to take off
the tag?", "Who is he trying to impress?", and so on.

The situation is the same with regard to the use of linguistic signs. Your usage of the
word *fruit* will certainly attract surprise and sanction if you arrive at the picnic with a
basket of muffins and say "Here, I brought some fruit." The same is true if you arrive
with a basket of pumpkins, even though a pumpkin is—technically—a "fruit," just not
in the normative sense relating to the kind of fruit one brings to a picnic.[4]

The point that we wish to make with regard to linguistic signs is this. Because linguistic signs—as form-meaning mappings—are both revealed and constituted by the
responses that they elicit (in the enchronic frame of social interaction), *and* because
we are held accountable for social actions done by the use of any sign in interaction,
then word meanings will necessarily be regimented by social norms of a general kind.
It should be clear, then, that we regard linguistic norms as social norms, if only because all norms must be social in the sense we discuss in the preceding. It might be
possible to distinguish between *pragmatic norms* (regulating the metalingual or proce-
dural functions of language) and *semantic norms* (regulating the referential function of
language), if taken as two aspects of a synchronic system of social norms that surround

---

[3] We have invented this term for the intended meaning (Latinate *ab-* "away from"; *-liminal* "at a
threshold"), as no appropriate word seems to exist.

[4] It can be argued here that the English word *fruit* is polysemous: $fruit_1$ is the everyday sense, covering
apples, pears, bananas, etc., while $fruit_2$ is the technical sense, covering the reproductive body of any seed
plant; this meaning difference can be seen in the two word's different grammatical distribution; *the fruit* may
refer to either, while *some fruit* could probably only be used with $fruit_1$. The two meanings will be normatively appropriate in different contexts.

communication. But the essence of our argument is that semantic norms are ultimately distilled from—i.e., caused by—norms of social interaction of a general kind. In the next section we look at cases in which people are held to account for their linguistic behavior in interaction insofar as their linguistic behavior contravenes norms of conversation: for example, the norm that if one is asked a question, one should respond to that question. In the section after that, we look at cases in which people dispute the appropriateness of a word that has been used in conversation, effectively invoking linguistic norms of proper application to reference.

3. Orientation to Norms in Language Usage

Language use in the enchronic frame is regimented by norms. For a simple example, consider the expectation that when you are greeted (e.g., "Good morning") you should greet in return (see Sacks and Schegloff 1973; Heritage 1984). If you greet in return, this will not attract special attention, but if you fail to do so, this will be noticed, and inferences will be made. You can be held to account for not greeting in return. Of the accounts that you might then give, some will be acceptable (e.g., you didn't hear the first greeting) while others will not (e.g., you didn't feel like greeting back). This indicates that account-giving is itself also a normatively organized form of behavior. Another example is asking questions. When you are asked a question you should respond, preferably with an answer to the question you have been asked. As predicted, evidence of these expectations can be observed in situations where the normatively appropriate behavior is missing. Here is an example from a tape recording of a group therapy session (from Schegloff 1992, 1310):

(1) GTS[5]

01 Rog:	It's always this uhm image of who I am
02	'n what I want people to think I am.
03	(0.2)
04 Dan:	And somehow it's unrelated to what's going on

---

[5] The transcribed examples discussed throughout this essay are drawn from a large corpus of recordings made over many years (those labeled "NB" are some of the oldest and were made in the late 1960s). The conventional labeling involves a title composed of an identifying name such as, e.g., "NB" (an acronym for "Newport Beach") or "Virginia" sometimes followed by details as to the location of the fragment within the collection or recording (e.g., "TG, 6:01–42" indicates TG transcript, page 6, lines 01 through 42). A title such as "Chubak workplace collection" indicates a one-off example provided by another researcher (i.e., Chubak). Some of the examples are taken from previous publications, in which case we indicate this with an in-text citation (e.g., Schegloff 1992).

Examples are presented using the transcription conventions originally developed by Gail Jefferson. For present purposes, the most important symbols are the period (".") which indicates falling and final intonation, the question mark ("?") indicating rising intonation, and the square parentheses ("[" and "]") marking the onset and resolution of overlapping talk between two speakers. Equal signs ("="), which come in pairs—one at the end of a line and another at the start of the next line or one shortly thereafter—are used to indicate that the second line followed the first with no discernable silence between them, i.e. it was 'latched' to it. Numbers in parentheses (e.g. "(0.5)") indicate silence, represented in tenths of a second. Finally, colons are used to indicate prolongation or stretching of the sound preceding them. The more colons, the longer the stretching. For an explanation of other symbols, see Enfield and Sidnell 2017.

05	at the moment?
06 Rog:	Yeah. But t(h)ell me is everybody like that or
07	am I just out of [it.
08 Ken:	[I- Not to change the subject
09	but-
10 Rog:	Well <u>don't</u> change [the subject. <u>An</u>swer me.
11 Ken:	[No I mea- I'm on the subject.
12	I'm on the subject. But- I- I mean "not to
13	interrupt you but-" uh a lotta times I'm sitting
14	in class, I'll start- uh I could be listening.

In lines 06 and 07 Roger asks, "But tell me is everybody like that or am I just out of it?" The fact that this is in the form of a question sets up a strong normative expectation that an answer be provided next, and when this is apparently not forthcoming—i.e., when the norm is violated—in lines 08 and 09, Roger is evidently within his rights to sanction Ken and invoke his entitlement to be answered, as seen in line 10. In Ken's subsequent response he explicitly acknowledges Roger's entitlement.

The norms that operate across sequences of question and answer cannot be reduced to notions of etiquette or politeness. This is supported by evidence from cases in which deviations from those norms lead to conversational inferences. If the norms were merely about politeness, then inferences licensed by deviations from them should be limited to attribution of "impoliteness," "rudeness," etc. But in fact the inferences observed in such cases are more nuanced. Where a response is not provided at all, a questioner may take this to suggest that the recipient did not *hear*. Where a response is given but no *answer* is provided, this might be explained by the inference that the recipient does not *know*. Consider the following case, in which the matter of politeness is not relevant to the problem of young Roger's failures to answer his mother's questions (Drew 1981, 249):

(2)

01 Mom:	What's the time- by the clock?
02 Roger:	Uh
03 Mom:	What's the time?
04	(3.0)
05 Mom:	(Now) what number's that?
06 Roger:	Number two
07 Mom:	No it's not
08	What is it?
09 Roger:	It's a one and a nought

Another example shows evidence of a norm that the person who has been asked a question is the person who should respond to it, even if another person is able to answer it (from Stivers and Rossano 2010):

Reina asks Tamaryn whether her boyfriend's mother calls to talk to her on the phone (line 1). Tamaryn fails to answer the question in the course of the following 1.0 second (line 2), but at that point co-present Sandra quips "No that('d)/('ll) be wastin' minutes" (line 3).

(3) Stivers, Hairdresser

```
            [((R gazing in T's direction; T off camera))
1 REI:      [Does she call you and conversate wit'=ju on your phone?,
2           (1.0)
3 SAN:      No that('d)/('ll) be wastin' minutes.
4           (0.5)
5 SAN:      [Th-
6 REI:      [>Ta- I want Tamaryn tuh answer the damn question.< Don't
7           [answer for (h)[her
8 SAN:      [O(kay)        [I'm sorry.
9 REI:      ((leaning towards Sandra)) Oh no it's okay.
10 TAM:     She called once to see if my mother had thrown a
11          fit but no: other than that_
```

Although Sandra's response (line 3) is formally type-matched (Schegloff and Sacks 1973) and type-conforming (Raymond 2003)—and is thus a normatively appropriate thing to say in context—it is nonetheless treated as failing, because it is not said by the appropriate person (Austin 1962). Reina does two things in response. First, she indirectly sanctions Tamaryn for not answering (indirect only in that the turn is nominally addressed to Sandra): ">Ta- I want Tamaryn tuh answer the damn question.< " Second, she directly sanctions Sandra for answering on Tamaryn's behalf: "Don't answer for her" (lines 6–7). This sanctioning elicits an apology from Sandra and, ultimately, the production of an answer from Tamaryn (lines 10–11).

More subtle displays of accountability to the norm that a question should receive an answer from its addressee are seen in cases where an addressee, unable to provide the information requested, accounts for not answering by responding with "I don't know." In (4), Guy has phoned Jon to arrange a game of golf in the afternoon. In the following excerpt he is asking Jon whether a mutual acquaintance, Brown, might be able to join them. At line 12, Guy asks "think he'd like to go?" and Jon replies with "I don't know" and follows up by suggesting that he could "go by and see," thereby going some way to fulfilling his obligation by indicating a willingness to obtain the information that has been requested (and an orientation to the norms that make this relevant, namely the norms surrounding proper behavior in relation to the asking of questions in conversation).

(4) NB 1.1 1:05

```
04 Guy:    I:ss uh: Bro:wn down-e?
05         (.)
06 Jon:    Yeah he's do:wn,
07 Guy:    Think he'd like to[↑go?
08 Jon:                       [Played golf with im yesterday et San
09         Clemente.
10 Guy:    Yih di:[d.hh
11 Jon:           [Uh huh?
12 Guy:    Think he'd like tih go:?
13 Jon:    u-I: uh,h I don't ↑kno:w,
14         uh:heh heh hu:h huh ·hhh Ah(h)'ll I(c) I c'd go by ed see:,
```

More subtle still are cases in which a person who is apparently unable to provide the requested information responds by adding information that they *do* know. In (5) Lottie is asking Emma whether Emma's son-in-law Hugh will accompany her daughter for a future visit.

(5) NB I. 6

```
46 Lot:    Hugh gonna (.) be with 'er?
48 Emm:    hhhh I don' kno::w
49         (0.4)
50 Emm:    I don't know. She's comin do:wn (.) ü- (.) dri:ve down by
51         'erse:lf so:,
```

Emma, evidently unwilling to commit to a yes or no response, first replies in line 48 with "I don't know" before going on to say in line 50 what she *does* know, namely that her daughter will "drive down by herself." Emma thereby implies that Hugh will not be coming, yet without answering definitively, and thereby avoiding being account-able (perhaps later on) for having said either way.

In each of the preceding cases, the respondent is dealing with norms of language use, and associated patterns of expectation and accountability. Each respondent is thus displaying a clear orientation to the norms that organize sequences of question and response.

The preceding examples have illustrated normative requirements for people to respond in specific ways to certain kinds of speech acts. Before ending this section, we consider a broader kind of normative constraint on responding, having to do with the accountability that an addressee has for showing an appropriate type of understanding of a linguistic utterance. This is striking because linguistic utterances are known to be semantically much more vague than the specific meanings they convey in context (Grice 1989). In principle, a simple utterance like *I had a flat tire* could be understood in many ways, but there is a "normal" reading, and this normal reading will be assumed unless otherwise signaled (Levinson 2000; Enfield 2015, 102–9). This means that the *recipient* will be accountable for knowing what it means in the normal sense, and if they act otherwise, this will show the hallmarks of a departure from social norms. Consider this example from Garfinkel's report of his students' breaching experiments:

(6) Garfinkel (1967, 42):
The subject was telling the experimenter, a member of the subject's car pool, about having had a flat tire while going to work the previous day.

(S) I had a flat tire.
(E) What do you mean, you had a flat tire?

She appeared momentarily stunned. Then she answered in a hostile way: 'What do you mean, "What do you mean"? A flat tire is a flat tire. That is what I meant. Nothing special. What a crazy question!'

The example shows that rather than the speaker being held to account for having been too vague, the addressee is held to account for having queried what was meant. As the example has partly to do with the conventional meanings of referential expressions, this leads us into the topic of the next section.

4. Orientation to Norms in the Use of Words

While norms of conversational behavior of the kind described in the previous section are clear candidates for focus in research on the normative nature of linguistic *usage*, much work on norms and language has to do with the normative nature of the linguistic *code*. We argue that the coded meanings of words are regimented by norms in the same ways as things like the proper handling of answering questions, discussed earlier. The basic point is that if you use a word, you are socially accountable for intending to convey its conventional meaning. So, for instance, if a mother describes her teenage daughter as "a child" she is accountable for having characterized her with the set of properties that this description conventionally entails. Consider the following example. Virginia, a teenage girl, is challenging her mother's decision not to allow her to work in the family shop. Virginia cites the fact that Mom had allowed her sister Beth to work in the shop at a similar age. In the course of justifying her decision, Mom obliquely describes Virginia as a "child" (line 06)—at line 08, Virginia objects to this.

(7)★ Virginia, 5:07–20, qt. 2:20

```
01 Virginia:    ˙hh Well Beth didn' Beth get tih work b'fore she
02              was sixteen?=
03 Mom:         =No::! I'd- (0.2) I would let her wrap presents
04              an' packages et Christmus an:'- °times we needed
05              somebady.° ˙hh >But people
06              just don't want< (0.4) chu:ldren (0.2) waiting
07              on[('um).
08 Virginia:    [I'm not a chi:::ld! ((shrilly))
```

Here, then Virginia objects to the use of the word "child" and treats this as in incorrect description, thus explicitly holding Mom to account for having inaptly applied the word. The conventional meaning of the word provides a normative ground for disputing the appropriateness of Mom's utterance.

Different words are often applied to the same referent, conveying very different construals: climate change *denier* versus *skeptic, freedom fighter* versus *terrorist, spared me that* versus *denied me that, dog* versus *mutt*. We select different linguistic formulations to fit the actions we mean to make with our utterances (Stivers 2007).

A simple and familiar illustration is when choice of words can portray an action as either intentional (culpable) or not (an accident). Sidnell and Barnes (2013, 331) give an example in which two children are playing with blocks. When the structure falls, one child screams, leading the supervising adult to complain, *Guys, too loud*. This occasions an excuse from the child, who assigns responsibility to the other by saying *She poked it*. The other child counters with *I tapped it*. Here, the coded semantics of the English words *poke* versus *tap*—clearly different in meaning, but both plausible for reference to certain situations—are used strategically for potentially consequential ends.[6] Whether it is explicitly articulated, as in this example, or not, as is more often the case, the linguistic expressions by which reference is accomplished in any instance of interaction are necessarily *selected* from among various possible, contextually adequate, extensionally accurate, yet intensionally divergent, expressions (e.g., in *That's my*

---

[6] See Schegloff (1972), Sacks and Schegloff (1979/2007), Stivers (2007). Enfield (2012) presents an extended example showing how references to times can be tailored to the action being crafted with talk, comparing, for example, *this time tomorrow* versus *about midday* versus *about lunch time*, and *over Christmas* versus *since December 24* versus *during the last week*.

dog, the word *dog* is selected from among equally possible, accurate expressions such as *poodle, pooch, pet, baby, boy, little guy, best friend, constant companion*, and so on).

Norms governing word selection are obviously of various sorts and operate over relations of granularity (*this week* vs. *today* vs. *this morning* vs. *9:30 am*, US vs. *Alabama* vs. *Georgia*), hyponymy/hypernymy (*dog* vs. *poodle*), perspective (*my wife's nephew* vs. *my mother-in-law's grandson*) and others. In each case, the context-situated choice between equally accurate forms may be regimented by norms of appropriateness, which then ultimately feed back into building the community norms of what those words should be taken to mean.[7]

A way of understanding lexical meaning is that whenever a word is used, that word will dependably invoke a definable core idea in the minds of people who hear the word being used (Wierzbicka 1996, 24 and passim; Goddard 1998; Enfield 2015, 3–4). A speaker will be accountable for having intended to convey this core meaning, which is to say that the speaker will be unable to plausibly deny that she had wanted to invoke this understanding in the other. And a listener will be accountable for having understood the word with that meaning, as long as he claims, explicitly or implicitly, to have understood the utterance in which the word was used. Suppose, again, that John says to Mary *I'll bring some fruit*, and Mary replies *OK*. If in fact John arrives with muffins (or pumpkins), he will be accountable for having lied or misspoken (or could give the reason that he'd changed his mind or forgotten; appealing to some alternative "normalizing" of the problem). He won't be able to defend what he had said earlier, a fact that is explained with reference to a core meaning of the English word *fruit*. Something similar applies to Mary. If John brings a pineapple, she can later assert that she hadn't expected this (John didn't say it would be a pineapple). But she can't later assert that she hadn't expected, for example, that he would bring something that people could eat (even though John didn't specify it would be *edible* fruit). More accurately: If she were to assert that she hadn't expected it to be fruit, she would be accountable for the inconsistency between this and her explicit signal of understanding in the response she had given to John (she said: "OK"). This is similar to an example given by Harvey Sacks: If I invite you for "drinks" you can expect no dinner, but if I invite you for dinner you can guess there will be wine, etc. (and you can indeed express surprise or sanction me for not giving you anything to drink). Drew (1992) provides good examples from courtroom interaction, such as this one, in which a question is directed to a defendant in a rape case:

---

[7] The mechanisms by which micro-level linguistic behavior (in enchrony) leads to macro-level creation of community conventions (in diachrony) are well known (see Enfield 2014), but are beyond our scope in this chapter.

(8)

A: *Did he sit with you?*

B: *He sat at our table.*

What is at issue is the difference between the meaning of *with us* (implying he was part of our social unit) versus *at our table* (implying spatial proximity only). In the example, B is effectively refusing to be held to account for having said that *He sat with us.* This connects back to the earlier discussion of answering questions: if you don't answer, then inferences may be drawn, so in order to direct or contain those inferences, you answer but modify. (See also Ehrlich and Sidnell 2006 and Stivers and Hayashi 2010 for more examples along these lines.)

Also consider cases in which the specific sense of the word is not obvious given its application in context, as in the use of "done" in line 07 of the following:

(9) Chubak workplace collection

07 Stef: h so when are you done with Porter.

08   (1.5)

09 Mike: whaddayah mean by "done"?

10 Stef: hhh h like when can you remove yourself

11   from that process.

Consider also cases in which the normative appropriateness of a word's usage is bluntly questioned: "It wasn't X it was Y!" Here is an example:

(10)

Grandma to grandchild: *Careful don't run!*

Grandchild: *I'm not running, I'm jogging!*

This case is about imposing a construal on a scene. The grandchild is effectively saying that she will not let "run" stand as a description of a scene that she might have some accountability for (e.g., if she trips and hurts herself, it can be said that she should not have been running). Of course it's not merely a matter of free will as to which word is accepted as appropriate, if the available facts unambiguously determine that the referent situation was truthfully describable as "run" and not "jog."[8] We also know that linguistic description itself can have effects on the psychology of perception (or on our conception of perception): for example, when a single scene is described to one

---

[8] Note, however, that the difference in appropriateness of alternative descriptions often has to do with the psychological state of an agent and so is not readily accessible. It is often the job of law courts to determine such distinctions.

person as a car "hitting" into another versus "crashing" into another, the person's estimation of the speed of the crash is different (Loftus and Palmer 1974).

With more space, we would say more about issues of entitlement here, matters of who has the right to say whether a description has been appropriately used or not. Sidnell and Barnes (2013) argue that such rights flow, primarily, from epistemic authority over the content of assertions.[9] They find that people are normatively entitled to describe their *own private experience* in whatever way they see fit. They may be called out for being dramatic or blasé but they will not, under normal circumstances, have those first-person-exclusive-access descriptions replaced or corrected by others. Psychotherapy represents an interesting and revealing exception in which the therapist is entitled and, indeed, expected to know the mind of the other better than he knows it himself (Peräkylä 2013)—a very unusual state of affairs. In this context we find that therapists routinely treat the patient's description of his own experience as potentially problematic and even requiring correction.

The larger point is this. It is not just that word meanings are regulated by norms, but that people are motivated to enforce such norms even in the most mundane and informal of settings, and they are differently entitled to do so. This might help us to define just what we should mean by saying that humans are the normative animal.

Before finishing this section, we would like to note that it is not just others who hold speakers accountable to norms that govern the appropriate use of words. Speakers also hold themselves so accountable. This underlies their own process of selection of words in such a way as to ensure they are generally appropriate. This process is seldom visible to us, but occasionally a speaker makes her self-accountability to such norms public in her own talk (often in order to achieve various social-interactional effects; see Jefferson 1974). Here is an example from a conversation in which two people are discussing the lecturers they have in university classes:

(11) TG, 6:01–42

01 Bee: Yeah, this fella I have- 'fella' this *man* –

02   He has- . . . -who I have for

03   linguistics is really too much

---

[9] There are two types of authority that a person might have to make a given assertion. Someone with *source-based authority* will actually know more about the matter than other people present. Someone with *status-based authority* may be treated as authoritative on a matter because of his social status, irrespective of his actual knowledge (Enfield 2013, 121–4).

Bee initially uses the form *fella* to refer to the instructor/professor of her linguistics class. She subsequently replaces *fella* by *man*. However, before she does this, she repeats the word *fella* as if quoting herself disparagingly, thereby commenting on her earlier usage and drawing attention to her own lapse and apparent violation of a norm: a person who is your professor is not appropriately referred to by a term such as *fella*. This is because the meaning of the word *fella* conventionally implies a level of informality and familiarity that does not characterize the relation between teacher and student. In this example, Bee calls attention not only to the norms governing the appropriate use of words but also, perhaps, to her own distance from the university environment and her lack of familiarity with its norms of social relations.

In another example, Emma is talking to her sister Lottie about a man she admires. She first describes him as a "viral man," but recognizing her error apparently as she says it, corrects to "virile," explicitly announcing that that was the word she wanted. In this way Emma exposes her own error as well as the selection process behind it, one that seems to have led her to use a word that is not totally within the vernacular.

(12) NB IV, 13 −2:40

01 Emm: Here's Mister Black older than any of them

02   . . . He's such a <u>VIRAL</u> man

03   <u>vir</u>ile the- the word I wanted (0.3) and uh (0.3)

04   (0.2) B<u>a</u>rbra said h<u>e</u> looked awfully bad b'

05   though of course <u>H</u>ugh didn't say he looked so ba:d but uh: . . .

So to summarize, in this section we have explored the fact that there are norms that govern word usage and meaning, and there are also norms governing the way in which such normatively prescribed word meanings are enforced and regulated. People not only hold others accountable to observing these norms, but also hold themselves so accountable. In these ways, the norm-governed flow of sequences of social interaction provides a matrix in which norms of language are used for regimenting the use of language, and thereby concretizing these norms in the form of semantic conventions.

5. Conclusion

If the meanings of things people say are defined, at least in part, by real processes of interpretation, the parts of interpretation that matter are the public parts; i.e., the observable interpretants that we produce, including both practical and linguistic actions as responses to things people say. These interpretants, which are not just interpretations of other signs but are also signs in themselves, are central to the normative organization of behavior. They are both *tools for*, and *objects of*, public evaluation of the appropriateness and effectiveness of linguistic signs in social contexts. In this way, normative behavior is at the core of linguistic meaning, in the sense of both pragmatic practice and semantic code.

No special theoretical or conceptual framework is needed for understanding this dynamic normative view of linguistic meaning. It can be clearly grounded in a neo-Peircean semiotic framework that is independently needed for understanding how the use of language in social interaction is organized (see Kockelman 2005, 2013; Enfield 2013). The framework has three key concepts of special relevance to the issues we have discussed here: first, *enchrony* (the causal-temporal frame that foregrounds the responsive and projective properties of any utterance in a social exchange); second, *status* (the set of normatively regimented rights and duties that define any social relation); and third, *agency* (the combination of flexibility in goal-oriented behavior and accountability for the planning, execution, and results of that behavior).

Linguistic norms are ultimately grounded in enchronic accountability. Every next move is—whether explicitly or implicitly—either a sanction of, or an acceptance of, the linguistic items that came in the prior move (Garfinkel 1967; Heritage 1984). There is a tyranny of accountability (Enfield and Sidnell 2017, 201): If you are going to achieve your pragmatic goals, your choice of methods for doing so are constrained by norms insofar as you will need to avoid doing what is surprising or likely to cause sanction (i.e., what is non-normative). This is because any non-normative behavior will, firstly, attract attention at a meta-level to what you are saying/doing, and thus risk derailment of the pragmatic project you are using language for, and secondly, risk failure of your goal due to inviting unwanted inferences as to your communicative intent. This follows naturally from the norm-defining conditions of subliminality, abliminality, and inference-vulnerability. Thus, language shows the hallmarks of any normative social behavior.

14

Can There Be Linguistic Norms?

Anne Reboul

1. Introduction

This chapter addresses the question of whether there are linguistic norms. From a philosophical point of view, this raises two preliminary questions: What are *norms*? And what are *linguistic* norms? To begin with the first question, the notion of *norm* implies that relative to a certain range of activity, there are criteria of correctness that are largely if not universally shared in a community. And it suggests that these criteria originate in the community, i.e., that, in one way or another, they have a social origin. In other words, regularities of behavior inside that community are largely due to the fact that the community has consensual criteria for correct action in a number of areas and to the fact that the individual members of the community usually comply with these criteria when they act. These criteria, having a social origin, are norms.[1]

Inside such a framework, *linguistic* norms are norms that pertain to linguistic activities, i.e., the production and interpretation of utterances (be they publicly produced or produced as internal discourse). They have to do not with what you are allowed to say or are prohibited from saying (these are usually social norms), but with how you say it.

From what has just been said, one would expect norms to differ from one community to the next, and a first way of looking at the question of whether there are linguistic norms is to look at whether regularities of linguistic behavior are universal or community-specific. An additional criteria should be in which way the putative norms have originated in the community and whether they play a causal role in the observed regularities of linguistic behavior inside a community.

---

[1] I am aware that there are other, less demanding, notions of what a norm is, which do not presuppose that norms have a social origin, or that they can be explicitly represented by the individuals in the community. Given the emphasis on human normativity in the present volume, however, I think that the informal definition of norms given in the preceding is the relevant one.

But a final and rather important consideration is whether, supposing all the previous criteria to be satisfied, the norms in question are really limited to linguistic behavior, or if they are just the linguistic by-products of more general norms, having to do with, e.g., rationality.

A less central, but not uninteresting question, is whether some norms of behavior, non-linguistic in nature, end up being grammaticalized, i.e., manifested as part of the structure of language.

2. Levels of Regularities in Linguistic Behavior

As said earlier, a strong indication of the existence of norms is the existence of regularities in behavior. This, however, is only a first step, given that regularity of behavior may have non-normative explanations: for instance, typically, people walk by moving their legs in a highly regular fashion, but this is due to anatomical and motor constraints, not to norms. But let us begin with regularities of linguistic behaviors and where one should look for them.

A first level is the structural level, the level which is responsible for semantic compositionality and which encompasses both syntactic and semantic structures. It is arguably the level at which human language differs from all other animal communication systems. There has been (and still is) an intense debate as to whether this level of linguistic compositionality is universal or whether it is language-specific. An important point to note is that the apparent diversity of linguistic structure is not a definitive argument in favor of the language-specificity of linguistic compositionality. Be that as it may, the diversity of languages seems to give support to the notion that there are linguistic norms.

Basically, there seem to be several possibilities:

A. There are linguistic universals, which are not normative, but constrained by the structure of the human brain; but, among these non-normative constraints, there are linguistic norms specific to each language, which cause the regularities of behaviors observed in the linguistic activities (at the structural level) of the individuals of the corresponding community;
B. There are no linguistic universals; language is norm-regulated through and through;
C. The apparent diversity is largely an illusion, and there is no need for norms at all.

This is not the place to argue for or against the existence of universals at the level of linguistic structure. Rather, it is interesting to have a look at whether the two normative hypotheses (A and B) can actually be maintained relative to the notion of norms developed in the preceding.

For something to be a norm (rather than a mere regularity of behavior), it has to satisfy the following conditions:

- It is a criterion for correctness of action that is universally or at least widely shared in the community;
- It has a social origin;
- Individual members usually comply with it and sanction deviations;
- It is the explanation for the regularities of behavior observed.

There are several important aspects here: the first one is that, precisely because norms are criteria for correctness of action, it may be the case that behavior that is incorrect will manifest itself from time to time (in other words, actions that flout the norm are possible). There is more, however: when incorrect action is produced, one would expect it to be the result of a choice, as is the case, for instance, in the moral domain. One may know how one ought to behave, but choose not to comply with the moral norm concerned. In a similar way, regarding linguistic structure, one knows how one ought to construct one's utterances, but one chooses not to comply. This presupposes that speakers have some sort of awareness of the norms in question. Even if, more often than not, they comply with them automatically, they are able to formulate them if asked to do so (in much the same way as, though we do not usually have to think about what we are doing when we refrain from taking others' possessions, we can still explicitly formulate the relevant ethical norm).

It appears, however, that this is not the case regarding the regularities of linguistic behavior at the structural level. There, when we are speaking our mother tongue, we not only usually produce utterances without thinking about how we ought to construct them, we find it rather difficult to say what rules we follow in doing so. This, obviously, may be different for second languages, when the speaker is not an early bilingual. However, in that case, the speaker also does not belong to the community in which the putative linguistic norms apply, so it is hardly a case in point. In other words, though there are undubitably structural regularities of linguistic behavior associated with specific languages, they do not seem amenable to a normative explanation.

It may be objected that speakers belonging to the same community may apply to one another's utterances normative appraisals, regarding the correctness of their syntax. Why should such appraisals, clearly normative in nature and bearing on linguistic behavior, not be considered as the outward manifestation of linguistic norms? As linguists have pointed out, this is, indeed, a normative behavior, but one that has more to do with social hierarchy and levels of language than with linguistic structure per se (they have more to do with how to behave in "polite" society than with anything else). And additionally, those strictures are not based on any knowledge of the structures involved at the structural and compositional level, but rather on ill-informed beliefs about them.[2]

Another level at which it seems that norms are likely to appear is the level of language use in communication. There have been a number of proposals regarding norms for language use, from turn-taking to politeness, but these seem at best to be very weakly linguistic, if linguistic at all. A more promising area is the recovery of implicit meaning.

3. Implicit Meaning

Implicit meaning is a promising ground for the discovery of linguistic norms for two reasons: the first one is that implicit communication seems much more widespread than was thought in the early years of philosophy of natural language; the second is that one of the more influential accounts of how hearers recover implicitly communicated information, the Gricean logic of conversation, relies on what looks very much like a set of norms for linguistic communication.

There is nevertheless a tension between these two reasons: the extension of the domain of implicit meaning, as detailed for instance in contextualism, is much more widespread than was thought by Grice (1989) and, as a result, it strongly upsets the Gricean distinction between what is said and what is communicated, or, in another formulation, between semantic meaning (linguistically determined) and speaker meaning (depending on the communicative intentions of the speaker). It appears that indeed this distinction is hard to maintain if pragmatic inferences play a role in determining not only what the speaker intended to communicate implicitly, but also what the explicit content of his utterance is.

On the other hand, this might be seen as reinforcing the case for linguistic norms. If even explicit communication has to go through a pragmatic interpretation to be recovered and if pragmatic interpretation relies on norms for linguistic communication, it seems that norms largely govern the interpretation of linguistic communication. Moreover, as these norms are usually considered as ruling over the speaker's linguistic behavior, this also constrains linguistic production, not only linguistic interpretation. So there are two main questions relative to the existence of linguistic norms:

- whether or not these norms can account for the recovery of the content of the utterance up to and beyond implicatures or presuppositions;

---

[2] This, incidentally, is why linguistics is not *prescriptive*, but *descriptive*.

- supposing that they do, whether or not the norms in question can be said to be *linguistic*, that is, specific to language, rather than instances of more general norms that apply beyond linguistic communication.

And here, it is useful to note that we can go beyond implicit communication and the Gricean approach, to speech act theory. Speech act theory (Austin 1962; Searle 1969) was instrumental in showing that utterances are acts more or less on a par with other physical acts, a part of human behavior like any other.

There are, again, two aspects here. According to speech act theory, utterances are to be considered as acts on par with, e.g., kicking a ball. In other words, utterances have to be explained in the same way as other acts, or behavioral items, through the intentional stance (see Dennett 1989). In other words, they should be explained in terms of the psychology of belief and desire/intention, i.e., theory of mind. This, indeed, is where speech acts and the logic of conversation meet: both, in highly different ways, come to the fundamental importance of intentions in linguistic communication.

Despite this, the differences between speech act theory, especially in its later Searlian version, and the Gricean logic of conversation, are deep. The first and most obvious one is that speech act theory (in its Searlian version at least) is a conventional theory: an illocutionary act has the illocutionary force it has through the meaning conventions of the language in which it is produced. Indeed, Searle rewrote the definition of meaning$_{NN}$ to make it conventional: the speaker still intends to produce an effect in his hearer through the recognition of this intention by the hearer (as in the Gricean definition), but Searle added the proviso that this recognition should be realized through the semantic conventions of the language in which the utterance was produced. This triggered a protest by Grice (1989), pointing out that this was a travesty of what he had in mind with the notion of meaning$_{NN}$.

For speech act theory, in this Searlian version, we thus find ourselves confronted with the idea that explicit, semantic meaning is due to linguistic conventions that might conceivably be couched in normative terms (but see section 4 of this chapter). Another possibility lies in the felicity conditions of the various types of speech acts. But there, whether they are or are not norms, it is unlikely that they are *linguistic* norms. Most of them are institutional, rather than linguistic. If you want someone to obey your order, you had better make sure you only order about people over whom you have some power. Otherwise, they will have no reason to obey. And so on for other kinds of speech acts.

So let us turn back to the Gricean logic of conversation (see Grice 1989). As is well-known, Grice proposed to explain, not how explicit meaning (what is *said*) is recovered through semantic conventions, but how implicit meaning (what is *communicated*), or conversational *implicatures*, are recovered. This, Grice proposed, was done through the hypothesis that speakers comply with a principle of cooperation (see Grice 1989, 26–7):

Cooperative principle:
Contribute what is required by the accepted purpose of conversation.
This principle is declined in a number of maxims:

Maxim of Quality:
Make your contribution true; so do not convey what you believe false or unjustified.

Maxim of Quantity:
Be as informative as required.

Maxim of Relation:
Be relevant.

Maxim of Manner:
Be perspicuous; so avoid obscurity and ambiguity, and strive for brevity and order.

On the face of it, it might be thought that these maxims, which do seem amenable to the constraints drawn out in the preceding for something to be a norm, are specific to linguistic communication, hence are linguistic norms.

Are the maxims criteria for correctness of action universally or at least widely shared in the community? The first thing to note is that the maxims (or the Cooperative Principle) are not community-specific. They are, if anything, universal and were intended as such by Grice. However, and this is where the use of language in communication differs from linguistic structure, they seem accessible to consciousness. When asked, ex post facto, why they produced such and such an utterance, there is a strong intuition that people would come up with very much the set of maxims Grice proposed. Indeed, some of them have a venerable history: for instance, as noted by Horn (2009), the Maxim of Manner was anticipated by classical rhetorical works since Greek antiquity. Again, the Maxim of Quality sounds self-evident, and has indeed been a staple of ethical works. And it is not clear in which way the Maxims of Quantity and Relation differ from the Maxim of Manner. In other words, there is no reason to doubt that these Maxims are public knowledge.

It is less clear in which way they have a social origin. The very fact that there is a good chance that they are universal makes it unlikely that they are the product of a social deliberation: if anything, they seem to be a preliminary condition for any social deliberation.

The third criterion, the fact that individual members comply with it, introduces a new complication. Clearly, on a Gricean account, given the fertility of human imagination when it is used in linguistic interpretation, hearers will always be able to come up with an interpretation, however outlandish, that will be consistent with the idea that the speaker has complied with the Maxims. In other words, it is not clear how a speaker could manage not to comply with the Maxims outside of lies. There are other complications, however.

Grice postulated that hearers take the notion that speakers comply with the cooperative principle and the attendant maxims as a hypothesis that will govern their interpretive process. The main idea is that hearers will attribute speaker meaning to the speaker's utterance on the constraint that the speaker, no matter how unlikely it seems, has complied with the maxims. Let us take a classical example, one that has been much discussed in contemporary pragmatics—including experimental pragmatics (Noveck 2000; Noveck and Posada 2003; Bott and Noveck 2004; Noveck and Reboul 2008):

(1)   The pianist played some of Beethoven's sonatas yesterday evening.

This is usually interpreted as follows:

(2)   The pianist played some, but not all, of Beethoven's sonatas yesterday evening.

The reasoning is based on the idea that the speaker of (1) is complying with the Maxim of Quantity (Be as informative as required): the speaker used the word *some*. But she could have used the word *all*. Given that she didn't, and on the hypothesis that she complies with the Maxim of Quantity, she used *some* because she could not have used *all*. Hence, she intended her hearer to recognize her intention to communicate that the pianist did not play all Beethoven's sonatas (based on the hypothesis that she complies with the Maxim) and the interpretation of the utterance in (1) is the implicature in (2).

However, as has been repeatedly pointed out by both Neo-Griceans (Levinson 2000; Horn 2006, 2007, 2009) and Post-Griceans (Sperber and Wilson 1995), this is a highly costly and unlikely psychological process. Though some form of pragmatic inference has to take place to take the hearer from the utterance in (1) to the implicature in (2), it can hardly include the hearer's speculating explicitly on the speaker's intention *as part of the interpretation process*. Though the Gricean interpretation is in keeping with the idea that utterances are interpreted, as other acts are, through theory of mind, the quickness of utterance production and interpretation makes it unlikely. There is slightly more than that, however.

On a Gricean interpretation, and equally on a Neo-Gricean interpretation, every time a speaker who could have used the word *all* chooses to use the word *some*, the utterance should be interpreted along the lines of (2), i.e., as communicating *not all*. While Gricean accounts will go through the fairly laborious process described earlier, some Neo-Gricean accounts (see Levinson 2000) usually go for something much simpler: a default account, according to which *some* is interpreted by default as *not all*. It is only when the implicature is explicitly defeated, as in utterance (3), that the default interpretation is abandoned in favor of the basic semantic interpretation, i.e., *some and maybe all*:

(3)   The pianist played some, and indeed all, of Beethoven's sonatas yesterday evening.

According to that analysis, no complex attribution of intentions to the speaker is necessary.

Beyond the adjudication between the Gricean and the Neo-Gricean accounts, there is a consequence for the idea that Gricean maxims could be seen as norms. Though that is a possible hypothesis for the Gricean account, it is not for the Neo-Gricean account, where everything happens in the hearer at a subpersonal level. This is less damaging that it might seem, however, as Neo-Gricean accounts are only intended to apply to implicatures with a lexical trigger (i.e., in (1) the word *some*). Such lexically triggered implicatures are usually called by Neo-Griceans (following the distinction made by Grice 1989) *Generalized Conversational Implicatures.*

There are other non-lexically triggered implicatures, as shown by the following example:

(4)   Anne lives somewhere in Burgundy, I believe.

This is usually interpreted as indicating that the speaker does not know where exactly in Burgundy Anne lives. There is, however, no specific word that conveys the implicature. Rather, it is the utterance as a whole that does. Such implicatures are usually called by Neo-Griceans *Particularized Conversational Implicatures.* And it is here that the other alternative account of implicatures, the Post-Gricean account, comes into play.

While the Neo-Gricean account aims at accounting only for Generalized Conversational Implicatures and ignores Particularized Conversational Implicatures where the usual Gricean account could apply, Post-Gricean accounts (Sperber and Wilson 1995) reject the distinction. Their analysis is supposed to apply indifferently to Generalized and Particularized Conversational Implicatures. And, though it is highly different from the Neo-Gricean account, it leaves no room for the basic Gricean account and rejects both the Cooperative Principle and the Maxims. In other words, it does not allow for a normative view of linguistic communication.

The only "principle" on which Post-Griceans rely is a cognitive principle which is declined in a cognitive and a communicative version, the Principle of Relevance, according to which both cognitive and interpretive systems function in such a way as to maximize cognitive benefits and minimize cognitive costs. This means that cognitive processes (including interpretive processes) will follow the least effortful paths. As can be seen, there is no room here for anything on a par with social norms. Indeed, and this is a major departure from both Gricean and Neo-Gricean accounts, Post-Griceans claim that, far from being automatic, Generalized Conversational Implicatures, just as Particularized Conversational Implicatures, are only drawn when the context makes it mandatory. This is because they are more costly than the semantic interpretation (*some and maybe all*) is and thus are not accessed unless necessary.

Here, it may be time to look back and assess these various accounts of implicatures. As it turns out, there have been, since the beginning of the present century, a number of experimental studies that have targeted Generalized Conversational Implicatures (e.g., Noveck 2000; Noveck and Posada 2003; Bott and Noveck 2004; Noveck and Reboul 2008). These have contradicted both the Gricean and the Neo-Gricean accounts. The Gricean account is contradicted by the fact that even in fairly favorable contexts, the implicatures are far from being systematically drawn (in the best of cases, up to 80% of the time, still far from ceiling). The Neo-Gricean account is, in addition, contradicted by the fact that these experiments have shown that, as predicted by the Post-Gricean account, implicatures are, indeed, costly to recover.

In other words, though the Post-Gricean account is not verified, it has a far greater empirical support than do its two rivals. It could, however, be argued, that, as Particularized Conversational Implicatures have been barely investigated from an experimental perspective, there is no reason to think that for such cases, the Gricean account does not apply. If this were the case, then one might defend the idea that there are indeed linguistic norms, or at least norms specific to linguistic communication (which would, thus, be arguably linguistic).

There are, however, two problems with this view:

- The Maxims are specific to communication, but they may apply as well to non-linguistic as to linguistic communication, as long as communication is under voluntary control *and whether or not it is conventionalized*;
- According to Grice himself, the Principle and the Maxims are general rules governing rational interaction, which, as we shall see, gives the notion of Cooperation involved a less altruistic slant than is usually thought.

None of the maxims can reasonably be said to be restricted to linguistic communication. Let us begin with the Maxim of Quality, making one's contribution true. There is no reason to think that it cannot apply to non-verbal communication. Suppose that a murderer asks where his intended victim has gone, and that you point to the right, while the potential victim is escaping to the left. You have flouted the Maxim of Quality, which applies to your non-verbal communication just as it would have applied had you said "He's taken the street to the right." Basically, the same kind of reasoning applies for all other maxims, and I will not go into details here.

The main consequence is that the Maxims, whether they are or are not norms, are not specialized in linguistic communication, but apply to all intentional communication, whether verbal or non-verbal. In other words, even if they are *norms*, they are not *linguistic* norms.

As said earlier, the second problem is that Grice did not see the Principle and the Maxims as linguistic norms, but as general principles for rational interaction.[3] This has raised a problem, mostly to do with work on the evolution of language. The Cooperative Principle has been widely interpreted as altruistic, though few people have bothered to say exactly what they mean by that. This, however, has nothing obvious about it. The first thing to note is that cooperation is a behavior, while altruism is a pro-social tendency. Even supposing that Grice was right about the Cooperative Principle being the mainspring of rational interaction, that does not entail anything about the supposed altruism of human communicative behavior, unless one supposes that Cooperation in the Gricean sense is uniquely tied to an altruistic, pro-social attitude. Is that the case?

Trivers (2002) has proposed definitions for *altruism, mutualism,* etc. His definitions were couched in terms of inclusive fitness, in keeping with his evolutionary approach. We will limit ourselves to altruism and mutualism and couch the definitions in economic rather than biological terms:

> *Altruism*: An action A is altruistic if and only if it is costly to its perpetrator and beneficial to its target.
> *Mutualism*: An action A is mutualistic if and only if it is beneficial to both its perpetrator and its target.

As a matter of clarification, other social and less pro-social (positive) attitudes are possible, but as they are not relevant here, I will leave them aside. It should be clear that Cooperation can be either altruistic or mutualistic. So, there is no reason to necessarily associate Gricean Cooperation and Altruism. Indeed, a look at the Maxims should be enough to convince the reader that, if anything, Gricean Cooperation is mutualistic. In any communicational interaction, the speaker is trying to produce a given effect in her hearer and it is thus in her interest to make it possible for the hearer to identify that intention (following the definition of meaning$_{NN}$). Reciprocally, unless the hearer entirely discounts any communication from that source as unworthy of his attention, it is in the hearer's interest to recover the speaker's intention and make the necessary

---

[3] Indeed, Grice (1989) himself gave examples of the domain of application of the Principle and the maxims that have nothing to do with linguistic communication (e.g., two people collaborating in repairing a car engine).

interpretive effort. Thus, on the face of it, any communication is mutualistic. In itself, that very fact pleads for the Gricean view on the conversational maxims: they are basically norms for rational interaction, not linguistic norms.

This is not only entirely central for the discussion relative to the existence of linguistic norms, but also highly important for any discussion about the evolution of language. It has too often been supposed that altruism had to evolve before language could, given that the Cooperative Principle is the heart of linguistic communication. As the previous discussion has shown, this is less obvious than is usually thought. And, additionally, as just discussed, it is doubtful that the Cooperative Principle is altruistic. It makes much better sense to suppose it to be mutualistic. If this is the case, no special account has to be produced for the evolution of pro-social attitudes necessary for language evolution, as mutualism, in contrast to altruism, is entirely consistent with natural selection, and is, indeed, very widespread in nature. But, and more centrally relevant to the present topic, and that is another difference from altruism, there is no need to postulate norms that have to be obeyed for mutualism.

4. Semantic Norms

As said earlier, linguistic norms are unlikely to be found in linguistic structure and compositionality, but there is a possibility that they could be found in lexical semantics. In other words, the meaning of words (what they refer to) is determined by norms. This raises two different questions:

- whether words can refer on their own (Searle [1969] notoriously claimed that words do not refer, people do, when using words in utterances);
- whether, if they can, the way they do refer depends on specific norms.

Regarding the first question, one could argue that some words do refer on their own: this would, for instance, be the case for *de jure* referring words, that is, for words that are rigid designators (Kripke 1972), for instance proper names. This, however, reduces rather drastically the domain where these norms apply. Additionally, linguists often consider proper names to be an addition to language rather than really part of it. Of course, other words can refer, but they do not do so in isolation. For instance, definite descriptions can be used *descriptively* (in which case they do not refer), or *referentially* (in which case they do), but in such cases, their referring is due more to semantic compositionality (which was discussed before and found to be non-normative) and to speaker's intention than to semantic norms specific to the word. So the prospects of a normative account of lexical reference are not as good as might be thought.

Let us concentrate on the best candidates for semantic norms, i.e., rigid designators, and their paradigmatic example, proper names. Proper names are rigid designators in as much as they refer to the same individual in all possible worlds where that individual exists. The account given by Kripke, who introduced the notion, relies on the notion of a causal chain, beginning with an explicit act of baptism (not necessarily in the religious sense, obviously), through which the individual acquires the proper name concerned. Then other individuals, whether they were present or not at the baptism, will call her by that name, through hearing her called by the name. One might argue for the existence of norms at two levels: when the name is bestowed on its bearer, and when it is picked up by new individuals along the causal chain. One could argue that a baptism bestows a name through a norm and that it is also because the individuals who pick up the name comply with a norm enjoining them to use for a given individual the name by which others call her that the causal link can be built.[4]

Indeed, one might argue that, even though words that are not rigid designators do not refer to specific objects on their own, they are nevertheless learned by, e.g., young children, through the same basic normative mechanisms as those just described for rigid designators. This, however, given what is known by now about lexical acquisition, is highly doubtful. First words are produced at the mean age of 11 months (Bloom 2002). Though there are "principles" that seem to govern lexical acquisition, these principles have nothing to do with what was described earlier for rigid designators. They are to the effect that words attach to whole objects rather than their parts, and to the effect that if an unknown word is produced in the child's presence, the child will associate it with an object for which she has no word yet. Apart from the fact that the child behaves as if she follows such principles, but is not able to formulate them, which makes them dubious candidates for norms, these cannot be lexical norms: if they were, any object could only be given one name or be categorized at only one level (while my cat Ramses is a cat, a feline, a mammal, a non-human animal, an animal, a physical object, etc.); and we would not have names for parts of objects (which would ban words such as *leg, arm, hand, head, lid, wheel,* etc.). Unsurprisingly, neither of these principles, which are cognitive in nature and part of what has been dubbed the language-ready brain, are articulated in any community as lexical norms.

So this seems to leaves us with the fairly limited case of rigid designators. Yet, from the fact that the principles that constrain and guide lexical acquisition are not norms, it does not follow that the use of the lexicon, once acquired, is not constrained by norms.

In Chapter 13 in this volume, Enfield and Sidnell propose to examine linguistic norms in the following two ways:

"1. Norms regulate language use in the flow of conversation.[5]

2. Norms play a causal role in the conventionalization of word meanings." (Enfield and Sidnell, this volume, 265)

---

[4] I should point out that Kripke's analysis is not social in any way.

[5] I will not comment on this first point as I take it that both their view, according to which "because conversation is a socially cooperative activity, with each move we make we are *accountable* for the appropriateness

Regarding the use of words, they claim that ". . . if you use a word, you are socially *accountable* for intending to convey its conventional meaning" (this volume, 272, emphasis added). In other words, the use of words is governed by a norm.

This claim seems similar in interesting ways to Burge's analysis in a widely quoted paper, "Individualism and the Mental" (1979), to which I will now turn. Burge's argument rests on a three-step demonstration based on a double-barrelled thought experiment. The thought experiment begins with a patient (let us call him Arthur) who has many of the attitudes (beliefs) normally associated with "arthritis." He (correctly) believes that he has arthritis, that it is more painful in his hands and wrists than in his knees, etc. *He also (incorrectly) believes that he has "arthritis" in the thigh.* This is incorrect because arthritis is an inflammation of the joints, not of the muscles.

The second part of the thought experiment concerns Twin Arthur. Twin Arthur is wholly identical with Arthur in all particulars, including their personal life histories and beliefs. The only difference is social: Twin Arthur lives in a group where "arthritis" covers not only inflammation of the joints, but all the varieties of rheumatism, among them pains in the thigh. Thus, the main difference between Arthur and Twin Arthur is that the former is in error, while the latter is not. Why is that?

On the face of it, the answer seems obvious: because Arthur's use of "arthritis" does not comply with the common standard, while Twin Arthur's does. This is not exactly what Burge says, however. Burge says that the difference lies in the fact that Arthur is actually speaking and thinking about arthritis, while Twin Arthur actually is not (his utterances and thoughts are about something else). The notion of *incomplete understanding* plays an important role in Burge's argument: Arthur has an incomplete understanding of "arthritis," while Twin Arthur does not. Again, this is because Arthur's notion of "arthritis" targets arthritis, while Twin Arthur's does not.

Note that what this implies (and this is the third step in Burge's demonstration) is that, though Arthur and Twin Arthur, on the face of it, seem to share the same set of beliefs and thoughts, *in fact, they do not.* This is because Arthur's beliefs and thoughts are about arthritis, while Twin Arthur's are not. Not having the same target, their respective sets of beliefs and thoughts are disjoint (they do not have the same contents).

Burge's argument seems relevant in that, like Enfield and Sidnell, he appears to have a normative view of meaning. As a matter of fact, he discusses the issue of normativity in the postscript to "Individualism and the Mental." Burge notes that the main issue here is the question of *representational success*. He takes *veridicality* to be a constitutive standard of representational success, which can be formulated as follows: any utterance, in virtue of being representational, has truth- or correctness conditions. This veridicality standard is a norm, but not, according to him, a social norm, as it is

---

of our contribution" (Enfield and Sidnell, this volume, 266; their emphasis), and their examples are amenable to a Gricean approach, i.e., they do not mandate an approach in terms of *linguistic* norms.

independent of the speaker's intentions: it is both necessary and a priori. Rather, it is a natural norm, not a man-made or human norm.

In other words, it is not a norm in the sense I outlined in section 1. Is it exactly what Enfield and Sidnell have in mind when they talk of the speaker being *accountable* for using words as convention dictates? Not really, and it might seem that there is room, in addition to Burge's norm of veridicality for a social norm to the effect that speakers are *bound* to use words in accordance with the linguistic conventions active in their respective linguistic communities. However, this raises new problems: on the one hand, this seems too strong; on the other, it is not clear that such a social norm is necessary.

It is too strong because it basically excludes a lot of utterances, as can be seen if we turn to the use of words in tropes (metaphor, metonymy, irony, understatement, etc.). When John drops his glass of wine, splashing wine all over Mary's clothes and she exclaims "Oh, brilliant!," she is not using "brilliant" in accordance with its conventional meaning.[6] It also seems unnecessary, given the veridicality norm (which is not a human norm). Thus, it is not clear that an extraneous social norm has any utility for communication. Basic individual prudentiality toward communicative success is enough.

A last possibility is that it is the link between words and their meanings itself that is a norm. Given that lexical meaning is generally regarded as *conventional*, this raises the intricate question of what the difference between a norm and a convention is. In keeping with other chapters in the present collection (see, e.g., Mertens, this volume, 108), I think that the difference is that conventions, though social in origins, are subject to prudential individual considerations (if your use of words is such as to make your utterances impossible to understand, you have failed in your communicative goal), while deviation from social norms is typically the object of social sanctions, sanctions applied by peers. Not complying with a convention, as Arthur does, on the other hand, will merely lead to a correction: his doctor will tell him that he does not have arthritis in the thigh, because arthritis is an inflammation of the joints, not of the muscles.

So, while lexical meaning is conventional, it is not subject to norms.

5. Taking Stock

Up to now, we have examined the claim that there are linguistic norms at several levels:

- at the level of linguistic structure and semantic compositionality, and the conclusion was that this is an unlikely place to find linguistic norms;
- at the level of speech acts, where the conclusion was that, whatever norms there are, they are more institutional than linguistic in nature;

---

[6] Note that this does not mean that the conventional meaning plays no part in the interpretation. Nevertheless, Mary is not using "brilliant" to convey that John's action was, in any way, brilliant.

- at the level of implicit communication, where, again, the conclusion was that it was unlikely that norms are involved, and that if they are, they are presumably not linguistic in nature;
- finally, if there are norms in lexical meaning, they are limited to rigid designators that, arguably, are not truly part of the lexicon of any language.

So there seems to be very limited scope for authentically linguistic norms. There is, however, another possibility, not for the existence of linguistic norms, but for a measure of grammaticalization of non-linguistic, social norms.

6. Non-Linguistic Norms in Linguistic Structure

This final section comes back to the evolution of language and, more precisely, targets the social environment in which it occurred. There can be no certainty as to when exactly this happened, but there is a fairly wide (and reasonable) consensus that language had to be in place when the so-called Upper Paleolithic Revolution occurred, circa 50,000 years ago. Agriculture did not begin until 15,000 years ago at the earliest, which entails that language developed in forager (hunter-gatherer) societies. Such societies have been characterized (by, e.g., Givon 2002), as *societies of intimates* (by contrast with the *societies of strangers*, in which we live nowadays in developed countries).

Societies of intimates have the following features (see Givon 2002, ch. 9):

- The group is small (50–150 group members);
- It relies on a foraging (hunter-gatherer) economy;
- It lives on a restricted territorial distribution (10–20 miles radius of range);
- It has a restricted gene pool (the social grouping is kin-based);
- It enjoys cultural uniformity,
- as well as informational homogeneity and stability, with three major features: there is generic culturally shared world knowledge, a shared current situation, and episodic knowledge of the specific action and communication of individuals in the group;
- The leadership structure is deeply consensual, rather than hierarchical;
- Social cooperation is strongly restricted to in-groupers and excludes out-groupers.

What is more, societies of intimates follow rules for linguistic communication to the effect that one ought to avoid giving explicit information about past events, identifying participants by names, being identified as a source of information, being identified as the author of a prediction, citing one's source of knowledge, and using explicit negative statements. As Givon points out, these prohibitions make sense in a society in which there is very little privacy, a strong egalitarian ethos leading to punishment for braggarts and for aggressive behavior, as well as to the search for consensus rather than confrontation, no matter how long it may take.

These norms are clearly *not* linguistic norms. But one interesting question, if language, as is likely, evolved in societies of intimates, is whether such rules have left traces in our contemporary languages, or, in other words, whether some linguistic phenomena can be traced back to such non-linguistic norms.

I want to suggest here that the very existence of some forms of implicit communication, such as scalar implicatures and presuppositions, seems especially fitted to allow people to communicate what they intend to communicate and to facilitate doing so while complying with such prohibitions. Presuppositions allow one to make something common knowledge, all the while pretending that it already was common knowledge, which means that no source is invoked. It also allows one to give implicit information about past events (through so-called aspectual verbs). Implicatures allow one to contradict someone implicitly rather than explicitly, all the while avoiding presenting oneself as responsible for what is being communicated.

I will not develop this point any further, but this, I think, is where we find traces of non-linguistic norms on communication in linguistic phenomena.

7. Conclusion

The general conclusion is that there are no linguistic norms, apart from the putative and fairly marginal possibility of rigid designators being normatively produced. However, it is possible that some linguistic phenomena, such as varieties of implicit communication, may be the trace in language of non-linguistic but communicative norms that were once operative in the societies of intimates where language first evolved.

15

The Normativity of Meaning Revisited

Hans-Johann Glock

> Everybody goes on about norms. Cows go "moo!," philosophers go "norm!"
>
> —FODOR (2008, 203)

"Norm" has become a buzzword in contemporary philosophy. But the obsession with normativity extends much further. According to anthropologists, the "human species is addicted to rule making" (Fox 2014, 13), a view widely echoed in the social sciences more generally (Antweiler, Chapter 4 in this volume). It is also becoming increasingly popular within the behavioural and cognitive sciences (Schmidt and Rakoczy, Chapter 6 in this volume), and is gaining a foothold in evolutionary theory (Kappeler, Fichtel, and van Schaik, Chapter 3 in this volume). Finally, normativity has always been a central topic of linguistics.

Ever since language has been studied in a systematic manner, it has widely been regarded as a *rule-guided activity*. Whether this view is correct is pivotal to an adequate understanding of language. Normativity also epitomizes two fundamental controversies about human beings and their place in the world.

The first is between *naturalism* and *normativism*. Naturalists hold that there is no genuine knowledge outside natural science (epistemological naturalism), and that the spatio-temporal phenomena studied by natural science exhaust reality (ontological naturalism). Normativists object that logic, knowledge, and language, among other things, depend on norms that cannot be captured by the factual descriptions and causal explanations of natural science.

The second conflict pits *individualism* against *communitarianism*. According to individualists, the basic linguistic phenomenon is the idiolect, the language of an individual. According to communitarians, the fundamental phenomenon is that of a public language guided by shared conventions. Communitarians treat a language as a social practice or institution which is more than the sum of individual speakers or idiolects. Both debates have profound repercussions for our self-image. Natural languages are the most striking and arguably the most fundamental characteristics of human as opposed to animal communities. Whether they have an irreducible normative dimension is central to the question of what distinguishes us from animals. It also sets decisive parameters for explaining the origins of language. Furthermore, individualism is hospitable to the idea of an extremely fragmented society. Members of a group not only hold diverse beliefs and values; they need not even share a common language. Communitarians, by contrast, insist that they must share at least a linguistic medium in which to express conflicting viewpoints. Because they treat language as an intersubjective practice, they also acknowledge and deplore phenomena such as "language death" (Evans 2010).

The orthodox division of semiotics distinguishes three types of linguistic rules, as follows: *syntactic* rules concern the combination of linguistic expressions, in particular word-arrangement within sentences; *semantic* or *lexical* rules determine the meaning or sense of words and sentences; *pragmatic* rules concern the use of words in communication, e.g. the speech-acts we perform by uttering sentences or principles of cooperative communication. This trichotomy should not be treated as rigid, since the meaning of a sign cannot be neatly separated from either its combinatorial possibilities or its use. But I shall bracket such complications and concentrate on *semantic* normativity. More specifically, I shall focus on *lexical* or *literal* meaning, the meaning expressions have in a language, as opposed to *speaker meaning*, i.e. what individuals mean by an expression on a given occasion.

1. Historical Background

Semantic norms were central to the ancient Greek contrast between *physis* and *nomos*, between what is natural, unalterable, and universal on the one hand, and what is cultural, contingent on human decisions, and context-dependent on the other. In the *Cratylos* Plato toyed with the idea that for each kind of object there is a "correct" name which resembles the things it names. Ever since Aristotle, however, there has been a broad consensus on two points. First, having a specific meaning is not a feature of a sign—of an acoustic or typographic phenomenon—*per se*; instead, it is constituted by the sign's relation to something else (see also section 9 in this chapter). Secondly, signs mean what they do as a result of human mental acts or conventions rather than natural law. This consensus is epitomized by Peirce's distinction between three different types of signs—indices based on causal relations (as in "These clouds mean rain"); icons based on similarity (e.g. pictorial representations); and symbols based on conventions (as in "*sesquipedalius* means '1 and ½ feet' in Latin").

The normative aspects of the meaning possessed by symbols came to the fore through Wittgenstein's later work. According to Wittgenstein, the meaning of an expression is not an object it stands for, but "its use in the language" (1953, § 43). At the same time, he (like Chomsky afterwards) criticized behaviourist and causal theories of meaning (e.g. Ogden and Richards 1923). Such theories explain meaning by reference to its use. But the operative conception of use is purely causal. The meaning of a word is equated with the conditions which *cause* a speaker to utter it and/or the *effects* which such utterances have on hearers.

Wittgenstein's alternative is normativist. The meaning of an expression depends not on how it is actually understood, but on how *it is to be understood* within a linguistic community. What is semantically relevant is neither the causes nor the effects of using an expression, nor the intentions with which speakers utter it, but the *correct* use of an expression. Accordingly, linguistic meaning depends on general *rules*. These rules provide standards for the correct use of expressions, and thereby determine what it makes sense to say with the help of these expressions.[1]

Kripke (1982) portrays Wittgenstein as devising a "sceptical paradox" that questions the possibility of distinguishing between following and violating a rule, and thereby casts doubt on the very phenomenon of meaning. According to "Kripkenstein," there is no set of facts that determines what rule R a speaker S is following in using an expression *e* and hence what S means by *e*. For all facts about S's use of *e* up to time *t* are compatible not just with R but also with an alternative R', which requires the same actions as R up to *t*, yet different ones after *t* (see Miller and Wright 2002; Kusch 2006; Glock 2014a).

A tempting avenue for blocking the paradox invokes *dispositions*. Following (understanding and accepting) a rule is a potentiality. S means something specific by *e* because even after any time *t*, S *would* use *e* in a certain fashion. But dispositionalism cannot do justice to the normative character of rules in general and meaning in particular. Dispositions can sustain predictions about what *will* occur, yet not statements about what *should* occur or what is *correct*. Instead, we judge *by reference to the rule* whether someone is disposed to act in accordance with it (Waismann 1965, chs. 7, 18; Kripke 1982, 22–37).

Dispositionalists have responded that what S means is determined by how S is predisposed to use *e under ideal conditions*. They characterize the semantically constitutive dispositions as those which are not subject to interference like disease or malfunction, or as those which are in line with the biological function and hence the evolutionary history of the pertinent cognitive system (Millikan 1990). Yet no set of conditions, however propitious to an individual's performance or crucial to the emergence of

---

[1] There are also "unruly" Wittgensteinians, who maintain that the idea of meaning as use militates against rather than requires that meaning be intrinsically normative. The first to incorporate this view into a sustained account of meaning was Horwich (1998a, esp. ch. 8). My reasons for insisting that Wittgenstein was a normativist are stated in Glock (2010, 88–91).

the pertinent cognitive system, can *guarantee* that an answer is correct—unless, that is, conditions *count as ideal* only if they engender the *correct* answer. In that case, however, the explanation of what constitutes correctness is circular.

One option at this juncture is to deny that the normativity of meaning is genuine in the first place. It has become increasingly popular, especially among naturalists trying to defuse the challenge posed by normativity. Drawing on Davidson and Chomsky, anti-normativists have questioned received views about the connection between meaning and rules. The remainder of this chapter is devoted to the lively ensuing debate. Starting out from a distinction between different respects in which lexical meaning might be normative, I defend the idea of semantic normativity against some recent challenges.[2]

2. Norms and Rules: A Brief Explanation

"Norm" and "rule" both hail from Latin and signify a standard (originally, a carpenter's ruler). In philosophy, at any rate, there is no generally entrenched clear-cut distinction between the two. Both can be used to signify either the average or usual level of attainment or a standard used to judge or assess something, in particular conduct. The two are not the same: what is normal or usual need not meet a pertinent standard, and vice versa. The same holds for "law," which may be a descriptive *law of nature* or a non-descriptive *law of state*.

Our topic is norms in the second sense. They differ from statements of mere regularities or natural laws in four interrelated respects.

First, they do not (merely) describe or explain behaviour; they set standards, in particular standards against which behaviour can be assessed as correct or incorrect. If planets turn out to follow paths other than elliptical ones, it is Kepler's Laws rather than the movement of the planets which needs revision. By contrast, if I drive on the right-hand side it is my driving rather than the Traffic Code which is at fault. The *direction of fit* is from world (action) to mind (norm).

Secondly, as the idea of fit implies, "to follow a rule" is an *achievement*-verb. And this possibility of success implies the possibility of failure. There is a difference between an agent *A* actually following a rule and her merely believing that she does.

Thirdly, although rule-following presupposes a regularity in behaviour, there is a difference between merely *regular* and *rule-guided* behaviour. If *A* follows a rule R in Φ-ing, R must be part of *A*'s reason for Φ-ing, and more specifically, for Φ-ing in a particular manner. Accordingly, rule-following is a type of goal-directed and indeed *intentional* behaviour.

---

[2] In Chapter 14 in this volume, Reboul weighs in on the other side of the controversy. But I have not made a deliberate attempt to address her specific worries, instead concentrating on developing a positive case against already published animadversions widely regarded as decisive.

Fourthly, and relatedly, whereas human agents can be irredeemably ignorant of regularities in their behaviour, they must be *potentially aware* of the rules they are following, albeit in a minimalist sense (Glock 2003, ch. 7). *A* can be clueless as to *why a rule R has been adopted*. But *A* must be able to recognize R itself as a reason for Φ-ing. To be sure, agents often follow rules without explicitly consulting them even in *foro interno*, as in the case of proficient chess-players. In many cases, they will be able to specify these rules when prompted. But there are exceptions, not least as regards language. For example, competent speakers may be incapable of explaining the difference between terms like "automatically" and "inadvertently," or between "bottle" and "jar." However, even in these cases, linguistically gifted agents will standardly be *capable of recognizing* formulations of the relevant rules, provided that these are couched in suitable terms. At the very least, *A* must be able to explain her Φ-ing as "the done thing," or "how we do things around here," i.e. by reference to the *existence* of a rule, a standard that is to be followed. In an analogous manner, even *non-linguistic* subjects can manifest that their Φ-ing is more than a regularity, namely by recognizing and sanctioning deviations (see section 8).

The first feature is equally present in desires; and all four are common to commands, orders, and requests. A fifth feature sets norms apart, namely that they are inherently *general*. Although norms are commonly restricted to certain types of subject and types of situation (context-sensitive), they govern an unlimited multiplicity of occasions (occasion-neutral).

Finally, there is a difference between a rule and its linguistic expression—a *rule-formulation*. A rule need not be expressed linguistically, and one and the same rule may be expressed in different ways. In short, a *norm* is a general standard that provides a reason for action and against which actions can be assessed as correct or incorrect.

These points are in line with the way in which "norm," "normative," and "rule" tend to be used outside of debates about semantic normativity. They should be acceptable to participants of those debates. But insofar as anti-normativists rely on more demanding conceptions of normativity, my quarrel with them is partly terminological. That is not to say *merely* terminological. As a normativist, I feel that it matters how terminology is used, and in particular whether familiar terms are employed in an established and clear fashion. Be that as it may, my main ambition is not to show that anti-normativists are mistaken, given their understanding of normativity. It is to make out a case for the claim that meaning *is* normative according to the conception set out here.

3. Dimensions of Semantic Normativity

Within the debate over the "normativity of meaning," one must distinguish various claims. Three of them concern linguistic meaning.

3.1. Bare Normativity of Meaning (BNM)

e is meaningful   ⇒ [conceptually entails]   there are conditions for the
correct use of e.

If an expression e is meaningful, then there must be conditions for its correct application. "Suppose the expression 'green' means *green*. It follows immediately that the
expression 'green' applies correctly only to these things (the green ones) and not to
those (the non-greens). The fact that the expression means something implies, that
is, a whole set of *normative* truths about my behaviour with that expression: namely,
that my use of it is correct in application to certain objects and not in application to
others" (Boghossian 1989, 148).

3.2. Rule-Based Normativity of Meaning (RNM)

e is meaningful   ⇒   there are *rules* for the use of e.

Etymologically, "norm" is roughly synonymous to "rule." Occasionally, however,
"normativity" is employed widely, for all phenomena that can be assessed for *correctness* according to a *standard*, with rules understood more specifically as standards
guiding *action*. According to RNM, meaning requires rules of use, since the correctness conditions of BNM are laid down by such rules.

3.3. Prescriptive Normativity of Meaning (PNM)

e is meaningful   ⇒   there are prescriptions for e's use.

PNM is stronger than RNM, since not all rules prescribe what one ought to do.
    In contemporary debates, normativity claims concerning the meaning of linguistic
expressions are intertwined with claims concerning the *content*—the concepts or
thoughts—expressed by employing expressions. One of them is Dummett's (1981,
300) suggestion that *assertion* presupposes the existence of certain rules, notably that an
assertion should aim to be true.

3.4. Normativity of Content: Assertion (NCA)

A asserts that p ⇒   there are rules for asserting that p.

The other concerns the content of *beliefs* rather than assertoric utterances.

3.5. Normativity of Content: Belief (NCB)

A believes that p ⇒   there are rules for believing that p.

Accordingly, our topic divides as follows (see Figure 15.1).

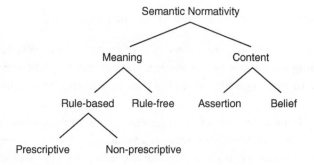

Figure 15.1

I shall leave aside NCA and NCB (see Glock 2014a). Instead, the final sections discuss the issue whether meaning presupposes conventions, shared arbitrary rules.

3.6. Conventionality of Meaning (CM)

e is meaningful ⇒   there are conventions for using e.

4. Truth and Meaning

Anti-normativists tend to grant BNM. That an expression has a specific meaning implies that there are conditions for its *correct* use. At the same time they confront normativism with a *dilemma*: either the operative conditions are *not really normative*; or they are *not in fact constitutive of meaning*, i.e. they do not follow from an expression being meaningful (Glüer and Wikforss 2009). BNM is supposed to fall under the first horn; RNM and especially PNM under the second.

A popular way of capturing the idea that expressions require conditions of correct application is as follows:

(BNM$_1$) e means F ⇒ $\forall x$ (it is correct to apply e to $x \leftrightarrow x$ is f)

(where e is a general term, F gives its meaning, and f' is that feature in virtue of which e applies to an object x). The consequent of BNM$_1$ provides the scheme for a "semantic principle" of the kind employed in formal semantics. A first anti-normativist objection runs: "correct" in (BNM$_1$) is not genuinely normative, since it is simply a place-holder for "true"; "it is correct to apply e to x," in other words, boils down to e *holds true of x* (Boghossian 2005; Hattiangadi 2007, 51–61).

This objection cannot be countered by pointing out that semantic principles *give rise* to norms, since the same holds of descriptive statements. For one thing, they can give rise to technical norms, given additional premises of a normative kind. Thus

(1) Compact fluorescent lamps consume less energy than standard light bulbs

may give rise to norms requiring the fitting of compact fluorescent lamps, given a norm requiring energy savings. For another, one can criticize statements and actions by reference to statements like (1) no less than by reference to semantic principles.

At the same time, by dint of its connection with truth, holding true is what Parfit (1997) calls "normatively relevant." If a predicate holds true of something, this constitutes a proposition being true. And that has implications for what it is correct to believe or do. What is more, whereas the normative implications of (1) depend on specific normative preferences, those of truth have an anthropological dimension: they arise from fundamental features of human thought and action. We need to modify, i.e. *correct* our beliefs and activities in the light of what is the case, of things being thus-and-so. This in turn reflects the fact that how things are is essential to how we should pursue our goals (Horwich 1998b, 44–6; Glock 2003, 131–6).

The first anti-normativist objection also assumes that semantic norms would have to be norms of truth, norms to the effect that one ought to think and state what is true. That assumption is shared by most normativists (e.g. Blackburn 1984, 281–2). Yet the contrast between correct and incorrect applies to language in a variety of ways, and their connection to the notion of meaning differs. In particular, one can use a word meaningfully, in a sentence with a sense that expresses a thought, without that thought being *either* true *or* justified. This crucial difference between truth and meaning emerges when one distinguishes types of *mistakes* that people can make in using words.[3] First, in the run-up to a by-election to the House of Commons a candidate once said,

(2) I know that I cannot win this seat.

There was nothing wrong with (2) either linguistically or factually. Yet she made a dreadful mistake, because it is not politic to admit to such dim prospects. Next consider Tony Blair's notorious statement in the House of Commons

(3) Iraq is capable of deploying weapons of mass destruction within 45 minutes of an order by Saddam Hussein.

There was nothing amiss linguistically with (3), yet it was both unjustified and false. Now turn to George W. Bush's

---

[3] I approach linguistic norms via deviations, just as Mertens (Chapter 5 in this volume) does with respect to social norms.

(4)   You teach a child to read, and he or her will be able to pass a literacy test.

Here we are confronted with a linguistic mistake. But it is of a syntactic rather than semantic kind. *Au contraire*, once we correct for that error, (4) is analytic, at least on a certain understanding of "teach" and "literacy." In spite of involving a solecism, therefore, (4) shows Bush at the very height of his semantic powers. That is more than can be said of

(5)   I am mindful not only of preserving executive powers for myself, but for my predecessors as well.

Here Bush's travails are semantic. (5) betokens not lack of factual knowledge, but an insufficient grasp of the meaning of at least one of the two terms "preserving" and "predecessors."

There is a fundamental contrast between saying something false or unjustified—as in (3)—and saying something meaningless—as in (5). Some uses of words are mistaken *solely* because of *what these words mean*, irrespective of any other facts, syntactic rules, or social expectations. Conversely, one can apply a word in a way which is *semantically correct*—based on a proper understanding of its meaning—without applying it correctly in the sense of saying something *true*, namely if one errs about pertinent facts (Glock 2014b; cf. Whiting 2013).

The meaning of *e* is constituted by a rule that specifies the *condition f* under which *e* applies to *x*. Whether a speaker S violates that rule depends *not* on whether *x* actually satisfies *f*—that is a matter of fact/knowledge rather than meaning/understanding. Instead, it depends on whether S applies (or withholds) *e* on the grounds that *x* does (or does not) satisfy condition *f*. If S assents to

(6)   George W. Bush is a predecessor of Bill Clinton

S commits a factual mistake if he does so on the grounds that the former was US president before the latter; S commits a semantic mistake if he does so on the grounds that George W. Bush's presidency postdates that of Bill Clinton.

Whether a sentence expresses a rule depends not on its linguistic *form*, but on whether it has a normative *function*, either in general or on a given occasion of utterance. Consequently rule-formulations need not contain a deontic verb. And formulations of linguistic rules need not be metalinguistic statements that mention the expressions for which they specify a rule. By these lights, all *explanations of meaning* are semantic rules, including not just definitions in the formal or material mode, but also recursive and ostensive definitions, colour-charts and conversion-tables, explanation by exemplification, and analytic propositions (see Glock 1996, 129–35). For instance, both

(7)   The term 'drake' means *male duck*.

and

(8)   A drake is a male duck.

are standardly used to explain what "drake" means. Because they function as
explanations, (7) and (8) have a normative role: we can criticize and justify our use of
"drake" by reference to them.

5. Correctness and Normativity (BNM)

Focusing on the explanations we actually employ in teaching, justifying, and
criticizing the use of expressions (dictionary explanations included) avoids serious
distortions (Glock 2003, ch. 5). Unfortunately, such an anthropological perspective
is alien to the genre of formal semantics that most contributors to the debate about
the normativity of meaning subscribe to. For the sake of argument, I shall nonetheless follow them in discussing our topic by reference to "semantic principles." At
the same time, to preserve some connection with the reality of linguistic exchange,
I shall ignore disquotational principles and address principles that are at least suitable as explanations of meaning in actual practice. For "drake," such a principle
might read:

(9)   It is correct to apply 'drake' to x iff x is a male duck.

Most anti-normativists concede

$$(\text{BMN}_{drake})\ (7)\ \Rightarrow\ (9)$$

At the same time they deny that (9) has a bona fide normative status. A first objection
is that the alleged semantic norms boil down to mere "descriptive facts" concerning
linguistic behaviour (Glüer 2001). However, we must distinguish between (9), which
standardly expresses a norm, from something like

(10)   In English, it is correct to apply 'drake' to an object x iff x is a male duck.

(10) can be used to invoke a norm *within* the Anglophone community. But it can also
be used as an empirical "norm-proposition" to the effect that this community follows
that norm (von Wright 1963, viii, 108). In that capacity, (10) states a fact about the
behaviour of Anglophones. It does so, however, only because the Anglophone speech

community accepts a certain norm, a standard for the correct use of "drake." That is to say, (10) is a true factual statement about normative behaviour precisely because (9) expresses a norm.

One could respond, however, that (10) describes linguistic practice as more norm-laden than it is (Davidson 2005, 109–12). All we really have is

(11)   Among a certain population, most people tend to apply 'drake' to an object x only if x is a male duck.

(11) is indeed bereft of normative implications. But there is more to linguistic practice than statistical regularity. We do not just tend to apply "drake" to male ducks. We also *explain* the term as a label for male ducks, and we *criticize* and *justify* our use of the term by reference to statements like (7) to (9). Applying "drake" to x on the grounds that x is a female duck or a male fox counts as (semantically) incorrect, a symptom of deviant understanding.

Semantic principles—aka explanations of meaning—determine what counts as an instance of a general term e, and *thereby* what constitutes, respectively, correct or incorrect, meaningful and nonsensical uses of e. Insofar as they are used normatively, namely as instruments of instruction, correction, or justification between participants of a practice, they differ from empirical statements about those participants following a rule, irrespective of whether or not a context is explicitly specified.

It is widely assumed that adjectives like "correct" or "mistaken" are normative (Blackburn 1984, 286–7), even among those sceptical about the normativity of meaning (Boghossian 2003, 35; Fodor 2008, 205). A second anti-normativist objection questions this assumption.

Now, a serviceable explanation of correctness is derived from the *OED* and runs:

(COR) x is correct iff x is in accordance with an acknowledged standard.

This standard may be part of a specific system of evaluation appropriate to x, as when we speak of correct academic dress. Or it may be a general standard expressing certain demands, e.g. on prudential or moral conduct. Either way, there must be a standard specifying conditions under which x counts as correct.

At this juncture it is tempting to think that calling x correct is merely to state that it satisfies these conditions, and hence that the concept lacks normative aspects after all. But in characterizing x as correct we do not just or even primarily ascribe to x the *features* specified in the relevant standard. In the first instance, we characterize x as *meeting a standard* of positive evaluation. The term "correct" is not purely descriptive or factual, but *evaluative*. Indeed, unlike other evaluative terms, e.g. "good," it carries the further implication that failure to meet this standard is not merely undesirable, but provides grounds for *intervention*. After all, the verb "to correct" means to set right, rectify, or amend. Applying the *terms used in the standard* may be purely descriptive, but applying "correct" is *not*. By the same token, to call something incorrect is not only to evaluate it negatively; if something is incorrect, one has grounds for *correcting* it. For instance, no normative force attaches to the statement that a person is not wearing a cap and gown. Given the standards of correct academic dress, however, not wearing them on certain official occasions constitutes being dressed incorrectly, and is there-fore liable to be corrected.

This lesson carries over to semantic normativity. According to anti-normativists, "To say that some use of a term is 'correct' is . . . merely to describe it in a certain way—in light of the norm or standard set by the meaning of the term" (Hattiangadi 2006, 225). To be sure, categorizing something by reference to the defining features of a drake has no normative implications *per se*. To deny that an object x possesses the defining features of a drake, for instance, is not to characterize x as fit for correction. But the "norm or standard set by the meaning" of "drake" makes reference to these features, just as the standard for correct academic dress makes reference to cap and gown. And to categorize applying "drake" to x on the grounds that x is a female duck as incorrect has direct normative implications, since it characterizes that application as fit for correction.

To assess an assertion or belief as false is to present it as fit for epistemic correc-tion. Similarly, to assess an utterance as meaningless, nonsensical, or a malapropism is to present it as fit for semantic correction. Admittedly, on particular occasions a speaker may intend to assert something false, to commit linguistic mistakes, or to utter nonsense. In that eventuality what she does may be correct relative to a dif-ferent standard—a prudential or moral one, for example. If that standard is more important in the situation, what she does may also be correct in an "all things considered" sense. But this does not detract from the fact that she is violating se-mantic or epistemic norms. In semantic principles "correct" is not used in this "all things considered" sense. Conversely, the general norms of rationality presupposed in that usage are not constitutive of the meaning of normal expressions like "drake," even though they feature in the semantic norms governing expressions like "reason-able" or "rational."

6. Meaning and Constitutive Rules

Even if (9) has a bona fide normative status vis-à-vis linguistic performances, RNM may go wrong in portraying it as a genuine *rule* (Stainton 1996, 139–42; Glüer and Pagin 1999). After all, it does not oblige or even entreat us to apply the term "drake" to an object in a particular situation.

Some rules, however, instead of prescribing a certain form of behaviour, lay down what a thing *must be like* to satisfy a certain description. Prime examples are the beloved EU norms concerning, for example, what qualifies as chocolate or the rules of games like chess. These norms lay down *what counts as* chocolate or as castling, without requesting anyone to produce or buy chocolate, or to castle.

This "definitory aspect" of certain rules (Baker and Hacker 1984, 259) is connected to the familiar distinction between "regulative" and "constitutive" rules (Searle 1969). Regulative rules advise one on how to pursue in an optimal fashion an activity that can be specified independently of the rule. Constitutive rules are partly definitive of the activity in question. What goes on at dinner parties can be described as eating independently of the rules of etiquette. What goes on when people move certain pieces across a board, by contrast, cannot be described as castling, checking, mating, or, more generally, as playing chess, independently of rules like "The king cannot castle out of a check" or "The king is mate if it is in check in such a way that no move will remove it from being in check." These rules constitute the game of chess, unlike regulative rules like "Do not relinquish control of the centre." Even someone who disregards the latter does not cease to play chess; he will just play chess badly, at least in standard cases.

It cannot be denied that constitutive rules make up a *bona fide* and indeed *paradigmatic* type of rule or norm. Otherwise one would have to insist that rule books do not really contain rules and that the law of contract does not really contain norms.[4] But are semantic principles a kind of constitutive rule?

One of the main arguments in favour of normativism is that linguistic utterances are subject to both regulative and constitutive rules in roughly the same way as chess moves. Someone who calls his superior an "idiot" is imprudent. And someone who indulges in lengthy explanations when requiring urgent help is imprudent because of violating a regulative rule governing the pragmatics of linguistic communication. But he does not commit a linguistic mistake. By contrast, someone who violates rules of syntax, e.g. by failing to conjugate properly or by violating rules of word order, or lexical rules, e.g. by calling an ambiguous statement ambidextrous, commits a linguistic mistake (Schroeder 1998, § 12).

One must not take the analogy between a language and a game too far, however. Thus Dummett has maintained that there is a convention whereby in making an assertion speakers aim at truth, just as there is a convention according to which in making a move in chess, players aim at the stipulated point of the game, i.e. checkmating. By this token, truth is the aim of assertion, just as checkmating is the aim of chess (1981, 296–8). But while we justly complain about insincere assertions, that complaint makes

---

[4] Indeed, as regards games, regulative rules are commonly known as "strategies" or "tactics" rather than "rules" (see Dawson 1950).

no reference to constitutive rules of a specific language. We do not say, "In French one doesn't lie, whereas in English it's ok," as we might say, "In draughts, one doesn't mate, whereas in chess one does" (Schroeder 1998, § 21).

Dummett could reply that the assertion rule extends to *all* languages in which assertions are made, just as rules of inference extend to all languages in which inferences can be expressed. Just as the latter can be regarded as constitutive both of inference and of the meaning of logical constants across languages, the rule to aim at truth could be regarded as constitutive both of the speech act of assertion and of the relevant force indicators across languages. But even if this response works for the case of inference, in that transformations of sentences violating the rules of inference do not strictly speaking count as inferences, it definitely fails for the case of assertion. Even *insincere* statements still count as assertions, otherwise we could not complain about insincere assertions in the first place. What is constitutive of asserting is only that the speaker *presents* herself as sincere (Glock 2014).[5]

Anti-normativists might further protest that someone who violates a constitutive rule of chess is no longer playing chess, while someone who violates the alleged constitutive rules of English is still speaking English. This qualm, however, is dubious on both counts. It is implausible to insist that a game involving a single incorrect move no longer counts as chess. Conversely, although someone who commits a mistake may still speak English, the *mistake itself* does not count as English. It is quite common to react to a serious mistake by protesting, "That's not English!" And someone who commits many such mistakes can be said not to be speaking English.

At the same time the objection contains a kernel of truth concerning the *criteria of identity* for languages, i.e. of the practices for which linguistic rules are supposed to be constitutive. The margin of tolerance for deviation is far greater and less well defined in the case of natural languages than in the case of chess. There is a simple though important reason for this: the constitutive rules of natural languages do *not* form a precise and stable system.

That natural languages are not spoken according to rigid and precise rules is a lesson ignored by Davidsonians and Chomskians, who deny that any two people ever speak the same language. They rightly note that "if no two speakers ever share the very same vocabulary items or observe exactly the same rules of grammar there

---

[5] An analogous response can be given to Fodor's objection that "it doesn't seem that languages are a lot like games after all: queens and pawns don't mean anything, whereas 'dog' means dog. That's why, though you can't translate the queen into French (or, a fortiori, into checkers), you can translate 'dog' into 'chien'" (Fodor 1998, 36). Like words, chess pieces have a meaning in the sense of having a significance or function within the framework of the game. And while there is no strict analogue to translation, elements of different games—notably of different card-games—can have equivalent or similar functions in their respective contexts.

will be no formally precise, syntactic and semantic characterization of the language spoken by a given community" (Smith 1998, 307–71). Yet this only entails that linguistic communities do not share a language on the assumption that languages are individuated by such formally precise characterizations. That is obviously not how we individuate natural languages like Basque or French, either in everyday parlance or in linguistics. Consequently there is no reason to suppose that, strictly speaking, members of a linguistic community do not share a language, provided that we use "language" in the established way (Glock 2003, 250–9).

7. Semantic Principles and Prescriptions

PNM invites a further anti-normativist worry: semantic principles lack the action-guiding force of genuine rules. The latter, it is often maintained, are deontic injunctures about what one *ought to do* (Boghossian 2003; Hattiangadi 2006). This complaint is fuelled by a difference between constitutive and regulative rules. The former have the general form

(CR$_1$) X counts as Y in context C

or, regarding actions

(CR$_2$) Φ-ing counts as Ψ-ing in context C.

By contrast, regulative rules have the form

(RR) One must Ψ in context C (Ψ in context C!)

One can rephrase all regulative rules as constitutive rules:

(CR$\star$) Not Ψ-ing in C counts as incorrect.

But the reverse transformation is not possible. Therefore, qua constitutive rules, semantic principles appear not to play a role in steering linguistic behaviour.

However, the regulative to constitutive transformation yielding (CR$\star$) exploits the action-guiding force of the label "correct." By the same token, therefore, constitutive rules specifying what count as "correct," such as (9), are *ab initio* action-guiding. Furthermore, constitutive rules, including linguistic ones, give rise to *hypothetical* imperatives.

(HI) If you want to Ψ in context C, you must Φ.

For instance, in the military raising one's right hand to the head constitutes greeting a superior. Since it is a regulative rule to greet superiors, this gives rise to the rule to raise one's right hand to the head when encountering a superior.

Now, for linguistic and non-linguistic acts alike, Φ-ing is often only one of several possibilities to Ψ in C. Even in such cases, however, constitutive rules play a role in practical inferences, inferences that lead to an intention or decision to Φ in C.

(Conative Premise)	I want to Ψ in C
(Constitutive Premise)	Φ-ing counts as Ψ-ing in C
(Practical Conclusion)	I shall (let me) Φ!

For instance, saying *Grüezi mitenand* counts as greeting a group of two or more in Zurich; I want to greet a group of two or more in Zurich; therefore I shall say *Grüezi mitenand*. By contrast to theoretical inferences, the conclusion is a sufficient rather than necessary condition for the combination of the premises. But this holds of practical inferences in general; consequently it does not constitute an objection against the idea that constitutive rules can guide action.

A more serious worry is that purely descriptive statements can take the place of the constitutive premise (see section 4). So where is the special normative dimension? The answer is: unlike purely descriptive statements, constitutive rules *invoke a normative practice*, namely a convention according to which Φ-ing *is to count as* Ψ-ing in C. For those who are part of such a practice, the constitutive rules have clear-cut *regulative* consequences. They *ought to* treat X / Φ-ing as Y / Ψ-ing in C. Officials in the EU must treat certain food-stuffs as chocolate. Competent speakers of English must accept (7) to (9) as *correct* explanations of "drake"; by the same token they must accept as *true* calling x a drake iff x is a male duck. Otherwise they disqualify themselves as competent users of "drake"; and if they diverge permanently from all constitutive rules of English, they cease being members of the speech community.

This does not exhaust the normative dimension of meaning. As we have seen, by laying down conditions under which terms of a language can be applied, semantic principles *also* lay down conditions under which certain utterances are *correct*. For instance, by specifying what counts as a drake, explanations like (7) or (8) *also lay down* what counts as using the term "drake" in a correct, in the sense of meaningful, way—a point which comes out in statements like (9). Such statements support *prohibitions*. We can justify

(12)   You ought not to apply "drake" to a female duck or a male fox.

by reference to (9). More generally, we often say

(13)   You shouldn't call that . . . , because it's not . . .

Even among regulative rules, finally, there are not just *prescriptive* "norms of obliga-tion" (von Wright 1963) or "mandatory norms" (Raz 1978) of the form

(MN) A ought to ϕ in condition C

There are also *permissive* norms of the form

(PN) A is entitled to ϕ in condition C

Entitlements presuppose a background of prohibitions. Such a background is pro-vided by injunctions like (12) and (13), even though the immediate sanctions for violating them may be confined to correction and ridicule. Some theorists have suggested that permissions reduce to obligations, either because they are the mere absence of obligations or because they are obligations on others not to interfere. The second claim does not pose a threat to regarding permissions as rules, since it merely relocates their normative trajectory. The first ignores two points. We can invoke per-missive norms in defence of Φ-ing; this goes beyond merely averring that there is no proscription on Φ-ing, especially if there are prohibitions in the vicinity, e.g. against Ψ-ing in C or Φ-ing in conditions other than C. Furthermore, we can adduce these norms to *explain* our F-ing even in the absence of any challenge.

It is common to employ explanations like (7) and (8) as permissive norms. I can appeal to a definition like (7) in defending or explaining my use of "drake." If chal-lenged why I call a male duck a drake I can defend myself by saying that "drake" means *male duck* (see also Whiting 2009). Furthermore, explanations of meaning also function as transformation or inference rules. Thus ostensive definitions are substitu-tion rules. "This ☞ is red," for instance, entitles one to pass from "My bike has this ☞ colour" to "My bike is red" (Wittgenstein 1974, 88–91, 202). Similarly (7) is consti-tutive of the meaning of "drake" by virtue of licensing transitions between empirical propositions (Sellars 1963b; Brandom 1994). Thus we can appeal to (7) in support of an inference like

(14)   Donald is a male duck, therefore Donald is a drake

without recourse to any non-linguistic facts.

A final criticism of (PNM) revolves around the idea that genuine norms must be or imply *categorical imperatives* (e.g. Bilgrami 1993, 135). Unlike merely hypothetical imperatives, such imperatives are independent of any desires or goals that the addressee might have. Now, a speaker can violate semantic prohibitions like (12) by lying. [6] Yet

---

[6] This claim is defensible *au pied de la lettre*. Semantic prohibitions like (12) can be violated by lying, namely if a speaker who knows that x is a female duck or that x is a male fox nonetheless asserts that x is

this only shows that they are genuine rules, something one can obey or fail to obey. What disqualifies semantic prohibitions from being categorical is that they can be overridden by other rules *in certain situations*. Kant notwithstanding, however, this arguably holds for all imperatives.

In any event, that an imperative is not categorical does *not* entail that it lacks normative force altogether. The opposite view is fuelled by the prejudice that a genuine "ought" must indicate an "all things considered" obligation. Yet in our normative discourse we recognize the possibility of *bona fide* yet *prima facie* or *pro tanto* obligations. In cases in which we cannot both Φ and Ψ, we frequently deliberate:

(15)   On the one hand I ought to Φ, on the other I should Ψ

RNM would be threatened if injunctions like (12) could be overridden simply by "a desire to lie or deceive" (Hattiangadi 2006, 231–2; Glüer and Wikforss 2009, 2). But lying is something one ought not to do! The ultimate rationale for this prohibition has a profound anthropological dimension. Lying undermines the trust essential to human communication and interaction. Indeed, a practice of uniformly insincere assertions cannot even be consistently conceived (Glock 2014b). Although the prohibition to lie can be overridden by more pressing obligations in certain situations, its validity is *not* simply contingent on the speaker's desire or decision to speak the truth. One is not entitled to lie simply because one feels like it.

8. Conventions: A Brief Explanation

According to Lewis (1969), conventions are communal regularities of behaviour that arise within "coordination problems," problems of arriving collectively at a particular course of action in situations where other courses of actions are equally feasible, provided that they are adopted collectively. The regularity is sustained not just by complex beliefs and preferences concerning those who are party to the convention, but also by a common knowledge that they have these beliefs and preferences.

This account does not capture what we standardly mean by a convention. For one thing, many conventions, for example most rules of etiquette and custom, do not solve problems of coordination (Gilbert 1989, ch. 6). Worse still, some of them positively create such problems. Think of the convention to buy presents for Christmas and the

---

a drake. But it ignores an important point which Severin Schroeder (forthcoming) has raised against both the anti-normativist appeal to lying and against normativists like Whiting and myself. Lying per se flouts semantic norms only when one lies about semantic norms. One does not normally commit a semantic mistake by lying. The relation between semantic normativity and various forms of insincerity is an intriguing topic to which I cannot do justice here.

resulting chaos in shopping areas. For another, Lewis demands far too much from those party to a convention. He is prepared to bite the bullet of accepting that "children and the feeble-minded" cannot be governed by conventions (1969, 62, 75). But the problem runs deeper. By and large, people do not entertain the complex beliefs and desires concerning members of large and often unspecified groups around which his definition revolves (von Savigny 1988, § 8). While Lewis goes wrong in requiring from the subjects complex beliefs and desires, Gilbert goes wrong in lumbering them with explicit joint commitments. Both are overly intellectualistic. They ignore the Humean insight into the importance of custom and habit. The substratum of conventions is regularities of behaviour that have become so entrenched and internalized as to give rise to normative expectations.

For these reasons I favour a weaker definition of conventions (elaborated in Glock 2010). It starts out from a proposal by Hart (1961, 54–6). Following Hart, in a group G a behavioural regularity R is a *shared rule* iff

(a)   it is rare for members of G to deviate from R

(b)   if members of G deviate from R, they are subject to sanctions, including the verbal sanction of being criticized

(c)   these sanctions are generally accepted by members of G.

Hart adds an additional requirement. Members of G regard R from an "internal point of view," that is, they avoid deviating from it not just for reasons of prudence, notably for the sake of avoiding sanctions. But this is too demanding (von Savigny 1988, ch. 2). Although as a matter of fact no rule-following practice may be stable if compliance with it is based exclusively on sanctions, this is not part of the *concept* of a rule that is in force within a certain community.

However, as I stressed earlier, behaviour is guided by rules only if these provide the agent's reasons for proceeding as they do. Therefore we need to preserve one element of Hart's additional requirement:

(d)   members of G abide by R for a reason (which can either be the communal regularity itself or the sanctions associated with deviations).

Even if (a)–(c) provide an acceptable definition of the concept of a *shared rule*, however, they do not capture the concept of a *convention*. For they apply equally to shared *prudential* rules, such as the rule not to go out into the rain unprotected. Conventions are shared rules that satisfy an additional requirement:

(e)   it would have been feasible for members of C to proceed according to a different regularity R′ without incurring substantial disadvantages

As Lewis noted, the terms "convention" and "conventional" carry a connotation of *arbitrariness*: there is no such thing as "the only possible convention" (1969, 70).

This point has to be handled with care. First, it does not preclude some conventions from being superior to others. Systems of measurement are arbitrary, yet the metric system is superior to the imperial one. Secondly, to say that a regularity R is arbitrary in the sense of (e) is not say that it would be convenient or even feasible to alter it. It may be unfeasible for most of the world to switch from driving on the right to driving on the left, yet this is a convention nonetheless. That is why (e) speaks counterfactually about the past. Thirdly, mere feasibility is not enough. It is feasible in principle to *abandon* many of the rules of the criminal code, yet these are clearly not conventional in the same sense in which some other legal rules are, not to mention the rules of etiquette. Fourthly, we have to distinguish the convenience or feasibility of other regularities from the convenience or feasibility of other sanctions. It would not be convenient or even feasible to impose the death penalty for every breach of etiquette, yet it might be convenient to adopt a different etiquette. Finally, not all arbitrary shared rules would commonly count as conventions. Consider for instance the absurd rules dictated by tyrants—e.g. having to sing the International at the end of every meeting. It may seem that these are not conventions, because they are accepted solely because of fear of sanctions. This may suggest that by contrast to shared rules in general, conventions feature something like Hart's internal point of view. But while we would tend to speak of *diktats* rather than conventions here, we would not regard the latter term as inappropriate.

In summary, my definition runs: a convention is a *shared, arbitrary rule*. It is a *rule* because it provides reasons for regular behaviour either directly or because of sanctions—(d). It is a *shared* rule because conformity is widespread in a community, because deviations are subject to normative reactions, and because these reactions are generally accepted—(a) to (c). And it is arbitrary because a different rule might have been adopted—(e).

9. Language and Convention

Expressions (acoustic or typographic signs) do not have an *intrinsic* meaning. Rather, what they mean is determined by how they are used. As a result, what a linguistic expression means is arbitrary in the following respects:

- in different languages, different words are used to mean one and the same thing;
- one and the same linguistic form can mean different things in different languages (e.g. "link" in English and German);
- we could in principle use words to mean something different from what they in fact mean.

The debate between individualists and communitarians over (CM) therefore turns on whether arbitrary semantic principles must be shared between speaker and hearer, or, more generally, between the members of a linguistic community. Individualist opponents of (CM) argue as follows: if the meaning of an expression *e* in a language L is determined or constituted by the use speakers make of *e*, the meaning of *e* cannot at the same time prescribe a certain use to the speakers of L. Accordingly, the idea that the use of *e* is governed by shared lexical norms is a lapse into the Platonist picture according to which "the meanings of words are magically independent of the speaker's intentions" (Davidson 1990, 310).

But one must distinguish between the use an individual speaker makes of *e*, and the use that the linguistic community makes of it. *Communal* use may *constitute* meaning, while *individual* use is *responsible* to it. From this perspective, the existence of lexical norms and their independence from the utterances and intentions of individual speakers is no more mysterious than the existence of legal norms and their independence from the acts and motives of individual agents.

Individualists standardly grant that we tend to speak as others do, while insisting that this is for extrinsic social reasons that are inessential to linguistic communication (e.g. Bilgrami 1993, 136). Thus agents may conform to a linguistic regularity or convention for extrinsic, i.e. prudential reasons, namely to be understood by or be in line with the majority. As a result, anti-normativists contend, the regularity itself cannot have an intrinsic normative status.

The objection is subject to a *reductio ad absurdum*. A variant of its premise holds even for the most obviously normative phenomena, such as prescriptive rules or commands. A shopkeeper can be honest *both* because it pays off through establishing trust in her customers *and* because she feels duty-bound. Accordingly, if the objection were sound, there would hardly be any intrinsic normative phenomena. Furthermore, the objection goes wrong because it fails to distinguish between the normative status of a rule on the one hand, and the various reasons agents may have for abiding by or disregarding a rule on the other.

Although conventions need not serve any prudential purposes, they can. In such cases one can engage in a certain behaviour both because of a convention *and* because it is in one's interest. For example, we are well advised to drive on the left in Britain simply to avoid accidents. Yet this has no tendency to show that it is not a convention to drive on the left (Schroeder 1998, § 15). There is no *general* linguistic convention to do or speak as others do.[7] Rather, there are conventions to use particular words in specific ways. And it is in general prudent to speak as others do, i.e. to follow the generally

---

[7] Any such rule would be prudential (a point of agreement with anti-normativists like Reboul, cf. this volume, 292) and highly defeasible. But there *may* be normative expectations of conformity of an implicit and diffuse kind, arising from enculturation and participation in a joint linguistic practice.

accepted conventions, because otherwise you are liable to be misunderstood or to be excluded from linguistic communication.

Confronted with such normative aspects of our linguistic behaviour, some anti-normativists worry *both* about their differing from paradigmatic cases like moral imperatives *and* about their not being distinctively linguistic. One should firmly resist this "Heads I win, tails you lose!" tactic. The crucial point remains. Linguistic meaning is normative in a perfectly familiar and respectable sense: it presupposes rules/conventions that are constitutive of the meaning of specific expressions and that resist reduction to prudential or moral norms about behaviour in general. This is of course perfectly compatible with these *sui generis* rules/conventions sharing *some* features with non-semantic or non-linguistic norms; indeed, it is difficult to fathom how they could qualify as norms unless they did.

10. Convention and Communication

A weightier objection to (CM) is that knowledge of or adherence to shared rules is neither necessary nor sufficient for successful linguistic communication. For malapropisms, spoonerisms, and similar infelicities are not merely common, but commonly understood (Davidson 2005, chs. 8–9). In appropriate circumstances, we have no difficulty in understanding Mrs Malaprop's remark, "A nice derangement of epitaphs," as meaning "a nice arrangement of epithets." The question remains whether such understanding does not rely on a background of shared conventions after all. For one thing, from the fact that people can deviate sometimes, it does not follow that they could always deviate. It is difficult to see how we might all be constantly committing malapropisms without communication breaking down. For another, while we are often, albeit by no means always, capable of understanding semantic infelicities, this may be limited to recognizable and, in some way, intelligible *deviations* from a shared norm. Finally, in the case of malapropisms, what we understand is what speakers *meant to say*, not what *they actually said* or the literal meaning of the expressions they uttered.

Individualists rightly point out that communication can succeed even between individuals who do not share a language, even passively. In interactions with foreigners, we sometimes communicate by way of facial expressions, gestures, and intonation. The moot question is whether there is or could be communication by *language* without semantic conventions, based solely on a mutual process of ingenious mutual interpretation of speaker's meanings. Our concept of language is not sufficiently clear-cut to provide a definite answer. But verbal communication without conventions, and hence without literal meaning, would definitely be incapable of expressing the fine-grained thoughts we can express in natural languages. This is crucial to the unique role such languages play for human beings. They allow us to express and communicate complex thoughts even to strangers, people of whose beliefs, intentions, and desires we are largely ignorant. Semantic conventions may not be part of the essence of linguistic communication, yet nevertheless are required by the anthropological function language has for our species of social primates. Finally, the debate about shared intentionality (Gilbert 1996) suggests that obligations can arise from the structure of a practice that we participate in. By these lights, an obligation to speak as others do can result from our participation in the practice of linguistic communication, a practice we engage in willy-nilly, as a result of enculturation.

11. Conventions and the Phylogenesis of Language

While an appeal to conventions can explain legal norms, by pain of regress it cannot explain language in the same manner, because enunciating conventions presupposes language (Russell 1921, 190; Davidson 1984, 280). Nevertheless, given that there is a difference between a rule and its linguistic formulation, there can be *implicit* rules that guide our communicative behaviour without having been enunciated or being consciously consulted (Brandom 1994, ch. 1; Glock 2003, 92–5, 247–8). Language probably arose when cooperative activities put a premium on the intentional and regular use of signals, a communicative practice that gradually became subject to mutual normative expectations and sanctions (Tomasello 2008). But it remains to be shown how this process can be conceptualized and explained without assuming that the subjects possess mental faculties of a kind that in turn presuppose language.

Davidson has advanced an argument that would rule out such an explanation *ab initio*.

(P$_1$)   All conventions (implicit ones included) presuppose
          beliefs and intentions about the beliefs and intentions of
          others

(P$_2$)   Beliefs and intentions about the beliefs and intentions of
          others presuppose language

(C)   All conventions presuppose language

(P$_1$) holds given the definition by Lewis that Davidson is building on. But it is implausible for my weaker conception, which demands only that the participants be capable of intentional action and of beliefs and attitudes towards the *behaviour* of others. For sanctions can in this context be understood without reference to the intentions of those who impose them, namely as adverse reactions to a deviation from a regularity. Linguistic communication began when the regular use of signals started to provide individuals with reasons for verbal behaviour and then became subject to normative reactions and sanctions.

In any event, (P₂) is wrong. *Pace* Davidson, non-linguistic creatures can have not just beliefs and intentions, but also beliefs and intentions concerning the beliefs and intentions of others. A majority of animal psychologists maintains that great apes have such beliefs, since they pass some false belief tests and engage in tactical deception like the hide and peek strategy. Many of the most promising genetic theories of both language evolution (Rizzolatti and Arbib 1998; Tomasello 1999) and language acquisition (Bloom 2000) take mind-reading abilities to be a prerequisite for language. Even if they are wrong, however, the a priori circularity objection founders. (P₂) is not a conceptual truth, since we can clearly conceive of non-linguistic hominins that display beliefs about mental states of their con-specifics (Glock 2000). And the notion of a shared rule devised in section 8 can be operationalized for non-linguistic creatures. To show this in detail, however, must be left to another occasion.[8]

---

[8] Sections 3–5 are derived from parts of Glock (2014a). For comments and assistance I am grateful to Kai Büttner, Javier Kalhat, and Meret Polzer, as well as to audiences in Zurich and Prague. Special thanks are due to the participants of the 2013 and 2014 "The Normative Animal" meetings at Münster, first and foremost to the editors Kurt Bayertz and Neil Roughley for their suggestions and forbearance.

PART V

Afterword

16

Normative Guidance, Deontic Statuses, and the Normative Animal Thesis

Neil Roughley

According to H. L. A. Hart, there is a "whole distinctive style of human thought, speech and action which is involved in the existence of rules" (Hart 1961, 88). If such rules pervasively and essentially structure human social, moral, and linguistic practice, and if they are moreover created, upheld, and enforced by the human beings to whom they apply, then we have strong support for the claim that humans are indeed essentially normative animals in a strong sense. It might, then, be the case that our nature as social, moral, and linguistic animals is explained by, or grounds in this more basic fact.

The various positions developed in the chapters of this book dedicated to "normative" features of each of these overlapping areas of human activity suggest different responses to this basic anthropological hypothesis. A natural way to approach the hypothesis is via the relationship of social norms to the standards in play in linguistic and morally relevant behaviour. The strategy of moving from social norms to the other two areas suggests itself here because of the lack of reasonable controversy as to whether there are social norms that play a decisive role in structuring human behaviour (cf. this volume, Chapter 1, 16ff.). Whether, and in what respects we should think of moral principles and linguistic rules as analogous to, or even as a sub-class of, social norms is then a natural way to approach our question. Its answer depends in the first instance on the analysis of the nature and function of social norms.

In what follows, I will begin with an assessment of the extent to which social norms can fulfil such a paradigmatic function. I will then proceed to discuss two features whose instantiation would be key to the truth of the core claim of the normative animal thesis: that humans regulate their behaviour in line with what they take to be their rights and obligations (NA2: this volume, Chapter 1, 13).

The first is behavioural regulation of the relevant type, which I take to be that of intentional guidance. The second concerns the concepts of obligations and of related normative statuses, to which human agents orientate their action in exercising such intentional guidance. The elucidation of both features responds to key challenges to the normative animal thesis raised in the contributions to this volume. It may appear both that there is no plausible mechanism of intentional guidance that can explain the relevant sort of conformity to normative strictures and that there is no plausible generic concept of obligation that could figure in all three areas foregrounded in the volume. I will argue that we have reasons to be optimistic that both of these challenges can be met. In the final section of this afterword, I return to the normative animal thesis and argue that, although further research in various areas is required, it may indeed turn out that the thesis picks out a key structural feature of the human life form.

1. Social Norms as Paradigms

The contributions to this volume contain both broad and narrow conceptions of social norms. Kappeler, Fichtel, and van Schaik (this volume, 68-72), like Mertens (105-115), distinguish social norms from conventions, where the latter are arbitrary, a feature manifested either in the belief of relevant agents that other rules would have been possible or in the fact that conformity is established by pure imitation without insight into utility. Mertens further excludes from the category any rules that are institutionally, for instance, legally framed, thus breaking the connection between the regulation of small-scale everyday interaction, on the one hand, and institutional regulations, on the other, a connection that is taken to be analytically decisive by Hart and Gilbert. Clearly, the narrower the concept of social norms at issue, the less plausible will be any analogies with other standards. Most obviously, if conventions are not social norms and if the decisive linguistic standards are conventions, there will be a conceptual gap between the two kinds of case.

Nevertheless, even if we begin with such narrow conceptualisations, there remains the possibility that there is a basic generic concept that is specified when we turn to particular types of activity, or to the subjection of activities to particular types of standards. To be clear on this structural point: it is unimportant whether the adjective "social" is used to pick out a broad set of norms that might be distinguished as "informal" and "formal," as "conventions," "laws," "traditions," and "customs," or whether "social" norms are thought of as a class on the same classificatory level as the members of the latter grouping and the generic concept is picked out by some other qualifier, say "societal." What is decisive for a discussion of the normative animal thesis is whether there is plausibly some corresponding generic class of norms and, if so, what their defining and perhaps characteristic features are.

If, as Glock proposes (313-5), conventions are a type of social rules or norms whose differentia specifica lies in the arbitrary character of their content, this leaves the structure constitutive of social norms untouched. In contrast, both Mertens and Kappeler et al., whilst emphasising the arbitrary character of conventions, add a further feature they take to be definitive of norms, but not necessarily present in conventions. This is an attitudinal feature that Kappeler et al. call a "sense of oughtness" (79) and which Mertens characterises as a strong sense of "obligation" (109). Similarly, Schmidt and Rakoczy (124) see normative attitudinising as involving representations of "oughtness," which they associate with a self-understanding as the bearer of obligations. These characterisations raise the question of whether, when an agent takes it that she ought to do something for reasons not deriving from social norms, this involves no such "sense of oughtness." Moreover, if such a sense and a sense of obligation are taken to be equivalent, this assumes that the concept of obligation at work is considerably weaker than that frequently invoked. Hart, for instance, takes it that obligations are the mark of only some social rules that are particularly important for the society and are thus reinforced by particularly insistent reactive attitudes. However, it seems clear that the normative animal thesis requires some generic concept, property, or sense of ought that can play a role in social, moral, and linguistic contexts. It will need to be open for weaker understandings than that often taken to be decisive for *moral obligation*, but it will also need to be more robust than the mere notion of *"ought"* as it figures in *all practical deliberation* (cf. Chapter 1, 8-10).

One way in which the relevant notion might be given substance has appeared to be in terms of reactions to non-conformity to the relevant standards. Accounts of this kind have to avoid the problem of circularity, which arises because they need to presuppose standards, which in turn raises the question of what it is that sets the standards. Clearly, the answer cannot be in terms of the reactions to the standards' contravention. There is perhaps an important difference here between reactions that are essentially intentional, reactions that often go under the labels "punishment" and "sanction," and attitudinal or emotional reactions that may occur spontaneously. Whilst reactions of this latter kind may, like reactions of the former kind, presuppose the standards, it is also conceivable that they derive from pre-normative dispositions.

Such reactive features are central to the approach developed by Schmidt and Rakoczy. Moreover, Antweiler's discussion (96-8) of normative socialisation by means of the inculcation of strong negative emotional dispositions could be understood as evidence for a view that sees emotions as standard setters. However, adducing strong emotions would significantly restrict the extension of the relevant concept of social norms. Antweiler's own distinction between "mores" and "folkways," where the latter appear also describable as "conventions," indicates that not all broadly "social" or "cultural" norms should be understood in this way. On the other hand, Schmidt and Rakoczy's work both on children's protest at the infraction of game norms and on their tendency to incorrectly infer norms concerning the way "things are done" (125-8) provides evidence that emotions may also be at work in apparently insubstantial everyday cases. Such protest might be thought to be descended from primates' spontaneous aggressive reactions in dyadic interaction contexts, where such reactions, as reported by Kappeler et al., effectively discourage others from repeating or completing unwanted behaviour (75).

Whether or not such reactions are taken to *set* the relevant standards, there is a general consensus that some such emotional or more directly observable behavioural tendencies are at least *epistemic criteria* for the presence of social norms in the wider sense. A further candidate for such a role in the case of social norms is that of behavioural regularities. Kappeler et al., Antweiler, Mertens, van Schaik and Burkart Enfield and Sidnell, Reboul, and Glock all take it that relevant forms of repeated action on the part of a society's members are at least epistemically necessary for us to appropriately talk of "social norms."[1] Those regularities may be thought to necessarily *result from* the application of the standards, if those standards are to count as social norms. Alternatively, it might be thought that it is the behavioural regularities that do the standard-*setting*. A third possibility is that the behavioural regularity is simply a *criterially unconnected* second feature that must be conjoined with the existence of the standards for them to count as social norms.

Glock takes it that both the first and the second kind of relationship hold. From a genealogical point of view, he claims that the standards come into being as a result of the habituation and internalisation of regular behaviour (313). This seems to amount to an assertion of the conjunctive necessity of behaviour and relevant attitudes. Glock also agrees with Mertens, Kappeler et al., Antweiler, Reboul, and Enfield and Sidnell that, where standards exist and apply, there will be corresponding behaviour of the norms' addressees.

However, if the concept of a social norm requires such efficacy in its implementation, this is one feature that is ill-suited to serve as a paradigm for all types of norms. Although such general efficacy may be a plausible feature of linguistic conventions, it seems to be no necessary part of the concept of moral principles. Indeed, as was pointed out in Chapter 1 of this volume (19), Hart himself retracts it as a general condition on a broader type of social norm that includes legal rules.

2. Normative Action Guidance

Whether or not social norms are necessarily expressed in regularities of behaviour, the question of how they guide their addressees' action, when they do, is paramount. The contributors to the volume offer varying thoughts on this issue. In the chapters

---

[1] See this volume, 70-2, 77-80, 91-2, 105-7, 139, 146, 266-7, 279-81, 298-9.

by Mertens, and by Enfield and Sidnell, there is emphasis on the fact that the relevant form of guidance requires no actual conscious thought, that guidance being "unthematic" (116) or "subliminal" (266). As both of these characterisations are negative, they shed little light on the mechanisms that are doing the work.

Antweiler refers to proposals from cognitive science, according to which norms function as "scripts" (95), i.e. mental representations taken to be responsible for automatic forms of action and largely unamenable to conscious access. Such proposals might be thought to do the explanatory work required. However, they don't look particularly promising as accounts of the normative guidance of intentional action, i.e. of action that its agent takes herself to be performing for reasons provided by the norms. Reboul argues that at least the capacity to formulate the relevant norms must be in place (281, 290). These fairly demanding requirements restrict significantly the cases of behaviour that might be thought to count as resulting from norm- or rule-following, in particular excluding much behaviour guided by the constraints of linguistic compositionality. Glock, in contrast, sees as sufficient the ability to recognise that a certain form of behaviour is "the way things are done," an ability that is at work where what he thinks of as implicit rules are followed (299). Where the agent is able to repeat the behaviour of other agents, it is fairly easy to see how this explanation works. In such cases, there is a clear sense in which the behaviour itself can be taken to do the standard-setting. Where, however, the agent has to compose her behavioural contribution anew, there remain questions as to how Glock's recognitional ability fulfils the explanatory role he assigns it.

This point is applicable to all accounts according to which the triggering of reactive attitudes to non-conformity is epistemically sufficient to confirm the subscription of the reacting agent to the relevant norm, a position that unites most of the contributions to the volume. There has to be some connection between the causes of such reactions and whatever it is that explains the actions that are guided by the norms. An obvious candidate is that the reactions are further manifestations of the attitudes responsible for actions that follow the norm. Moreover, if it is claimed that the mode of existence of the norms is essentially that of collective attitudinising, there would appear to be potential here for closely connected accounts of the metaphysics of social norms and both rule-following action and critical reactions to the non-conformity of relevant agents.

However, such a model might be thought to run head-on into the problem insisted on by Reboul and which Glock's notions of implicit rules and associated recognitional capacities are intended to avoid. Clearly, if a necessary condition for the existence of a norm consists in the implementation of attitudes, in particular shared attitudes, on the part of the members of a population, as Kappeler et al., Schmidt and Rakoczy, Bayertz, Steinfath, and I all argue,[2] the action-guiding role of the relevant

---

[2] Cf this volume, pages 69-72, 122-3, 162-5, 188-90, 241-2.

attitudes cannot be dependent on their being conscious. One model that might be able to deal with the problem is the model of virtual guidance that is sketched in Chapter 1 (33), according to which attitudes, whether conscious or not, only need play a role where problems with habitual conformity arise. Such a model in turn raises the question as to the precise relationship between the explanation of habitual norm conformity and conscious rule following: does behaviour of both kinds have the same kinds of causes? Might the distinction between dispositional and occurrent attitudes carry sufficient explanatory weight or is automatic norm conformity to be explained by completely different kinds of psychological mechanisms? If the latter, how is the claim to be upheld that the action is guided by taking the norm to provide a reason?

These questions, which point to a key action-theoretic dimension of the normative animal thesis, are given particular emphasis in the discussion of linguistic norms, both here and in the body of the literature. Nevertheless, it ought to be clear that the same questions are pertinent both for social and moral norms. It would, for example, be obviously false to claim that moral principles are generally adhered to as a result of immediately antecedent conscious choices to act in accordance with them.

As is well known, Kant made a big thing of a distinction between acting "in accordance with duty" and acting "out of duty," insisting that only actions of the latter pedigree have moral worth (Kant 1788, 67f.). If an agent only acts out of duty when she in the situation consciously chooses to act because of what she takes to be a valid principle, then there will be an extremely restricted number of actions with moral worth. We may or may not agree with Kant's evaluative claim that actions with natural motivational sources such as empathy can have no such moral worth. What is decisive for our purposes here is what looks to be an explanatory claim. It seems that Kant is claiming that actions performed in line with moral prescriptions because the agents have developed corresponding automatic orientations in the course of their upbringing are not performed "out of duty." However, there is a clear and important sense in which such actions do involve following relevant moral orientations. Indeed, these cases appear to be the decisive ones for the development and maintenance of coherent—and decent—moral communities. Kant himself thought that it was an open question whether any human actions have ever had "moral worth." There can, however, be no question that very many human agents, in acting, frequently take it that their actions satisfy relevant moral constraints, just as they frequently take it that their utterances conform to relevant linguistic constraints. Hence, the key questions concerning the following of linguistic rules also require an answer from authors who think that morally right action involves following moral principles.

The jury is still out on whether a satisfactory explanation of rule-, or norm-following can be provided that will meet three central desiderata here: first, it ought to cover both cases in which explicit choice is involved and in which the relevant action is automatic. Second, it should nevertheless be sufficiently unitary to count as an explanation of a single type of behaviour, a concern that is particularly pressing for a causal theory of action. Third, it would need to clarify whether, and, if so, why we should take the behaviour thus explained as intentional in both choice-based and automatic cases. Perhaps, as suggested in the preceding (and cf. Chapter 1, note 21), a form of virtual intentionality might suffice.

3. Deontic Statuses

A further key point on which clarity is required in order to assess the normative animal thesis concerns the statuses conferred by norms. Social norms assign statuses that we may describe as "obligations" or "duties," as "rights" or "entitlements," as "permissions" or "allowances," and as "prohibitions" or "proscriptions." These may be expressed in terms of "oughts," although "oughts" need no such deontic backing, as some, in particular the all-things-considered "ought," ground in the balance of reasons, whether or not those reasons themselves ground in norms. Moreover, everyday usage would appear to assume a difference in strength between what is picked out by some of these terms. "Entitlement," for instance, may be taken to be weaker than "right," in as far as rights are thought to correlate with "duties." Certainly, in everyday speech, people don't talk very much about "duties" outside explicit institutional contexts. In this, everyday talk differs from the talk of moral philosophers, who traditionally use the terms "obligations" and "duties" to pick out one of their central topics. And although it seems natural to say that someone is obligated or has a duty to—or "must"—help others in desperate need, it sounds hopelessly overdramatic to declare that speakers of English have a duty not to call a whale a fish. The question raised by the normative animal thesis is whether we have a sufficiently unified set of statuses in the social, moral, and linguistic dimensions to justify seeing them as providing the same kinds of orientation for behaviour in each of these dimensions. We shouldn't rule out the possibility that there may be a generic set of statuses for which everyday language does not have generic terms.

In this section, I will begin by clarifying why the mere orientation to standards cannot be sufficient for our purposes here. I will then go on to discuss two ways in which additional conditions may be thought to be sufficient for the kinds of deontic statuses which would need to be in play across the board for the normative animal thesis to be true, or interestingly true. Both construals work once again with the fact that non-adherence to the relevant standards tends to trigger attitudinal or behavioural reactions on the part of other agents. However, they cash out the importance of such reactions for deontic statuses in very different ways.

3.1. Standards

Begin, then, with the fact that humans generally orientate their behaviour to *standards*. This is in itself an anthropologically significant feature of their intentional action. However, it doesn't only apply to intentional action: we at least frequently see our emotions as more or less appropriate to relevant standards. Importantly, intentional action can be guided by the striving to satisfy standards where doing so isn't a matter of meeting an obligation. The exercise of skills by a boxer, a poet, or a salesman generally involves, as Ryle pointed out, the "observance of rules or canons" (Ryle 1949, 46–8).[3] But this is not because the boxer, poet, or salesman is obligated by those standards. Clearly, then, the applicability of standards, that is, of reason-providing criteria, is insufficient to ground obligations. The basic reason for this is that the standards for skilled performance are, by and large, standards for goodness or excellence of performance, even though a certain level of abjectness in performance might justify the rejection of the claim that the agent is boxing, producing poetry, or functioning as a salesman at all.

In discussing what he calls "bare normativity," Glock is explicit that the relevant standards are standards of *correctness*, from whose infringement, he claims, it follows that others have a reason to intervene and "correct" the performance in question (306). Clearly, this doesn't entail that anyone has a *decisive* reason for corrective action. Whether the reason has this status will depend on other features of the situation, not least on the importance of the standard in question. Once this is taken into account, however, inadequate boxing or application of sales techniques seem to share this reason-generating feature. Nevertheless, such reasons only come into play for very specific agents, such as the boxer's or salesman's trainer, perhaps for other employees of the firm the salesman works for, or for the agents themselves. This in turn derives from the fact that meeting the standards tends to be only of importance for agents who have set themselves to meet them, where the relevant agents may be some sort of collective, such as a sales company. Meeting the standards in play is their business and, ceteris paribus, theirs alone.

Standards of correctness, in contrast to standards of goodness, are categorical, rather than scalar. The latter can be met more or less well, whereas the former can be met or missed. They can, of course, be missed by a smaller or bigger margin, differences which may be significant for the evaluation of the case. Nevertheless, a miss is a miss, whereas performances viewed in the light of standards of goodness are often labelled

---

[3] Although learning to walk involves developing a "natural" ability for humans, that doesn't entail that there are no standards in play here. Does the joke in Monty Python's Ministry of Silly Walks sketch ground in the contravention of such standards (in a context where the conformity to standards is taken to be paramount) or in the conceit that there are such standards, although plausibly no such standards exist?

with adverbial qualifiers such as "quite," "fairly," "not very," "very," "extremely," and so on.

Where standards of correctness are set by collective attitudinising or perhaps by collective practices, the standard setters satisfy NA3 (Chapter 1, 13). Where the standards are a priori, as is plausible for the standards of rationality, this will not be so. Now add to this difference the fact that we don't think of the requirements of rationality as generating obligations, although they certainly can require behaviour of us or tell us what we ought to do. This conjunction might suggest that obligation hangs together with the way in which socially set standards are instituted. As is repeatedly emphasised in the contributions to this volume, the existence of norms goes hand in hand with particular kinds of reaction to their contravention. These might be arranged in an ascending order of *obtrusiveness* or *insistence*.

3.2. Obtrusiveness

At the bottom of the scale, we might place the tendency of such contraventions to be noticed, what Enfield and Sidnell call "abliminality," and their tendency to generate putative explanations on the part of observers (267). Such tendencies don't necessarily interfere with the further behaviour of the norm-breaker, although, where they are part of linguistic turn-taking sequences that involve her, they will tend to have an effect on her next move.

Reactions that may tend to exert a greater influence on the infractor might be emotional reactions such as surprise, amusement, or pity, where these are openly expressed. Note, though, that where such reactions affect the agent whose behaviour causes them, this will be for the same reason that they influence an agent who does anything merely out of the ordinary. Someone who is sensitive to being laughed at or pitied for doing something out of the ordinary will presumably be so whether that behaviour is simply statistically unusual or whether it fails to meet some standards.

The reactions that have generally been taken to be intimately connected with norm contravention are reactions that Strawson labelled the "reactive attitudes." Although Strawson used the label to cover a wider set, the attitudes that are taken by several of the contributors, in particular by Steinfath and myself, to be key here are resentment, indignation, and guilt. Their occurrence and expression tends to be seriously disruptive of relationships, in the last case, of an agent's relationship to herself.

Finally, there are various forms of intentional reaction to the infraction of norms that can come in differing strengths. Criticism may involve a simple evaluation of an action on the basis of its contravening the norm or may go much further, moving from an assessment of the action to a global assessment of the agent (cf. Antweiler, 97). Protest against a particular action may also be more or less emotional, expressing reactive attitudes and may again develop into protest against agents, not just their actions (cf. Schmidt and Rakoczy, 129-31). At the top end of the scale, the practice of institutional or sub-institutional deliberate sanctioning, which may consist in a mere cold shoulder, in complete exclusion from some social context, or in explicit punishment of one form or another, is also typically associated with many norms.

Hart's claim that we begin appropriately to talk of "obligations" when the social pressure to conformity reaches a certain level of insistence or seriousness (Hart 1961, 86f.) presumably entails that obligations come into play beyond some seriousness threshold in the kinds of practices just depicted. Thus understood, there are some contexts in which it is clearly inappropriate to talk of obligations (Hart names etiquette and the conjugation of verbs), others where it is clearly appropriate, and a set of vague cases somewhere in between. Such an account, however, seems to make the introduction of the term "obligation" merely a linguistic label for part of a practice marked by particular kinds of interpersonal disturbances, where the practice otherwise has pretty much the same structure. If this is correct as an analysis of everyday terminology and if the normative animal is indeed an animal that in the relevant dimensions of its behaviour orients itself to normative statuses we label as obligations, then clearly our linguistic activity would not be thus covered and the thesis would be massively weakened.

3.3. Accountability

There is, however, another way of interpreting the same material that would be much more accommodating to a broader understanding of "obligation" and thus to the normative animal thesis. This interpretation might start with a claim of Stephen Darwall's, underscored by Steinfath, according to which the concept of obligation is internally bound up with that of *accountability*. Darwall contrasts the relationship to standards taken on where accountability is in play with the relationship taken on to standards which have no such internal relation to accountability. As an example of the latter, Darwall names the standards of logic. Clearly, we get things right or wrong in the light of these standards. Consequently, criticism of logical mistakes may be appropriate. However, we are not accountable to anyone for our logical performances, unless there are additional moral or social standards, for instance, standards of due care, that apply (Darwall 2006, 26f.).

If this is correct, then perhaps the hallmark of obligation lies in the relationship of the relevant normative statuses to accountability. Moreover, perhaps it may be worth investigation whether different species of obligation have internal connections to different modes of accountability. The various kinds of reactions to the contravention of standards might then turn out to be relevant not because of the degree of their intrusiveness, but rather in virtue of constituting different ways of holding accountable. A suggestion in this direction can be gleaned from the contributions to this volume because Steinfath's remarks on moral accountability (107-8) are echoed by Enfield and Sidnell's claim that linguistic norms are at core devices that ground accountability (266).

The essence of moral accountability on Darwall's account is *answerability*: holding to account involves demanding from the infractor either a justification of her action, an excuse that shows why blaming misses the target, or else acceptance of blame. Acceptance of moral blame involves coming to feel guilt, which Darwall takes to be equivalent to the acceptance of the appropriateness of resentment or indignation of others (Darwall 2018, 298ff.). Its non-acceptance, on the other hand, involves the address of justifications or excuses to the blaming party.

According to such an account, then, moral accountability has two features that are decisive for our question. First, its *currency* is a specific set of emotional reactions and, second, it is essentially a matter of *interactive address* focussed on reasons for and against the appropriateness of such reactions. If an analysis along these lines is correct and if obligation and accountability are internally related, then the following structure suggests itself as supporting the normative animal thesis: accountability might be a generic matter of interactive address that presupposes reasons for that address and demands reasons from the addressee, where insufficient provision of reasons by the addressee is taken to justify reactions that exert some kind of pressure. Different species of accountability might be distinguished by varying currencies, that is, by differences in the reactions for and against which the reasons count. Differing reactive currencies and types of relevant reasons might in turn be connected to differing species of obligation.

It is certainly plausible that there are forms of social accountability that parallel those in the moral case. Clearly, if we are working with a broad conception of social norms, the decisive reaction types are going to be differentiated according to the more specific types of social norms in play. Accountability in terms of the penal law involves being required to provide excuses or justifications in the face of the threat of institutional punishment. Accountability for one's behaviour in view of informal social norms will involve reasons for and against reactions that overlap strongly with the reactions decisive for moral accountability. Mertens mentions disapproval, ignoring, and the termination of cooperation (102). These may all result in moral cases, although at least the latter two may be thought to be secondary relative to the key feature of blame. The relationship between blame and what is sometimes called "moral disapproval" is, on the other hand, no doubt contestable. The ontogenetic studies reported by Schmidt and Rakoczy involve similar forms of more or less emotionally coloured "protest" in both moral and non-moral cases (125-6, 130-1; cf. also Kappeler et al., 75).

There are various proposals as to how one should differentiate here between the moral and the merely social case. Alongside Mertens's distinction in terms of the universality or cultural specificity of the norms themselves, a proposal that coincides with one of Turiel and Dahl's parameters, there are a number of suggestions as to how the structure of the accountability relation itself differs. Brennan et al., who claim that the creation of accountability relations is the central function of norms (Brennan et al. 2013, 36ff.), argue that the difference between moral and social norms lies in the types of values the three variables in the structure *X is accountable to Y in virtue of Z* can have. X, they claim, is in the moral case all individuals, in the social case, the individual members of a particular social group; Y they take to be all other individuals in the former case, the members of the group in the latter; and Z, they believe, is intrinsic properties of individual agents where we are dealing with moral accountability, but shared group membership where the accountability is social (Brennan et al. 2013, 87ff.). This is a useful schema, which ties in closely with the proposals of social domain theory, as well as with the results on differential responses to infractions of moral and game rules presented by Schmidt and Rakoczy (130). It is no doubt also a schema for which different authors represented in this volume would propose different values, particularly where moral accountability is at issue. In line with his grounding of morality in collective intentionality, Steinfath may take Y, in the moral case, to be all members of an individual's "moral community"; Bayertz and perhaps van Schaik and Burkart might be prepared to simply substitute all the members of the society or cultural group of which the individual is a member.

In spite of the differences in views as to how one should precisely fill out the schema, there is a strong plausibility to the claim that it applies to both social and moral norms. In order that the claim can support the normative animal thesis, the relevant modes of accountability need to be seen as connected to normative statuses that can be labelled "obligations" in a sense that is perhaps wider than that labelled by the everyday term, but one that appears operative in the relevant areas of our practices.

The more controversial step would then be to go on to claim that our linguistic, in particular our semantic behaviour is structured by an analogous set of "obligations" that are internally bound up with comparable forms of accountability. On the basis of our discussion so far, the relevant linguistic practices should be bound up with *demands for reasons* where standards of correctness are not met; the reasons should be reasons concerning the appropriateness or inappropriateness of some *specifiable type of negative reaction* to the non-conformity; and there should be plausible types of values for the *variables in the schema* proposed by Brennan et al.

Enfield and Sidnell present claims at two levels concerning the roles of norms and accountability in human linguistic practices, roles that they see as bound up with the applicability of the terms "obligation," "duty," "right," and "entitlement." At the level of pragmatics, they argue that social norms ground accountability relations in the infrastructure of linguistic interaction. These norms concern such matters as conversational turn-taking, the social acceptability of chosen lexical items, and also their referential correctness. At the level of semantics, Enfield and Sidnell claim that social pressures associated particularly with accountability in the latter kinds of case lead to a kind of social precipitation of semantic conventions (265-6).

The key to Enfield and Sidnell's conception is their understanding of holding to account. To hold to account here is to require from a speaker that she "give an account," that is, an explanation of failure to meet the standards for kinds of response and for contents of those responses (276-8). At first blush, this proposal may appear to be far removed from the kind of reason-giving foregrounded in a model of the kind developed by Darwall for moral accountability. Providing an explanation, it might be thought, is very different from providing justification. Moreover, reason giving in a deontic moral context will often involve invoking meta-norms for the applicability of first-order norms, for instance the norm that ought implies can. However, as Enfield and Sidnell argue, the explanations required in linguistic interaction are also themselves subject to standards of appropriateness, standards that do seem to include conditions on ability. Moreover, appropriateness here is narrowly circumscribed by the fact that the requirements on linguistic responding apply specifically to sequences involving two or more agents.

A central difference between the linguistic case, as conceived by Enfield and Sidnell, and the moral case is that, whereas the contexts of moral norm transgression and the contexts of moral blame are often separate, linguistic norm transgression and the corresponding holding to account are generally part of the same interactive sequence. This also has consequences for the answer to the question as to the kinds of responses that constitute holding to account. According to Enfield and Sidnell, the responses will themselves be linguistic in nature. They will frequently involve explicit criticism, claims of inappropriateness, or directives aimed at bringing about a new, corrected performance. They are also often inexplicit, as when a respondent simply expresses exasperation or swaps interlocutors, rather than continuing the original exchange.

The interactive context and linguistic form of both potential norm infractions and holding to account entail further that a move that aims to hold another speaker to account is itself subject to the constraints of accountability. Thus, someone contesting another speaker's description of her or of her action may well be motivated by the desire not to be held accountable for the appropriateness of the first speaker's description. That is, she may be denying that the properties thus picked out are indeed instantiated by her or her action, in order to pre-empt her being held to account for being or acting that way (275). This is, again, a significant difference from the moral case. Of course, when A blames B morally for something that the latter has done, A may be doing so in order to pre-empt herself being held accountable for the consequences of B's action. However, such cases don't manifest anything like a general structure of moral accountability, whereas linguistic accountability, as an essential attribute of sequential interaction, is, according to Enfield and Sidnell, in play with every move in the development of such sequences.

How, finally, should the values in Brennan et al.'s accountability schema be filled in for the linguistic case according to such a model? The persons held accountable are clearly all speakers of a particular language and the feature in virtue of which they are held accountable is simply their capacity to speak the language. And it seems correct to see them as accountable to their linguistic community, although there are, as Glock points out (309), difficulties in individuating linguistic communities. In spite of the difficulties in specifying precise membership conditions, it seems clear that minority groups or subcultures can create linguistic counter-communities, within which smaller scale conventions and associated patterns of accountability are in place.

Of course, there is a sense in which our interactions involve accountability to our co-agents, rather than to any broader communities, whether we are thinking in terms of moral, social, or linguistic communities. A particular person who is most directly affected—by attacks on her integrity, by disturbances in action coordination, or by semantic confusion—will have a special entitlement to call out an agent who brings about such circumstances through norm infraction. Nevertheless, the case of norms sustained between only two persons will be exceptional and part of the entitlement of the sufferer from such infractions will concern the capacity to call on other members of the relevant community to confirm the stability of the accountability relation thus invoked.

If something along these lines is correct, then there is a sense in which "obligations" of a generic or formal kind, alongside "rights" of a comparable status, are indeed central features of linguistic, like social and moral behaviour. Obligations and rights thus understood would be normative statuses internally bound up with accountability relations. This would be the case even though both the *contents* of those obligations and the substantial features of the associated accountability *relations* would differ significantly.

Even if this is accepted, there remains a particularly large gap between the obtrusiveness of moral and social accountability on the one hand, and linguistic accountability on the other. Whereas moral accountability is a high-profile feature of our everyday life, linguistic accountability may tend to disappear under our social-perceptual radar. This may be because of its omnipresence in every move in linguistic interaction; it may be because of the linguistic nature of both holding to account and of that for which agents are accountable; and it may be because of the easy reversibility of many linguistic norm infractions, whose amendment may result from the lightest of corrective touches. These points might be best understood as marking superficial differences that don't tell against there being deeper structural commonalities in accountability relations. These commonalities would then support a generic understanding of the kind of deontic structures required for there to be obligations in play across the board where social, moral, and linguistic standards of correctness are pertinent.

4. Normative Animals?

Two of the biggest obstacles to the truth of the normative animal thesis—that of an explanation of intentional, yet largely inexplicit norm conformity and that of formal concepts of the key normative statuses—may, then, have solutions. Making the thesis stick would, however, require further work on a number of fronts.

First, we would need to examine in some detail the four kinds of relation between potentially normative animals and norms that were distinguished in Chapter 1, section 2.3. Paradigmatic social norms seem to uncontroversially instantiate all four relations: they apply to the relevant creatures (NA1); they are used by those creatures to regulate their behaviour (NA2); they are created and upheld by those creatures (NA3); and they are enforced by them (NA4).

Of these relations, NA2 is key for the normative animal thesis. We have discussed in some detail what the regulation of one's behaviour with a view to satisfying the relevant norms might consist in, or alternatively, how precisely their guiding our behaviour should be understood to be implemented psychologically. As it seems clear that there must be an answer to this question for the case of social norms, it is unlikely that there is a principled reason why NA2 cannot be true. The claim that NA2 holds across the board encounters, as Kompa's and Reboul's contributions to this volume (Chapters 12 and 14) show, particular resistance with respect to linguistic behaviour. In view of the proposed alternative, nativist explanations and in view of both the complexity and inaccessibility of some of the standards for speakers of a language, there might be some value in normativists and non-normativists going head to head on specific kinds of test cases. It is perhaps not unlikely that different aspects of linguistic behaviour might be shown to be susceptible to alternative kinds of explanations.

This point raises a second key question for the normative animal thesis. This concerns the extension and importance of normative dimensions in each of the three areas named—in particular in linguistic and moral behaviour. The suggestion just mooted for the linguistic dimensions of our behaviour is that in some of these speakers may be guided by the goal of conforming to standards, whereas other features of their speech and understanding are to be explained differently. As far as the moral dimensions of our behaviour are concerned, we require an answer to two questions: first, how much of morality is obligation-based? For Bayertz, morality is entirely a matter of moral obligation (156); Turiel and Dahl may concur (199). Steinfath's advances the slightly weaker view that obligation is morality's core, if not its entirety (177). Virtue ethicists would demur. Second, do obligations necessarily ground in norms? An affirmative answer to this question is assumed in all the discussions of moral norms in the volume, with the exception of my own, where I suggest that at least some obligations may be particularistic, i.e. irreducibly situation-specific (242). If this were to be correct, moral normativity or deonticity might share with its social and linguistic relatives the key features of guiding intentional action and being internally connected to accountability, even though, unlike them, it doesn't necessarily ground in norms.

Return again to the relations NA1 to NA4. Note that, as NA1 need not be true in order for NA2 to be true, humans could be normative animals in an important sense even if, for example, an error theory of moral obligation and a nativist theory of linguistic—or indeed moral—standards were to be correct. In either of these cases, what might be created, upheld, and enforced would not be standards of moral or linguistic correctness, as NA3 and NA4 specify, but rather standards that agents mistakenly take to determine correctness in these areas. The overall view that would correspond to such a conjunction of positions would be that, whereas humans are socially normative animals, they are in other key areas perhaps better characterised as pseudo-normative animals.

In the case of social norms, the distinction between NA3 (creating and upholding) and NA4 (enforcing) may seem fairly blurred, as abstention from norm-enforcement may effectively contribute to the norm's dissolution. This is not necessarily the case, however, when we turn to moral and linguistic norms. Certainly, a realist about deontic moral facts may think both that the norms that make the relevant propositions true are not created by humans in any important sense, and that human agents expend a lot of energy enforcing those norms. According to such a view, the existence of the normative facts and the extent to which they are conformed to are two entirely different questions. This distinction is also reconstructed by my own account, according to which, although facts about moral obligation are dependent on certain psychological facts, those facts may hold independently of widespread behavioural conformity to the obligations (241-2).

That linguistic standards exist is uncontroversial. That these standards count as norms isn't. My discussion of accountability in section 3.3 is an attempt to show why at least some of the relevant standards should be classified as norms. In her rejection of any such claim, Reboul ties the existence of standards as norms to their fulfilling NA3 (279), which she, in contrast to Enfield and Sidnell (266), and Glock (313), also denies (287, 289, 292). Importantly, the concept of creation at work in NA3 need in no sense entail intentionality, but might itself ground in dispositions with some kind of evolutionary explanation. Some such model might have the potential to mediate between sub-personal and normative explanations of linguistic behaviour.

A final question that would need answering in order to provide clarity on the normative animal thesis concerns not the internal structure of the three dimensions discussed in this volume, but their extension and significance within the human form of life as a whole. Although it seems clear that the social, moral, and linguistic orientations of humans are central to the way they live their lives, there are undoubtedly other forms of orientation that are candidates for similar discussions. The reason for focussing on the three dimensions foregrounded in this volume derives from the traditional significance that has been attached to each of them as potentially distinguishing marks of the human form of life. A complete assessment of the normative animal thesis would, then, naturally require an additional discussion of forms of orientation and evaluation picked out by other traditional characterisations of what has often been thought of as the human essence.

Clearly, rationality, as a central candidate for that role, would require such discussion. The requirements of rationality appear relatively uncontroversially to fulfil NA1, but, as a priori requirements, not to fulfil NA3. The question as to the extent and the way in which they guide behaviour may appear not necessarily to receive answers that parallel those given for the norms that have been our focus. As conforming to the norms of rationality is essentially bound to our attempting to satisfy our own self-interest, enforcement of those norms is, to a significant extent, presumably something we do primarily with respect to our own behaviour and, outside contexts of education and upbringing, relatively rarely with respect to that of others (cf. Chapter 1, section 2.3, 13–15). If this is so, then guiding one's own behaviour in view of the requirements and enforcing them may, over a wide range of cases, be one and the same. Hence, the extent to which, and the way in which we are rational animals might turn out to be significantly different from the extent and ways in which we are social, moral, and linguistic animals.

This result would not need to be seen as weakening the claims of the normative animal thesis, for which NA2 is the key condition. Where we have a group of requirements for which this condition is satisfied and where it is backed by the satisfaction of NA4, we can ask whether their satisfaction of these two conditions pervasively structures the way the members of a species characteristically lead their lives. An affirmative answer to this question would presuppose the solution of the problem of normative action guidance. Its affirmative answer would in turn support the normative animal thesis if the claim were accepted that a generic conception of normative statuses were applicable to requirements of each type.

If the way humans live their lives involves pervasive intentional guidance by conceptions of normative statuses internally bound up with accountability relations, and if humans are pervasively concerned to bring about conformity to those statuses in interaction with conspecifics, where those statuses are of a generic kind that takes social, moral, and linguistic specifications, then humans are normative animals. The sense in which the normative animal thesis is true would be strengthened where, as in social norms, humans are also the originators of the statuses and where the reality of those statuses plausibly explains the conceptions that guide their behaviour.

References

Abu-Lughod, L. 1993. *Writing Women's Worlds: Bedouin Stories.* Berkeley: University of California Press.

Aharoni, E., Sinnott-Armstrong, W., and Kiehl, K. A. 2012. Can Psychopathic Offenders Discern Moral Wrongs? A New Look at the Moral/Conventional Distinction, *Journal of Abnormal Psychology* 121: 484–97.

Alexander, R. D. 1987. *The Biology of Moral Systems.* Hawthorne, NY: Aldine de Gruyter.

Alonso, F. M. 2009. Shared Intention, Reliance, and Interpersonal Obligations, *Ethics* 119: 444–75.

Alsberg, P. 1922. *In Quest of Man: A Biological Approach to the Problem of Man's Place in Nature.* Oxford: Pergamon 1970.

Anderson, J. R., Kuroshima, H., Takimoto, A., and Fujita, K. 2013. Third-Party Social Evaluation of Humans by Monkeys, *Nature Communications* 4: 1561.

Anscombe, G. E. M. 1957. *Intention.* Oxford: Basil Blackwell 1976².

——— 1958. Modern Moral Philosophy, *Philosophy* 32: 1–19.

Antweiler, C. 2012a. *Inclusive Humanism: Anthropological Basics for a Realistic Cosmopolitanism.* Göttingen: V&R Unipress and Taipei: National Taiwan University Press.

——— 2012b. On Cultural Evolution: A Review of Current Research toward a Unified Theory of Societal Change, *Anthropos* 107: 217–27.

——— 2015. Local Knowing as a Universal Social Product: A Model and a Case from Southeast Asia, in P. Meusburger and L. Suarsana (eds.). *Ethnic and Cultural Dimensions of Knowledge.* Berlin: Springer, 1–22.

——— 2016. *Our Common Denominator: Human Universals Revisited.* New York: Berghahn Books.

Apicella, C. L., Marlowe, F. W., Fowler, J. H., and Christakis, N. A. 2012. Social Networks and Cooperation in Hunter-Gatherers, *Nature* 481: 497–501.

Arbib, M. 2005a. From Monkey-Like Action Recognition to Human Language: An Evolutionary Framework for Neurolinguistics, *Behavioral and Brain Sciences* 28: 105–67.

——— 2005b. The Mirror System Hypothesis: How Did Protolanguage Evolve? in Tallermann and Gibson 2012, 21–47.

——— 2012. Mirror Systems: Evolving Imitation and the Bridge from Praxis to Language, in Tallermann and Gibson 2012, 207–25.

Aristotle (Hist. an.) [1996⁶]. *History of Animals* (Hist. an.). In *The Complete Works of Aristotle.* Ed. Jonathan Barnes. Princeton, NJ: Princeton University Press, Vol. 1, 774–993.

——— (Pol.) [1995⁶]. *Politics* (Pol.). In *The Complete Works of Aristotle.* Princeton, NJ: Princeton University Press. Vol. 2, 1986–2129.

Aureli, F., Fraser, O. N., Schaffner, C. M., and Schino, G. 2012. The Regulation of Social Relationships, in Mitani et al. 2012, 531–51.

Aureli, F., and Schaffner, C. M. 2002. Relationship Assessment through Emotional Mediation, *Behaviour* 139: 393–420.

Aureli, F., Schaffner, C. M., Boesch, C., Bearder, S. K., Call, J., Chapman, C. A., Connor, R., Di Fiore, A., Dunbar, R. I. M., Henzi, S. P., Holekamp, K., Korstjens, A. H., Layton, R., Lee, P.,

Lehmann, J., Manson, J. H., Ramos-Fernandez, G., Strier, K. B., and van Schaik, C. P. 2008. Fission-Fusion Dynamics: New Research Frameworks, *Current Anthropology* 49: 627–54.

Austin, J. L. 1962. *How to Do Things with Words*. Oxford: Clarendon Press 1975².

Baier, A. C. 1995. *Moral Prejudices: Essays on Ethics*. Cambridge, MA: Harvard University Press.

Baier, K. 1958. *The Moral Point of View: A Rational Basis of Ethics*. Ithaca, NY: Cornell University Press.

Baker, G., and Hacker, P. M. S. 1984. *Language, Sense and Nonsense*. Oxford: Blackwell.

Baldassarri, D., and Grossman, G. 2011. Centralized Sanctioning and Legitimate Authority Promote Cooperation in Humans. *Proceedings of the National Academy of Sciences* 108: 11023–7.

Baron-Cohen, S. 2011. *Zero Degrees of Empathy: A New Theory of Human Cruelty*. London: Penguin.

Bastian, M. L., Zweifel, N., Vogel, E., Wich, S. A., and van Schaik, C. P. 2010. Diet Traditions in Wild Orangutans, *American Journal of Physical Anthropology* 143: 175–87.

Bateson, M., Nettle, D., and Roberts, G. 2006. Cues of Being Watched Enhance Cooperation in a Real-World Setting, *Biology Letters* 2: 412–14.

Bateson, P., and Laland, K. N. 2013. Tinbergen's Four Questions: An Appreciation and an Update, *Trends in Ecology and Evolution* 28: 712–18.

Batson, C. D. 2014. Empathy-Induced Altruism and Morality: No Necessary Connection, in H. Maibom (ed.). *Empathy and Morality*. Oxford; New York: Oxford University Press, 41–58.

Baumard, N., André, J.-B., and Sperber, D. 2013. A Mutualistic Approach to Morality: The Evolution of Fairness by Partner Choice, *Behavioral and Brain Sciences* 36: 59–78.

Baumeister, R. F., and Tierney, J. 2011. *Willpower: Rediscovering the Greatest Human Strength*. New York: Penguin Press.

Baumrind, D. 2013. Is Milgram's Deceptive Research Ethically Acceptable? *Theoretical and Applied Ethics* 2: 1–18.

Bayertz, K. (ed.). 2005. *Die menschliche Natur. Welchen und wieviel Wert hat sie?* Paderborn: Mentis.

—— 2010. Moral Normativity Is (Naturally) Grown, in U. J. Frey, C. Störmer, and K. P. Windfuhr (eds.). *Homo Novus—A Human Without Illusions*. Berlin, Heidelberg: Springer, 183–91.

Beisner, B. A., and McCowan, B. 2013. Policing in Nonhuman Primates: Partial Interventions Serve a Prosocial Conflict Management Function in Rhesus Macaques. *PLOS ONE* 8: e77369. doi: 10.1371/journal.pone.0077369.

Benedict, R. 1934. *Patterns of Culture*. Boston: Houghton Mifflin.

Bennardo, G., and De Munck, V. C. 2014. *Cultural Models: Genesis, Methods, and Experiences*. Oxford; New York: Oxford University Press.

Bermudez, J. L. 2003. *Thinking without Words*. Oxford: Oxford University Press.

Bernhard, H., Fischbacher, U., and Fehr, E. 2006. Parochial Altruism in Humans, *Nature* 442: 912–15.

Bicchieri, C. 2006. *The Grammar of Society: The Nature and Dynamics of Social Norms*. New York: Cambridge University Press.

Bicchieri, C., and Chavez, A. 2010. Behaving as Expected: Public Information and Fairness Norms, *Journal of Behavioral Decision Making* 23: 161–78.

Bicchieri, C., and Muldoon, R. 2011. Social Norms. *Stanford Encyclopedia of Philosophy*. http://plato.stanford.edu/entries/social-norms.

Bickerton, D. 2009. *Adam's Tongue: How Humans Made Language, How Language Made Humans*. New York: Hill and Wang.

—— 2014. *More than Nature Needs: Language, Mind, and Evolution*. Cambridge, MA: Harvard University Press.

Bilgrami, A. 1993. Norms and Meaning, in R. Stoecker (ed.). *Reflecting Davidson*. Berlin; New York: de Gruyter, 121–44.

Bittner, R. 2002. An Action for Two, in G. Meggle (ed.). *Social Facts and Collective Intentionality*, Frankfurt am Main: Hansel-Hohenhausen, 35–42.

Blackburn, S. 1984. The Individual Strikes Back, *Synthese* 58: 281–301.

Blair, R. J. R. 1995. A Cognitive Developmental Approach to Morality: Investigating the Psychopath, *Cognition* 57: 1–29.

—— 1997. Moral Reasoning and the Child with Psychopathic Tendencies, *Personality and Individual Differences* 22: 731–9.

Blair, R. J. R., Finger, E., and Marsh, A. 2009. The Development and Neural Bases of Psychopathy, in M. de Haan and M. R. Gunnar (eds.). *Handbook of Developmental Social Neuroscience*. New York: Guilford Press, 419–34.

Blair, R. J. R., Jones, L., Clark, F., and Smith, M. 1995. Is the Psychopath Morally Insane? *Personality and Individual Differences* 19: 741–52.

Blair, R. J. R., Mitchell, D., and Blair, K. 2005. *The Psychopath: Emotion and the Brain*. Malden, MA: Blackwell.

Blair, R. J. R., Monson, J., and Frederickson, N. 2001. Moral Reasoning and Conduct Problems in Children with Emotional and Behavioural Difficulties, *Personality and Individual Differences* 31: 799–811.

Bloom, P. 2000. *How Children Learn the Meaning of Words*. Cambridge, MA: MIT Press.

—— 2012. Moral Nativism and Moral Psychology, in M. Mikulincer and P. R. Shaver (eds.). *The Social Psychology of Morality: Exploring the Causes of Good and Evil*. Washington, DC: American Psychological Association, 71–89.

—— 2013. *Just Babies: The Origins of Good and Evil*. New York: Random House.

Boehm, C. 1999. *Hierarchy in the Forest: The Evolution of Egalitarian Behavior*. Cambridge, MA: Harvard University Press.

—— 2012. *Moral Origins: The Evolution of Virtue, Altruism, and Shame*. New York: Basic Books.

—— 2018. Collective Intentionality: A Basic and Early Component of Moral Evolution, *Philosophical Psychology* 31: 680–720.

Boesch, C., and Boesch, H. 1989. Hunting Behavior of the Wild Chimpanzees in the Taï National Park. *American Journal of Physical Anthropology* 78: 547–73.

Boghossian, P. 1989. The Rule-Following Considerations, in Miller and Wright 2002, 141–87.

—— 2003. The Normativity of Content, *Philosophical Perspectives* 13: 31–45.

—— 2005. Is Meaning Normative? in C. Nimtz and A. Beckermann (eds.). *Philosophy—Science—Scientific Philosophy*. Paderborn: Mentis, 205–18.

Bok, S. 1979. *Lying: Moral Choice in Public and Private Life*. New York: Vintage Books 1999.

Bonanno, G. A., and Keltner, D. 2004. The Coherence of Emotion Systems: Comparing On-Line Measures of Appraisal and Facial Expressions, and Self-Report, *Cognition and Emotion* 18: 431–44.

Bott, L., and Noveck, I. A. 2004. Some Utterances Are Underinformative: The Onset and Time Course of Scalar Inferences, *Journal of Memory and Language* 51: 437–57.

Bouchard, D. 2013. *The Nature and Origin of Language*. Oxford: Oxford University Press.

Bowles, S. 2006. Group Competition, Reproductive Leveling, and the Evolution of Human Altruism, *Science* 314: 1569–72.

—— 2012. Warriors, Levelers, and the Role of Conflict in Human Social Evolution, *Science* 336: 876–9.

Bowles, S., and Gintis, H. 2011. *A Cooperative Species: Human Reciprocity and Its Evolution.* Princeton, NJ: Princeton University Press.

Boyd, R., Gintis, H., Bowles, S., and Richerson, P. J. 2003. The Evolution of Altruistic Punishment, *Proceedings of the National Academy of Sciences* 100: 3531–5.

Boyd, R., and Richerson, P. J. 2005. *The Origin and Evolution of Cultures.* New York: Oxford University Press.

—— 2006. Culture and the Evolution of the Human Social Instincts, in Enfield and Levinson 2006, 453–77.

—— 2009. Culture and the Evolution of Human Cooperation, *Philosophical Transactions of the Royal Society of London B* 364: 3281–8.

Brandom, R. B. 1994. *Making It Explicit: Reasoning, Representing and Discursive Commitment.* Cambridge, MA: Harvard University Press.

—— 1997. Replies, *Philosophy and Phenomenological Research* 57: 189–204.

Brandt, R. 1979. *A Theory of the Good and the Right.* Oxford: Oxford University Press.

Bratman, M. 2009. Modest Sociality and the Distinctiveness of Intention, *Philosophical Studies* 144: 149–65.

—— 2014. *Shared Agency: A Planning Theory of Acting Together.* Oxford: Oxford University Press.

Bräuer, J., Call, J., and Tomasello, M. 2006. Are Apes Really Inequity Averse? *Proceedings of the Royal Society B* 273: 3123–8.

—— 2009. Are Apes Inequity Averse? New Data on the Token-Exchange Paradigm, *American Journal of Primatology* 71: 175–81.

Bräuer, J., and Hanus, D. 2012. Fairness in Non-Human Primates? *Social Justice Research* 25: 256–76.

Brennan, G., Eriksson, L., Goodin, R. E., and Southwood, N. 2013. *Explaining Norms.* Oxford: Oxford University Press.

Briggs, J. L. 1998. *Inuit Morality Play: The Emotional Education of a Three-Year Old.* New Haven, CT: Yale University Press.

Brink, D. O. 1989. *Moral Realism and the Foundations of Ethics.* Cambridge: Cambridge University Press.

Broome, J. 2013. *Rationality through Reasoning.* Malden, MA; Oxford: Wiley Blackwell.

Brosnan, S. F. 2006. Nonhuman Species' Reactions to Inequity and Their Implications for Fairness, *Social Justice Research* 19: 153–85.

—— 2013. Justice- and Fairness-Related Behaviors in Nonhuman Primates, *Proceedings of the National Academy of Sciences* 110: 10416–23.

—— 2014. Precursors of Morality: Evidence from Oral Behavior in Non-Human Primates, in M. Christen, C. van Schaik, J. Fischer, M. Huppenbauer, and C. Tanner (eds.). *Empirically Informed Ethics: Morality Between Facts and Norms.* Cham: Springer International, 84–98.

Brosnan, S. F., and de Waal, F. B. M. 2003. Monkeys Reject Unequal Pay, *Nature* 425: 297–9.

—— 2014. Evolution of Responses to (Un)fairness, *Science* 346: 1251776, 1–9.

Brosnan, S. F., Schiff, H. C., and de Waal, F. B. M. 2005. Tolerance for Inequity May Increase with Social Closeness in Chimpanzees, *Proceedings of the Royal Society B* 272: 253–8.

Brosnan, S. F., Talbot, C., Ahlgren, M., Lambeth, S. P., and Schapiro, S. J. 2010. Mechanisms Underlying Responses to Inequitable Outcomes in Chimpanzees, Pan Troglodytes, *Animal Behaviour* 79: 1229–37.

Brown, D. E. 2000. Human Universals and Their Implications, in N. Roughley (ed.). *Being Humans: Anthropological Universality and Particularity in Transdisciplinary Perspectives.* Berlin; New York: Walter de Gruyter, 156–74.

Brügger, R. K., Schmalzried-Kappeler, T., and Burkart, J. M. 2018. Reverse Audience Effect on Helping in Cooperatively Breeding Marmosets, *Biology Letters* 14: 20180030, 1–5.

Bshary, R. 2010. Cooperation between Unrelated Individuals: A Game Theoretic Approach, in P. M. Kappeler (ed.). *Animal Behaviour: Evolution and Mechanisms.* Heidelberg: Springer, 213–40.

Bunnag, J. 1971. Loose Structure: Fact or Fancy? Thai Society Re-examined, *Journal of Siam Society* 59: 1–23.

Burge, T. 1979. Individualism and the Mental: Postscript to "Individualism and the Mental," in *Foundations of Mind. Philosophical Essays*, Vol. II. Oxford: Clarendon Press 2007, 100–81.

Burkart, J. M., Allon, O., Amici, F., Fichtel, C., Finkenwirth, C., Heschl, A., Huber, J., Isler, K., Kosonen, Z. K., Martins, E., Meulman, E. J., Richiger, R., Rueth, K., Spillmann, B., Wiesendanger, S., and van Schaik, C. P. 2014. The Evolutionary Origin of Human Hyper-Cooperation, *Nature Communications* 5: 4747, 1–9.

Burkart, J. M., Brügger, R. K., and van Schaik, C. P. 2018. Evolutionary Origins of Morality: Insights from Nonhuman Primates, *Frontiers in Sociology* 3: 1–12. doi: 10.3389/fsoc.2018.00017.

Burkart, J. M., Hrdy, S. B., and van Schaik, C. P. 2009. Cooperative Breeding and Human Cognitive Evolution, *Evolutionary Anthropology: Issues, News, and Reviews* 18: 175–86.

Burling, R. 2012. Words Came First: Adaptations for Word-Learning, in Tallermann and Gibson 2012, 406–16.

Burnham, T. C., and Hare, B. 2007. Engineering Human Cooperation: Does Involuntary Neural Activation Increase Public Goods Contribution? *Human Nature* 18: 88–108.

Call, J., and Tomasello, M. 2008. Does the Chimpanzee Have a Theory of Mind? 30 Years Later, *Trends in Cognitive Sciences* 12: 187–92.

Camerer, C. F. 2003. *Behavioral Game Theory: Experiments in Strategic Interaction.* Princeton, NJ: Princeton University Press.

Campbell, M. W., and de Waal, F. B. M. 2014. Chimpanzees Empathize with Group Mates and Humans, but Not with Baboons or Unfamiliar Chimpanzees. *Proceedings of the Royal Society B* 281: 20140013, 1–6.

Campos, J. J., Walle, E. A., Dahl, A., and Main, A. 2011. Reconceptualizing Emotion Regulation, *Emotion Review* 3: 26–35.

Cancian, F. 1975. *What Are Norms? A Study of Beliefs and Action in a Maya Community.* Cambridge: Cambridge University Press 2009.

Cant, M. A. 2011. The Role of Threats in Animal Cooperation, *Proceedings of the Royal Society of London B* 278: 170–8.

Cant, M. A., and Young, A. J. 2013. Resolving Social Conflict among Females without Overt Aggression, *Philosophical Transactions of the Royal Society of London B* 368: 20130076, 1–13.

Carassa, A., and Colombetti, M. 2014. Interpersonal Responsibilities and Communicative Intentions, *Phenomenology and the Cognitive Sciences* 13: 145–59.

Casler, K., Terziyan, T., and Greene, K. 2009. Toddlers View Artifact Function Normatively, *Cognitive Development* 24: 240–7.

Chapais, B. 1995. Alliances as a Means of Competition in Primates: Evolutionary, Developmental, and Cognitive Aspects, *Yearbook of Physical Anthropology* 38: 115–36.

—— 2013. Monogamy, Strongly Bonded Groups, and the Evolution of Human Social Structure, *Evolutionary Anthropology* 22: 52–65.

Chartrand, T. L., and van Baaren, R. 2009. Human Mimicry, *Advances in Experimental Social Psychology* 41: 219–74.

Cheney, D. L., and Seyfarth, R. M. 1990. *How Monkeys See the World: Inside the Mind of Another Species*. Chicago: University of Chicago Press.

Chibnik, M. 1981. The Evolution of Cultural Rules, *Journal of Anthropological Research* 37: 256–86.

Chomsky, N. 1968. *Language and Mind*. New York: Harcourt, Brace & World.

—— 1980. *Rules and Representations*. New York: Columbia University Press.

Chomsky, N., and Halle, M. 1968. *The Sound Pattern of English*. New York: Harper & Row.

Chrisman, M. 2016. *The Meaning of 'Ought': Beyond Descriptivism and Expressivism in Metaethics*. Oxford: Oxford University Press.

Christen, M., and Glock, H.-J. 2012. The (Limited) Space for Justice in Social Animals, *Social Justice Research* 25: 298–326.

Chudek, M., and Henrich, J. 2011. Culture-Gene Coevolution, Norm-Psychology and the Emergence of Human Prosociality, *Trends in Cognitive Sciences* 15: 218–26.

Claidière, N., and Whiten, A. 2012. Integrating the Study of Conformity and Culture in Humans and Nonhuman Animals, *Psychological Bulletin* 138: 126–45.

Clark, A. 2008. *Supersizing the Mind: Embodiment, Action, and Cognitive Extension*. Oxford: Oxford University Press.

Clay, Z., and Zuberbühler, K. 2012. Communication during Sex among Female Bonobos: Effects of Dominance, Solicitation and Audience, *Scientific Reports* 2: 291.

—— 2014. Vocal Communication and Social Awareness in Chimpanzees and Bonobos, in Dor et al. 2014, 141–56.

Clayton, N. S., Dally, J., Gilbert J., and Dickinson, A. 2005. Food-caching by Western Scrub-Jays (Aphelocoma californica) Is Sensitive to the Conditions at Recovery, *Journal of Experimental Psychology: Animal Behavior Processes* 31: 115–24.

Clayton, N. S., Emery, N., and Dickinson, A. 2006. The Rationality of Animal Memory: Complex Caching Strategies of Western Scrub Jays, in Hurley and Nudds 2006, 197–216.

Cleckley, H. 1941. *The Mask of Sanity: An Attempt to Clarify Some Issues about the So-Called Psychopathic Personality*. St. Louis: C.V. Mosby 1950.

Cloud, D. 2014. *The Domestication of Language: Cultural Evolution and the Uniqueness of the Human Animal*. New York: Columbia University Press.

Clutton-Brock, T. H., and Parker, G. A. 1995. Punishment in Animal Societies, *Nature* 373: 209–16.

Cole, P. M., Barrett, K. C., and Zahn-Waxler, C. 1992. Emotion Displays in Two-Year-Olds During Mishaps, *Child Development* 63: 314–24.

Collier, K., Bikel, B., van Schaik, C. P., Manser, M. B., and Townsend, S. W. 2014. Language Evolution. Syntax before Phonology? *Proceedings of the Royal Society B* 281: 20140263, 1–7. doi: 10.1098/rspb.2014.0263.

Collins, E. F., and Bahar, E. 2000. To Know Shame: Malu and Its Uses in Malay Society. *Crossroads. An Interdisciplinary Journal of South East Asian Studies* 14: 35–62.

Condillac, É. B. de. 2001. *Essay on the Origin of Human Knowledge* (Cambridge Texts in the History of Philosophy), edited by Hans Aarslef. Cambridge: Cambridge University Press.

Conry-Murray, C. 2009. Adolescent and Adult Reasoning about Gender Roles and Fairness in Benin, West Africa, *Cognitive Development* 24: 207–19.

Corballis, M. C. 2012. The Origins of Language in Manual Gestures, in Tallermann and Gibson 2012, 382–6.

Cords, M., and Aureli, F. 2000. Reconciliation and Relationship Qualities, in F. Aureli and F. B. M. de Waal (eds.). *Natural Conflict Resolution*. Berkeley: University of California Press, 177–98.

Cosmides, L. E., Tooby, J. E., Fiddick, L., and Bryant, G. A. 2005. Detecting Cheaters, *Trends in Cognitive Sciences* 9: 505–6.

Crofoot, M. C., and Wrangham, R. W. 2010. Intergroup Aggression in Primates and Humans: The Case for a Unified Theory, in Kappeler and Silk 2010, 171–96.

Csibra, G., and Gergely, G. 2009. Natural Pedagogy, *Trends in Cognitive Sciences* 13: 148–53.

—— 2011. Natural Pedagogy as Evolutionary Adaptation, *Philosophical Transactions of the Royal Society B: Biological Sciences* 366: 1149–57.

Cummins, D. D. 1998. Social Norms and Other Minds: The Evolutionary Roots of Higher Cognition, in D. D. Cummins and C. Allen (eds.). *The Evolution of Mind*. Oxford: Oxford University Press, 30–50.

Currie, G. 1998. Pretence, Pretending and Metarepresenting, *Mind and Language* 13: 35–55.

Dahl, A. 2014. Definitions and Developmental Processes in Research on Infant Morality. *Human Development* 57: 241–9.

—— 2016. Infants' Unprovoked Acts of Force toward Others. *Developmental Science* 19: 1049–57.

Dahl, A., and Campos, J. J. 2013. Domain Differences in Early Social Interactions, *Child Development* 84: 817–25.

Dahl, A., and Freda, G. 2017. How Young Children Come to View Harming Others as Wrong: A Developmental Analysis, in J. Sommerville and J. Decety (eds.). *Social Cognition: Development across the Life Span*. New York: Routledge, 151–84.

Dahl, A., Campos, J. J., and Witherington, D. C. 2011. Emotional Action and Communication in Early Moral Development, *Emotion Review* 3: 147–57.

Dahl, A., Sherlock, B. R., Campos, J. J., and Theunissen, F. E. 2014. Mothers' Tone of Voice Depends on the Nature of Infants' Transgressions, *Emotion* 14: 651–65.

Dahl, A., Gingo, M., Uttich, K., and Turiel, E. 2018. Moral Reasoning about Human Welfare in Adolescents and Adults: Judging Conflicts Involving Sacrificing and Saving Lives. *Monographs of the Society for Research in Child Development, Serial No. 330*, 83, 1–109.

DaMatta, R. 1979. *Carnivals, Rogues, and Heroes: An Interpretation of the Brazilian Dilemma*. Transl. J. Drury. Notre Dame, IN; London: University of Notre Dame Press 1991.

Dancy, J. 1993. *Moral Reasons*. Oxford: Blackwell.

—— 2004. *Ethics without Principles*. Oxford: Oxford University Press.

Darwall, S. 2006. *The Second-Person Standpoint: Morality, Respect and Accountability*. Cambridge, MA: Harvard University Press.

—— 2013a. Bipolar Obligation, in S. Darwall (ed.). *Morality, Authority and Law: Essays in Second-Personal Ethics I*. Oxford: Oxford University Press, 20–39.

—— 2013b. Moral Obligation: Form and Substance, in S. Darwall (ed.). *Morality, Authority and Law: Essays in Second-Personal Ethics I*. Oxford: Oxford University Press, 40–51.

—— 2013c. Morality's Distinctiveness, in S. Darwall (ed.). *Morality, Authority and the Law: Essays in Second-Personal Ethics I*. Oxford: Oxford University Press, 3–19.

—— 2018. Empathy and Reciprocating Attitudes, in Roughley and Schramme 2018, 291–305.

Darwin, C. 1871. *The Descent of Man and Selection in Relation to Sex*. Princeton, NJ: Princeton University Press 1981.

Davidson, D. 1982. Communication and Convention, in Davidson 1984, 265–80.

—— 1984. *Inquiries into Truth and Interpretation*. Oxford: Oxford University Press.

—— 1990. The Structure and Content of Truth, *Journal of Philosophy* 87: 297–328.

—— 1994. The Social Aspect of Language, in B. McGuiness and G. Olivieri (eds.). *The Philosophy of Michael Dummett*. Dordrecht: Springer, 1–16.

—— 2005. *Truth, Language and History*. Oxford: Oxford University Press.

Dawson, L. H. 1950. *Hoyle's Games Modernized*. London: Routledge and Kegan Paul.

Day, K. 2014. The Right to Literacy and Cultural Change: Zulu Adolescents in Post-Apartheid Rural South Africa, *Cognitive Development* 29: 81–94.

Deaner, R. O., Isler, K., Burkart, J., and van Schaik, C. P. 2007. Overall Brain Size, and Not Encephalization Quotient, Best Predicts Cognitive Ability across Non-Human Primates, *Brain Behavior and Evolution* 70: 115–24.

De Caro, M., and Macarthur, D. (eds.) 2010. *Naturalism and Normativity*. New York: Columbia University Press.

Dediu, D., and Levinson, S. C. 2013. On the Antiquity of Language: The Reinterpretation of Neandertal Linguistic Capacities and Its Consequences, *Frontiers in Psychology* 4: 1–17. doi: 10.3389/fpsyg.2013.00397.

—— 2014. The Time Frame of the Emergence of Modern Language and its Implications, in Dor et al. 2014, 184–95.

Deigh, J. 2011a. Reactive Attitudes Revisited, in C. Bagnoli (ed.). *Morality and the Emotions*. New York: Oxford University Press, 197–216.

—— 2011b. Psychopathic Resentment, in A. Konzelmann Ziv et al. (eds.). *Self-Evaluation*. Dordrecht: Springer, 155–69.

—— 2018. Is Empathy Required to Make Moral Judgments? in N. Roughley and T. Schramme (eds.). *Forms of Fellow Feeling: Empathy, Sympathy, Concern and Moral Agency*. Cambridge: Cambridge University Press, 245–64.

della Mirandola, P. 1846. *On the Dignity of Man*, transl. of *Oratio de hominis dignitate* by C. J. Wallis. In *On the Dignity of Man, On Being and the One, Heptaplus*. Indianapolis, IN: Bobbs Merrill 1965, 1–34.

DeLoache, J., and Gottlieb, A. (eds.) 2000. *A World of Babies: Imagined Childcare Guides for Seven Societies*. Cambridge: Cambridge University Press.

Dennett, D. C. 1989. *The Intentional Stance*. Cambridge, MA: MIT Press.

de Quervain, D. J.-F., Fischbacher, U., Treyler, V., Schellhammer, M., Schnyder, U., Buck, A., and Fehr, E. 2004. The Neural Basis of Altruistic Punishment, *Science* 305: 1254–8.

de Ruiter, J., Weston, G., and Lyon, S. M. 2011. Dunbar's Number: Group Size and Brain Physiology in Humans Re-Examined, *American Anthropologist* 113: 557–68.

Desalles, J.-L. 2014. Why Talk? in Dor et al. 2014, 284–96.

Deutsch, M., and Gerard, H. 1955. A Study of Normative and Informational Social Influences upon Individual Judgment, *Journal of Abnormal and Social Psychology* 51: 629–36.

de Waal, F. B. M. 1991. The Chimpanzee's Sense of Social Regularity and Its Relation to the Human Sense of Justice, *American Behavioral Scientist* 34: 335–49.

—— 1998. *Chimpanzee Politics: Power and Sex Among Apes*. Revised ed. Baltimore, MD: Johns Hopkins University Press.

—— 2006. *Primates and Philosophers: How Morality Evolved*. Princeton, NJ: Princeton University Press.

—— 2011. What Is an Animal Emotion? *Annals of the New York Academy of Sciences* 1224: 191–206.

de Waal, F. B. M., and Pollick, A. S. 2012. Gesture as the Most Flexible Modality of Primate Communication, in Tallermann and Gibson 2012, 82–9.

Diamond, J. 1997. *Guns, Germs, and Steel*. New York: W. W. Norton.

—— 2012. *The World Until Yesterday*. New York: Viking Press.

Diesendruck, G., and Markson, L. 2011. Children's Assumption of the Conventionality of Culture, *Child Development Perspectives* 5: 189–95.

Dindo, M., Whiten A., and de Waal, F. B. M. 2009. In-Group Conformity Sustains Different Foraging Traditions in Capuchin Monkeys (*Cebus apella*), *PLOS ONE* 4: e7858.

Donald, M. 1998. Mimesis and the Executive Suite: Missing Links in Language Evolution, in J. R. Hurford, M. Studdert-Kennedy, and C. Knight (eds.). *Approaches to the Evolution of Language*. Cambridge: Cambridge University Press, 44–67.

Dor, D., Knight, C., and Lewis, J. (eds.) 2014. *The Social Origins of Language*. Oxford: Oxford University Press.

dos Santos, M., Rankin, D. J., and Wedekind, C. 2010. The Evolution of Punishment through Reputation, *Proceedings of the Royal Society B* 278: 371–7.

Dretske, F. 1988. *Explaining Behavior: Reasons in a World of Causes*. Cambridge, MA: MIT Press.

Drew, P. 1981. Adults' Corrections of Children's Mistakes, in P. French and M. MacLure (eds.). *Adult-Child Conversations*. London: Croom Helm, 244–67.

—— 1992. Contested Evidence in Courtroom Examination: The Case of a Trial for Rape, in P. Drew and J. Heritage (eds.). *Talk at Work: Interaction in Institutional Settings*. Cambridge: Cambridge University Press, 470–520.

Dubreuil, B. 2010. *Human Evolution and the Origins of Hierarchies: The State of Nature*. New York: Cambridge University Press.

Dummett, M. 1981. *Frege: Philosophy of Language*. London: Duckworth.

Dunbar, R. I. M. 1992. Neocortex Size as a Constraint on Group Size in Primates, *Journal of Human Evolution* 20: 469–93.

—— 1996. *Grooming, Gossip, and the Evolution of Language*. London: Faber and Faber.

—— 2012. Gossip and the Social Origins of Language, in Tallermann and Gibson 2012, 341–5.

Dunbar, R. I. M., and Shultz, S. 2007. Evolution in the Social Brain, *Science* 317: 1344–7.

Dunn, J. 1988. *The Beginnings of Social Understanding*. Cambridge, MA: Harvard University Press.

Dwyer, S. 2006. How Good Is the Linguistic Analogy? *Culture and Cognition* 2: 237–56.

—— 2009. Moral Dumbfounding and the Linguistic Analogy: Methodological Implications for the Study of Moral Judgment, *Mind and Language* 24: 274–96.

Edgerton, R. B. 1985. *Rules, Exceptions and Social Order*. Berkeley: University of California Press.

Ehrlich, S., and Sidnell, J. 2006. "I Think That's Not an Assumption You Ought to Make." Challenging Presuppositions in Inquiry Testimony, *Language in Society* 35: 655–76.

Eisenberg, N. 2018. Empathy-Related Responding and Its Relations to Positive Development, in Roughley and Schramme 2018, 165–83.

Eller, J. D. 2012². *Cultural Anthropology: Global Forces, Local Lives*. New York; London: Routledge.

El Mouden, C., West, S. A., and Gardner, A. 2010. The Enforcement of Cooperation by Policing, *Evolution* 64: 2139–52.

Elster, J. 1990. Norms of Revenge, *Ethics* 100: 862–85.

Embree, J. F. 1950. Thailand: A Loosely Structured Social System, *American Anthropologist* 52: 181–93.

Enfield, N. J. 2007. Meanings of the Unmarked: How 'Default' Person Reference Does More than Just Refer, in N. J. Enfield and T. Stivers (eds.). *Person Reference in Interaction. Linguistic, Cultural and Social Perspectives*. Cambridge: Cambridge University Press, 97–120.

—— 2009. *The Anatomy of Meaning: Speech, Gesture and Composite Utterances*. Cambridge University Press.

—— 2010. *Human Sociality at the Heart of Language*. Nijmegen: Radboud Universiteit Nijmegen.

—— 2012. Reference in Conversation, in J. Sidnell and T. Stivers (eds.). *The Handbook of Conversation Analysis*. Malden, MA: Wiley-Blackwell, 433–54.

—— 2013. *Relationship Thinking: Agency, Enchrony, and Human Sociality*. New York: Oxford University Press.

—— 2014. *Natural Causes of Language: Frames, Biases, and Cultural Transmission*. Berlin: Language Science Press.

—— 2015. *The Utility of Meaning: What Words Mean and Why*. Oxford University Press.

Enfield, N. J., and Levinson, S. C. (eds.) 2006. *Roots of Human Sociality: Culture, Cognition and Interaction*. Oxford; New York: Berg.

Enfield, N. J., and Sidnell, J. 2014. Language Presupposes an Enchronic Infrastructure for Social Interaction, in Dor et al. 2014, 92–104.

—— 2017. *The Concept of Action*. Cambridge: Cambridge University Press.

Engel, P. 2011. Epistemic Norms, in S. Bernecker and D. Pritchard (eds.). *The Routledge Companion to Epistemology*. New York: Routledge, 47–57.

Engelmann, J. M., Herrmann, E., and Tomasello, M. 2012. Five-Year Olds, but Not Chimpanzees, Attempt to Manage Their Reputations, *PLOS ONE* 7. doi: 10.1371/journal.pone.0048433.

Engelmann, J. M., Clift, J. B., Hermann, E., Tomasello, M. 2017. Social Disappointment Explains Chimpanzees' Behavior in the Inequity Aversion Task. *Proceedings of the Royal Society B* 284: 20171502, 1–8. doi: 10.1098/rspb.2017.1502.

Enoch, D. 2011. *Taking Morality Seriously: A Defense of Robust Realism*. Oxford University Press.

Evans, N. 2010. *Dying Words*. Oxford: Wiley.

Evers, H. D. (ed.) 1969. *Loosely Structured Social Systems: Thailand in Comparative Perspective*. New Haven, CT: Yale University, Southeast Asian Studies.

Falk, D. 2004. Prelinguistic Evolution in Early Hominins. Whence Motherese? *Behavioral and Brain Sciences* 27: 491–503.

—— 2012. The Role of Hominin Mothers and Infants in Prelinguistic Evolution, in Tallermann and Gibson 2012, 318–21.

Fehr, E., and Fischbacher, U. 2004a. Social Norms and Human Cooperation, *Trends in Cognitive Sciences* 8: 185–90.

—— 2004b. Third-Party Punishment and Social Norms, *Evolution and Human Behavior* 25: 63–87.

Fehr, E., and Schmidt, K. 1999. A Theory of Fairness, Competition and Cooperation, *Quarterly Journal of Economics* 114: 817–68.

Feinberg, J. 1974. Noncomparative Justice, *The Philosophical Review* 83: 297–338.

—— 1980. *Rights, Justice, and the Bounds of Liberty: Essays in Social Philosophy*. Princeton, NJ: Princeton University Press.

Fenson, L., Dale, P. S., Reznick, J. S., Bates, E., Thal, D. J., and Pethick, S. J. 1994. Variability in Early Communicative Development, *Monographs of the Society for Research in Child Development* 59.

Ferraro, G. P., and Andreatta, S. 2014[10]. *Cultural Anthropology. An Applied Perspective*. St. Paul: Wadsworth Thomson Learning.

Fessler, D. M. T. 1995. *A Small Field with a Lot of Hornets: An Exploration of Shame, Motivation, and Social Control*. Ph.D. dissertation. San Diego: University of California.

—— 2004. Shame in Two Cultures: Implications for Evolutionary Approaches. *Journal of Cognition and Culture* 4: 207–62.

—— 2007. From Appeasement to Conformity: Evolutionary and Cultural Perspectives on Shame, Competition, and Cooperation, in J. L. Tracy, R. W. Robins, and J. P. Tangney (eds.). *The Self-Conscious Emotions: Theory and Research*. New York: Guilford Press, 174–93.

Fessler, D. M. T., and Gervais, M. 2010. From Whence the Captains of Our Lives: Ultimate and Phylogenetic Perspectives on Emotions in Humans and Other Primates, in Kappeler and Silk 2010, 261–80.

Fessler, D. M. T., and Holbrook, C. 2014. Marching into Battle: Synchronized Walking Diminishes the Conceptualized Formidability of an Antagonist in Men, *Biology Letters* 10. http://rsbl.royalsocietypublishing.org/content/10/8/20140592.

Fessler, D. M. T., and Navarrete, C. D. 2004. Third-Party Attitudes toward Sibling Incest: Evidence for Westermarck's Hypothesis, *Evolution and Human Behavior* 25: 277–94.

Finlay, S. 2014. *Confusion of Tongues: A Theory of Normative Language*. Oxford: Oxford University Press.

—— 2019. Defining Normativity, in D. Plunkett, S. Shapiro, and K. Toh (eds.). *Dimensions of Normativity*. Oxford: Oxford University Press, 187–219.

Firth, R. 1952. Ethical Absolutism and the Ideal Observer, *Philosophy and Phenomenological Research* 12: 317–45.

Fischer, J. 2012. *Affengesellschaft*. Berlin: Suhrkamp.

Fitch, T. W. 2010. *The Evolution of Language*. Cambridge: Cambridge University Press.

Flack, J. C., and de Waal, F. B. M. 2000. 'Any Animal Whatever': Darwinian Building Blocks of Morality in Monkeys and Apes, *Journal of Consciousness Studies* 7: 1–29.

—— 2007. Context Modulates Signal Meaning in Primate Communication, *Proceedings of the National Academy of Sciences USA* 104: 1581–6.

Flack, J. C., de Waal, F. B. M., and Krakauer, D. C. 2005. Social Structure, Robustness, and Policing Cost in a Cognitively Sophisticated Species, *The American Naturalist* 165: E126–39.

Flack, J. C., Krakauer, D. C., and de Waal, F. B. M. 2005. Robustness Mechanisms in Primate Societies: A Perturbation Study, *Proceedings of the Royal Society B: Biological Sciences* 272: 1091–9.

Flack, J. C., Girvan, M., de Waal, F. B. M., and Krakauer, D. C. 2006. Policing Stabilizes Construction of Social Niches in Primates, *Nature* 439: 426–9.

Fodor, J. 1998. *Concepts: Where Cognitive Science Went Wrong*. Oxford: Clarendon Press.

—— 2008. *LOT 2: The Language of Thought Revisited*. Oxford: Oxford University Press.

Foot, P. 1958–9. Moral Beliefs. *Proceedings of the Aristotelian Society. New Series* 59: 83–104.

Fox, K. 2014[2]. *Watching the English: The Hidden Rules of English Behaviour*. London: Hodder and Staughton.

Freud, S. 1930. *Civilization and Its Discontents*. New York: Norton 1961.

Frijda, N. H. 1988. The Laws of Emotion, *American Psychologist* 43: 349–58.

Fung, H. 1999. Becoming a Moral Child: The Socialization of Shame among Young Chinese Children, *Ethos* 27: 180–209.

Gabennesch, H. 1990. The Perception of Social Conventionality by Children and Adults, *Child Development* 61: 2047–59.

Galef, B. G., and Whiskin, E. E. 2008. 'Conformity' in Norway Rats? *Animal Behaviour* 75: 2035–9.

Garfinkel, H. 1967. *Studies in Ethnomethodology*. Upper Saddle River, NJ: Prentice Hall.

Gazzaniga, M. S., Ivry, R. B., and Mangun, G. R. 2013[4]. *Cognitive Neuroscience: The Biology of the Mind*. New York: W. W. Norton.

Geertz, H. 1961. *The Javanese Family: A Study of Kinship and Socialization*. New York: Free Press of Glencoe.

Gehlen, A. 1950. *Man: His Nature and Place in the World*. Transl. C. McMillan and K. Pillemer. New York: Columbia University Press 1988.

Geraci, A., and Surian, L. 2011. The Developmental Roots of Fairness: Infants' Reactions to Equal and Unequal Distributions of Resources, *Developmental Science* 14: 1012–20.

Gergely, G., and Csibra, G. 2006. Sylvia's Recipe: The Role of Imitation and Pedagogy in the Transmission of Cultural Knowledge, in Enfield and Levinson 2006, 229–55.

Gert, B. 2005. *Morality: Its Nature and Justification*. Revised ed. Oxford: Oxford University Press.

Gibbard, A. 1990. *Wise Choices, Apt Feelings*. Oxford: Clarendon Press.

—— 2012. *Meaning and Normativity*. Oxford: Oxford University Press.

Gilbert, M. 1989. *On Social Facts*. Princeton, NJ: Princeton University Press.

—— 1990. Walking Together: A Paradigmatic Social Phenomenon, *Midwest Studies in Philosophy* 15: 1–14.

—— 1996. *Living Together*. Lanham, MD: Rowman and Littlefield.

—— 2000. *Sociality and Responsibility: New Essays in Plural Subject Theory*. Lanham, MD: Rowman and Littlefield.

—— 2003. The Structure of the Social Atom: Joint Commitment as the Foundation of Human Social Behavior, in F. Schmitt (ed.). *Socializing Metaphysics: The Nature of Social Reality*. Lanham, MD: Rowman and Littlefield, 39–64.

—— 2014a. Considerations on Joint Commitment, in M. Gilbert (ed.). *Joint Commitment: How to Make the Social World*. Oxford: Oxford University Press, 37–57.

—— 2014b. Shared Values, Social Unity, and Liberty, in M. Gilbert (ed.). *Joint Commitment: How to Make the Social World*. Oxford: Oxford University Press, 181–206.

Gingo, M., Roded, A., and Turiel, E. 2017. Authority, Autonomy, and Deception: Evaluating the Legitimacy of Parental Authority and Adolescent Deceit. *Journal of Research on Adolescence* 27: 862–77.

Givón, T. 2002. *Bio-Linguistics: The Santa Barbara Lectures*. Amsterdam: John Benjamins.

Glock, H.-J. 1996. *A Wittgenstein Dictionary*. Oxford: Blackwell.

—— 2000. Animals, Thoughts and Concepts, *Synthese* 123: 35–64.

—— 2003. *Quine and Davidson on Language, Thought and Reality*. Cambridge: Cambridge University Press.

—— 2010. Does Language Require Conventions? in P. Frascolla, D. Marconi, and A. Voltolini (eds.). *Wittgenstein: Mind, Meaning and Metaphilosophy*. Basingstoke: Palgrave Macmillan, 85–112.

—— 2014a. Meaning and Rule Following, in J. D. Wright (ed.). *International Encyclopedia of the Social and Behavioral Sciences*, Vol. 14. Amsterdam: Elsevier, 841–9.

—— 2014b. Unintelligibility Made Intelligible, *Erkenntnis* 80: 111–36.

Glüer, K. 2001. Dreams and Nightmares: Conventions, Norms, and Meaning in Davidson's Philosophy of Language, in P. Kotatko, P. Pagin, and G. Segal (eds.). *Interpreting Davidson*. Stanford, CA: CSLI Publications, 53–74.

Glüer, K., and Pagin, P. 1999. Rules of Meaning and Practical Reasoning, *Synthese* 118: 207–27.

Glüer, K., and Wikforss, Å. 2015a. The Normativity of Meaning and Content. *Stanford Encyclopedia of Philosophy*. ed. E. N. Zalta. https://plato.stanford.edu/entries/meaning-normativity.

—— 2015b. Meaning Normativism: Against the Simple Argument, *Organon F* 22, suppl. issue: 63–73.

Göckeritz, S., Schmidt, M. F. H., and Tomasello, M. 2014. Young Children's Creation and Transmission of Social Norms, *Cognitive Development* 30: 81–95.

Goddard, C. 1996. The "Social Emotions" of Malay (Bahasa Melayu), *Ethos* 24: 426–64.

—— 1998. *Semantic Analysis: A Practical Introduction*. Oxford: Oxford University Press.

Goffman, E. 1971. *Relations in Public: Microstudies of the Public Order*. With a new introduction by Philip Manning. New Brunswick, NJ; London: Transaction 2010.

Goodenough, W. H. 1961. Comments on Cultural Evolution, *Daedalus* 9: 521–8.

Goody, J. 1986. *The Logic of Writing and the Organization of Society*. Cambridge: Cambridge University Press.

Gottlieb, G. 1991. Experiential Canalization of Behavioral Development: Theory, *Developmental Psychology* 27: 4–13.

Gould, S. J. 1977. *Ontogeny and Phylogeny*. Cambridge, MA: Belknap Press.

Gould, S. J., and Lewontin, R. C. 1979. The Spandrels of San Marco and the Panglossian Paradigm: A Critique of the Adaptationist Programme, *Proceedings of the Royal Society of London. Series B. Biological Sciences* 205: 581–98.

Greene, J. D., Sommerville, R. B., Nystrom, L. E., Darley, J. M., and Cohen, J. D. 2001. An fMRI Investigation of Emotional Engagement in Moral Judgment, *Science* 293: 2105–8.

Greene, M. 1965. *Approaches to Philosophical Biology*. New York; London: Basic Books.

Grice, H. P. 1957. Meaning, in Grice 1989, 213–23.

—— 1967. Logic and Conversation, in Grice 1989, 22–40.

—— 1989. *Studies in the Way of Words*. Cambridge, MA: Harvard University Press.

Gros-Louis, J. 2004. The Function of Food-Associated Calls in White-Faced Capuchin Monkeys, *Cebus capucinus*, from the Perspective of the Signaller, *Animal Behaviour* 67: 431–40.

Grueter, C. C., Chapais, B., and Zinner, D. 2012. Evolution of Multilevel Social Systems in Nonhuman Primates and Humans, *International Journal of Primatology* 33: 1002–37.

Guala, F. 2012. Reciprocity: Weak or Strong? What Punishment Experiments Do (and Do Not) Demonstrate, *Behavioral and Brain Sciences* 35: 1–59.

Gürerk, Ö., Irlenbusch, B., and Rockenbach, B. 2006. The Competitive Advantage of Sanctioning Institutions, *Science* 312: 108–11.

Guvenc, G. 2011. *Women's Construction of Familial-Gender Identities and Embodied Subjectivities in Saraycik, Turkey*. Unpublished Manuscript. Isik University, Istanbul, Turkey.

Habermas, J. 1998. A Genealogical Analysis of the Cognitive Content of Morality, in C. P. Cronin and P. De Greiff (eds.). *The Inclusion of the Other: Studies in Political Theory*. Cambridge, MA: MIT Press.

Haidt, J. 2001. The Emotional Dog and Its Rational Tail: A Social Intuitionist Approach to Moral Judgment, *Psychological Review* 108: 814–34.

—— 2007. The New Synthesis in Moral Psychology, *Science* 316: 998–1002.

—— 2012. *The Righteous Mind: Why Good People Are Divided by Politics and Religion*. New York: Pantheon Books.

Haidt, J., and Bjorklund, F. 2008. Social Intuitionists Answer Six Questions about Moral Psychology, in W. Sinnott-Armstrong (ed.). *Moral Psychology*, Vol 2: *The Cognitive Science of Morality: Intuition and Diversity*. Cambridge, MA: MIT Press, 181–217.

Haidt, J., and Joseph, C. 2008. The Moral Mind: How Five Sets of Innate Intuitions Guide the Development of Many Culture-Specific Virtues, and Perhaps Even Modules, in P. Carruthers, S. Laurence, and S. Stich (eds.). *The Innate Mind*, Vol. 3: *Foundations and the Future*. New York: Oxford University Press, 367–91.

Haidt, J., Koller, S. H., and Dias, M. G. 1993. Affect, Culture, and Morality, or Is It Wrong to Eat Your Dog? *Journal of Personality and Social Psychology* 65: 613–28.

Haidt, J., Bjorklund, F., and Murphy, S. 2000. *Moral Dumbfounding: When Intuition Finds No Reason*. Unpublished manuscript.

Haley, K. J., and Fessler, D. M. T. 2005. Nobody's Watching? Subtle Cues Affect Generosity in an Economic Game, *Evolution and Human Behavior* 26: 245–56.

Hamilton, M. J., Milne, B. T., Walker, R. S., Burger, O., and Brown, J. H. 2007. The Complex Structure of Hunter-Gatherer Social Networks, *Proceedings of the Royal Society of London B* 274: 2195–202.

Hamlin, J. K. 2013. Moral Judgment and Action in Preverbal Infants and Toddlers: Evidence for an Innate Moral Core, *Current Directions in Psychological Science* 22: 186–93.

Hamlin, J. K., and Wynn, K. 2011. Young Infants Prefer Prosocial to Antisocial Others, *Cognitive Development* 26: 30–9.

Hansen, K. P. 2009. *Kultur, Kollektiv, Nation*. Passau: Verlag Karl Stutz.

Hare, B., and Tomasello, M. 2004. Chimpanzees Are More Skillful in Competitive than in Cooperative Cognitive Tasks, *Animal Behaviour* 68: 571–81.

Hare, R. D. 1991. *The Hare Psychopathy Checklist—Revised*. Toronto: Multi-Health Systems.

—— 1993. *Without Conscience. The Disturbing World of the Psychopaths among Us*. New York: Guilford Press.

Hare, R. D., Neumann, C. S., and Widiger, T. A. 2012. Psychopathy, in T. A. Widiger (ed.). *The Oxford Handbook of Personality Disorders*. New York: Oxford University Press, 478–504.

Hare, R. M. 1952. *The Language of Morals*. Oxford: Clarendon Press.

—— 1981. *Moral Thinking: Its Levels, Method, and Point*. Oxford: Clarendon Press.

Harman, G. 1977. *The Nature of Morality: An Introduction to Ethics*. New York: Oxford University Press.

Harnad, S. 2012. From Sensorimotor Categories and Pantomime to Grounded Symbols and Propositions, in Tallermann and Gibson 2012, 387–92.

Hart, H. L. A. 1961. *The Concept of Law*. Oxford University Press 1994^2.

—— 1994. Postscript to *The Concept of Law*, in Hart 1961, 238–76.

Hattiangadi, A. 2006. Is Meaning Normative? *Mind and Language* 21: 220–40.

—— 2007. *Oughts and Thoughts: Rule-Following and the Normativity of Content*. Oxford: Clarendon Press.

Haun, D. B. M., and Over, H. 2013. Like Me: A Homophily-Based Account of Human Culture, in P. J. Richerson and M. Christiansen (eds.). *Cultural Evolution*. Cambridge, MA: MIT Press, 75–85.

Haun, D. B. M., Rekers, Y., and Tomasello, M. 2012. Majority-Biased Transmission in Chimpanzees and Human Children, but Not Orangutans, *Current Biology* 22: 727–31.

Hauser, M. D. 1992. Costs of Deception: Cheaters Are Punished in Rhesus Monkeys (*Macaca mulatta*), *Proceedings of the National Academy of Sciences USA* 89: 12137–9.

—— 2006. *Moral Minds: How Nature Designed Our Universal Sense of Right and Wrong*. New York: Ecco.

Hauser, M. D., Chomsky, N., and Fitch, T. W. 2002. The Faculty of Language: What Is It, Who Has It, and How Did It Evolve? *Science* 298: 1569–79.

Haviland, W. A., Prins, H. E. L., McBride, B., and Walrath, D. 2014[14]. *Anthropology: The Human Challenge*. Belmont, CA: Wadsworth Cengage.

Hechter, M., and Opp, K. D. 2001. *Social Norms*. New York: Russell Sage Foundation.

Helwig, C. C. 1995. Adolescents' and Young Adults' Conceptions of Civil Liberties: Freedom of Speech and Religion, *Child Development* 66: 152–66.

—— 1997. The Role of Agent and Social Context in Judgments of Freedom of Speech and Religion, *Child Development* 68: 484–95.

Helwig, C. C., Hildebrandt, C., and Turiel, E. 1995. Children's Judgments about Psychological Harm in Social Context, *Child Development* 66: 1680–93.

Henrich, J., McElreath, R., Barr, A., Ensminger, J., Barrett, C., Bolyanatz, A., Cardenas, J. C., Gurven, M., Gwako, E., Henrich, N., Lesorogol, C., Marlowe, F., Tracer, D., and Ziker, J., 2006. Costly Punishment across Human Societies, *Science* 312: 1767–70.

Henrich, J., Ensminer, J., McElreth, R., Barr, A., Barrett, C., Bolyanatz, A., Cardenas, J. C., Gurven, M., Gwanko, E., Henrich, N., Lesorogol, C., Marlowe, F., Tracer, D., and Ziker, J. 2010. Markets, Religion, Community Size, and the Evolution of Fairness and Punishment, *Science* 327: 2480–4.

Henrich, J., Heine, S., and Norenzayan, A. 2010. The Weirdest People in the World? *Behavioral and Brain Sciences* 33: 61–83.

Heritage, J. 1984. *Garfinkel and Ethnomethodology*. Cambridge: Polity Press.

Hervé, H. F., Hayes, P. J., and Hare, R. D. 2003. Psychopathy and Sensitivity to the Emotional Polarity of Metaphorical Statements, *Personality and Individual Differences* 35: 1497–507.

Hill, K. R. 2002. Altruistic Cooperation during Foraging by Ache [*sic*], and the Evolved Predisposition to Cooperate, *Human Nature* 13: 105–28.

—— 2009. Animal "Culture," in K. N. Laland and B. G. Galef (eds.). *The Question of Animal Culture*. Cambridge, MA: Harvard University Press, 269–87.

Hill, K. R., Walker, R. S., Božičević, M., Eder, J., Headland, T., Hewlett, B., Hurtado, A. M., Marlowe, F., Wiessner, P., and Wood, B. 2011. Co-Residence Patterns in Hunter-Gatherer Societies Show Unique Human Social Structure, *Science* 331: 1286–89.

Hinde, R. A. 1976. Interactions, Relationships and Social Structure, *Man* 11: 1–17.

Hobbes, T. 1651. *Leviathan*, edited by Richard Tuck. Cambridge University Press 1991.

Hockett, C. 1960. The Origin of Speech, *Scientific American* 203: 88–111.

Hoffman, M. L. 1982. Development of Prosocial Motivation: Empathy and Guilt, in N. Eisenberg (ed.). *The Development of Prosocial Behavior*. New York: Academic Press, 281–313.

—— 2000. *Empathy and Moral Development: Implications for Caring and Justice.* Cambridge: Cambridge University Press.

Hohfeld, W. N. 1913. Some Fundamental Legal Conceptions as Applied in Judicial Reasoning, *Yale Law Journal* 23: 16–59.

—— 1917. Fundamental Legal Conceptions as Applied in Judicial Reasoning, *Yale Law Journal* 26: 710–70.

Hollis, M. 1994. *The Philosophy of Social Science: An Introduction.* Cambridge University Press.

Holmes, J. 1891. Opinion on the Case of *Goode* v. *Riley*, May 19, 1891, Supreme Judicial Court of Massachusetts. Citation: 153 Mass. 585, 28 N. E. 228.

Homans, G. C. 1961. *Social Behavior.* New York: Harcourt Brace and World.

Hopper, L. M., Schapiro, S. J., Lambeth, S. P., and Brosnan, S. F. 2011. Chimpanzees' Socially Maintained Food Preferences Indicate Both Conservatism and Conformity, *Animal Behaviour* 81: 1195–202.

Hopper, L. M., Spiteri, A., Lambeth, S. P., Schapiro, S. J., Horner, V., and Whiten, A. 2007. Experimental Studies of Traditions and Underlying Transmission Processes in Chimpanzees, *Animal Behaviour* 73: 1021–32.

Hoppitt, W., and Laland, K. N. 2012. *Social Learning: An Introduction to Mechanisms, Methods and Models.* Princeton, NJ: Princeton University Press.

Horn, L. R. 2006. The Border Wars: A Neo-Gricean Perspective, in K. Heusinger and K. Turner (eds.). *Where Semantics Meets Pragmatics.* Oxford: Elsevier, 21–48.

—— 2007. Neo-Gricean Pragmatics: A Manichaean Manifesto, in N. Burton-Roberts (ed.). *Pragmatics.* London: Palgrave Macmillan, 158–83.

—— 2009. WJ-40: Implicature, Truth, and Meaning, *International Review of Pragmatics* 1: 3–34.

Horn, S. S. 2003. Adolescents Reasoning about Exclusion from Social Groups, *Developmental Psychology* 39: 71–84.

Horne, C. 2001. Sociological Perspectives on the Emergence of Norms, in Hechter and Opp 2001, 3–34.

Horwich, P. 1998a. *Meaning.* Oxford University Press.

—— 1998²b. *Truth.* Oxford University Press.

Hrdy, S. B. 2009. *Mothers and Others: The Evolutionary Origins of Mutual Understanding.* Cambridge, MA: Harvard University Press.

Hull, D. 1978. A Matter of Individuality, *Philosophy of Science* 45: 335–60.

—— 1984. Historical Entities and Historical Narratives, in C. Hookway (ed.). *Minds, Machines and Evolution: Philosophical Studies.* Cambridge: Cambridge University Press, 17–42.

—— 1986. On Human Nature, *Proceedings of the Philosophy of Science Association* 2: 3–13.

Hume, D. 1739–40. *A Treatise of Human Nature*, edited by L. A. Selby-Bigge. Oxford: Clarendon Press 1978.

Hurford, J. R. 2012a. *The Origins of Grammar: Language in the Light of Evolution*, vol. II. Oxford University Press.

—— 2012b. The Origins of Meaning, in Tallermann and Gibson 2012, 370–81.

Hurley, S. 2008. The Shared Circuits Model (SCM): How Control, Mirroring, and Simulation Can Enable Imitation, Deliberation, and Mindreading, *Behavioral and Brain Science* 31: 1–58.

Hurley, S., and Nudds, M. (eds.). 2006. *Rational Animals?* Oxford: Oxford University Press.

Hyman, H. H., and Sheatsley, P. B. 1953. Trends in Public Opinion on Civil Liberties, *Journal of Social Issues* 9: 6–16.

Jackendoff, R. 2002. *Foundations of Language: Brain, Meaning, Grammar, Evolution*. Oxford: Oxford University Press.

Jacobson, D. 2012. Moral Dumbfounding and Moral Stupefaction, in M. Timmons (ed.). *Oxford Studies in Normative Ethics*, Vol. 2. Oxford: Oxford University Press, 289–316.

Jefferson, G. 1974. Error Correction as an Interactional Resource, *Language in Society* 2: 181–99.

Jensen, K., Call, J., and Tomasello, M. 2007a. Chimpanzees Are Rational Maximizers in an Ultimatum Game, *Science* 318: 107–9.

—— 2007b. Chimpanzees Are Vengeful but Not Spiteful. *Proceedings of the National Academy of Sciences* 104: 13046–50.

Johnson, A. W., and Earle, T. 2000². *The Evolution of Human Societies: From Foraging Group to Agrarian State*. Redwood City, CA: Stanford University Press.

Joyce, R. 2006. *The Evolution of Morality*. Cambridge, MA: MIT Press.

Kacelnik, A. 2006. Meanings of Rationality, in Hurley and Nudds 2006, 86–106.

Kaiser, I., Jensen, K., Call, J., and Tomasello, M. 2012. Theft in an Ultimatum Game: Chimpanzees and Bonobos Are Insensitive to Unfairness, *Biology Letters* 8: 942–5.

Kalish, C. W. 2005. Becoming Status Conscious: Children's Appreciation of Social Reality, *Philosophical Explorations* 8: 245–63.

Kamilar, J. M., and Baden, A. L. 2014. What Drives Flexibility in Primate Social Organization? *Behavioral Ecology and Sociobiology* 68: 1677–92.

Kamilar, J. M., and Cooper, N. 2013. Phylogenetic Signal in Primate Behaviour, Ecology and Life History, *Philosophical Transactions of the Royal Society of London B* 368: 20120341, 1–10.

Kant, I. 1785. *Groundwork of the Metaphysics of Morals*. Transl. and ed. M. Gregor and J. Timmermann. Cambridge: Cambridge University Press 2012.

—— 1788. *Critique of Practical Reason*. Transl. M. Gregor, ed. A. Reath. Cambridge: Cambridge University Press 2015.

—— 1798/1800. *Anthropology from a Pragmatic Point of View*. Transl. and ed. R. B. Louden. Cambridge: Cambridge University Press 2006.

Kaplan, H., Hooper, P. L., and Gurven, M. 2009. The Evolutionary and Ecological Roots of Human Social Organization, *Philosophical Transactions of the Royal Society B* 364: 3289–99.

Kappeler, P. M. 2012. The Behavioral Ecology of Strepsirrhines and Tarsiers, in Mitani et al. 2012, 17–42.

Kappeler, P. M., and Silk, J. B. (eds.) 2010. *Mind the Gap: Tracing the Origins of Human Universals*. Oxford: Oxford University Press.

Kappeler, P. M., and van Schaik, C. P. 2002. Evolution of Primate Social Systems, *International Journal of Primatology* 23: 707–40.

Kappeler, P. M., and Watts, D. P. 2011. *Long-Term Field Studies of Primates*. Heidelberg: Springer.

Kappeler, P. M., Silk, J. S., Burkart, J., and van Schaik, C. 2010. Primate Behavior and Human Universals: Exploring the Gap, in Kappeler and Silk 2010, 3–15.

Kappeler, P. M., Barrett, L., Blumstein, D. T., and Clutton-Brock, T. H. 2013. Constraints and Flexibility in Mammalian Social Behaviour: Introduction and Synthesis, *Philosophical Transactions of the Royal Society of London B* 368: 20120337, 1–10.

Kawai, N., Yasue, M., Banno, T., and Ichinohe, N. 2014. Marmoset Monkeys Evaluate Third-Party Reciprocity, *Biology Letters* 10. http://rsbl.royalsocietypublishing.org/content/10/5/20140058.

Kearney, M. 1984. *World View*. Novato, CA: Chandler and Sharp.

Keeley, L. H. 1988. Hunter-Gatherer Economic Complexity and "Population Pressure": A Cross-Cultural Analysis, *Journal of Anthropological Archaeology* 7: 373–411.

Keesing, R. M., and Strathern, A. J. 1998³. *Cultural Anthropology. A Contemporary Perspective*. Fort Worth, TX: Harcourt Brace College.

Kelemen, D. 1999. The Scope of Teleological Thinking in Preschool Children, *Cognition* 70: 241–72.

—— 2004. Are Children "Intuitive Theists"? Reasoning about Purpose and Design in Nature, *Psychological Science* 15: 295–301.

Kelly, D., Stich, S., Haley, K. J., Eng, S. J., and Fessler, D. M. T. 2007. Harm, Affect, and the Moral/Conventional Distinction, *Mind and Language* 22: 117–31.

Kelman, H. C. 1958. Compliance, Identification, and Internalization: Three Processes of Attitude Change, *Journal of Conflict Resolution* 2: 51–60.

Kemmerling, A. 2001. Gricy Actions, in G. Cosenza (ed.). *Paul Grice's Heritage*. Turnhout: Prepols, 73–99.

Kendal, R., Hopper, L. M., Whiten, A., Brosnan, S. F., Lambeth, S. P., Schapiro, S. J., and Hoppitt, W. 2015. Chimpanzees Copy Dominant and Knowledgeable Individuals: Implications for Cultural Diversity. *Evolution and Human Behavior* 36: 65–72.

Kennett, J. 2006. Do Psychopaths Really Threaten Moral Rationalism? *Philosophical Explorations* 9: 69–82.

Kenward, B. 2012. Over-Imitating Preschoolers Believe Unnecessary Actions Are Normative and Enforce Their Performance by a Third Party, *Journal of Experimental Child Psychology* 112: 195–207.

Keupp, S., Behne, T., and Rakoczy, H. 2013. Why Do Children Overimitate? Normativity Is Crucial, *Journal of Experimental Child Psychology* 116: 392–406.

Kiehl, K. 2008. Without Morals: The Cognitive Neuroscience of Criminal Psychopaths, in W. Sinnott-Armstrong (ed.). *Moral Psychology*, Vol. 3: *The Neuroscience of Morality: Emotion, Brain Disorders and Development*. Cambridge, MA: MIT Press, 119–50.

Killen, M., and Rutland, A. 2011. *Children and Social Exclusion: Morality, Prejudice, and Group Identity*. New York: Wiley-Blackwell.

Killen, M., and Smetana, J. G. (eds.) 2006. *Handbook of Moral Development*. Mahwah, NJ: Lawrence Erlbaum.

Killen, M., Lee-Kim, J., McGlothlin, H., and Stagnor, C. 2002. How Children and Adolescents Value Gender and Racial Exclusion, *Monographs of the Society for Research in Child Development* 67.

Kim, J. M. 1998. Korean Children's Concepts of Adult and Peer Authority and Moral Reasoning, *Developmental Psychology* 34: 947–55.

Kim, J. M., and Turiel, E. 1996. Korean and American Children's Concepts of Adult and Peer Authority, *Social Development* 5: 310–29.

Kluckhohn, C. K. M., and Kelly, W. H. 1945. The Concept of Culture, in Ralph Linton (ed.). *The Science of Man in the World Crisis*. New York: Columbia University Press, 78–105.

Knight, C., and Lewis, J. 2014. Vocal Deception, Laughter, and the Linguistic Significance of Reverse Dominance, in Dor et al. 2014, 297–314.

Knight, C., and Power, C. 2012. Social Conditions for the Evolutionary Emergence of Language, in Tallermann and Gibson 2012, 346–9.

Kochanska, G. 1994. Beyond Cognition: Expanding the Search for the Early Roots of Internalization and Conscience, *Developmental Psychology* 30: 20–22.

Kockelman, P. 2005. The Semiotic Stance, *Semiotica* 157: 233–304.

—— 2013. *Agent, Person, Subject, Self: A Theory of Ontology, Interaction, and Infrastructure*. Oxford: Oxford University Press.

Koentjaraningrat, R. M. 1984. *Javanese Culture*. Singapore: Institute of Southeast Asian Studies and Oxford University Press 1990.

Kohlberg, L. 1969. Stage and Sequence: The Cognitive-Developmental Approach to Socialization, in D. A. Goslin (ed.). *Handbook of Socialization Theory and Research*. Chicago: Rand McNally, 347–480.

—— 1971. From Is to Ought: How to Commit the Naturalistic Fallacy and Get Away with It in the Study of Moral Development, in T. Mischel (ed.). *Psychology and Genetic Epistemology*. New York: Academic Press, 151–235.

Kompa, N. 2010. Contextualism in the Philosophy of Language, in K. Petrus (ed.). Meaning *and Analysis: New Essays on H. P. Grice*. Basingstoke: Palgrave Macmillan, 288–309.

Korsgaard, C. M. 1996. *The Sources of Normativity*. Cambridge: Cambridge University Press.

—— 1997. The Normativity of Instrumental Reason, in G. Cullity & B. Gaut (eds.). *Ethics and Practical Reason*. Oxford: Clarendon Press, 215–54.

Koski, S. E., and Sterck, E. H. M. 2010. Empathic Chimpanzees: A Proposal of the Levels of Emotional and Cognitive Processing in Chimpanzee Empathy, *European Journal of Developmental Psychology* 7: 38–66.

Kottak, C. P. 2013[15]. *Anthropology: Appreciating Human Diversity*. New York: McGraw-Hill.

Krämer, H. 1992. *Integrative Ethik*. Frankfurt am Main: Suhrkamp.

Krause, J., and Ruxton, G. D. 2002. *Living in Groups*. Oxford: Oxford University Press.

Krebs, D. L. 2008. Morality: An Evolutionary Account, *Perspectives on Psychological Science* 3: 149–72.

Krebs, J. R., and Dawkins, R. 1984. Animal Signals, Mind-Reading and Manipulation, in J. R. Krebs and N. B. Davis (eds.). *Behavioural Ecology: An Evolutionary Approach*. Oxford: Blackwell, 380–402.

Kripke, S. A. 1972. *Naming and Necessity*. Amsterdam: Springer.

—— 1982. *Wittgenstein on Rules and Private Language: An Elementary Exposition*. Oxford: Blackwell.

Kroeber, A. L., and Kluckhohn, C. M. 1952. *Culture: A Critical Review of Concepts and Definitions*. Cambridge, MA: Harvard University Press.

Kronfeldner, M., Roughley, N., and Töpfer, G. 2014. Recent Work on Human Nature: Beyond Traditional Essences, *Philosophy Compass* 9: 642–52.

Kummer, H., and Cords, M. 1991. Cues of Ownership in Long-Tailed Macaques, *Macaca fascicularis*, *Animal Behaviour* 42: 529–49.

Kusch, M. 2006. *A Sceptical Guide to Meaning and Rules*. Chesham: Acumen.

Kusserow, A. 2004. *American Individualism: Child-Rearing and Social Class in Three Neighborhoods*. New York: Palgrave Macmillan.

Laland, K. N., and O'Brien, M. J. 2011. Cultural Niche Construction: An Introduction, *Biological Theory* 6: 191–201.

Laland, K. N., Odling-Smee, J., and Feldman, M. 2000. Niche Construction, Biological Evolution, and Cultural Change, *Behavioural and Brain Sciences* 23: 131–75.

Laland, K. N., Odling-Smee, J., Hoppitt, W., and Uller, T. 2012. More on How and Why: Cause and Effect in Biology Revisited, *Biology and Philosophy*: 719–45. doi: 10.1007/s10539-012-9335-1.

Lamm, E. 2014. Forever United: The Co-Evolution of Language and Normativity, in Dor et al. 2014, 267–83.

Lancy, D. F. 2015². *The Anthropology of Childhood: Cherubs, Chattel, Changelings*. Cambridge: Cambridge University Press.

Langergraber, K. E., Boesch, C., Inoue, E., Inoue-Murayama, M., Mitani, J. C., Nishida, T., Pusey, A., Reynolds, V., Schubert, G., Wrangham, R. W., Wroblewski, E., and Vigilant, L. 2011. Genetic and 'Cultural' Similarity in Wild Chimpanzees, *Proceedings of the Royal Society B: Biological Sciences* 278: 408–16.

Laupa, M., Turiel, E., and Cowan, P. A. 1995. Obedience to Authority in Children and Adults, in M. Killen and D. Hart (eds.). *Morality in Everyday Life: Developmental Perspectives*. Cambridge: Cambridge University Press, 131–65.

Lazarus, N. 1991. *Emotion and Adaptation*. New York: Oxford University Press.

Leroi-Gourhan, A. 1964/5. *Gesture and Speech*. Cambridge, MA: MIT Press 1993.

LeVine, R. A., Dixon, S., LeVine, S., Richman, A., Leiderman, P. H., Keefer, C. H., and Brazelton, T. B. 1994. *Child Care and Culture: Lessons from Africa*. Cambridge: Cambridge University Press.

LeVine, R. A., and New, R. S. (eds.) 2008. *Anthropology and Child Development" A Cross-Cultural Reader*. Malden, MA: Blackwell.

LeVine, R. A., and Norman, K. 2001. The Infant's Acquisition of Culture: Early Attachment Re-Examined in Anthropological Perspective, in C. C. Moore and H. F. Matthews (eds.). *The Psychology of Cultural Experience*. Cambridge: Cambridge University Press, 83–104.

Levinson, S. C. 2000. *Presumptive Meanings: The Theory of Generalized Conversational Implicature*. Cambridge, MA: MIT Press.

Lewis, D. 1969. *Convention: A Philosophical Study*. Oxford; Malden, MA: Blackwell 2002.

—— 1975. Languages and Language, in K. Gunderson (ed.) *Language, Mind and Knowledge*. Minneapolis: University of Minnesota Press, 3–35.

Lickliter, R., and Honeycutt, H. 2010. Rethinking Epigenesis and Evolution in Light of Developmental Science, in M. S. Blumberg, J. Freeman, and S. R. Robinson (eds.). *Oxford Handbook of Developmental Behavioral Neuroscience*. Oxford: Oxford University Press, 30–47.

Locke, J. 1790. *An Essay Concerning Human Understanding*, edited with an introduction by P. H. Nidditch. Oxford: Clarendon Press 1975.

Loftus, E. F., and Palmer, J. C. 1974. Reconstruction of Automobile Destruction: An Example of the Interaction between Language and Memory, *Journal of Verbal Learning and Verbal Behavior* 13: 585–9.

Lohse, K., Gräfenhain, M., Behne, T., and Rakoczy, H. 2014. Young Children Understand the Normative Implications of Future-Directed Speech Acts, *PLOS ONE* 9: e86958.

Lucke, D. M. 2014². Norm und Sanktion, in G. Endruweit, G. Trommsdorff, and N. Burzan (eds.). *Wörterbuch der Soziologie*. Konstanz; München: UVK and UVK/Lucius, 338–42.

Lull, J. 2000². *Media, Communication, Culture: A Global Approach*. New York; Chichester: Columbia University Press.

Luncz, L. V., and Boesch, C. 2014. Tradition over Trend: Neighboring Chimpanzee Communities Maintain Differences in Cultural Behavior Despite Frequent Immigration of Adult Females, *American Journal of Primatology* 76: 649–57.

Luncz, L. V., Mundry, R., and Boesch, C. 2012. Evidence for Cultural Differences between Neighboring Chimpanzee Communities, *Current Biology* 22: 922–6.

Machery, E., and Mallon, R. 2010. Evolution of Morality, in J. M. Doris and the Moral Psychology Research Group (eds.). *The Moral Psychology Handbook*. Oxford: Oxford University Press, 3–46.

Mackie, J. L. 1977. *Ethics: Inventing Right and Wrong*. London: Penguin Books 1990.

—— 1982. *The Miracle of Theism: Arguments for and against the Existence of God*. Oxford: Oxford University Press.

Magnis-Suseno, F. 1981. *Javanische Weisheit und Ethik. Studien zu einer östlichen Moral*. Munich; Vienna: R. Oldenbourg.

Maibom, H. 2008. The Mad, the Bad and the Psychopath, *Neuroethics* 1: 167–84.

Markus, H. R., and Kitayama, S. 1991. Culture and the Self: Implications for Cognition, Emotion, and Motivation, *Psychological Review* 98: 224–53.

Marlowe, F. W. 2005. Hunter-Gatherers and Human Evolution, *Evolutionary Anthropology* 14: 54–67.

—— 2009. Hadza Cooperation: Second-Party Punishment, Yes; Third-Party Punishment, No, *Human Nature* 20: 417–30.

—— 2010. *The Hadza: Hunter-Gatherers of Tanzania*. Berkeley: University of California Press.

Massen, J. J. M., Sterck, E. H. M., and de Vos, H. 2010. Close Social Associations in Animals and Humans: Functions and Mechanisms of Friendships, *Behaviour* 147: 1379–412.

Maynard Smith, J., and Harper, D. 2003. *Animal Signals*. Oxford: Oxford University Press.

Maynard Smith, J., and Szathmary, E. 1995. *The Major Transitions in Evolution*. Oxford: Oxford University Press.

McClosky, M., and Brill, A. 1983. *Dimensions of Tolerance: What Americans Believe about Civil Liberties*. New York: Sage.

McDowell, J. 1979. Virtue and Reason, in McDowell 1998, 50–73.

—— 1984. Wittgenstein on Following a Rule, in McDowell 1998, 221–62.

—— 1985. Values and Secondary Qualities, in McDowell 1998, 131–50.

—— 1998. *Mind, Value and Reality*. Cambridge, MA: Harvard University Press.

McKeever, S., and Ridge, M. 2006 *Principled Ethics: Generalism as a Regulative Ideal*. Oxford: Oxford University Press.

Mead, M. 1928. *Coming of Age in Samoa*. New York: Morrow 1971.

Meijers, A. W. M. 2003. Can Collective Intentionality Be Individualized? *American Journal of Economics and Sociology* 62: 167–83.

Mensing, J. F. 2002. *Collectivism, Individualism, and Interpersonal Responsibilities in Families: Differences and Similarities in Social Reasoning between Individuals in Poor, Urban Families in Colombia and the United States*. Unpublished doctoral dissertation. Berkeley: University of California.

Mercader, J., Barton, H., Gillespie, J., Harris, J., Kuhn, S., Tyler, R., and Boesch, C. 2007. 4,300-Year-Old Chimpanzee Sites and the Origins of Percussive Stone Technology, *Proceedings of the National Academy of Sciences USA* 104: 3043–8.

Mertens, K. 2013. Soziale Dimensionen der Normativität. Perspektiven einer phänomeno-logischen Analyse handlungskonstitutiver und sozialer Normen, in D. Lohmar and D. Fonfara (eds.). *Soziale Erfahrung*. Hamburg: Felix Meiner Verlag, 145–64.

Meyer, P. 2010. *Menschliche Gesellschaft im Licht der Zweiten Darwinschen Revolution. Evolutionäre und kulturalistische Deutungen im Widerstreit*. Münster: Lit Verlag.

Michael, J., and Székely, M. 2018. The Developmental Origins of Commitment, *Journal of Social Philosophy* 49: 106–23.

Milgram, S. 1963. Behavioral Study of Obedience, *Journal of Abnormal and Social Psychology* 67: 371–8.

—— 1974. *Obedience to Authority*. New York: Harper and Row.

Milinski, M. 2006. Reputation, Personal Identity and Cooperation in a Social Dilemma, in P. M. Kappeler and C. P. Van Schaik (eds.). *Cooperation in Primates and Humans: Mechanisms and Evolution*. Heidelberg: Springer, 265–78.

Mill, J. S. 1861. *Utilitarianism*, in Mill (ed.). *On Liberty and Other Essays*. Oxford: Oxford University Press 1991, 129–201.

Miller, A., and Wright, C. (eds.) 2002. *Rule-Following and Meaning*. Chesham: Acumen.

Miller, S. 1997. Social Norms, in G. Holmström-Hintikka and R. Tuomela (eds.). *Contemporary Action Theory*, Vol. 2: *Social Action*. Dordrecht/Boston/London: Kluwer, 211–27.

—— 2001. *Social Action: A Teleological Account*. Cambridge: Cambridge University Press.

Millikan, R. G. 1990. Truth, Rules, Hoverflies, and the Kripke-Wittgenstein Paradox, *Philosophical Review* 99: 323–53.

—— 2006. Styles of Rationality, in Hurley and Nudds 2006, 117–26.

Mitani, J. C., Call, J., Kappeler, P. M., Palombit, R. A., and Silk, J. B. (eds.). 2012. *The Evolution of Primate Societies*. Chicago: University of Chicago Press.

Mithen, S. 2005. *The Singing Neanderthals: The Origins of Music, Language, Mind, and Body*. London: Weidenfeld and Nicholson.

Moffett, M. W. 2013. Human Identity and the Evolution of Societies, *Human Nature* 24: 219–67.

Moghaddam, F. M. 2002[2]. *Social Psychology: Exploring Universals across Cultures*. New York: W. H. Freeman.

Monroe, K. R., Martin, A., and Ghosh, P. 2009. Politics and an Innate Moral Sense: Scientific Evidence for an Old Theory? *Political Research Quarterly* 62: 614–34.

Moors, A., and Scherer, K. R. 2013. The Role of Appraisal in Emotion, in M. D. Robinson, E. R. Watkins, and E. Harmon-Jones (eds.). *Handbook of Cognition and Emotion*. New York: Guilford Press, 131–55.

Mulcahy, N., and Call, J. 2006. Apes Save Tools for Future Use, *Science* 312: 1038–40.

Münch, R. 1987. Parsonian Theory Today: In Search of a New Synthesis, in A. Giddens and J. H. Turner (eds.). *Social Theory Today*. Stanford, CA: Stanford University Press, 116–55.

Munroe, R. L., and Munroe, R. H. 2001. Comparative Approaches to Psychological Anthropology, in C. C. Moore and H. F. Mathews (eds.). *The Psychology of Cultural Experience*. Cambridge: Cambridge University Press, 223–37.

Nagel, T. 1986. *The View from Nowhere*. New York: Oxford University Press.

Nanda, S., and Warms, R. L. 2015[3]. *Culture Counts: A Concise Introduction to Cultural Anthropology*. Belmont, CA: Wadsworth Thomson Learning.

Neff, K. D. 2001. Judgments of Personal Autonomy and Interpersonal Responsibility in the Context of Indian Spousal Relationships: An Examination of Young People's Reasoning in Mysore, India, *British Journal of Developmental Psychology* 19: 233–57.

Nesse, R. 2013. Tinbergen's Four Questions, Organized: A Response to Bateson and Laland, *Trends in Ecology and Evolution* 28: 681–2.

Nettle, D., Cronin, K. A., and Bateson, M. 2013. Responses of Chimpanzees to Cues of Conspecific Observation. *Animal Behaviour* 86: 595–602.

Newman, G. 1976. *Comparative Deviance: Perception and Law in Six Cultures.* New York: Transaction.

Nichols, S. 2002. Norms with Feeling: Towards a Psychological Account of Moral Judgment, *Cognition* 84: 221–36.

—— 2004. *Sentimental Rules: On the Natural Foundations of Moral Judgment.* Oxford: Oxford University Press.

Niedenzu, H.-J. 2012. *Soziogenese der Normativität. Zur Emergenz eines neuen Modus der Sozialorganisation.* Weilerswist: Velbrück Wissenschaft.

Norenzayan, A., and Heine, S. J. 2005. Psychological Universals: What Are They and How Can We Know? *Psychological Bulletin* 131: 763–84.

Noveck, I. A. 2000. When Children Are More Logical Than Adults: Experimental Investigations of Scalar Implicature, *Cognition* 78: 165–88.

Noveck, I. A., and Posada, A. 2003. Characterizing the Time Course of an Implicature: An Evoked Potentials Study, *Brain and Language* 85: 203–10.

Noveck, I. A., and Reboul, A. 2008. Experimental Pragmatics: A Gricean Turn in the Study of Language, *Trends in Cognitive Sciences* 12: 425–31.

Nucci, L. P., Saxe, G. B., and Turiel, E. 2000. *Culture, Thought, and Development.* Mahwah, NJ: Lawrence Erlbaum.

Nucci, L. P., and Turiel, E. 1978. Social Interactions and the Development of Social Concepts in Preschool Children, *Child Development* 49: 400–7.

Nucci, L. P., and Weber, E. 1995. Social Interactions in the Home and the Development of Young Children's Conceptions of the Personal, *Child Development* 66: 1438–52.

Nussbaum, M. C. 1999. *Sex and Social Justice.* New York: Oxford University Press.

—— 2000. *Women and Human Development: The Capabilities Approach.* Cambridge: Cambridge University Press.

—— 2001. *Upheavals of Thought: The Intelligence of Emotions.* Cambridge: Cambridge University Press.

Ochs, E., and Schieffelin, B. 1984. Language Acquisition and Socialization: Three Developmental Stories, in R. Shweder and R. A. LeVine (eds.). *Culture Theory: Essays on Mind, Self and Emotion.* Cambridge: Cambridge University Press, 276–320.

Odling-Smee, J. F., Laland, K. N., and Feldman, M. W. 1996. Niche Construction, *The American Naturalist* 147: 641–8.

—— 2003. *Niche Construction.* Princeton, NJ: Princeton University Press.

Ogden, C. K., and Richards, I. A. 1923. *The Meaning of Meaning.* London: Kegan Paul.

Opp, K. D. 2015[2]. Norms, in J. D. Wright (ed.). *International Encyclopedia of the Social and Behavioral Sciences,* Vol. 17. Amsterdam: Elsevier, 5–10.

O'Toole, M. E. 2008. Psychopathy as a Behavior Classification System for Violent and Serial Crime Scenes, in H. Hervé & J. C. Yuille (eds.). *The Psychopath: Theory, Research and Practice.* Mahwah, NJ: Lawrence Erlbaum, 301–25.

Over, H., and Carpenter, M. 2009. Priming Third-Party Ostracism Increases Affiliative Imitation in Children, *Developmental Science* 12: F1–F8.

Pagel, M. 2012. *Wired for Culture: Origins of the Human Social Mind.* New York; London: W. W. Norton.

Parfit, D. 1997. Reasons and Motivation, *Proceedings of the Aristotelian Society,* suppl. vol. 71: 99–130.

Parsons, T. 1951. *The Social System.* London: Routledge & Kegan Paul.

Paul, A. W. 2006. Von der Natur der menschlichen Geselligkeit, in H. Schmidinger and C. Sedmak (eds.). *Der Mensch—ein "zôon politikón"? Gemeinschaft—Öffentlichkeit—Macht.* Darmstadt: Wissenschaftliche Buchgesellschaft: 71–84.

Payer, M. 2009. Ist Zuspätkommen unhöflich? Ein Blick auf andere Zeitkulturen, in A. Seemüller, T. G. Baudson, and M. Dresler (eds.). *Zeit in Wissenschaft, Philosophie und Kultur.* Stuttgart: S. Hirzel Verlag, 162–75.

Penn, D., Holyoak, K., and Povinelli, D. 2008. Darwin's Mistake: Explaining the Discontinuity between Human and Nonhuman Minds, *Behavioral and Brain Sciences* 31: 109–78.

Peoples, J. G., and Bailey, G. A. 2015[10]. *Humanity: An Introduction to Cultural Anthropology.* Stamford, CT: Cengage Learning.

Peräkylä, A. 2013. Conversation Analysis in Psychotherapy, in J. Sidnell and T. Stivers (eds.). *The Handbook of Conversation Analysis.* Malden, MA: Wiley-Blackwell, 551–74.

Peregrin, J. 2010. The Enigma of Rules, *International Journal of Philosophical Studies* 18: 377–94.

—— 2012. Inferentialism and the Normativity of Meaning, *Philosophia* 40: 75–97.

—— 2014. *Inferentialism: Why Rules Matter.* Houndmills, UK: Palgrave Macmillan.

Pereira, M. E. 1989. Agonistic Interactions of Juvenile Savannah Baboons. II. Agonistic Support and Rank Acquisition, *Ethology* 80: 152–71.

Perkins, S. A., and Turiel, E. 2007. To Lie or Not to Lie: To Whom and under What Circumstances, *Child Development* 78: 609–21.

Perry, S. 2009. Conformism in the Food Processing Techniques of White-Faced Capuchin Monkeys (*Cebus capucinus*), *Animal Cognition* 12: 705–16.

Perry, S., Baker, M., Fedigan, L., Gros-Louis, J., Jack, K., MacKinnon, K. C., Manson, J. H., Panger, M., Pyle, K., and Rose, L. 2003. Social Conventions in Wild White-Faced Capuchin Monkeys: Evidence for Traditions in a Neotropical Primate, *Current Anthropology* 44: 241–68.

Perry, S., and Manson, J. H. 2003. Traditions in Monkeys, *Evolutionary Anthropology* 12: 71–81.

Pettit, P. 1993. *The Common Mind: An Essay on Psychology, Society, and Politics.* New York: Oxford University Press.

—— 2008. Value-Mistaken and Virtue-Mistaken Norms, in J. Kühnelt (ed.). *Political Legitimization without Morality?* Dordrecht: Springer, 139–56.

Pettit, P., and Smith, M. 2004. The Truth in Deontology, in R. J. Wallace, M. Smith, and P. Pettit (eds.). *Reason and Value: Themes from the Moral Philosophy of Joseph Raz.* Oxford: Oxford University Press, 153–75.

Peuckert, Rüdiger. 2010[10]. Norm, soziale, in J. Kopp and B. Schäfers (eds.). *Grundbegriffe der Soziologie.* Wiesbaden: VS Verlag für Sozialwissenschaften/GWV Fachverlage GmbH, 215–18.

Piaget, J. 1932. *The Moral Judgment of the Child.* London: Routledge and Kegan Paul.

—— 1954. *The Child's Construction of Reality.* New York: Basic Books.

—— 1985. *The Equilibration of Cognitive Structures.* Chicago: University of Chicago Press.

Pika, S. 2014. Chimpanzee Grooming Gestures and Sounds, in Dor et al. 2014, 129–40.

Pinker, S. 1994. *The Language Instinct: The New Science of Language and Mind.* London: Penguin.

Plessner, H. 1928. *Die Stufen des Organischen und der Mensch.* Berlin; New York: de Gruyter 1975.

Popitz, H. 1980. *Die normative Konstruktion von Gesellschaft.* Tübingen: J. C. B. Mohr.

—— 2006. *Soziale Normen.* Frankfurt am Main: Suhrkamp.

Portmann, A. 1944. *A Zoologist Looks at Humankind.* Transl. J. Schaefer. New York: Columbia University Press 1990.

Power, C. 2014. Signal Evolution and the Social Brain, in Dor et al. 2014, 47–55.

Price, E. E., Lambeth, S. P., Schapiro, S. J., and Whiten, A. 2009. A Potent Effect of Observational Learning on Chimpanzee Tool Construction, *Proceedings of the Royal Society B: Biological Sciences* 276: 3377–83.

Price, S. A., and Brosnan, S. F. 2012. To Each According to his Need? Variability in the Responses to Inequity in Non-Human Primates, *Social Justice Research* 25: 140–69.

Prichard, H. A. 1912. Does Moral Philosophy Rest on a Mistake? in J. MacAdam (ed.). *Moral Writings*. Oxford: Clarendon Press 2002, 7–20.

Prinz, J. 2007. *The Emotional Construction of Morals*. Oxford University Press.

—— 2011. Is Empathy Necessary for Morality? in A. Coplan and P. Goldie (eds.). *Empathy: Philosophical and Psychological Perspectives*. Oxford: Oxford University Press, 211–29.

Prinz, J. J., and Nichols, S. 2011. Moral Emotions, in J. M. Doris and the Moral Psychology Research Group (eds.). *The Moral Psychology Handbook*. Oxford: Oxford University Press, 111–46.

Proctor, D., Williamson, R. A., de Waal, F. B. M., and Brosnan, S. F. 2013. Chimpanzees Play the Ultimatum Game, *Proceedings of the National Academy of Sciences* 110: 2070–5.

Pusey, A. E., and Wolf, M. 1996. Inbreeding Avoidance in Mammals, *Trends in Ecology and Evolution* 11: 201–6.

Quinn, N. 2005. Universals of Child Rearing, *Anthropological Theory* 5: 477–516.

Quinn, N., and Mageo, J. M. (eds.) 2013. *Attachment Reconsidered: Cultural Perspectives on a Western Theory*. New York: Palgrave Macmillan.

Raby, C. R., Alexis, D. M., Dickinson, A., and Clayton, N. S. 2007. Planning for the Future by Western Scrub Jays, *Nature* 445: 919–21.

Radcliffe-Brown, R. A. 1935. On the Concept of Function in Social Science, *American Anthropologist* 37: 394–402.

Raihani, N. J., Grutter, A. S., and Bshary, R. 2010. Punishers Benefit from Third-Party Punishment in Fish, *Science* 327: 171.

Raihani, N. J., Thornton, A., and Bshary, R. 2012. Punishment and Cooperation in Nature, *Trends in Ecology and Evolution* 27: 288–95.

Rainbolt, G. W. 1993. Rights as Normative Constraints on Others, *Philosophy and Phenomenological Research* 53: 93–111.

Rakoczy, H. 2008a. Pretence as Individual and Collective Intentionality, *Mind & Language* 23: 499–517.

—— 2008b. Taking Fiction Seriously: Young Children Understand the Normative Structure of Joint Pretence Games, *Developmental Psychology* 44: 1195–201.

Rakoczy, H., Brosche, N., Warneken, F., and Tomasello, M. 2009. Young Children's Understanding of the Context Relativity of Normative Rules in Conventional Games, *British Journal of Developmental Psychology* 27: 445–56.

Rakoczy, H., Clüver, A., Saucke, L., Stoffregen, N., Gräbener, A., Migura, J., and Call, J. 2014. Apes Are Intuitive Statisticians, *Cognition* 131: 60–8.

Rakoczy, H., Hamann, K., Warneken, F., and Tomasello, M. 2010. Bigger Knows Better: Young Children Selectively Learn Rule Games from Adults Rather than from Peers, *British Journal of Developmental Psychology* 28: 785–98.

Rakoczy, H., and Schmidt, M. F. H. 2013. The Early Ontogeny of Social Norms, *Child Development Perspectives* 7: 17–21.

Rakoczy, H., and Tomasello, M. 2007. The Ontogeny of Social Ontology: Steps to Shared Intentionality and Status Functions, in S. L. Tshohatzidis (ed.). *Intentional Acts and Institutional Facts*. Dordrecht: Springer, 113–37.

—— 2009. Done Wrong or Said Wrong? Young Children Understand the Normative Directions of Fit of Different Speech Acts, *Cognition* 113: 205–12.

Rakoczy, H., Warneken, F., and Tomasello, M. 2008. The Sources of Normativity: Young Children's Awareness of the Normative Structure of Games, *Developmental Psychology* 44: 875–81.

—— 2009. Young Children's Selective Learning of Rule Games from Reliable and Unreliable Models, *Cognitive Development* 24: 61–9.

Rantala, M. J., and Marcinkowska, U. M. 2011. The Role of Sexual Imprinting and the Westermarck Effect in Mate Choice in Humans, *Behavioral Ecology and Sociobiology* 65: 859–73.

Ratnieks, F. L. W., and Reeve, H. K. 1992. Conflict in Single-Queen Hymenopteran Societies: The Structure of Conflict and Processes That Reduce Conflict in Advanced Eusocial Species, *Journal of Theoretical Biology* 158: 33–65.

Rawls, J. 1955. Two Concepts of Rules, *The Philosophical Review* 64: 3–32.

—— 1971. *A Theory of Justice*. Oxford: Oxford University Press 1972.

Raymond, G. 2003. Grammar and Social Organization: Yes/No Interrogatives and the Structure of Responding, *American Sociological Review* 68: 939–67.

Raz, J. 1978. Reasons for Action, Decisions and Norms, in Raz (ed.). *Practical Reasoning*. Oxford: Oxford University Press, 128–43.

—— 2011. *From Normativity to Responsibility*. Oxford: Oxford University Press.

Reader, S. M., Hager, Y., and Laland, K. N. 2011. The Evolution of Primate General and Cultural Intelligence, *Philosophical Transactions of the Royal Society of London B* 366: 1017–27.

Reboul, A. 2011. A Relevance-Theoretic Account of the Evolution of Implicit Communication, *Studies in Pragmatics* 13: 1–19.

Richerson, P. J., and Boyd, R. 2005. *Not by Genes Alone: How Culture Transformed Human Evolution*. Chicago: University of Chicago Press.

Riedl, K., Jensen, K., Call, J., and Tomasello, M. 2012. No Third-Party Punishment in Chimpanzees, *Proceedings of the National Academy of Sciences* 109: 14824–9.

Rizzolatti, G., and Arbib, M. A. 1998. Language within Our Grasp, *Trends in Neurosciences* 21: 188–94.

Robertson, S. (ed.). 2009. *Spheres of Reason: New Essays in the Philosophy of Normativity*. Oxford: Oxford University Press.

Rochat, P. 2012. Self-Consciousness and "Conscientiousness" in Development, *Infancia y Aprendizaje* 35: 387–94.

Rodseth, L. 1998. Distributive models of culture: A Sapirian Alternative to Essentialism, *American Anthropologist* 100: 55–69.

Rodseth, L., Wrangham, R. W., Harrigan, A. M., and Smuts, B. B. 1991. The Human Community as a Primate Society, *Current Anthropology* 32: 221–54.

Röttger-Rössler, B. 2013. In the Eyes of the Other: Shame and Social Conformity in the Context of Indonesian Societies, in B. Sère and J. Wettlaufer (eds.). *Shame between Punishment and Penance*. Florence: Micrologus, 405–19.

Röttger-Rössler, B., Scheidecker, G., Jung, S., and Holodynski, M. 2013. Socializing Emotions in Childhood: A Cross-Cultural Comparison between the Bara in Madagascar and the Minangkabau in Indonesia, *Mind, Culture, and Activity* 20: 260–87. doi: 10.1080/10749039.2013.806551.

Rogers, L. J., and Kaplan, G. 1998. *Songs, Roars, and Rituals: Communication in Birds, Mammals and Other Species*. Cambridge, MA: Harvard University Press.

Rogoff, B. 2003. *The Cultural Nature of Human Development*. Oxford: Oxford University Press.

Rossano, F., Rakoczy, H., and Tomasello, M. 2011. Young Children's Understanding of Violations of Property Rights, *Cognition* 121: 219–27.

Rossano, M. J. 2012. The Essential Role of Ritual in the Transmission and Reinforcement of Social Norms, *Psychological Bulletin* 138: 529–49.

Roughley, N. 2003. Normbegriff und Normbegründung im moralphilosophischen Kontraktualismus, in A. Leist (ed.). *Moral als Vertrag?* Berlin; New York: de Gruyter, 213–43.

—— 2005. Was heisst "menschliche Natur"? Begriffliche Differenzierungen und normative Ansatzpunkte, in Bayertz 2005, 133–56.

—— 2011. Human Natures, in S. Schleidgen, M. Jungert, R. Bauer, and V. Sandow (eds.). *Human Nature and Self Design*. Paderborn: Mentis, 11–33.

—— 2016. *Wanting and Intending: Elements of a Philosophy of Practical Mind*. Dordrecht: Springer.

—— 2018a. The Empathy in Moral Obligation: An Exercise in Creature Construction, in Roughley and Schramme 2018, 264–90.

—— 2018b. From Shared Intentionality to Moral Obligation? Some Worries, *Philosophical Psychology*: 736–54. doi: 10.1080/09515089.2018.1486610.

Roughley, N., and Schramme, T. (eds.). 2018. *Forms of Fellow Feeling: Empathy, Sympathy, Concern and Moral Agency*. Cambridge: Cambridge University Press.

Rudolf von Rohr, C., Burkart, J. M., and van Schaik, C. P. 2011. Evolutionary Precursors of Social Norms in Chimpanzees: A New Approach, *Biology and Philosophy* 26: 1–30.

Rudolf von Rohr, C., Koski, S. E., Burkart, J. M., Caws, C., Fraser, O. N., Ziltener, A., and van Schaik, C. P. 2012. Impartial Third-Party Interventions in Captive Chimpanzees: A Reflection of Community Concern, *PLOS ONE* 7: e32494.

Rudolf von Rohr, C., van Schaik, C. P., Kissling, A., and Burkart, J. M. 2015. Chimpanzees' Bystander Reactions to Infanticide: An Evolutionary Precursor of Social Norms? *Human Nature* 26, 143–60.

Rudolph, W., and Tschohl, P. 1977. *Systematische Anthropologie*. München: Wilhelm Fink Verlag.

Russell, B. 1921. *The Analysis of Mind*. London: Allen and Unwin.

Ryle, G. 1949. *The Concept of Mind*. Harmondsworth, UK: Penguin 1970.

Sacks, H., and Schegloff, E. A. 1979/2007. Two Preferences in the Organization of Reference to Persons in Conversation and Their Interaction, in N. J. Enfield and T. Stivers (eds.). *Person Reference in Interaction: Linguistic, Cultural, and Social Perspectives*. Cambridge: Cambridge University Press, 23–8.

Sanderson, S. K. 2014. *Human Nature and the Evolution of Society*. Boulder, CO: Westview Press.

Sanz, C. K., Call, J., and Boesch, C. (eds.). 2013. *Tool Use in Animals: Cognition and Ecology*. Cambridge: Cambridge University Press.

Sapolsky, R. M., and Share, L. J. 2004. A Pacific Culture among Wild Baboons: Its Emergence and Transmission, *PLOS Biology* 2: e106.

Sartre, J.-P. 1946. *Existentialism Is a Humanism*. Transl. by A. Cohen-Solal. New Haven, CT: Yale University Press 2007.

Sayre-McCord, G. 2015. Hume and Smith on Sympathy, Approbation and Moral Judgement, in E. Schliesser (ed.). *Sympathy. A History*. Oxford: Oxford University Press, 208–46.

Scanlon, T. M. 1998. *What We Owe to Each Other*. Cambridge, MA: Harvard University Press.

Schank, R., and Abelson, R. P. 1977. *Scripts, Plans, Goals and Understanding: An Inquiry into Human Knowledge Structures*. New York: Lawrence Erlbaum.

Schegloff, E. A. 1972. Notes on a Conversational Practice: Formulating Place, in D. Sudnow (ed.). *Studies in Social Interaction*. New York: Free Press, 75–119.

—— 1992. Repair after Next Turn: The Last Structurally Provided Defense of Intersubjectivity in Conversation, *American Journal of Sociology* 97: 1295–345.

Schegloff, E. A., and Sacks, H. 1973. Opening Up Closings, *Semiotica* 7: 289–327.

Schino, G., and Aureli, F. 2010. Primate Reciprocity and Its Cognitive Requirements, *Evolutionary Anthropology* 19: 130–5.

—— 2017. Reciprocity in Group-Living Animals: Partner Control versus Partner Choice, *Biological Reviews* 92: 665–72.

Schmid, H. B. (ed.) 2009. *Plural Action. Essays in Philosophy and Social Science*. Dordrecht: Springer.

—— 2011. The Idiocy of Strategic Reasoning: Towards an Account of Consensual Action, *Analyse & Kritik* 33: 35–56.

Schmidt, M. F. H., Rakoczy, H., and Tomasello, M. 2011. Young Children Attribute Normativity to Novel Actions without Pedagogy or Normative Language, *Developmental Science* 14: 530–9.

—— 2012. Young Children Enforce Social Norms Selectively Depending on the Violator's Group Affiliation, *Cognition* 124: 325–33.

—— 2013. Young Children Understand and Defend the Entitlements of Others, *Journal of Experimental Child Psychology* 116: 930–44.

Schmidt, M. F. H., and Sommerville, J. A. 2011. Fairness Expectations and Altruistic Sharing in 15-Month-Old Human Infants, *PLOS ONE* 6: e23223.

Schmidt, M. F. H., and Tomasello, M. 2012. Young Children Enforce Social Norms, *Current Directions in Psychological Science* 21: 232–6.

Schnall, S., Haidt, J., Clore, G. L., and Jordan, A. H. 2008. Disgust as Embodied Moral Judgment, *Personality and Social Psychology Bulletin* 34: 1096–109.

Schnoell, A. V., Dittmann, M. T., and Fichtel, C. 2014. Human-Introduced Long-term Traditions in Wild Redfronted Lemurs? *Animal Cognition* 17: 45–54.

Schnoell, A. V., and Fichtel, C. 2012. Wild Redfronted Lemurs (*Eulemur rufifrons*) Use Social Information to Learn New Foraging Techniques, *Animal Cognition* 15: 505–16.

Schopenhauer, A. 1840. Preisschrift über die Grundlage der Moral, in L. Lütkehaus (ed.). *Werke in fünf Bänden, Bd. III*. Zürich: Haffmans 1988, 459–632.

Schramme, T. (ed.). 2014. *Being Amoral: Psychopathy and Moral Incapacity*. Cambridge, MA: MIT Press.

Schroeder, S. 1998. *Das Privatsprachenargument*. Paderborn: Schöningh.

—— Forthcoming. Semantic Normativity and Moral Obligation.

Schülke, O., Bhagavatula, J., Vigilant, L., and Ostner, J. 2010. Social Bonds Enhance Reproductive Success in Male Macaques, *Current Biology* 20: 2207–10.

Schweikard, D. P., and Schmid, H. B. 2013. Collective Intentionality. *Stanford Encyclopedia of Philosophy*. http://plato.stanford.edu/archives/sum2013/entries/collective-intentionality.

Schweizer, T. 1989. *Reisanbau in einem javanischen Dorf. Eine Fallstudie zur Theorie und Methodik der Wirtschafsethnologie*. Cologne and Vienna: Böhlau Verlag.

Scott-Phillips, T. C., Kirby, S., and Ritchie, G. R. S. 2009. Signalling Signalhood and the Emergence of Communication, *Cognition* 113: 226–33.

Scupin, R., and DeCorse, C. R. 2006[6]. *Anthropology: A Global Perspective*. Upper Saddle River, NJ: Pearson Prentice Hall.

Searle, J. R. 1969. *Speech Acts: An Essay in the Philosophy of Language*. Cambridge: Cambridge University Press.

—— 1979. *Expression and Meaning: Studies in the Theory of Speech Acts*. Cambridge: Cambridge University Press.

—— 1983. *Intentionality: An Essay in the Philosophy of Mind*. Cambridge: Cambridge University Press.

—— 1995. *The Construction of Social Reality*. London: Penguin.

—— 2001. *Rationality in Action*. Cambridge, MA: MIT Press.

—— 2010. *Making the Social World*. Oxford: Oxford University Press.

Sellars, W. 1963a. *Science, Perception and Reality*. London: Routledge and Kegan Paul.

—— 1963b. Some Reflections on Language Games, in Sellars 1963a, 321–58.

Sen, A. K. 1992. *Inequality Re-Examined*. Oxford: Clarendon Press.

—— 1999. *Development as Freedom*. New York: Alfred A. Knopf.

Seyfarth, R. M., and Cheney, D. L. 2012a. Primate Social Cognition as a Precursor to Language, in Tallermann and Gibson 2012, 59–70.

—— 2012b. Knowledge of Social Relationships, in Mitani et al. 2012, 628–42.

Shoemaker, D. W. 2011. Psychopathy, Responsibility and the Moral/Conventional Distinction, *Southern Journal of Philosophy* 49: 99–124.

Shweder, R. A., and Bourne, E. J. 1982. Does the Concept of Person Vary Cross-Culturally?, in A. J. Marsella and G. M. White (eds.). *Cultural Conceptions of Mental Health and Therapy*. Boston: Reidel, 97–137.

Shweder, R. A., Mahapatra, M., and Miller, J. G. 1987. Culture and Moral Development, in J. Kagan and S. Lamb (eds.). *The Emergence of Morality in Young Children*. Chicago: University of Chicago Press, 1–83.

Sidgwick, H. 1874. *The Methods of Ethics*. Indianapolis: Hackett 1981.

Sidnell, J. 2014. The Architecture of Intersubjectivity Revisited, in N. J. Enfield, P. Kockelman, and J. Sidnell (eds.). *The Cambridge Handbook of Linguistic Anthropology*. Cambridge: Cambridge University Press, 364–99.

Sidnell, J., and Barnes, R. 2013. Alternative, Subsequent Descriptions, in M. Hayashi, G. Raymond, and J. Sidnell (eds.). *Conversational Repair and Human Understanding*. Cambridge: Cambridge University Press, 322–42.

Silk, J. B. 2012. The Adaptive Value of Sociality, in Mitani et al. 2012, 552–64.

Silk, J. B., Beehner, J. C., Bergman, T. J., Crockford, C., Engh, A. L., Moscovice, L. R., Wittig, R. M., Seyfarth, R. M., and Cheney, D. L. 2009. The Benefits of Social Capital: Close Social Bonds among Female Baboons Enhance Offspring Survival, *Proceedings of the Royal Society of London B* 276: 3099–104.

—— 2010. Strong and Consistent Social Bonds Enhance the Longevity of Female Baboons, *Current Biology* 20: 1359–61.

Sinha, C. 2014. Niche Construction and Semiosis: Biocultural and Social Dynamics, in Dor et al. 2014, 31–46.

Skinner, B. F. 1971. *Beyond Freedom and Dignity*. New York: Knopf.

Skorupski, J. 1999. The Definition of Morality, in J. Skorupski (ed.). *Ethical Explorations*. Oxford: Oxford University Press, 137–59.

Skyrms, B. 2010. *Signals: Evolution, Learning, and Information*. Oxford: Oxford University Press.

Sloane, S., Baillargeon, R., and Premack, D. 2012. Do Infants Have a Sense of Fairness? *Psychological Science* 23: 196–204.

Slote, M. 2010. *Moral Sentimentalism*. Oxford: Oxford University Press.

Smetana, J. G. 1981. Preschool Children's Conceptions of Moral and Social Rules, *Child Development* 52: 1333–6.

—— 1984. Toddlers' Social Interactions Regarding Moral and Conventional Transgressions, *Child Development* 55: 1767–76.

—— 2006. Social-Cognitive Domain Theory: Consistencies and Variations in Children's Moral and Social Judgments, in Killen and Smetana, 119–53.

Smetana, J. G., and Braeges, J. L. 1990. The Development of Toddlers' Moral and Conventional Judgments, *Merrill-Palmer Quarterly* 36: 329–46.

Smith, A. 1759/90. *The Theory of Moral Sentiments*. Eds. D. D. Raphael and A. L. Macfie. Indianapolis: Liberty Fund 1982.

Smith, B. 1998. Language, Conventionality of, in E. Craig (ed.). *Routledge Encyclopedia of Philosophy*, vol. V. London: Routledge, 368–71.

Snell-Rood, E. C. 2013. An Overview of the Evolutionary Causes and Consequences of Behavioural Plasticity, *Animal Behaviour* 85: 1004–11.

Sommerville, J. A., Schmidt, M. F. H., Yun, J., and Burns, M. 2013. The Development of Fairness Expectations and Prosocial Behavior in the Second Year of Life, *Infancy* 18: 40–66.

Southwood, N. 2011. The Moral/Conventional Distinction, *Mind* 120: 761–802.

Spencer, J. P., Blumberg, M. S., McMurray, B., Robinson, S. R., Samuelson, L. K., and Tomblin, J. B. 2009. Short Arms and Talking Eggs: Why We Should No Longer Abide the Nativist-Empiricist Debate, *Child Development Perspectives* 3: 79–87.

Sperber, D., and Wilson, D. 1995². *Relevance: Communication and Cognition*. Oxford: Basil Blackwell.

Spittler, G. 1967. *Norm und Sanktion. Untersuchungen zum Sanktionsmechanismus*. Olten and Freiburg i. Br.: Walter Verlag.

Sripada, C. S. 2005. Punishment and the Strategic Structure of Oral Systems, *Biology and Philosophy* 20: 767–89.

Sripada, C. S., and Stich, S. 2006. A Framework for the Psychology of Norms, in P. Carruthers, S. Laurence, and S. P. Stich (eds.). *The Innate Mind*, Vol. 2: *Culture and Cognition*. Oxford: Oxford University Press, 280–301.

Stainton, R. J. 1996. *Philosophical Perspectives on Language*. Peterborough: Broadview.

Sterck, E. H. M., Watts, D. P., and van Schaik, C. P. 1997. The Evolution of Female Social Relationships in Nonhuman Primates, *Behavioral Ecology and Sociobiology* 41: 291–309.

Sterelny, K. 2012. *The Evolved Apprentice: How Evolution Made Humans Unique*. Cambridge, MA: MIT Press.

—— 2016. Deacon's Challenge: From Calls to Words. *Topoi* 35: 271–82.

—— 2018. Language: From How-Possibly to How-Probably? in R. Joyce (ed.). *The Routledge Handbook of Evolution and Philosophy*. New York: Routledge, 120–35.

Stivers, T. 2007. Alternative Recognitionals in Person Reference, in N. J. Enfield and T. Stivers (eds.). *Person Reference in Interaction: Linguistic, Cultural, and Social Perspectives.* Cambridge: Cambridge University Press, 73–96.

Stivers, T., and Hayashi, M. 2010. Transformative Answers: One Way to Resist a Question's Constraints, *Language in Society* 39: 1–25.

Stivers, T., and Rossano, F. 2010. Mobilizing Response, *Research on Language and Social Interaction* 43: 3–31.

Stouffer, S. 1955. *Communism, Conformity and Civil Liberties.* New York: Doubleday.

Strawson, P. F. 1962. Freedom and Resentment, in Strawson, *Freedom and Resentment and Other Essays.* New York: Routledge 2008, 1–28.

—— 1992. *Analysis and Metaphysics: An Introduction to Philosophy.* Oxford: Oxford University Press 2006.

Street, S. 2006. A Darwinian Dilemma for Realist Theories of Value, *Philosophical Studies* 127: 109–66.

—— 2016. Objectivity and Truth. You'd better Re-think it! *Oxford Studies in Metaethics* 11: 293–334.

Sunstein, C. R. 1996. Social Norms and Social Roles, *Columbia Law Review* 96: 903–68.

Tallermann, M., and Gibson, K. R. (eds.). 2012. *The Oxford Handbook of Language Evolution.* Oxford: Oxford University Press.

Taylor, C. 2016. *The Language Animal: The Full Shape of the Human Linguistic Capacity.* Cambridge, MA; London: Belknap Press of Harvard University Press.

Tennie, C., Call, J., and Tomasello, M. 2009. Ratcheting up the Ratchet: On the Evolution of Cumulative Culture, *Philosophical Transactions of the Royal Society B: Biological Sciences* 364: 2405–15.

Thierry, B. 2013. Identifying Constraints in the Evolution of Primate Societies, *Philosophical Transactions of the Royal Society of London B* 368: 20120342, 1–8.

Thompson, M. 2004. What Is It to Wrong Someone? A Puzzle about Justice, in R. J. Wallace, M. Smith, and P. Pettit (eds.). *Reason and Value: Themes from the Moral Philosophy of Joseph Raz.* Oxford: Oxford University Press, 333–84.

Thomson, J. J. 1971. A Defense of Abortion, in J. J. Thomson and W. Parent (eds.). *Rights, Restitution, and Risk.* Cambridge, MA: Harvard University Press 1986.

—— 2008. *Normativity.* Chicago; La Salle, IL: Open Court.

Tinbergen, N. 1952. Derived Activities: Their Causation, Biological Significance, Origin and Emancipation during Evolution, *Quarterly Review of Biology* 27: 1–32.

—— 1963. On Aims and Methods of Ethology. *Zeitschrift für Tierpsychologie* 20: 410–33.

Tomasello, M. 1999. *The Cultural Origins of Human Cognition.* Cambridge, MA: Harvard University Press.

—— 2003. *Constructing a Language.* Cambridge, MA: Harvard University Press.

—— 2008. *Origins of Human Communication.* Cambridge, MA: MIT Press.

—— 2009. *Why We Cooperate.* Cambridge, MA: MIT Press.

—— 2014. *A Natural History of Human Thinking.* Cambridge, MA: Harvard University Press.

—— 2016. *A Natural History of Human Morality.* Cambridge, MA: Harvard University Press.

Tomasello, M., and Call, J. 2006. Do Chimpanzees Know What Others See—or Only What They Are Looking At? in Hurley and Nudds 2006, 371–84.

Tomasello, M., and Moll, H. 2010. The Gap is Social. Human Shared Intentionality and Culture, in Kappeler and Silk 2010, 331–49.

Tomasello, M., and Vaish, A. 2013. Origins of Human Cooperation and Morality, *Annual Review of Psychology* 64: 231–55.

Tomasello, M., Carpenter, M., Call, J., Behne, T., and Moll, H. 2005. Understanding and Sharing Intentions: The Origins of Cultural Cognition, *Behavioral and Brain Sciences* 28: 675–91.

Tomasello, M., Melis, A. P., Tennie, C., Wyman, E., and Herrmann, E. 2012. Two Key Steps in the Evolution of Human Cooperation: The Interdependence Hypothesis, *Current Anthropology* 53: 673–92.

Trabant, J. 2008. *Was ist Sprache?* München: C. H. Beck.

Tracy, J. L., and Matsumoto, D. 2008. The Spontaneous Expression of Pride and Shame: Evidence for Biologically Innate Nonverbal Displays, *Proceedings of the National Academy of Sciences USA* 105: 11655–60.

Trivers, R. 2002. *Natural Selection and Social Theory: Selected Papers of Robert Trivers*. Oxford: Oxford University Press.

Trommsdorff, G. (ed.) 1989. *Sozialisation im Kulturvergleich*. Stuttgart: Ferdinand Enke Verlag.

Tugendhat, E. 1984. *Probleme der Ethik*. Stuttgart: Reclam.

—— 2001. Wie sollen wir Moral verstehen? In E. Tugendhat (ed.). *Aufsätze 1992–2000*, Frankfurt am Main: Suhrkamp.

Tuomela, R. 2007. *The Philosophy of Sociality: The Shared Point of View*. Oxford University Press.

Turiel, E. 1978. Social Regulations and Domains of Social Concepts, in W. Damon (ed.). *New Directions for Child Development*, Vol. 1: *Social Cognition*. San Francisco: Jossey-Bass, 45–74.

—— 1983. *The Development of Social Knowledge: Morality and Convention*. Cambridge: Cambridge University Press.

—— 2002. *The Culture of Morality: Social Development, Context, and Conflict*. Cambridge: Cambridge University Press.

—— 2006. The Development of Morality, in W. Damon, R. M. Lerner (eds.). *Handbook of Child Psychology*, Vol. 3: N. Eisenberg (ed.). *Social, Emotional, and Personality Development*. Hoboken, NJ: John Wiley and Sons, 789–857.

—— 2008a. Thought about Actions in Social Domains: Morality, Social Conventions, and Social Interactions, *Cognitive Development* 23: 126–54.

—— 2008b. Social Decisions, Social Interactions, and the Coordination of Diverse Judgments, in U. Mueller, J. I. Carpendale, N. Budwig, and B. Sokol (eds.). *Social Life, Social Knowledge: Toward a Process Account of Development*. Mahwah, NJ: Lawrence Erlbaum, 255–76.

—— 2010. The Development of Morality: Reasoning, Emotions, and Resistance, in W. F. Overton (ed.). *Cognition, Biology, and Methods across the Lifespan. Handbook of Life-Span Development*, Vol. 1. Editor-in-chief: R. M. Lerner. Hoboken, NJ: John Wiley and Sons, 554–83.

—— 2015. Moral Development, in W. F. Overton and P. C. M. Molenaar (eds.). *Handbook of Child Psychology and Developmental Science*, Vol. 1: *Theory and Method*. Hoboken, NJ: John Wiley and Sons, 484–523.

Turiel, E., and Gingo, M. 2017. Development in the Moral Domain: Coordination and the Need to Consider Other Domains of Social Reasoning, in N. Budwig, E. Turiel, and P. Zelazo (eds.). *New Perspectives on Human Development*. Cambridge: Cambridge University Press, 209–28.

Turiel, E., and Smetana, J. G. 1984. Social Knowledge and Social Action: The Coordination of Domains, in W. M. Kurtines and J. L. Gewirtz (eds.). *Morality, Moral Behavior, and Moral Development: Basic Issues in Theory and Research*. New York: John Wiley and Sons, 261–82.

Turiel, E., and Wainryb, C. 1998. Concepts of Freedoms and Rights in a Traditional Hierarchically Organized Society, *British Journal of Developmental Psychology* 16: 375–95.

Turiel, E., Killen, M., and Helwig, C. C. 1987. Morality: Its Structure, Functions, and Vagaries, in J. Kagan and S. Lamb (eds.). *The Emergence of Morality in Young Children*. Chicago: University of Chicago Press, 155–243.

Turiel, E., Perkins, S. A., and Mensing, J. F. 2009. *Judgments about Deception in Marital Relationships.* Unpublished manuscript, University of California, Berkeley.

Ullmann-Margalit, E. 1977. *The Emergence of Norms*. Oxford: Oxford University Press.

Vaish, A. 2018. Sophisticated Concern in Early Childhood. In Roughley and Schramme 2018, 216–42.

Vaish, A., Missana, M., and Tomasello, M. 2011. Three-Year-Old Children Intervene in Third-Party Moral Transgressions, *British Journal of Developmental Psychology* 29: 124–30.

van den Berghe, P. L. 1983. Human Inbreeding Avoidance: Culture in Nature, *Behavioral and Brain Sciences* 6: 91–102.

Vanderschraaf, P., and Sillari, G. 2013. Common Knowledge. *The Stanford Encyclopedia of Philosophy*, ed. E. N. Zalta: https://plato.stanford.edu/entries/common-knowledge.

van de Waal, E., Borgeaud, C., and Whiten, A. 2013. Potent Social Learning and Conformity Shape a Wild Primate's Foraging Decisions, *Science* 340: 483–85.

van Leeuwen, E. J. C., and Haun, D. B. M. 2013. Conformity in Nonhuman Primates: Fad or Fact?, *Evolution and Human Behavior* 34: 1–7.

——— 2014. Conformity without Majority? The Case for Demarcating Social from Majority Influences, *Animal Behaviour* 96: 187–94.

Vann, E. 2013. Culture, in J. G. Carrier and D. B. Gewertz (eds.). *The Handbook of Sociocultural Anthropology*. London: Bloomsbury, 30–48.

van Schaik, C. P. 2000. Infanticide by Male Primates: The Sexual Selection Hypothesis Revisited, in C. P. van Schaik and C. H. Janson (eds.). *Infanticide by Males and its Implications*. Cambridge: Cambridge University Press, 27–60.

——— 2012. Animal Culture: Chimpanzee Conformity? *Current Biology* 22: R402–4.

——— 2013. The Costs and Benefits of Flexibility as an Expression of Behavioural Plasticity: A Primate Perspective, *Philosophical Transactions of the Royal Society of London B* 368(1618): 20120339, 1–9.

——— 2016. *The Primate Origins of Human Nature*. Hoboken, NJ: Wiley & Sons.

van Schaik, C. P., and Burkart, J. 2018. The Moral Capacity as a Biological Adaptation: A Commentary on Tomasello, *Philosophical Psychology* 31: 703–21. doi: 10.1080/09515089.2018.1486608.

van Schaik, C. P., and Isler, K. 2012. Life-History Evolution, in Mitani et al. 2012, 220–44.

van Schaik, C. P., and Michel, K. 2016. *The Good Book of Human Nature: An Evolutionary Reading of the Bible*. New York: Basic Books.

van Schaik, C. P., Burkart, J. M., Jaeggi, A. V., and Rudolf von Rohr, C. 2014. Morality as a Biological Adaptation: An Evolutionary Model Based on the Lifestyle of Human Foragers, in M. Christen, C. van Schaik, J. Fischer, M. Huppenbauer, and C. Tanner (eds.). *Empirically Informed Ethics: Morality between Facts and Norms*. Zurich: Springer International, 65–84.

Vivelo, F. R. 1978. *Cultural Anthropology Handbook: A Basic Introduction*. New York: McGraw-Hill.

Vlastos, G. 1962. Justice and Equality, in R. B. Brandt (ed.). *Social Justice*. Englewood Cliffs, NJ: Prentice-Hall, 31–72.

von Savigny, E. 1988. *The Social Foundations of Meaning*. New York: Springer.

von Wright, G. H. 1963. *Norm and Action*. London: Routledge and Kegan Paul.

Wainryb, C. 1991. Understanding Differences in Moral Judgments: The Role of Informational Assumptions, *Child Development* 62: 840–51.

—— 1993. The Application of Moral Judgements to Other Cultures: Relativism and Universality, *Child Development* 64: 924–33.

Wainryb, C., and Turiel, E. 1994. Dominance, Subordination, and Concepts of Personal Entitlements in Cultural Contexts, *Child Development* 65: 1701–22.

Wainryb, C., Brehl, B. A., and Matwin, S. 2005. Being Hurt and Hurting Others: Children's Narrative Accounts and Moral Judgments of Their Own Interpersonal Conflicts, *Monographs of the Society for Research in Child Development* 70.

Waismann, F. 1965. *The Principles of Linguistic Philosophy*. London: Macmillan.

Wallace, R. J. 1996. *Responsibility and the Moral Sentiments*. Cambridge, MA: Harvard University Press.

—— 2011a. Konzeptionen der Normativität: Einige grundlegende philosophische Fragen, in R. Forst and K. Günther (eds.). *Die Herausbildung normativer Ordnungen. Interdisziplinäre Perspektiven*. Frankfurt am Main: Campus Verlag, 33–55.

—— 2011b. Dispassionate Opprobrium: On Blame and the Reactive Sentiments, in R. J. Wallace, R. Kumar, and S. Freeman (eds.). *Reasons and Recognition: Essays on the Philosophy of T. M. Scanlon*. Oxford: Oxford University Press, 348–72.

—— 2013. The Deontic Structure of Morality, in D. Bakhurst, B. Hooker, and M. Little (eds.). *Thinking about Reasons: Themes from the Philosophy of Jonathan Dancy*. Oxford: Oxford University Press, 137–67.

Walters, J. R., and Seyfarth, R. M. 1987. Conflict and Cooperation, in B. B. Smuts, D. L. Cheney, R. M. Seyfarth, R. W. Wrangham, and T. T. Struhsaker (eds.). *Primate Societies*. Chicago: University of Chicago Press, 306–17.

Watts, D. P. 2012. The Apes: Taxonomy, Biogeography, Life History, and Behavioral Ecology, in Mitani et al. 2012, 113–42.

Wedgwood, R. 2007. *The Nature of Normativity*. Oxford: Clarendon Press.

Weinrib, E. J. 1996. *The Idea of Private Law*. Cambridge, MA: Harvard University Press.

—— 2012. *Corrective Justice*. Oxford: Oxford University Press.

Weir, A. A. S., Chappell, J., and Kacelnik, A. 2002. Shaping of Hooks in New Caledonian Crows. *Science* 297: 981.

Weir, A. A. S., and Kacelnik, A. 2006. A New Caledonian Crow (Corvus moneduloides) Creatively Re-Designs Tools by Bending or Unbending Aluminium strips. *Animal Cognition* 9: 317–34.

Wellman, H. M., and Miller, J. G. 2008. Including Deontic Reasoning as Fundamental to Theory of Mind. *Human Development* 51: 105–35.

Werner, H. 1957. *Comparative Psychology of Mental Development*. New York: International Universities Press.

Whiten, A. 2012. Social Learning, Traditions, and Culture, in Mitani et al. 2012, 681–99.

Whiten, A., Goodall, J., McGrew, W. C., Nishida, T., Reynolds, V., Sugiyama, Y., Tutin, C. E. G., Wrangham, R. W., and Boesch, C. 1999. Cultures in Chimpanzees, *Nature* 399: 682–5.

Whiten, A., Horner, V., and de Waal, F. B. M. 2005. Conformity to Cultural Norms of Tool Use in Chimpanzees, *Nature* 437: 737–40.

Whiten, A., Spiteri, A., Horner, V., Bonnie, K. E., Lambeth, S. P., Schapiro, S. J., and de Waal, F. B. M. 2007. Transmission of Multiple Traditions within and between Chimpanzee Groups, *Current Biology* 17: 1038–43.

Whiting, D. 2009. Is Meaning Fraught with Ought? *Pacific Philosophical Quarterly* 90: 535–55.

—— 2013. What is the Normativity of Meaning? *Inquiry* 59: 219–38. doi: 10.1080/0020174X. 2013.852132.

Whiting, B. B., and Pope Edwards, C. 1988. *Children of Different Worlds: The Formation of Social Behavior*. Cambridge, MA: Harvard University Press.

Whiting, B. B., and Whiting, J. W. M., in collaboration with Longabaugh, J. W. M. 1975. *Children in Six Cultures: A Psycho-Cultural Analysis*. Cambridge, MA: Harvard University Press 2014.

Wich, S. A., Krützen, M., Lameira, A. R., Nater, A., Arora, N., Bastian, M. L., Meulman, E., Morrogh-Bernard, H. C., Atmoko, S. S. U., Pamungkas, J., Perwitasari-Farajallah, D., Hardus, M. E., van Noordwijk, M., and van Schaik, C. P. 2012. Call Cultures in Orang-Utans? *PLOS ONE* 7: e36180. doi: 10.1371/journal.pone.0036180.

Wierzbicka, A. 1996. *Semantics: Primes and Universals*. Oxford: Oxford University Press.

Wiggins, D. 1987. A Sensible Subjectivism, in Wiggins, *Needs, Values, Truth: Essays in the Philosophy of Value*. Oxford: Blackwell, 185–214.

Wikan, U. 1996. *Tomorrow, God Willing: Self-Made Destinies in Cairo*. Chicago: University of Chicago Press.

Wikforss, A. 2001. Semantic Normativity, *Philosophical Studies* 102: 203–26.

Williams, B. 1965. Ethical Consistency, in *Problems of the Self. Philosophical Papers 1956–1972*. Cambridge University Press 1973, 166–86.

Wilson, D. S. 2015. *Does Altruism Exist? Culture, Genes, and the Welfare of Others*. New Haven, CT: Yale University Press.

Wiltermuth, S. S., and Heath, C. 2009. Synchrony and Cooperation, *Psychological Science* 20: 1–5.

Winch, P. 1958. *The Idea of a Social Science and Its Relation to Philosophy*. London; New York: Routledge 2008.

Wittgenstein, L. 1930–32. *Wittgenstein's Lectures, Cambridge 1930–32*. Oxford: Basil Blackwell 1980.

—— 1953. *Philosophische Untersuchungen. Philosophical Investigations*. Transl. G. E. M. Anscombe. Oxford: Blackwell.

—— 1974. *Philosophical Grammar*. Transl. A. Kenny. Oxford: Blackwell.

Wrangham, R. W., and Glowacki, L. 2012. Intergroup Aggression in Chimpanzees and War in Nomadic Hunter-Gatherers, *Human Nature* 23: 5–29.

Wright, C. 1986. *Realism, Meaning, and Truth*. Oxford: Blackwell.

Wyman, E., and Rakoczy, H. 2011. Social Conventions, Institutions, and Human Uniqueness: Lessons from Children and Chimpanzees, in W. Welsch et al. (eds.). *Interdisciplinary Anthropology*. Berlin: Springer-Verlag, 131–56.

Wyman, E., Rakoczy, H., and Tomasello, M. 2009. Normativity and Context in Young Children's Pretend Play, *Cognitive Development* 24: 146–55.

Zahavi, A. 1975. Mate Selection: A Selection for a Handicap, *Journal of Theoretical Biology* 53: 205–14.

Zahn-Waxler, C., Radke-Yarrow, M., Wagner, E., and Chapman, M. 1992. Development of Concern for Others, *Developmental Psychology* 28: 126–36.

Zahn-Waxler, C., Schoen, A., and Decety, J. 2018. An Interdisciplinary Perspective on the Origins of Concern for Others: Contributions from Psychology, Neuroscience, Philosophy and Sociobiology, in Roughley and Schramme 2018, 185–215.

Zlatev, J. 2014. The Co-Evolution of Human Intersubjectivity, Morality, and Language, in Dor et al. 2014, 249–66.

Zuberbühler, K. 2012. Cooperative Breeding and the Evolution of Vocal Flexibility, in Tallermann and Gibson 2012, 71–81.

Name Index

Mertens, Karl, 41–43, 48–49, 322, 323, 324–25, 331
Milgram, Stanley, 52, 206–8
Mill, John Stuart, 177–78
Miller, Seumas, 105, 109, 114, 115, 118
Millikan, Ruth, 249

Nucci, Larry, 222
Nussbaum, Martha, 196

Peirce, Charles Sanders, 57
Pettit, Philip, 18, 182–83
Piaget, Jean, 124–25, 198, 204
Plessner, Helmuth, 4–5
Popitz, Heinrich, 105, 112, 113, 114
Portmann, Adolf, 41
Prinz, Jesse, 25, 222, 228

Rakoczy, Hannes, 43–45, 106–7, 125–26, 127–29, 130, 323–24, 331
Rawls, John, 237
Reboul, Anne, 57–59, 253–54, 263, 298, 325–26, 335, 336
Roughley, Neil, 53–54, 107, 123, 133, 188, 189

Sartre, Jean-Paul, 4–5
Scanlon, Thomas, 194
Schmidt, Marco, 43–45, 106–7, 125–26, 127–29, 130, 323–24, 331
Schopenhauer, Arthur, 159, 160–61
Searle, John, 21, 34, 36, 56, 283
Sellars, Wilfred, 33
Sen, Amartya, 196

Sidnell, Jack, 56–57, 59, 262–63, 276, 290, 292, 329, 330–31, 332–33
Smith, Adam, 15, 27, 31, 54, 230–32, 234, 238
Smith, Michael, 182–83
Sperber, Dan, 58–59
Steinfath, Holmer, 49–50, 229–30, 329, 330–32, 335–36
Strawson, Peter Frederick, 31, 50, 180, 187–88, 215–16, 229–30, 234, 329

Thompson, Michael, 179, 189
Thomson, Judith Jarvis, 8–9
Tomasello, Michael, 6, 20, 21–22, 27, 33–35, 36, 41, 44, 46, 47, 49, 54, 55, 125–26, 127–29, 130, 131–33, 141–42, 145, 162, 178, 191–92, 229–30, 240, 250–51, 255–56, 257, 259
Tugendhat, Ernst, 159
Turiel, Elliot, 28, 43, 50–53, 124–25, 222–24, 225, 331–32, 335–36

Van Schaik, Carel, 38, 45–47, 50–51, 54, 106–7, 239–40, 241–42

Wallace, Jay, 188, 193–94, 229–30
Weinrib, Ernest, 179
Werner, Heinz, 198
Williams, Bernard, 8–9
Wilson, Deirdre, 58–59
Winch, Peter, 106–7
Wittgenstein, Ludwig, 31, 36, 106–7, 227, 296–97

Subject Index